FREEDOM

FREEDOM:
Reassessments
and Rephrasings

Jose V. Ciprut, Editor

The MIT Press
Cambridge, Massachusetts
London, England

Phrygian Liberty Cap—worn by paleo-Christians, Yezidi Muslims, "The Three Wise Men," Mithra, Marianne, enfranchised slaves in Rome, revolutionaries in France, and patriots in the American War of Independence—is on the state flag of New York. —*Ed.*

Cover Concept and Design: Jose V. Ciprut

© 2008 Jose V. Ciprut

MIT Press books may be purchased at special quantity discounts for business or sales promotional use. For information, please e-mail special_sales@mitpress.mit.edu or write to Special Sales Department, The MIT Press, 55 Hayward Street, Cambridge, MA 02142.

This book was set in Palatino by SNP Best-set Typesetter Ltd., Hong Kong, and was printed and bound in the United States of America.

Library of Congress Cataloging-in-Publication Data

Freedom : reassessments and rephrasings / edited by Jose V. Ciprut.
    p.   cm
Includes bibliographical references and index.
ISBN 978-0-262-03387-9 (hardcover : alk. paper)—ISBN 978-0-262-53310-2 (pbk. : alk. paper)
1. Liberty—Congresses.   2. Liberty—Philosophy—Congresses.   3. Liberty—Religious aspects—Congresses.   4. Liberty—History—Congresses.   I. Ciprut, Jose V.
HM1266.F77   2009
123′.5—dc22

2008014399

10 9 8 7 6 5 4 3 2 1

For my beloved parents, to whom I owe my wings
M. Süzan Naon (Sept. 24, 1912–Aug. 1, 2005)
Vitali H. Çiprut (Feb. 17, 1903–Dec. 20, 1992)

"Ölüm Allahın emri, Ayrılık olmasaydı."
[Death's God's Will; pity there's separation.]

The grave in Akşehir/Turkey of the thirteenth century Sufî mystic Nasreddin Hodja paraphrases well the venerable confines of human freedom: a heavy bolt on a massive iron gate guards a sepulcher with no protective walls on any side of the tiny plot. Trespass is facile, yet no one transgresses. Why?

Hürriyete Doğru
[Towards Freedom]

Heeey
Ne duruyorsun be, at kendini denize:
Geride bekliyenin varmış, aldırma;
Görmüyor musun, her yanda hürriyet;
Yelken ol, kürek ol, dümen ol, balık ol, su ol;
Git gidebildiğin yere . . .

Orhan Veli Kanık, Turkish poet (1914–1950)

Easier Said Than Done . . .

Heeey
Why so still standeth ye, go throw thyself to the sea:
Never you mind those left behind, who wait for you;
Can't you tell, freedom beckons from all quarters;
Be sail, be oar, be rudder, be fish, or become water;
Go s'far away as you can flee . . .

Jose V. Ciprut ©

Contents

Preface and Acknowledgments

Tiny Appleworm was content. It had been told by its parent that it could roam all it wanted, that it was at liberty to explore its universe, free to partake of apple flesh and apple blood for as much its baby body could tolerate and for as long as its baby heart should desire . . . provided, of course, that it remain always on this side of the outer sanctum and well clear of The Peel. Now how ought I put it, our youthful worm was simply ecstatic: surely such apple-wide freedom was the best of all freedoms in the best of all possible worlds. "Not so, Papaworm?" Longjohn Appleworm was silent. And pensive. He did not deem the time had come to tell junior all the truth, and nothing but the truth at that. For how could a parent confide in its only child that cheap advice aside, once it, too, had stooped to infringe Rule Number One; that, as if straying too close to the Edge of Knowledge were not scary enough, the transgression of The Limit had proven even more creepy—it had divulged disturbing questions to which there were alas no soothing answers. And all that, for what? A useless innocent peep into a wholly unreachable realm: the Forbidden Territory. What good would it do to seek to explain? Would not the explanation now prove to be even more confusing than the infraction then, considering (a) that there were still myriad pears, oranges, and peaches under the sunny blue sky, out there; and (b) that Longjohn and the missus had long given up all hope and worry about how to get from here to there: over time, alternate concepts of 'freedom' had become for them wholly reprehensible rebellious ruminations to be placed under lock inside righteously repressive beliefs tightly wrapped in the ancient wisdom of honorably acknowledgeable, predeterminedly linear disenchantment.

This cross-disciplinary product holds the harvest of an interfaculty seminar conducted as part of an academic series of scholarly exchanges founded and directed by the editor in the collegial spirit implied by its name: *Cross-Campus Conversations (CCC) at Penn*. It proved to be a joy and a privilege to collaborate with my very distinguished participants, all of whom are respected for their insight-provoking erudition within their respective fields of academic research and/or professional practice. Without their loyal cooperation, and sustained faith and support, this complex product could not have materialized.

I would like to present special thanks to Dr. Greg Urban, Arthur Hobson Quinn Professor and then-Chair of the Department of Anthropology at the University of Pennsylvania, not only for extending to me helpful Visiting privileges that have greatly facilitated my varied duties as seminar convener, director, and editor, but also for taking an active interest and a productive part in our seminars, and thereby actually contributing to the operational, cross-communal, and intellectual fruition of yet another of our unconventional initiatives. My special thanks go also to Dr. Rogers E. Smith, C. H. Browne Distinguished Professor and then-Chair of the Department of Political Science at the University of Pennsylvania, for facilitating the continuation and completion of my editorial work on this project as Visiting Scholar at my old department. As a newcomer on Penn Campus, Dr. Smith sat in on two of my seminars, was introduced to arrays of colleagues from various disciplines and professions, could observe the design and the conduct to fruition of our pursuits, and was included as a participant in our end-of-term public panels. Shortly after my farewells to Penn, I learned that he will be chairing a new interdisciplinary program named DCC—"Democracy, Citizenship and Constitutionalism": a program that will generate a new theme each year, publish the results of its scholarly work, and stage spring conferences, too. And I find cause to rejoice. To Dr. Jay C. Treat, Director, Instructional Computing, School of Arts and Sciences at Penn, and to his merry troubleshooters go my sincere appreciation and thanks for the electronic blackboard network that facilitated my remote management of the project in a very sustained fashion.

This volume is being brought together at a point in life when I should have been spending even more quality time with my family. My deepest debt is therefore to the two women who shared my emotional universe, imparting to me the freedom to imagine I still could afford to do many things wholly my way, and enjoying my feigning to be doing just that. At this writing, alas, one of them is no more; may she rest in peace in the eternal embrace of the spouse she loved and she missed so much. And may the other continue to do what she does well—remain a source of strength, of love and inspiration, for many more happy and healthy years to come. Freedom is at its best, when shared, no matter that our days on Earth are counted.

Jose V. Ciprut

1

Freedom?
The Very Thought of It!

Jose V. Ciprut

In every freedom there nestles a voluntary form of enslavement. Humans meet their freedom under myriad guises; and between birth and death, liberation comes in many forms. Some have measured freedom in discrete instants,[1] others by the amount of justice it embodies,[2] the attitudes it affords,[3] the mistakes it forgives,[4] and the serious responsibilities that it entails.[5] Sören Kierkegaard once suggested that "people demand freedom of speech as a compensation for the freedom of thought which they seldom use." For U.S. politician Barry Goldwater, freedom was too precious a commodity to be entrusted in the hands of the indifferently semi-sovereign: "Extremism in the defense of liberty is no vice. And moderation in the pursuit of justice is no virtue." Lastly, when it comes to defending liberty, one "should never put on one's best trousers" when going out "to fight for freedom," warns Henrik Ibsen in *The Enemy of the People*.

In 1940, the town of Oswiecim in Poland became Auschwitz under the German Wehrmacht's occupation. The path to "freedom" for Jews, and also for Gypsies, in the model death camp at Auschwitz-Birkenau, passed through the cleansing/gassing facilities and the crematorium's smokestack, both serviced with exemplary *tüchtigkeit*.[6] The German death camp's wrought-iron entrance gate bore a black ornamental inscription. It read *"Arbeit Macht Frei"* (toil sets free). But that iron

---

1. Jeffrey Borenstein: ". . . that instant between when someone tells you to do something and when you decide how to respond."
2. Edmund Burke: "Whenever a separation is made between liberty and justice, neither, in my opinion, is safe."
3. Viktor Frankl: "The last of the human freedoms is to choose one's attitudes."
4. Mahatma Ghandi: "Freedom is not worth having if it does not include the freedom to make mistakes."
5. G. Bernard Shaw: "Liberty means responsibility. That is why most men dread it."
6. "Proficiency" in German.

dictum rested on an ironic conundrum: for those who had decreed "the final solution," as for those who triaged, processed, and dispatched the Jews to their "freedom" promptly upon arrival, *die Juden* were *"arbeitsunfähig"* (unsuited for work) to begin with. The automatic "liberation" of the frail, the sick, the newborn, and the elderly among those reaching their destination in cattle cars was a foregone conclusion. Healthy slaves could wait for their turn: all in good time. In this version of freedom, liberty was death; and life, a Hobson's choice. Not quite so for the American revolutionary in early colonial times, who felt free enough to perceive—indeed, to demand—a distinction twixt death and liberty.[7]

For the bard, by contrast, freedom is but a way of life—*chacun à sa façon*—"Like a bird on the wire, like a drunk in a midnight choir I have tried in my way to be free."[8] Some philosophers ideate freedom as a state; others view it as an ideal, the pursuit of which, by self and by other—whereas often projected in absolute terms—is neared relatively at best, if asymptotically at most. Not so for the embattled statesman and idealist man of faith, who perceives causal links among personal freedoms, societal democracy, and global peace, and for whom

[t]here is only one force of history that can break the reign of hatred and resentment, and expose the pretensions of tyrants, and reward the hopes of the decent and tolerant, and that is the force of human freedom . . . . Freedom, by its nature, must be chosen, and defended by citizens, and sustained by the rule of law and the protection of minorities . . . . [M]oral choice between oppression, which is always wrong, and freedom, which is eternally right . . . will not pretend that jailed dissidents prefer their chains, or that women welcome humiliation and servitude, or that any human being aspires to live at the mercy of bullies . . . . [R]ights must be more than the grudging concessions of dictators; they are secured by free dissent and the participation of the governed. In the long run, there is no justice without freedom, and there can be no human rights without human liberty . . . . Liberty for all does not mean independence from one another [but] relies on men and women who look after a neighbor and surround the lost with love . . . value the life [they] see in one another . . . and must always remember that even the unwanted have worth . . . . We have confidence because freedom is the permanent hope of mankind, the hunger in dark places, the longing of the soul . . . . When the [U.S.] Declaration of Independence was first read in public and the Liberty Bell was sounded in celebration, a witness said, "It rang as if it meant something." In our time it means something still. (Bush 2005)

---

7. Patrick Henry: "Give me liberty or give me death."
8. Leonard Cohen, Stranger Music Inc. (BMI). © Sony Music Canada.

In this cross-disciplinary volume, we reassess and rephrase the conceptualizations and theorizations of freedom and their appropriate applicability to daily practices. We situate our analytic-synthetic perspectives in historical contexts. This permits us to reinterpret and to update the elusive promise long attributed to this polyvalent and multifaceted thought. The framework bases itself on contemporary quests for meaning. The field-specific studies, besides having an insightful illustrative value, help to reconcile theory and practice, keeping the past, the present, and especially the possible future of that thought in mind. Here is how the authors voice their respective sensitivities, appreciations, and concerns in interconnecting arrays of thoughts and arguments, inside a shared ideational framework that quite correctly and completely can be paraphrased in six short words, a question mark, and a (muted) exclamation point, on this occasion: Freedom? Beware what you wish for(!)

Freedom and the Free Man

In chapter 2, Classicist Jeremy McInerney sets out to explore two notable features of the Classical Greek notion of freedom. The first is that *eleutheria*,[9] as a thought, entered political discourse at a precise moment: the time of the Persian Wars. The origins of Greek concepts of freedom, therefore, can be traced to a critical moment of self-definition for Greek culture. As the Greeks forcefully assert a Hellenic identity, "freedom" emerges as one of the defining characteristics of the Hellens. Somehow, the Greeks seem incapable of imagining freedom without its negative: Eastern despotism, and, more specifically, in the persona of the Persian Empire. This is perhaps most clearly displayed in Aeschylus's *Persae*, first performed only eight years after the Greek victory at Salamis. "Who is their king?" asks Atossa, the Persian queen, only to be answered by the Messenger, "They call no man king. They are a free people."

The second notable feature of *eleutheria*, as understood by the Greeks, is that freedom is not conceptualized as a right—certainly not as a universal right. One does not fight to win freedom, that is, to assert one's right to be free. Rather, for the Greeks, freedom is the condition enjoyed by a "free man." This is more than a tautology. Freedom is a status that derives from a host of actual and ethical factors. Most

---

9. Pronounced "e-leph-te-ri-a" in Greek.

important, it is a quality enjoyed by a citizen, a man, one enmeshed in the fabric of military, religious, and civic performances that constitute citizenship.[10] Poorly theorized, freedom is seen by the Greeks as connected to such civic and personal virtues as autonomy and autarchy, temperance and moderation. Aristotle's famous justification of slavery in the *Politics* identifies the free man with one who uses his rationality, as opposed to the slave who is a human creature that chooses not to use his rational faculties. Yet Aristotle's attempt to distinguish between the free and the enslaved according to temperament, skills, and abilities is atypical. For the most part, the Greeks are untroubled by the notion that a slave might be a human whose right to freedom has been denied. By conceptualizing freedom as a quality demonstrated by the actions of the free man, the Greeks were able to assert their own freedom while denying that of others.

Freedom, then, in the Greek context, cannot be divorced from a series of dialectical relations: Greek versus barbarian, and citizen versus slave. It is thus a contingent, not a universal, phenomenon.

It is conventional to see the Greeks as the source of modern notions of freedom; yet a closer inspection of Athenian culture reveals that the Classical understanding of freedom was not at all like its modern counterpart. For the Greeks, freedom was not a right but a privileged status—enjoyed by fully enfranchised, male adult citizens. The Greek understanding of freedom was conditioned by the omnipresence of slaves and by the realization that enslavement was the potential fate of every individual and community. Notions such as freedom of speech and freedom of privacy, conceived in modern times as rights requiring protection, were virtually unknown to the Greeks. Their nearest equivalents, for example, relate not to the right to speak but to the characteristic behaviors of free men: participation in civic life and democratic discourse. Freedom, in fact, served as a marker of inclusion within the democratic community. Fear of losing that freedom was played out in stories of enslavement, in which women served as the embodiment of "servitude."

The historical circumstances that made freedom a concern to the Greeks were the Persian invasions of the early fifth century. As a result of the Greeks' victory, freedom was established not as a private right but as a community's ideal, equivalent to autonomy. Freedom was not

---

10. For different perspectives on the evolution of this concept, see J. J. Mulhern, "The Political Economy of Citizenship: A Classical Perspective," or Edward L. Rubin, "The Dangers of Citizenship," or yet, Mark P. Gaige, "Citizen: Past Practices, Prospective Patterns," all in *The Future of Citizenship* (Ciprut 2008).

internalized by the Greeks as a matter of integrity or piety, as it would be later by Stoics and Christians; it came to be viewed as an inherent quality of the Greeks, as opposed to the innate servility of barbarians.

Boxed In, Boxed Out—Whither Freedom?

Communication expert Elvira Arcenas brings the discourse forward in time and looks at the tug-of-war within modern human aspirations, between our yearnings to be free and our longings for discipline and order at the same time. She explores how in this dialectical process it is possible actually to free our 'fettered' freedoms; this thereby helps her to envision alternate conceptions and practices of freedom.

We are "boxed in" by genetic inheritance, by culture, and by our own choices, she argues: the box can be as large as we can make it so that it includes as many people as possible. But inevitably, at least some people will be shut out. Boxes are defined by their suffocating walls which serve as limits; existence itself cannot but be bounded, lest it cease being simply "being." Likewise, human freedom is 'boxed in', if it is to be human at all. Within the confines of our box, we are free to act and to create. So, the question is no longer whether we are free, but what kind of freedom we have and want—or, rather, what kind of freedom is "worthy" of us as human beings?

Herein dwells the paradox: while we are free within the confines of our life's "box," we are forever seeking to be liberated from our limits. We can read our life's trajectory as more or less a conscious quest for an 'otherness'. Thus, drawn by the allure of the diversity with which life is so profuse, we may at our best moments aspire to get out of our human-made box, break out of the often boringly narrow cocoon of our self-interests, and propel ourselves into an exciting realm of uncommon encounters with hitherto unknown others, like us, if somewhat differently so in many respects. But then, often, electing homophily over heterophily, we may prefer to return to the relatively facile comforts of living and dealing with our "more similar" others, and opening our doors only to those of our own color, race, creed, or persuasion, for example. The freedom sensed within the familiar but correspondingly shallower boxes of our lives can be so self-absorbing that it can deprive us of the edifying surprises, the mind-stretching and self-renewing possibilities of communication with unknown others, who share our common humanity in their own fashion. But such freedom brings unease and feelings of guilt, which, for Kenneth Burke, are rooted in our individual inability to be "consubstantial" with other human beings. And so the tug-of-war goes on, between our being free as we think we are and our being desirous to be free as we think we would, should, or ought to want to be.

We face a dilemma: if we cannot free ourselves of our man-made existential "boxes," what alternatives do we have to become free? And even then, pray what would our merited or earned freedom be good for? Freedom seeks self-accomplishment. But one cannot "actualize" oneself without one's other(s). George Herbert Mead suggested that the self is "social": almost inexorably, we define each other reciprocally for better or worse. And thus, fulfilling the best in us is tantamount to fulfilling the best in others. This is called love, and the highest fulfillment of freedom is love. For love is not just sentiment, but a will to see the good in others come to fruition. It is an offering of oneself to others; what I give I do not lose, but allow to potentiate itself into becoming even more fruitful. Hence, to be free, I must be endowed to enable others' freedoms through my human love for them.

Although Dr. Arcenas is also a consecrated Catholic layperson, it is impossible to read her without thinking of the recollections of Viktor Frankl (1959, 1995), a Jewish survivor of Nazi extermination camps: "We who lived in concentration camps can remember the men who walked through the huts comforting others, giving away their last piece of bread. They may have been few in number, but they offer sufficient proof that everything can be taken from a man but one thing: the last of human freedoms—to choose one's attitude in any given set of circumstances—to choose one's own way."

Freedom that is fed by selfishness, by self-aggrandizement, is destined to sterility. And nothing is more self-destructive than sterility.[11]

---

11. Cf. Pablo Neruda (born in 1904, Nobel Laureate in Literature in 1971): "Muere lentamente quien no . . . encuentra gracia en si mismo . . . quien se transforma en esclavo del hábito . . . o bien no conversa con quien no conoce . . . quien evita una passión y su remolino de emociones, justamente éstas que regressan el brillo a los ojos y restauran los corazones destrozados . . . quien no arriesga lo cierto ni lo incierto para ir atrás de un sueño" [which I take to mean "dies slowly whoever does not find grace in oneself, who enslaves oneself to habit, or does not converse with a stranger, who eschews a passion for fear of its emotional swirls, the very ones that return to the eyes their shine and help restore shattered hearts, who does not jeopardize the certain or the uncertain in order to go behind a dream . . ."]. I was reminded of this passage when my childhood classmate—and, much later in life, friend—Ergun (through his wife, Rengin) Avunduk of Turkey serendipitously e-mailed to me a series of touching pictures at the time of this writing. Ergun and I studied humanities, trained as technologists, served as plant managers, engaged in industrial business on an intercontinental scale, and even went to Army Officers' School together prior to receiving our marching orders and going our separate ways to serve at the strangest of remote places—liberating experiences one and all.

If we fearlessly can recognize and unmask those unjust structures in our personal and social lives, imposed by historical accidents and institutional designs; if we can speak the truth where we see it, with the humility that comes via the awareness that we can be wrong; if we can choose other paths, however unconventional, that make life better for others; and if we can risk our lives so that others may have life abundantly, we are not merely acting *as if* we were free, but are, in fact, enabling others to be as free as possibly they can become, while also breaking down the oppressive walls around our personal and social lives and building a habitat worthy of humankind.

We need to "liberate" freedom fettered by greed and strife, by egoism and suspicion. To do it requires that we acknowledge the rich diversity of life—pure white *and* wholly pigmented, male *and* female, young *and* old, God-fearing *and* unbelieving, destitute *and* affluent. It is in this reciprocity, through shared humanity and self-giving, that freedom can be allowed to attain its fullest possible expression and longevity.[12]

Today, the conventional notion of human freedom as 'liberation from earthly obstacles that stand in the way of volition and desire' is being challenged by humanity's daily experience of myriad evolving aspects of the natural world, whether occasioned by modern structural necessities, or also by the novel communicative/relational character of human interactions. Even when that notion finds strong support in material realizations and, defying the barricades, the quest attains its objective, liberation invariably comes off hollow, as if it were an *accident de parcours*, devoid of "substance," in terms of modernized Aristotelian terminology. Such emptiness becomes evident in the urge to smash newer barriers, in the search for content apt to confer mass to form, and in the quest to impart a state of stable equilibrium to turbulent existence, for instance.

In chapter 3, Arcenas tackles the paradox of human freedom—"boxed in" by the determinacy and constraints of earthly conditions and yet incessantly seeking, by means both natural and cultural, to break out of the "box"—in a search for greater actualization of the human self. She sees the self, no matter how autonomous, as something that

---

12. In the lyrics of Piazzola's *Libertango*, this state of being has been idealized as follows: "Mi libertad es tango que baila en diez mil puertos / y es rock, malambo y salmo y es opera y flamenco. / Mi libertango es libre, poeta y callejero, / tan viejo como el mundo, tan simple como un credo." Or, as I interpret it: "My freedom is a tango that is danced at ten thousand ports, / it's rock, psalm, and creole malambo, and opera, too, and flamenco. / My libertango is unbound, all at once poet and hobo, / as ancient as old mother Earth, yet as simple as a credo."

cannot—and does not—exist without its *Altro* (its Other). As self and other mutually define and sustain each other, fulfillment via self-actualization is achieved in social interaction and through dialogue. The ideal form of dialogue for unity in diversity is human communion.

Her essay is structured into two main parts. The first part is on "whether" freedom. It describes some of the typical manifestations of being "boxed in," say, by biological, geopolitical, psychosocial, technological, global, and symbolic fences, illustrating the argument with examples of related attempts to destroy, redraw, or elude those boundaries. Our symbolic fences, erected tallest particularly through human language, often also embody the highest of challenges to human liberation when they are utilized to create social exclusions of all kinds. They are the most refractory, since habits of communicated thought often are more resistant to change. The potentiality for language to be a menace to freedom nevertheless also bears a promise for the fulfillment of freedom, where freedom fosters sincere and mutual efforts by self and other to go beyond words and to reach out to each other as members of a far-flung if inclusive human community.

The second part of Arcenas's chapter addresses the question of "whither" freedom. A break out, from human-made boxes via dialogical encounters, can help. Facilitated by the habit of reflection that of itself provides the necessary condition for self-awareness and the experience of intersubjectivity, dialogical encounters (Krippendorff 2000) offer context and condition for communion, by which our common humanity—transcending the natural, social, and cultural differences that box it in—can be experienced and enjoyed as a community of co-presences. With communion, or at least through a sincere effort to achieve it, freedom finally ceases to be just a flight from, or fight between obstacles, but a fulfillment of the human self which is not quite an island to itself. And in the twenty-first century, where else could one discover a better foundation for a free and democratic society than in the hearts and minds of citizens consciously working toward a more vibrant global communion?

Freedoms Lost, Freedoms Regained

David Williams and Jacques Barber are two psychologists practicing psychiatry. They view the practice of psychotherapy as an art. Just as in the practice of any other profession, from architecture to medicine, engineering to law, the psychotherapist's "art" is applied to the medium of human freedom—more specifically, to the individual person's apparent capacity for voluntary behavior, cognitive as well as physical.

Their chapter (chap. 4) provides a sense of how psychotherapists generally regard human freedom: its loss, its recuperation, the tools available to support its recovery, and the experience of working with it. They address "freedom" as a widely recognized attribute of individual human experience. Williams and Barber treat freedom as "the exercise of liberty"; they see in psychopathology a failure to exploit liberty fully, with the consequent attenuation of freedom. They discuss the concept of psychopathology in some detail, viewing it as the negative part of a continuum of well-being and self-management that begins with "serious mental disorder," continues through "ineffective utilization of liberty," and moves on to a positive side that ranges from "adequate" to "fully functioning." In the course of characterizing the regions of this spectrum of well-being, they reassess the concepts of "mental disorder" and "needless self-limitation."

As "freedom workers," psychotherapists have a variety of tools to choose from. Here discussed are those frequently used for interventions, the many ways of working with a person's biology, environment, feelings, voluntary behavior, and relational concerns included. The variety of tools comes with a matching array of rationales for their construction and use. Williams and Barber tread lightly past those, focusing instead on a generic conception of human nature based on cognitive science's "Theory of Mind" concept and on a strict definition of empathy as "the power of projecting one's personality into (and thus fully comprehending the object of) contemplation." Within this context, it is possible to address freedom as a human experience, whatever its scientific basis, and whatever the purpose of the experience might be. They illustrate the use of the psychotherapist's tools, and their impact on individuals, with examples from their own work as psychotherapists, explaining also how working with others' freedom impacts the therapists' access to their own.

The psychotherapist's practical experience with freedom makes a unique contribution to the general understanding of the concept. Freedom, an enigma to psychological science, is an important part of its healing practice. For those suffering from severe mental disorders, freedom must be restricted; for those with lesser impairment, the exercise of full personal freedom can be supported by interventions aimed at reducing the intrusion of needless self-limitations into the process of everyday living. In their chapter, Williams and Barber explore the way psychotherapists approach the topic of freedom: honoring the canons of cognitive science while also taking the time-honored subjective experiences of awareness and personal agency into account. They discuss the most common interventions available to psychotherapists as freedom workers: changing a person's environment through full or partial hospitalization, adjusting their biology through medication, and, through experience-based persuasion, altering the cognitive maps by which people create meanings that guide their lives. They relate these interventions to specific regions of the spectrum of self-management effectiveness, focusing on clinically significant dysfunction, disordered personality, and the various degrees of success people achieve as they attempt to produce a fully satisfactory experience of living. They propose that freedom can be usefully seen to involve an important subjective experience occurring *inside* individuals, as they go about reconciling the conflicting demands and opportunities found in the inner and outer worlds they perceive. The very experience of freedom influences the therapist's choice of interventions and provides a trustworthy beacon that guides psychotherapy as a process of liberation.

Viewed as an opportunity to exercise the possibilities that liberty permits, the experience of personal freedom affects those who provide psychotherapy as well as those who receive it: the therapist encounters costs but also benefits from the empathically based self-scrutiny that is a normal part of the therapy process. Focus on freedom as an experience reveals an impact quite distinct from its role as a *problématique* in the natural and social sciences.

Degrees of Freedom: Jazz and the Art of Improvisation

William Parberry is a professional musician: a director and performer of classical, choral, and jazz music. For him, freedom and music are very intimately related. Throughout the history of Western music, Classical music has been documented on paper. The composer, usually after numerous drafts over weeks, months, or sometimes years of labor, finally puts his *Deo gratias* on the final page and sends the work to his publisher. Such a creative process would represent the opposite of spontaneity, or freedom. Improvisation, on the other hand, is the ultimate expression of freedom in music, and only in jazz is the art of improvisation the central means by which the performer relatively freely communicates his music.

A recording of Beethoven's Fifth Symphony by the Boston Symphony Orchestra is not particularly different from a recording of the same composition performed by the Philadelphia Orchestra, because both ensembles are *trying* to interpret the symphony exactly (cf. Reise 2008) as Beethoven wrote it. But the 1939 recording of Coleman Hawkins's inspired sax solo on Johnny Green's "Body and Soul" is unique, never to be performed the same way again. Had Hawkins's solo not been recorded, the improvisation that he created, undocumented, would never have reached our ears. In jazz, the performer (Hawkins), not the composer (Green), determines the *quality* of the music: freedom is deeply personal, while also collectively liberating, beginning with its fleetingly perceived manifestation.

The only style of jazz that does not involve improvisation is ragtime, and it is the earliest documented style for that very reason. Written examples of ragtime and piano rolls predate the first recording of improvised jazz by the Original Dixieland Jazz Band in 1917. Once improvisation was captured on vinyl, music scholars and critics began to evaluate the jazz artists, and the recordings served as a teaching tool for young performers who were eager to learn the very difficult discipline of improvising jazz.

As the styles of jazz progressed through the twentieth century, the degree of freedom in improvisation changed from one period to the next. Curiously, the change was not always toward greater freedom as history moved forward. During the 1920s, Classic jazz (commonly called Dixieland jazz) contained abundant improvisation, both solo and ensemble; but in the decade that followed, the Swing era ushered in dance music, and written arrangements with brief improvised solos became the standard practice. Jazz reached a popular peak in the 1930s and early 1940s because it performed a function—catering to the millions of Americans whose primary leisure time activity was dancing. As a consequence, however, the jazz soloist felt restricted melodically and rhythmically because he was neither free to roam far from the popular tunes familiar to the listener, nor free to play complicated rhythmic patterns that might confuse the dancer. Bebop's progressive style in the forties and fifties broke away from the formula-ridden approach to improvisation in Swing. Young dancers in the 1950s chose Rock and Roll over the Swing era's "businessman's bounce," and jazz, no longer dance music, became nonfunctional—a chamber art, purely for listening. More than any other traditional style, Bebop required a high degree of skill in the art of improvisation. Kenny Clarke, one of the first drummers to play Bebop with the likes of Charlie Parker and Dizzy Gillespie, explained how difficult it was to keep pace with the masters of the new style: "We'd play Epistrophy or I've Got My Love To Keep Me Warm just to keep the other guys off the stand, because we knew they couldn't make those chord changes. We kept the riff-raff out and built our clique on new chords" (Parberry, chap. 5): but freedom cannot survive for long as mere *boutade*. For, a whim freedom is not—never was, and never could be.

From Classic jazz to Bebop, the art of improvisation varied in the amount of freedom that the artist had; the process was based on certain rules, such as matching the improvised phrases to specific chords that were written to the original melody, for example, the chords that Johnny Green wrote to "Body and Soul." The greatest degree of freedom is reached when the jazz artist improvises without having to observe those traditional rules. Two styles, Modal jazz and Free jazz, both beginning in 1959 with the albums *Kind of Blue* by Miles Davis (trumpet) and *The Shape of Jazz to Come* by Ornette Coleman (sax), abandon traditional chord progression for improvisation based on a modal scale (Davis) or no scale at all (Coleman). Released from a regularly recurring pattern of chords, the rhythm section was also freed, since an audible timing factor that kept track of when chords changed was no longer needed. The improviser in these avant-garde styles could experiment melodically, harmonically, and rhythmically, without any preset conditions or conventions. Initially, the sixties saw a reduction in the sale of jazz recordings because the progressive sounds of Modal and Free jazz were not accessible to the average listener. Today, however, with the help of jazz scholars, the charlatans have been weeded out, and the recordings of premier avant-garde performers such as Miles, John Coltrane, Eric Dolphy, and Charles Mingus are staples in the collections of open-minded listeners. To those who would question that the increase in freedom was a positive development in the art of improvisation, one need only point to *Kind of Blue*, now the most critically acclaimed and largest selling album in the history of jazz.

In his chapter on freedom in music William Parberry describes the history of jazz improvisation, which, more than any other musical genre, represents an artist's immediate—hence free—expression in the creative process. By tracing the changes in improvisation through the evolution of jazz styles in the nineteenth century, he explains the varying degrees of freedom that have occurred. Any music that accompanies dance is functional; and hence jazz improvisation was limited by the demands of that function from 1917 (the first recording of improvised jazz) to the decline of the Swing era in the late 1940s. During the first half of the twentieth century, rhythmic, melodic, and harmonic conventions controlled the amount of freedom that the improvising artist had. In the early 1940s, Bebop arose as an alternate, nonfunctional style of jazz, running concurrently with Swing. Bebop and the rapid succession of styles that followed formed a body of music that was "art for art's sake": the modern era of jazz. The greater freedoms accessible to jazz musicians, as improvisation progressed without the restrictions of the dance, led to the gradual removal of musical conventions, until an impression of total freedom was reached with the arrival of Free jazz in the 1960s. As the archetype of free expression by the improvising artist, however, Free jazz was neither commercially nor artistically successful. Instead, those modern styles that offered the artist freedom with a modicum of traditional theory or sonority seemed to endure. On the market for sounds, might there be practical bounds to free expression? The 1959 recording of *Kind of Blue*, still the largest selling jazz album, supports just such a conclusion: that complex improvisation by skilled artists, when set in a traditional structure or familiar sonority, results in a more successful communication between musician and listener than if the need for intelligibility were overlooked. While the freedom expressed in the art of jazz improvisation may seem unique, the same conclusion drawn here would apply to any art. Greater artistic freedom generally elicits a corollary abatement in appreciation on the part of one's audience in poetry, literature, painting, and Classical music, just as it does in jazz. Yet, unlike the other arts, jazz improvisation is a spontaneous creation, and as such, it is the most temporal of the arts, with a uniquely ephemeral beauty. Demanding unusual musical skills from the artist and nothing short of acute listening skills from the audience, jazz will always remain the purest form of free artistic expression.

Freedom and Risk

As a mathematician engaged in the formulation of risk, and in the definition of optimal proactive responses to unforeseeable factors that can threaten operational freedoms under conditions of uncertainty, Paul Kleindorfer views the area of decision making under risk to be at the center of many problems in business strategy, public policy, and individual choice. Theory about such choices in all of these contexts foresees a set of primitives, or givens, underlying particular decision acts: values and preferences of the decision maker, alternatives, feasibility constraints, beliefs about uncertain events that may influence the outcome, and mental models linking alternatives and possible scenarios to potential outcomes. The decision maker is imagined to reflect on possible futures, given the alternatives, and to choose among alternatives to achieve some positive confluence with the decision maker's values and preferences. In reality, of course, decision making under risk does not present itself in such neat terms; and a rich literature, both theoretical and empirical, has noted over the years the many ways in which actual decision making departs from a quasi-rational view of consistent execution of decision acts, governed by some underlying paradigm of choice. The first point to note about the "freedom *to* risk," therefore, is the need to agree that the nature of actual choice (in Herbert Simon's words) is only "boundedly rational," comprising many systematic and understandable flaws that are present and predictable about actual choice under uncertainty. What to do about this is somewhat perplexing and has given rise to several puzzles, especially in the public arena where the state has limited rights to intervene, to sanction, or to constrain choices in many areas—from market activity to pension planning to setting environmental standards. A typical puzzle is the one posed by Cass Sunstein in his work on social norms under the rubric of "libertarian paternalism," a term that attempts to capture the idea of granting freedom-to-risk to appropriately informed and mature agents in the polity, while still reserving for the state the right to "frame" the problem and to insist on certain features of decision contexts in order to improve overall outcomes. This is but one of many issues that surround the basic problem of allowing mature and free adults in a society the right to choose and to risk in the process, while also constraining their choice problems in ways that the paternalistic state must argue are reasonable interventions. Given all of this, Kleindorfer highlights in his opening comments of chapter 6 some of the classic limitations of human decision makers in risky choice problems, buttressing his argument with examples that illustrate in the public policy arena the tensions between an excess of liberty and an excess of paternalism.

His chapter examines whether the presence of uncertainty and risk imparts any restrictions or limits to the notion that "freedom" is tantamount to unconstrained "liberty to choose." His basic thesis is that there are such palpable limits and that these derive both from the limitations and biases that humans exhibit in decision making and from whatever restrictions society chooses to impose on allowed outcomes. For example, in situations involving personal bankruptcy, society may deem it unacceptable that an individual or his or her dependents be required to meet obligations that may be so large as to imply long-term penury if these obligations are honored. These social constraints on the outcomes of free choice under uncertainty are complicated even further by behavioral biases that represent systematic departures of human choice from certain rational ideals. The central issue that then arises is whether the state, the family, or other entities acting as surrogates of the state or the family should be given the power to constrain such choices in a manner that is intended to "de-bias" individual choices—protecting the individual from herself, as it were. If de-biasing individual choices is considered a desirable option, then a whole range of social and personal interventions come into view. In one sense, such de-biasing arises naturally, if society is required to bear the burden of poor choices by its members, or even of good choices that may entail unlucky outcomes. At the same time, however, the nature and extent of constraints imposed in the name of correcting individual decision biases may affect the scope and nature of freedom that individuals have in specific contexts. The chapter explores this issue, for individual choices—such as insurance and pension planning—as well as for social choices, involving the design of social safety nets for individuals who may experience bad outcomes from their choices. He concludes the essay with a discussion of issues of legitimation that arise when the state intervenes in personal choice, and he notes from this the balance that must be struck between freedom and risk.

Liberation and Freedom in Jewish Liturgy and Practice

Rabbi Levi Haskelevich is a Lubavitcher.[13] He argues that at the very start of this new millennium, just as humankind began to think it was

---

13. Popularly known as the Loubavitch, the Chabad movement, in opposition to the Hassidism grounded on the human heart and on human sentiments, once so very widely practiced by the less cultivated masses in Ukraine and Volhinia, restored to its place of pride the human intellect as an instrument of Ashkenazic Jewish religious life. Chabad's principal sphere of influence was Russia, where human knowledge had always been fostered. Chabad eased Hassidism's return to the rabbinical tradition.

relearning how to live in peaceful coexistence, and contemplating transforming some of its deadliest swords into benign ploughshares, a new kind of threat impacted the world scene, vying to turn box cutters and jumbo jets full of people and fuel into deadly weapons in order to hijack the hard-earned freedoms of civilian society, out of ill-guided motives to ill-conceived intents. Now blinded by hate and intoxicated by blood, this ancient new enemy is selflessly suicidal, heartlessly self-destructive, and mindlessly self-deluded about his destination, dreaming of an erotic paradise in which his feckless soul, freed at last from his faceless frame, will be rewarded in heaven for causing death, for inflicting injury and suffering to hundreds of thousands of innocents, including many faithful Muslims. This bitter faithless foment, this senseless Armageddon devoid of divine justification, goes against the values of any religion. Is the human soul really so evil? How has this come to be? This war is forcing the civilized world to reassess its basic values of liberty, equality, and human brotherhood. Hence, it makes perfect sense for this chapter to look to the Mother of all monotheistic religions for an answer to the question: "What is the meaning of Freedom, and what is the true nature of the Soul?"

The concept of freedom in Judaism goes back to the very early days of Israel as a nation: to the Exodus from Egypt. For Jews everywhere, freedom is a sacred concept; celebrated with religious ceremonies during Passover, it is but a way of life in daily context. Freedom is the ability to articulate one's conscience, or true will. Freedom has many levels, depending on the intellectual horizon of a person's mind and the spiritual elevation of his soul. If man's human content is created in the Image of his Creator, then man's innermost meaning of freedom can reside only in the acknowledgment of his true innate Self.

The yearning in man's Heavenly Soul for becoming one with one's Creator is meditated in *Tefillah*—prayer. Prayer is self-education. It sets the Spirit free of the body's lowly animal cravings. Through such learning, and hence by association with the Creator's Wisdom and Will, man accomplishes his life's mission. This inner Wisdom, the Jew finds in the Torah. It is when the Torah is engraved on the tablets of his heart that he senses he is truly free.

The ancient Hebrew prophets knew that a liberated world would be filled with perfect wisdom—the knowledge of God. For how else could there endure prosperous and peaceful coexistence between the wolf and the lamb? Filled with knowledge of High Wisdom, the Creator's wisdom, man will discover his ultimate freedom by knowing Creation and Source, not by inventing his liberty through the defeat and demise of others.

Human Freedom: A Christian Understanding of Salvation as Liberation

Jesuit Fr. Roger Haight is a scholar of systematic and historical theology. His review of Paul Knitter's work (2002), under the title "Placing Christianity in a Pluralistic World" (Nov. 8, 2002) in the *National Catholic Reporter*, reminded us that Christian theology of religion asks such questions as: "Are all religions equal? Does Christianity supersede all other religions? Is there some way to state clearly how one should relate to Jesus Christ in today's world that strikes a balance between these two extremes?"; that "no set of questions engages Christian theologians today more"; and that "no questions have more practical relevance in the most religiously pluralistic country in the world"— the United States of America. In that article, Fr. Haight summarized Knitter's four models as housing "a collection of theologians who may live on different floors but share the same roof": First, ironically from right to left, the 'replacement model' "understands Christianity to supersede all religions. Typical of some evangelical Christians, this view underlines the importance of the biblical witness for theology, the centrality of Christ relative to a real need for salvation. But it appears unrealistic to most mainline Christians today." To its left, "the 'fulfillment model' represents Vatican II and the mainline Protestant position in holding that Christ recapitulates and brings to perfection the salvific power that exists in other religions. Some versions of this view assert the distinct truth and salvific value of other religions, but its critics ask how one can assert real openness to other religions at the same time as the absoluteness of Jesus Christ." Third in that line-up, "the 'mutuality model' regards other religions on a rough par with Christ and Christianity, so that the revelation and truth of all have to be taken seriously as mutually exercising a claim to respect, understanding, and even normalcy. The vision reflects a new situation of a humanity actually interacting, sharing really distinct versions of the truth in a mutually critical way. Some critics believe this wipes out traditional Christological claims." As the last one, "the 'acceptance model' is a study in paradox. It begins with the premise of a new recognition of how deep cultural, linguistic, and religious differences really are: no more commonality among religions; autonomy and difference reign.

This fixation on difference then becomes the premise for each religion harboring its own absolute claims, unassailed, which leads to a re-assertion of pre-modern and modern claims of Christian supremacy." But in an earlier short essay, titled "Jesus and Salvation: An Essay in Interpretation" (1994), Fr. Haight had already made it clear that central to all models of Christianity, past, present, and future, is the concept of salvation. I transcribe his words with his advance permission: from a historical perspective, the experience of Jesus as savior is the very basis from which the Christian movement sprang. This religion arose and continues to exist because Christians experience Jesus as a bringer of God's salvation. In its narrow sense of defining the status of Jesus before God and human beings, Christology depends upon soteriology.[14] Yet, despite this centrality and importance, the Church has never formulated a conciliar definition of salvation, nor has it provided a universally accepted conception. This is not necessarily something negative, but it still leaves us with a pluralism in the domain of the theology of salvation, the meaning of which remains open and fluid. The meaning of salvation *is* elusive: like time, every Christian knows its meaning—until asked to explain it. Because of its centrality, the problems that surround the concept of salvation are rendered even graver. Indeed, many of the traditional expressions of how Jesus saves are expressed in myths that no longer communicate to educated Christians; some are even offensive. And some of the traditional theological "explanations" of salvation through Christ do no better. Often treatments of salvation are largely devoted to rehearsing tradi-tional theories or presenting models or types that seem to inject some order into the disarray. But no one can assume that these are credible today, and too little attention is given to intelligible present-day reinterpretation.

Given the pluralism of conceptions, is there a way to establish sys-tematically a center of gravity on the salvation mediated by Jesus that will be clear and definite, but open and not exclusive? In the face of the confusion about the nature of salvation, can one formulate the present-day questions and inner crises to which Jesus provides a sal-vific answer? And given the incredibility of the mythological language when it is read at face value, can one find a symbolic formulation of this doctrine that is closer to actual human experience today?

---

14. Soteriology is the study of the doctrine of salvation. It is derived from the Greek word *soterios* (salvation). Some of its topics concern atonement, imputation, and regen-eration in Christianity. For more details, see any dictionary of theology.

Because salvation in its religious sense can come only from God, many of the theories of salvation that emerged after the first century in both the Greek and Latin traditions focused on Jesus as a divine figure, or on the divinity of Jesus. Moreover, their language drifted away from the concrete historical ministry of Jesus. On the one hand, these theories are beginning to sound unrealistic: even when they are interpreted symbolically they are much too far removed from ordinary experience to command respect. On the other hand, this situation is reinforced by present-day historical consciousness and its proneness to highlight the humanity of Jesus. How does the prominent place that the historical Jesus is assuming in Christology come to bear upon salvation theory? More deeply, how is the salvation mediated by Jesus to be understood within the framework of a historicist imagination?

These issues serve as a backdrop for the main query that guides Roger Haight's chapter for our volume (chap. 8) as an attempt at interpretation. In his contribution, Professor Haight discusses an understanding of salvation from the viewpoint of its relationship to liberation and human freedom. The chapter unfolds in two parts: first, the author sets the logic of the problem and the method of approach; next, he provides a constructive theological interpretation, before closing.

Framing the Discussion

The language of salvation is close to the core of Christian faith and to the believer's self-understanding. For Christians, Jesus is the savior. If human existence is understood fundamentally as a form of freedom, it is this very freedom that is saved. How then should such process be understood?

This discussion is set within a framework that contains a number of problems. Several Christian teachings connected with salvation seem archaic and thus complicate the discussion in modern times. The very conception, for instance, of an original sin and a fall of humankind portrays a pervasive negativity; and yet a dark side does indeed seem intrinsic to human freedom. Another background conception provides a division between two spheres of human existence—one, natural; and the other, supernatural—that accompanies Christianity as a religion based on revelation; and yet human beings do have experiences of contingency and gratuity and gift that signal transcendence. Still another problem area emerges with the idea of redemption occurring at a precise moment as if it were a historical transaction; and yet

Christians, rather consistently, do look back to Jesus of Nazareth as the answer to the religious question. The central issue that these cumulative questions pose, both to Christians themselves and to those who inquire from outside the circle of Christian faith, regards the intelligibility of this salvation in a time marked by a heightened sense of historicity, the social construction of consciousness, and the sheer diversity of religious beliefs.

As the theological method for addressing the meaning of salvation shapes the logic and affects the intelligibility of the response, Fr. Haight continues the discussion with brief statements about the nature of theological language as intrinsically symbolic but not "merely" so. The phrase "a hermeneutical method of critical correlation" summarizes the elements of the reasoning process to follow. That process appeals to two principal sources: the first evokes common human experience; the second invokes standard Christian symbols. The former appeal seeks to make the language broadly intelligible, whereas the latter makes it Christian. These two sources for reflection are brought into intimate conjunction with each other, each criticizing and illumining the other, and thereby generating an interpretive discussion.

In sum, the first part highlights four problems that surround the Christian language of salvation: (1) a tendency toward a dualism of a natural and a supernatural order of history; (2) a pervasive negativity portrayed in a doctrine of sin; (3) the incredibility of a salvation for all, wrought in a single moment of history; and (4) the problematic character of extending the religious idea of salvation into the public social order. To address these problems, Roger Haight brings up the symbolic character of religious language and employs a hermeneutical method of critical correlation between historical Christian symbols and present-day experience.

Salvation as Liberation of Human Freedom

The constructive interpretation of salvation as a liberation of innate human freedom unfolds in four stages, each of which takes a classical Christian symbol and elicits its meaning through a brief phenomenology of human experience.

First, the symbol of creation refers primarily not to something that God did "in the beginning" but to the permanent power of being that holds finitude in existence and on which all things are most absolutely dependent. The doctrine implies that there is no "space" between God and the physical world, that the presence of God to reality is personal, benevolent, and loving, and that this is the basis for the language of God as Spirit at work in the world. The doctrine of creation by a loving creator entails a divine will for human flourishing and fulfillment, and yet creation is intrinsically characterized by finitude and death.

Second, the symbol of sin refers not to objective evil but, as Augustine and, more recently, Paul Ricoeur have shown, to a condition of human freedom itself prior to the exercise of choice and decision. This is described on both the personal and the social levels, for these two dimensions of human freedom cannot be separated, and the analysis helps to provide a context within which the very notion of salvation will be meaningful.

Third, the root meaning of the Christian symbol of salvation draws from the basic religious questions of why human existence is at all, and of what it is for. In the late twentieth century, the meaning of salvation has been portrayed as liberation: liberation in this world, discussed in that section; and final or eschatological liberation, discussed in the following section. On the personal level, salvation may be construed as liberation of human freedom from internal bondages such as egoism, and the release of freedom toward altruistic values. On the social level, salvation may be interpreted as a solidarity that enhances the freedom of groups and supports a common good. In the measure in which, beyond law and its enforcement, these require also transcendent power—which is marked by gratuity and comes as gift—they can be construed as Salvation. In this view of salvation, Jesus is not considered as its efficient cause but as its revealer, a view that, among others, is supported by the Christian Bible called the New Testament.

Fourth, heaven is an eschatological symbol that appeals to hope. Neither faith nor hope is the equivalent of knowledge, but both have cognitive aspects. Hope is faith based in some form of religious experience reaching into the future. And although the future remains absolutely unknown, it is imagined on the basis of a projection of faith experience in the present. On this logic, therefore, salvation as fulfillment in the future has meaning on the basis of faith in the present. But as future, it draws the present into a wider horizon of meaning that promises to redeem the innocent suffering of the past and the future.

In sum, these four symbols are interlocking; and their only validation is that—for a whole body of ordinary Christians—they redeem ultimate meaning for human freedom from an alternative of sheer contingency. Here, they are phenomenologically discussed in terms of the experience they elicit for Christians: creation, sin, salvation, and heaven. Each one of these interlocking symbols conveys elements of the meaning of the fundamental narrative that defines Christian identity and gives an account of salvation in Christian terms. Hence, this chapter provides both a reinterpretation of the meaning of the Christian symbol of salvation relative to human freedom and its liberation; and, no less, a definition of how the symbol appeals to human praxis. For the Christian imagination, the symbol of salvation itself is able to redeem ultimate meaning for human freedom from alternatives of sheer contingency.

Theorizing Freedom

In chapter 9, political scientist Nancy Hirschmann examines the concept of freedom in the discipline of political theory. In the middle of the twentieth century, noted Oxford philosopher Isaiah Berlin developed two concepts of liberty, which he called negative and positive liberty, and which have since dominated contemporary political thinking. Hirschmann's chapter articulates the differences between these two models as a difference between the external factors of freedom (conditions that prevent or enable one in doing what one wants) and the internal factors of desire and will. The latter elements tend to be ignored by contemporary political theorists, who instead focus on debates over what constitutes an external barrier to freedom (for instance: is poverty a barrier to freedom, or is it simply an inevitable condition that defines the limits of certain people's ability?). This inattention to the internal aspects arguably stems from Berlin's thinly veiled hostility to them specifically, and to positive liberty more generally: because of Cold War politics, the internal dimensions of freedom once were associated with totalitarian mind control, whereas Western liberal democracy was seen as providing for the maximum amount of freedom from restriction to develop one's own mind. Not only does this naively ignore the ways in which class, race, and gender construct desire for Western liberal citizens, but it also ignores the historical foundations of Berlin's typology.

Attention to the internal dimensions of desire, and of will, is warranted, as these play important roles in the theories of the major figures of the modern canon, ranging from Hobbes and Locke to Kant and Mill. In these theories, both desire and will are "socially constructed" through the production of individuals and citizens, who are taught to want the right things. Attending to the canon of freedom theory thus shows that

Berlin's fundamental conceptualization of freedom into negative and positive components is intellectually correct—but that, rather than treating them as opposing structures, we must recognize each of the components as embodying a complementary half of a single, unified conception of freedom.

Freedom and Culture

The central proposition of anthropologist Greg Urban's chapter (chap. 10) is that freedom is a metacultural concept: simultaneously *part of* culture (for being socially learned and transmitted) yet also *about* culture (for representing a reflection on what guides human action). As such, one goal of his chapter is to place the concept of freedom within the context of other possible reflections on what guides human action.

One finds a good illustration, if fictionalized example, of the strong contrast between an idea of freedom and any other metacultural conceptualization of action in the film *Lawrence of Arabia*: When Lawrence, an Englishman, is told by Sherif Ali, a Bedouin Arab, that he should not concern himself with a (tragic) event in this world because "it is written"—meaning preordained by God—he retorts that "nothing is written." Later, after Lawrence has displayed remarkable stamina in crossing the Nefud desert and defeating the Turks at Aqaba, Ali concedes: "for you, Aurens, truly nothing is written."

Although freedom can be viewed as one among an array of possible cultural conceptions of human action and what guides action, another question of interest in Greg Urban's chapter is what active role such a concept plays in shaping culture, not merely in reflecting on it. Metaculture in general being an active force affecting the motion of culture through the world, Urban asks: What are the peculiarities of the freedom concept as it affects culture? His hunch is that freedom goes along with—and facilitates an idea of—change, innovation, and modernity.

Instead of emphasizing how present action is determined by what comes from the past—by our received ways of doing things—freedom emphasizes the differences between past and present conduct. While the freedom concept is part of culture, and hence received from the past, it focuses conscious attention on emergence, on both the possibility and the reality of the desirable new, sometimes at the expense of its undesirable counterpart. Such a focus is crucial to the dissemination of culture where one is endeavoring (as in the case of corporations) to move new culture (new products) into existing pathways.

Freedom has a peculiar property as metaculture: it is used to inhibit the flow of another culture. This peculiar twofold character explains its tendency to move around the globe and to be taken up by people who find reason to resist the imposition of other culture(s). Looked at from the point of view of cultural motion, several among the earlier philosophical attempts to grapple with freedom in relation to culture—such as those by Kant and Habermas—make sense. But the limitations of those and other single-level accounts of freedom become also apparent: they all fail to grasp adequately freedom's paradoxical qualities; in particular that, although freedom is about the absence of constraint, it also presents itself as a duty, and hence as a kind of constraint. These paradoxical qualities make sense from the point of view of freedom as simultaneously cultural and metacultural. A metacultural account also provides a window to the possible futures of the freedom concept. Greg Urban's chapter is just such an account.

Shades of Freedom in America

There is no more powerful a word in the American vocabulary than "freedom." Long before Jamestown, Thomas More in "Utopia" (1516) saw the New World as a place unencumbered by the past, and thus free to be the site of a perfect society—a society free of the greed and the ambition that produced oppression in Europe. The Puritans came to Massachusetts Bay not only to escape the established Church but also to build a biblical Commonwealth, a "city on a hill," so all the world could see how God meant for people to live. Theirs was a commitment to God, in whose service is perfect freedom. When the Jubilee Year, the 50th anniversary, of the Charter of Liberties (1702) approached, the Pennsylvania legislature decided to commission a bell to celebrate this guarantor of home rule, adopting a verse from Leviticus as the adequate inscription: "Proclaim Freedom throughout the land." That bell, probably rung to mark the formal adoption of the Declaration of Independence, was not known as the Liberty Bell until the 1830s, when the Abolitionists adopted it as their symbol of the quest for a very different kind of individual liberty.

Meanwhile, the revolutionary generation had transformed the religious sense of mission into an earthly experiment in democracy, a simultaneous commitment to both freedom and equality, a very perilous balancing act. One can understand the Civil War as a conflict between two very different meanings of freedom: on one side, the individual freedom of human beings from slavery; and, on the other side, the freedom of local communities to determine their own laws and customs.

Freedom is such an appealing concept that almost all serious social conflict in the United States eventually gets expressed as a battle between opposing understandings of freedom. Robber barons insisted on their freedom to make contracts with individual laborers, while workers insisted on their right to organize and oppose the tyranny of the bosses. On the heels of the Great Depression, Franklin Delano Roosevelt and Winston Churchill announced in the Atlantic Charter a worldwide goal of "freedom from want." Shortly after World War II, the Civil Rights movement insisted on "Freedom Now," meaning the abolition of segregation and a more vague demand of equal opportunity. In turn, the counterculture of the 1960s wanted freedom of the individual from the constraints of bourgeois culture. Given this rich history, it is not surprising that U.S. intervention in the Fertile Crescent was known as "Operation Iraqi Freedom."

A scholar of American history in general, and of the history of the U.S. South and of the 1960s in particular, Sheldon Hackney in his chapter for this volume (chap. 11) describes and explains these various meanings of freedom in their historical context.

He views "freedom"—the most powerful word in the American vocabulary—as clearly implicated in the meaning of the U.S. American identity. It is in the nation's founding documents, patriotic songs, and the rhetoric of its leaders. The problem is that, historically, it has meant very different things at different times and places and to different individuals and groups. For the New England Puritans, it was the freedom *to* build in the "wilderness" a society that would abide by God's explicit wishes, in which conforming individuals would be free of sin. The "liberty" inscribed on the Liberty Bell had to do with local control in the colony as opposed to the power of the Proprietor in England, though its meaning was later converted by the Abolitionists to freedom *from* being individually enslaved. The Civil War, for the North, was about preserving the union and freeing the slaves; while, for the South, it was about states' rights and local control. Freedom has signified the absence of governmentally imposed rules, and it has meant government aid to the individual person in overcoming obstacles to success. Throughout the history of the United States, Americans have prized the freedom *of* self-invention. Hence, the dialogical relationship between individualism and community is one of the principal themes of American history; and a constant problem has been the recognized need to reconcile freedom and order. The only way to do this successfully has been to recognize individual freedom *as* a community enterprise, one that depends for its health and longevity on the sustained active commitment of the citizenry.

Outside In/Inside Out: The Ordering of Liberty in a Globalizing International Political Economy

In an *Alumni Bulletin* received from my undergraduate Alma Mater—the (erstwhile American) Robert College of Istanbul—the text of an award-winning essay by a young undergraduate woman on the complexity ensconced in the modern dilemma of having to choose between freedom and security sets out to interpret a phantasmagoric work of fine art: "There is a painting by the Belgian surrealist René Magritte," notes the author,

depicting the concept of human liberty as a room with one window opening onto a bright blue sky with clouds like puffs of smoke and another onto a Renaissance-style female nude. In the middle of the boxlike room, where the three walls are as intimidating as the windows are liberating, there is a cannon aimed at the viewer of the painting. Magritte's perspective on human liberty invites reflection on the concepts of freedom versus security . . . a central dilemma for thinkers who have aimed at creating the best form of state. How far can a state *allow* its individuals to be free? Is there, or should there be a limit to freedom, and where and how can a state *draw the line* between what is a necessary limit to freedom and what would be described as an infringement upon the 'natural' rights of human beings? In modern societies the cannon has been turned towards 'the other', who is intruding upon the scene with different notions of liberty, as well as to the window depicting the infinity of the sky, which can be interpreted as the freedom of society as a whole.[15]

The terrorist attacks of September 11, 2001, in New York and Washington, D.C., on edifices symbolic of U.S. monetary and military power, and the composition of the perpetrators, made one lesson very clear: nation-states no longer possess a monopoly on warfare or on warlike violence (see Ciprut 2001). Nineteen individuals, with a mere several hundred thousand dollars, inflicted more damage and took more lives

---

15. (Pamuk 2007) My italics to accentuate my reading of a young twenty-first-century citizen's vision of *freedom vs. security* in terms of *state-run democracy as natural setting.*

in one day than the mightiest of armies normally would. This new reality—the very fact that individuals can possess statelike force without the tethers of a geographic base and/or the habitual restraints of a national polity—poses not only a direct and serious primary threat to national/international order, but potentially and indirectly a parallel menace to democratic freedoms, too, considering that commensurate responses on the part of democratic and open societies would have to wield the kind of decisive power that criminal entities merit, require, and understand. This new demand imparts to democratic citizenship a *global* meaning—an expansive ethic of freedom that, at its very best, stands on *individual* shoulders, yet, through unity in a higher aspiration, and diversity in wherewithal or technique, makes of humanity an indivisibly inclusive whole, at once free *and* secure.

In chapter 12, jurist Viet Dinh, who has had a significant role in the formulation of the U.S. Patriot Act, takes the reader through the development of the sovereign nation-state as the well-established building unit of political organization, the more intelligibly next to expose the threat that transnational terrorism explicitly presents to an international order predicated upon national sovereignty. His outside-in analysis is complemented with an inside-out reexamination of how patriotism—or, put less unabashedly, nationalism—contributes to the safeguard of sovereignty and to the upholding of international order. He takes care to express some thoughts on where all of this may lead; and, more important perhaps, *whereto* a willed recommitment to national sovereignty and dedication to national ideals should *not* lead a democratic nation and an open (yet principled) society such as the United States of America.

Dinh contends that, when predicated on a healthy foundation of nationalism able and willing to act in defense of their own societal democratic freedoms, strong nation-states thereby also can provide a powerful impediment to acts or threats of worldwide terrorism out to hurt personal and societal freedoms regionally and globally, as well.

Beyond Ideology, Toward a New Ethic of Freedom?

Kevin Cameron is a scholar in the field of political theory and law. In chapter 13 he attempts to carve out a new ethic of freedom, beyond the limits placed on freedom through ideological constructions of the "good." Thus it concerns the interrelation between transcendental freedom and ideological interpellation. In particular, he examines the possibilities for freedom against the backdrop of terms laid out by the dominant ideology that accompanies the political-economic process known as globalization. In the face of ideological hegemony, he argues that ideological definitions of freedom tend to cloud the relationship between reason and freedom so central to more rigorous definitions of freedom such as the one offered in Kant's critical philosophy. In this manner, ideology functions to impart to heteronomous acts (non-free acts in the Kantian sense) the appearance of being transcendentally free acts. The goal of ideology, then, is to prevent the subject from recognizing itself as free in any way other than that prescribed by ideology. The rigor of Kant's definition of freedom may not prevent it from being susceptible to ideological constrictions.

To overcome this possible shortcoming in Kant's theory, Cameron first ascertains whether one can supplement it with Kierkegaard's notion of the "teleological suspension of the ethical." Next, he investigates whether, by means of Kierkegaard's understanding of faith, he can begin to situate an agent that actually transcends the confines of the ideological determination of the "good" and thus begins to determine the grounds of its own freedom. Lastly, he applies this theory both to the contemporary process of globalization and to the hegemonic ideology accompanying that process, in order to seek and maybe even to find a nonideological space for freedom, one beyond that of the political-economic hierarchy offered by crass globalism.

Conclusion

And this brings us to the end of this introductory chapter. One may ask: How do these chapters interrelate? They do so by intimately interlinking the past, present, and future of what is understood by liberty, at the individual, societal, and global levels of analysis along perspectives and within contexts that, moreover, help to expose the different and differently evolving meanings of freedom and their implications and consequences across time and space for all of the stakeholders. One may also ask: What—if any—is the unifying central message of the resultant narrative? That freedom has both objective external and subjective internal components which are not always nor necessarily in harmony within, let alone between or among, their neat categorical groupings; that history, therapy, spirituality, faith, prayer, improvisation, risk, culture, ideology, law, politics, etc., . . . each has its own ways of addressing one or more aspect(s) of this multifaceted thought that freedom is; and that the greater one's exposure to such complex poly-valence is, the greater becomes the probability of attaining and emitting even higher, deeper, and broader freedoms likely to reward the one and the many across time and space.

References

Bush, George W. (2005) U.S. President's Second Inaugural Address, January 20, 2005.

Ciprut, Jose V. (2001) "Introduction: The Quest for Certainty and the Newer Equations of Security," in Jose V. Ciprut, Editor, *Of Fears and Foes: Security and Insecurity in an Evolving Global Political Economy*, Westport, CT: Praeger.

Ciprut, Jose V., Editor (2008) *The Future of Citizenship*, Cambridge, MA: The MIT Press.

Frankl, Viktor Emil (1959) *From Death-Camp to Existentialism*, Boston: Beacon Press.

——— (1995) *Was nicht in meinen Büchern steht: Lebenserinnerungen*, Munich: Quintessenz.

Haight, Roger (1994) "Jesus and Salvation: An Essay in Interpretation," *Theological Studies* 55:225–251.

——— (2002) "Placing Christianity in a Pluralistic World," Book Review, *National Catholic Reporter*, November 8.

Knitter, Paul F. (2002) *Introducing Theologies of Religion*, Maryknoll, NY: Orbis Books.

Krippendorff, Klaus (2000) "Ecological Narratives: Reclaiming the Voice of Theorized Others," in Jose V. Ciprut, Editor, *The Art of the Feud: Reconceptualizing International Relations*, Westport, CT: Praeger.

Pamuk, Zeynep (2007) "Freedom, Security and Multiculturalism in Modern Societies," senior-class essay submitted to the Fifteenth Philosophy Olympiads, held in Antalya, Turkey, May 2007. Full text available at: http://portal.robcol.k12.tr/Default.aspx?pgID=357.

Reise, Jay (2008) "Context, Choice, and Issues of Perceived Determinism in Music" (on the idea of connectedness as context), in Jose V. Ciprut, Editor, *Indeterminacy: The Mapped, the Navigable, and the Uncharted*, Cambridge, MA: The MIT Press.

2   Freedom and the Free Man

Jeremy McInerney

Writing on the Constitution of the United States, Senator Charles Mathias Jr. observed: "The historical and philosophical roots of the Constitution run very deep. We have been nourished by a long tradition of thought reaching back to the ancient Greeks" (Mathias 1995, 85–86). But beyond a passing reference to Plato and Aristotle, U.S. Senator Mathias goes no further in his exploration of the connections between the Constitution and antiquity. And with good reason. Although the Constitution was drafted "to secure the Blessings of Liberty," the gap between the Greek notion of freedom *(eleutheria)* and our understanding of the concept is so wide that easy comparisons are dangerously misleading. For example, if one were to ask, how might Classical thinkers have reacted to the government's controversial antiterrorism legislation, the Patriot Act? one quickly realizes that it is a question almost impossible to answer. In the first place, the very idea that legislation could be promulgated by an entity such as "the government," separate from the community, cannot even be put in words, in Greek. The nearest that Greek can come to translating "government" is *politeia*, but all it means is a constitutional arrangement. One can speak of an oligarchic or democratic *politeia*, but the laws are the laws, either enacted by semimythical figures like Solon or passed by vote in the Assembly.

Aside from the institutional differences between direct Athenian democracy and, say, the U.S. American Republican system, there is an even more profound conceptual divide separating us moderns from the ancient Greeks. The modern idea of freedom is rooted in a belief in universal rights, an understanding of freedom quite alien to the Greeks (Ostwald 1996). The huddled masses yearn to be free—free from oppression, free from hunger, free to assemble, to worship, to speak and . . . to carry handguns. It is such positive and negative freedoms that are the subjects of Berlin's influential essay on the two concepts of liberty (Berlin 2002). And it is these freedoms that are enshrined in the first ten amendments to the U.S. Constitution, promulgated as the Bill of Rights in 1791. In each of these instances, we understand that the individual is free when her right to act in a certain way is not curtailed or impeded, and the state may be called "free" to the degree to which it protects these personal freedoms. At the root of the Classical conception, on the other hand, was a much simpler understanding: *eleutheria* was the opposite of slavery. This is what Moses Finley (1983, 233) called "the simple slave-free antinomy."

From this profound difference between Classical and modern understandings of freedom stems a variety of further important distinctions. For example, unlike the Kantian notion of freedom "as the basis for self-reflective conduct in the world" (see Urban, chap. 10 in this book), in Classical Athens freedom was neither a right nor a source of agency, but a status. Just as it was defined by its exact opposite, slavery, so too was freedom given meaning by having a distinct field of operation: the community of citizens—not the individual agent. Freedom, for the Greeks, was part of a larger dialectic of inclusion in and exclusion from a community of peers. The slave was the most thoroughly excluded; the free adult male citizen was the greatest beneficiary of the system. As Eteocles remarks in Euripides' *Phoenissae* (520), "When I can rule, shall I be this man's slave?" In this chapter, I would like to explore that dialectic and to show how the Greek conception of freedom served as a marker and a means for distinguishing the beneficiaries of the social order from the disenfranchised. In important and distinctive ways the Classical understanding of freedom differed markedly from our own. The point of departure from the Classical model, we shall see, will occur in the post-Classical world, in the philosophical schools of the Hellenistic age and in the popular Christian literary genre of hagiography. In these two fields, freedom was transformed from a public status to a private virtue, a meaning it still holds today.

Slaves and Masters

The contrast between Classical and modern approaches to freedom can be best demonstrated by looking at freedom of expression. In the words of Robert Kennedy at Cape Town, on June 7, 1966: "The first element of individual liberty is the freedom of speech," which, as he explained, comprises "[t]he right to express and communicate ideas, to set oneself apart from the dumb beasts of field and forest; to recall governments to their duties and obligations; above all, the right to affirm one's membership and allegiance to the body politic—to society—to the men and women with whom we share our land, our heritage and our children's future."[1]

This is a fundamental right according to our conception of freedom, but not so for the ancient Greeks. To them, *isegoria*, the nearest Greek word to "freedom of speech" (an expression more literally descriptive of "equal speech"), is not a right but a mere characteristic—the mark of a free man, as member of the community of free men. A hallmark of the democratic Assembly was that its sessions opened with the herald's cry, "Who wishes to speak?" If one were removed from the community of free men, then the opportunity to speak freely quite understandably evaporated. Accordingly, an exile, divorced from the city of his free peers and constrained by the conditions of his exile, lost not the right but the opportunity to speak. When his mother asks, is exile hard, Polyneices, in Euripides' *Phoenissae,* answers, "One thing is the worst, you cannot speak openly." In response, Jocasta remarks that it is characteristic of a slave that he does not say what he thinks. Polyneices concludes that an exile must play the slave to get what he wants. The audience of free Athenian citizens no doubt concurred: freedom speaks, slavery conceals (cf. Parberry, chap. 5 in this book). And just as the exile is like a slave, unable to speak freely, so too only the free man can be expected to tell the truth willingly (see Hackney, chap. 11 in this book). To get the truth from a slave, one must torture him (duBois 1991).

The two statuses produce distinctive behaviors. In fact, it is the very behavior—not the question of rights—that fascinates the Athenian citizen. Slaves ought to look and behave like slaves and free men should look and behave like masters (see chapter by Williams and Barber on the idea of "thrownness"). A pamphlet by Pseudo-Xenophon, denouncing the democracy, complains about the confusion over status: "If it were customary for the slave to be beaten by the freeman, you would often strike an Athenian, believing that he was a slave, or a metic or a freedman. For the ordinary folk *(demos)* at Athens dress no better than do the slaves, and are in no way superior in appearance. . . . The slaves enjoy just as much freedom of speech as do the free" (Xen.

---

1. See http://www.americanrhetoric.com/speeches/rfkcapetown.htm.

Ath. Pol. 1:10–12). This last claim is tendentious, but is all the more telling for the anxiety that lies behind it. The ultimate criticism of the democracy was that it blurred the distinction between free and enslaved. The democrats criticized by Pseudo-Xenophon, however, were perfectly clear about slaves and their proper place. Each year the plays of Aristophanes, Eupolis, and the other comic poets treated the audience of free Athenians to a spectacle of lazy, wily slaves aping and mugging their way around the stage. Aristophanes' *Wasps* begins, typically, with Sosias and Xanthias, two slaves, asleep on stage:

SOSIAS. Xanthias, you idiot! What are you up to?
XANTHIAS. I'm learning how to relieve the Night Watch.
SOSIAS. Learning how to cop a hiding if the master catches you is more like it!
(Aristoph. *Vesp.* 1–3)

The casual references throughout fifth-century B.C.E. literature to beating or sexual exploitation, exaggerated upstairs/downstairs distinctions between the classes, and the threat of torture or banishment from the household to the mill or mines, all reflect a society in which the difference between the autonomy of the masterly and the servility of the enslaved was reinforced every day.

Only a small minority explored the possibility that these distinctions were more a matter of custom or behavior (Mulhern 2008) and were therefore not innate (Garlan 1988, 126–145). In his famous discussion of slavery in the *Politics*, Aristotle observes: "Some thinkers regard mastery as contrary to nature, since men are only free or slave because of convention, though they do not differ by nature. Accordingly, mastery is unjust, since it is based on force" (Arist. *Pol.*1.1253b). Such observations never amounted to an ancient abolitionist movement, although they prompted Aristotle to compose the most infamous section of his entire oeuvre, the defense of natural slavery in Book One of the *Politics* (1.1254a–1255a). Here Aristotle articulates the notion that nature consists of a series of agonistic relations: human versus animal, male versus female, free versus slave. Each of these had a *telos*, a function that was best accomplished when the superior partner dominated the inferior. Thus, a domesticated animal is better than a wild animal because it has come under the domination of a human master. The same principle, applied more broadly, justifies the male domination of the female, and the free man's domination of the slave. Accordingly, not only is slavery 'not a problem' but potentially it is part of an ideal relationship in which a fully realized man, the free man, who uses his

mental capacities, is in control of the slave—a human tool that is capable
of reason but does not use it (see Williams and Barber's distinction
between liberty and freedom, chap. 4 in this book). Hence, for Aristotle,
the definitive proof that a man *deserves* to be a slave is the fact that he
is a slave. The circularity of the argument aside, Aristotle's defense of
slavery reflects the universal assumption of the Greek world that
slavery is natural (Cartledge 1993, 126). As early as the eighth century
B.C.E., Homer had already depicted a heroic world, in which women
were offered as prizes at the funeral games of dead heroes, and Hesiod
had advised the Greek Everyman, "First get a house, and a woman,
then a plough-ox—a slave woman, not a wife, who can walk behind
it" (Hesiod *W&D* 405–406). Everywhere, and at every time, in ancient
Greece, slaves were the silent counterpoint to the free population. Most
slave owners did not bother to think about slavery as did Aristotle,
since they took it for granted. It remained an undertheorized institution, but provided a negative image of freedom. Where the slave was
silent and sullen, acting under compulsion and incapable of independence, the free man therefore was autonomous, self-reliant, 'open'.
Antinomy became antipathy.

Between the two statuses there is a *frisson*. Although it is reassuring
to cast the free man and the slave as opposites by nature, there is still
the recognition that free can become slave. This accounts for the fatal-
ism in some of the earliest references to freedom. In the *Iliad* and the
Odyssey, for example, whenever Homer speaks of "the day of freedom,"
he means the moment when a character is about to lose his or her
freedom (de Romilly 1989, 29–31; Raaflaub 1985, 29–32). Hector, for
example, imagines the day Andromache will be taken to Greece as a
slave, lamenting that she has no man to fend off "the day of slavery"
(*Il.* 6.455). It is a horrific fate, but the violation that Hector and Andromache ponder is more brutal and immediate than a question of the
denial of rights. Women are the spoils of war. Thus, Hector taunts the
dying Patroclus, "Did you really think you would sack my city, and,
snatching away their day of freedom, drive the Trojan women onto the
ships, to take them, back to your dear fatherland? Fool!" (*Il.*16.831).
Enslavement is the fate that befalls women. The male equivalent is to
be penetrated by a spear, or driven from the field by a taunt. Either
way, freedom is not a right but a status to be protected, a piece of cultural capital up for grabs.

Freedom was a privileged status, usually inherited. More important,
it was almost the same as citizenship, which was understood in

Classical Athens to entail active participation in the life of the community. Militarily, this involved service as either a hoplite or a rower. It was no coincidence that some ships in the Athenian navy were named *Eleutheria*, or that rowers on the state trireme, the *Paralos*, were all freeborn (Hansen 1996, 91–104; Strauss 1996, 313–325). Politically, freedom and citizenship meant attending the Assembly, the law courts, and the Council. As Pierre Vidal-Naquet (1995, 77) puts it briefly, "... in Athens liberty was strictly connected with participation." Citizenship, sometimes likened to membership of an exclusive club, was a status restricted to free adult males who, except in a few cases, were the sons of citizen fathers. And in the course of the fifth century B.C.E., Athenian attitude to citizenship grew even more anxious, resulting in restrictions, such as Pericles' citizenship law (Davies 1977–78, 105–121). As a result of this legislation, it became necessary for an Athenian to prove his status as a citizen and a free man by showing that both his father and mother were freeborn Athenians (Plut. *Pericles* 37.2). Men introduced their adolescent sons to their brotherhood at the Apatouria festival and, shortly after, to the other members of their *deme* (local community) for registration as a citizen (Parke 1977, 88–92). Cases from the law courts in the fourth century B.C.E. show that one way of pursuing a family feud was to charge that an individual never before had been introduced as such, or that the registration was fraudulent in some other way.

While citizenship is concrete—one either is or is not a citizen—the qualities that distinguish a free man are abstract. In fact, at the end of the fifth century B.C.E., Thucydides (2.35–46) puts into the mouth of Pericles a speech radiating an idealized view of the Athenians as free men: they are bold, enterprising, yet at the same time moderate, both in their pursuit of pleasure and in their physical training. Making an explicit comparison with the Spartans, Pericles presents the Athenians as models of *sophrosyne*—temperance—the ancient Greek 'virtue of virtues'. That speech, which is the clearest articulation of an Athenian ideology to survive in the literature of the Classical period, makes also a few claims about individual Athenians, one of which is most particularly instructive: "The freedom which we enjoy in our government extends also to our ordinary life. There, far from exercising a jealous surveillance over each other, we do not feel called upon to be angry with our neighbor for doing what he likes, or even to indulge in those injurious looks which cannot fail to be offensive, though they inflict no real harm" (Thuc. 1996 2.37.2).

This is not exactly a paean in praise of the right of privacy. Rather, it is an assertion that the community of free men manifests a tolerance of private difference. The emphasis is not on the right of the individual but on the latitude in the characteristic behavior of the group. The speaker is unambiguous: when it comes to the individual who withdraws from communal activity, the community of the free can have nothing but contempt. "For," Pericles is presumed to have said, "we regard the citizen who takes no part in these duties [i.e., in the citizenry's political and legal affairs] not as unambitious, but as useless" (2.40.2). This condemnation of private abstention or withdrawal demands two comments. First, it demonstrates that the quest for private and personal freedom—referred to by Elvira Arcenas as "self-actualization," in chapter 3 in this book—is a concept alien to the world of fifth-century B.C.E. Athens. And, second, it demonstrates that these sentiments differ markedly from the distinctively American, modern understanding of freedom, in which the individual is usually at odds with "the government." In the Athenian view, all free men share certain qualities, and their community is nothing more than the ideal individual replicated 20,000 times. There is no meaningful distinction between the Athenian and the government because the government is nothing more than the Assembly of free Athenians. Where one might rejoice that America is free, the ancient Athenian would have always quite casually stated that Athenians are free because, ideally, there is no qualitative difference between one Athenian and 1,000 Athenians. This is the ideal proclaimed by Thucydides' Pericles in the Funeral Oration, through the idea of a community wholly of integrated individuals: "In short, I maintain that our entire city is an education to Greece, and that individually each man among us would seem to me to be capable of handling any situation with grace and dignity."

In Classical Athens, where freedom was a matter of status rather than of individual ethics, the question of freedom was unambiguous; not without its anxieties, however. One obvious source of concern was the threat posed by living amid a servile population. Pseudo-Xenophon's complaint that one could not distinguish free from slave at Athens, divulges the very concern. Accounts on building, from the *Erechtheion,* show that work crews were often composed of free and servile working side by side. Not only were slaves in fact everywhere, but they were also believed to be everywhere, and in vast numbers: Classical sources speak of a servile population of 400,000. The implausibility of the figure only underscores the anxiety that produced it.

The fear of slaves was compounded by the phobia that somehow oneself could be reduced to slavery one day. Just as cities could be sacked and the populaces enslaved, so too could individuals be challenged in court—only to have their legitimacy, citizenship, and inheritance rights questioned by an accuser. One's freedom was never entirely secure. As a result, the 'free ancient Athenians' lived in a state of permanent disquiet from all possible and potential alternatives to their freedom (cf. Dinh, chap. 12 in this book). The venue for exorcizing such concerns, routinely for the ancient Greeks, was the theater. This explains why slavery figures appeared so prominently in so many plays. Since slavery was the opposite of the free man's station, the role is frequently gendered female, on stage as in epic. In Euripides' *Phoenissae*, for instance, Jocasta contemplates the besieging army around Thebes in her complaint of Capaneus:

This is the man who boasted he would give
the maidens of Thebes as spear captives to the women of Mycenae
and to the Trident of Lerna,
casting upon them servitude
to the waters of Poseidon and Amymone!
Never, never, O lady Artemis,
golden tressed offshoot of Zeus,
may I suffer this slavery!
(ll. 183–192, trans. Kovacs)

A second Euripidean play also named after its chorus of enslaved women, the *Trojan Women*, opens with Poseidon describing the apportioning of the Trojan women to their new Greek masters. Hecuba, the Queen, cries: "I am taken away as an aged slave from my house . . ." (l. 140). The chorus's song interrupts her:

A pang of fear is darting through
the women of Troy, who within these walls
bewail their slavery.
(ll. 156–158)

And the chorus sings for every captive slave when it cries out, "To whom am I, poor woman, assigned as a slave?" (l. 185). "Where will I serve as a slave, me an old woman," plaintively asks Hecuba (l. 192). The chorus contemplates its last view of Troy and remarks bitterly,

Greater troubles than these shall I have,
either brought to the bed of a Greek
(a curse on that night and its fate)

or going as a pitiable slave to draw water
from the sacred spring of Peirene.
(ll. 202–206)

This, at least, is preferable to ending up in Sparta, "the hateful, abode
of Helen, where as a slave I will encounter Menelaus, the sacker of
Troy" (ll. 211–213). Events will end up much worse: Polyxena, her
throat cut, a sacrifice at the tomb of Achilles; Cassandra claimed as the
bedmate of Agamemnon; Andromache allotted to Neoptolemos, son
of her husband's killer; and Hecuba, enslaved to Odysseus. In the
awful symmetry of these decisions the enslavement of the women
makes the Greek victory at every turn more hideous.

There is nothing comparable in Greek literature exploring the agony
of the male slave, yet the slave population was composed of both men
and women; so why was it that the Athenians found the enslavement
of women such a fascinating subject for tragedy? Displaced dread
seems the likeliest answer. "We are the slaves of a Dorian land," cries
the chorus of the *Trojan Women*. And for an audience of Athenian
men to contemplate this thought in 415 B.C.E., a few months after the
sack of Melos and in the middle of a thirty-year war with the Dorian
Spartans, must have been an unsettling experience. The *Trojan Women*
is part of a tradition of fifth-century B.C.E. works that examine the
typical uncertainties and contradictions of power, freedom, and empire,
by exploring the victim's point of view. For Greek poets and audiences,
Atossa and the Persian elders, the women of Troy, the Phoenician
women, the slave women attending Iphigenia, each and all, are examples of the weak, the powerless, and pointedly, the disenfranchised—
the vivid reminders of the privileged status of the free men, who
constitute the audience and sometimes the key characters of the drama.
Like slaves, women serve as the Other, representing the fate feared by
men, kept at arm's length, and rendered abject (duBois 1988, 159). The
abjection to which the Self (in the female) is subjected on stage is, in
fact, an enactment of the fear that the male audience has of the (servile)
Other in life. DuBois expresses it pithily: "In tragedy, women take the
place of men" (duBois 2003, 149).

Freedom and Autonomy

Greek conceptions of freedom, we have seen, did not grow out of a
tension between the state and the individual, but between a more basic
opposition of masters and slaves. Freedom was the distinguishing

feature of the members of the slave-owning class. Since there is little distinction between a free individual and a community of the free, the label of freedom is all too easily applied to entire communities. In this arena, freedom was genuinely contested. Early in the fourth century B.C.E., Athenians participated in negotiations with most of the rest of the Greek states to bring to an end two decades of fruitless war that had left Greece crippled and disunited. The Peace, though short lived, was guaranteed by the Persian king, who spoke explicitly of allowing the Greek states to enjoy autonomy. Any state possessing *autonomia* was recognized by all sides as living under their own laws, free of interference. This was the hallmark of a free people: they got to decide their own laws and constitution. "Freedom" and "autonomy" were quickly linked, becoming key terms in interstate diplomacy. The Athenians rebuilt their empire in the 380s B.C.E. by forging alliances that explicitly promised freedom and autonomy to new allies, until, in 377 B.C.E., the Athenians could go public with a general invitation to any Greek state to join their alliance. The invitation, known as the Aristoteles decree (*IG* II^2 143), contains, as part of the preamble, this clause: "In order that the Spartans may allow the Greeks to enjoy the peace in freedom and autonomy . . . ," and the decree goes on to specify how that freedom *and* autonomy are to be guaranteed. Each ally is to be free *and* autonomous, to have whatever constitution it desires, not to be subject to Athenian garrisons or military governors, and not to have to pay tribute. Here is a notion of negative freedom (i.e., *from* some limitation or restriction, as discussed by Nancy Hirschmann in chap. 9 in this book), not unlike our own today, yet—in the ancient Greek context—a concept operating only at the level of international relations between independent states—not at the level of the individual's personal, civil, or human rights within society.

The origins of this understanding of freedom, as something characteristic of states rather than a trait of individuals, lie in the seminal events at the beginning of the fifth century B.C.E. By defeating the Persians first in 490 B.C.E. at Marathon, and then again and again, in 480 B.C.E. and 479 B.C.E., at Salamis and Plataea, the Athenians had guaranteed their own freedom and autonomy, understandably remaining as they did—proud of their feat. When, in Aeschylus's *Persae*, first produced a mere eight years after Salamis, the Persian queen Atossa asks the chorus about the Athenians, "Who shepherds them? What master do their ranks obey?" The chorus replies, "Master? They are not called slaves to any man" (Aesch. *Pers.* 241–242). In sum, the Greeks cannot contemplate freedom separate from its shadow, slavery, so that the biggest threat of enslavement, a Persian conquest, thus necessarily results in a yet deeper emphasis on freedom as a Greek attribute. Freedom is the mark both of the individual, fortunate enough to enjoy that status, and of the community, made up of such individuals, and valiant enough to fight in its own defense. Thus, freedom has two fields of operation: as a marker distinguishing those at the top of the social order, and as an assertion of the city's status in relation to its foes. Yet, freedom is not an active component in the civic discourse *within* the city's political community, as it is for us today. External threats were seen always in terms of freedom and slavery, whereas internal conflict was understood routinely in terms of order and lawlessness.

Therefore, only external threats imperiled the freedom of the community. The threat was Persian, barbarian; and the victory over the Persians had the unfortunate effect of transforming triumph into triumphalism: in the century that followed, the Greeks would articulate the (almost Spartan) notion that it was the very hardness of Greece that bred a race of champions, while soft Persia became the home of soft men. In the *Menexenos*, Plato argued that the Athenians were pure born, with no admixture of barbarian blood, and that the spirit of freedom was sound and healthy among them as a result. Aristotle saw the Greek climate as the perfect balance—*between* hot and cold and wet and dry—producing the only race that could truly enjoy freedom, since it was a perfectly balanced people. But if only Greeks were the natural product of an environment that nurtured free men, then would other people not be inherently servile? An extraordinary passage in chapter 16 of the Hippocratic treatise *Airs, Waters and Places* insinuates how environmental determinism and ethnic stereotypes inflected the Greek notion of freedom: ". . . with regard to the pusillanimity and cowardice of the inhabitants, the principal reason the Asiatics are more unwarlike and of gentler disposition than the Europeans is, the nature of the seasons, which do not undergo any great changes either to heat or cold, or the like. . . . It is changes of all kinds which arouse understanding of mankind, and do not allow them to get into a torpid condition. For these reasons, it appears to me, the Asiatic race is feeble, and further, owing to their laws; for monarchy prevails in the greater part of Asia, and where men are not their own masters nor independent, but are the slaves of others, it is not a matter of consideration with them how they may acquire military discipline . . ."

This distinction, according to which freedom and servility were subsumed under the broader *alterité* of Greek versus barbarian, becomes a fixed feature of fourth-century B.C.E. public discourse. Year after year, the Athenians would listen to public speeches praising their ancestors' efforts in the Persian Wars. Isocrates was typical of this pandering rhetoric when he wrote, "Your ancestors prepared to wage war in defense of freedom, even as they forgave the rest of the Greeks for submitting to slavery" (Isoc. *Panegyricus* 95). In these panegyrics and funeral orations, the antithesis is always between Greek freedom and barbarian enslavement, as when Isocrates justifies Athenian imperial might by asserting that, during the seventy years of Athenian rule, the rest of the Greeks "experienced no tyrannies, were free in relation to the Persians, unaffected by civil strife and enjoyed universal peace" (Isoc. *Panegyricus* 106). The same dialectic left its mark in utopian literature. Plato's *Republic*, for example, addresses the issue of Greek/barbarian conflict. In Book Five, Plato's rhetorical question is, how should the soldiers of the ideal state deal with their enemy? Should they enslave them? The answer is rather Scottish: *this will depend* (here, on whether the ideal state is Greek or not and whether the enemy is Hellenic or not). The rhetoric is revelatory: "And therefore when Greeks fight with barbarians, and barbarians fight with Greeks, they will be described as being at war when they fight, and by nature enemies, and this kind of antagonism should be called war; but when Greeks fight with one another we shall say that Greece is then in a state of disorder and discord, they being by nature friends; and such enmity is to be called discord" (Plato *Rep.* 5.470C, trans. Jebb).

Plato concludes from these distinctions that it would be wrong to enslave other Greeks and that their land should not be devastated. Barbarians receive no such leniency. The distinction is not based on any sense of natural right or on the protection of freedom, but rather on the recognition that all Greeks are "united by ties of blood and friendship." It is the entire Greek community, therefore, that deserves protection from enslavement—because they are Greek. In Plato's utopia, freedom is protected—not because it is a human right, but only because you are Greek. In an ancient Greek community, therefore—and Plato does very explicitly state that his Republic is Greek, and thus civilized—freedom is simply part of the backdrop against which the principles of justice, good order, and the rule of law come into focus. Accordingly, Plato's *Republic* discusses justice, education, and social institutions such as marriage, without mentioning freedom even once. He does not need to. The men, who constitute the actors in his dialogue and in his audience, were all, all, free men. So, defining freedom made about as much sense for Plato as defining the state must have for Louis XIV.

Yet we run the risk of being misled. Freedom as a mark of all Greeks was a hortatory fiction. The Greeks who defeated the barbarians might have justifiably claimed to be free. This did not prevent the victorious Athenians from enslaving other Greeks. In the generation after the Persian Wars, the men who attended the first performance of Aeschylus's *Persae* in 472 B.C.E. were the very same soldiers and sailors who had forced Skyros into the Athenian Empire and had sacked Thasos when it tried to secede. And in the same century, the Athenians would order the execution of all the men at Mytilene, when that Greek city dared to rebel against the Athenian alliance. They meted out similar punishments to the Melians in 416 B.C.E. And if Athenians could kill and enslave other Greeks, so too did they risk being enslaved or killed by other Greeks: two Athenian armies ended up trapped in the quarries of Syracuse, where close to 7,000 men died in captivity (Thuc. 7.87). In 403 B.C.E., when news came that the Athenian fleet had been decisively wiped out at Aegospotami, the Athenians came perilously close to suffering the same fate they had inflicted on others. Xenophon describes the climate of terror in the city: ". . . during that night no one slept, all mourning, not for the lost alone, but far more for their own selves, thinking that they would suffer such treatment as they had visited upon the Melians, colonists of the Lacedaemonians, after reducing them by siege, and upon the Histiaeans and Scionaeans and Toronaeans and Aeginetans and many other Greek peoples" (Xen. *Hell.* 2.2.3).

There were serious discussions at the conference after the war at which the Thebans and Corinthians strongly argued that Athens should be utterly destroyed (Xen. *Hell.* 2.2.19). Although freedom could be bandied about as a slogan, even at the level of international relations there remained an elementary truth: freedom was tenuous. States could lose their freedom. If they did, this could mean more than just the loss of their precious independence. Entire populations could be massacred or sold into slavery.

Internalizing Freedom

Since freedom was not conceived of as a universal right but as a status—and one that came with no guarantees—it was almost impossible for freedom to be internalized. In this respect, modern understanding of freedom, in which freedom can be viewed as an aspect of individual liberty and highly personal autonomy (Williams and Barber, chap. 4 in this book), reveals more of an affinity to Christian hagiography than a compliance with Classical Greek notions of the term. In modern-day parlance and popular everyday understanding, freedom is a quality that is held synonymous with the indomitability of the human spirit—more so when tested by physical suffering. Films such as the *Shawshank Redemption* and *Braveheart* only reflect the influence of martyrology on our understanding of freedom as a quality of character and soul. The more an innocent soul suffers, the more his spirit triumphs over his oppressors'. As Mel Gibson's William Wallace writhes on a butcher's block, intestines being yanked from his still conscious body, he is called upon to foreswear his treasonous behavior and thereby (maybe) earn a quick death. The strings reach a crescendo and in his last breath the hero cries triumphantly, "Freedom!" Compare this with the *Passion of Saints Verissimus, Maxima and Julia:* "Their judge, in a clear public announcement, ordered a closed chamber to be prepared. Attendants entered, tied the martyrs up, binding their feet and gave them a flogging. The judge then ordered the frames of the racks to be shown to them. But not one of these actions terrified these companions of God, nor was more powerful than the promise [of salvation] at hand. It was as if the virtue of their souls was increasing as their bodies were wrecked, and their steadfast faith in God pressed forward to the blessed state promised them even as their suppliant steps stuttered and faltered" (Cat. Codd. Hagiogr. Lat. Col. 3809 A).

In both cases there is the same use of torture, not merely to test but to give authority to the victim. In the Christian literature this is to inspire faith (Bynum 1995). The use of torture, not merely to test but to give authority to the victim, is a staple of the great medieval compendium of martyr stories—Jacques de Voragine's *Golden Legend*, say, in which St. Lucy remarks to her executioners: "And therefore, if thou make my body to be defouled without mine assent, and against my will, my chastity shall increase double to the merit of the crown of glory. What thing that thou dost to the body, which is in thy power, that beareth no prejudice to the handmaid of Jesu Christ" (de Voragine, *Golden Legend*, Life of St. Lucy, trans. Caxton). Or, as St. Margaret puts it to her persecutor, Olibrius, "Thou shameless hound and insatiable lion, thou hast power over my flesh, but Christ reserveth my soul" (de Voragine, *Golden Legend*, Life of St. Margaret).

Yet the notion of freedom as the equivalent of the state of grace did not entirely supplant the earlier and simpler notion of freedom as the opposite of slavery. Even Augustine, whose Christian outlook leads him to discern a truer, divine freedom in Christ, still has a foot in the pagan camp and sees freedom in Classical terms. In Book One of *de libero Arbitrio Voluntatis*, for example, he lists those things that, in contrast to eternal things, are "things which may be called ours for a time." Listed are our bodies, freedom, our relatives, the state, honors, praise and favors, and finally possessions. Augustine defines this ephemeral freedom as, "not indeed true freedom which is reserved for those who are happy and abide by eternal law; rather I am speaking now of that freedom which men who have no masters think they possess and which men who wish to be free of human masters desire" (August. *de lib.* 109). Here is the conventional, truly Classical notion of freedom—that of the opposite of servitude. Accordingly, the Christian notion of spiritual freedom was laid over, but did not replace, the earlier, Classical notion. This layering is most fully exploited in the stories of saints like St. Agatha, St. Lucy, and St. Catherine, whose high social status is usually emphasized. St. Catherine, for example, is the daughter of King Costus and, after being orphaned, lives alone in a palace full of slaves and riches—until, that is, she is moved to begin her short career of good works, and of emperor baiting. After her execution, she is praised for maintaining her chastity in the face of the great personal freedom she enjoyed: "she had freedom without any that governed her in her palace" (de Voragine, *Golden Legend*, Life of St. Catherine). Thanks to her resistance to the temptations of freedom, she can advocate the Christian interpretation of freedom, when she admonishes the emperor: "If thou governest thyself by good courage thou shalt be a king, and if thou governest thee otherwise thou shalt be a servant." Freedom is no longer the status of the free man, but the integrity of the pious soul.

Although cinema and hagiography are both popular genres, this understanding of freedom, which equates it with dignity and personal courage, is by no means entirely lowbrow. Solzhenitsyn (in Amis 2002) recounts the story of the Polish engineer Jerzy Wegierski, a political prisoner in the camp at Ekibastuz, who participated in a hunger strike. When strikers saw one of the neighboring huts surrender, they broke down and wept, but not Wegierski: "But now—his face was distorted with rage, scorn and suffering, as he tore his eyes from that procession of beggars, and cried in an angry, steely voice: 'Foreman! Don't wake me for supper! I shan't be going!' He clambered up onto the top bunk,

turned his face to the wall—and didn't get up again. That night we
went to eat—but he didn't get up! He never received parcels, he was
quite alone, he was always short of food—but he wouldn't get up. In
his mind's eye the steam from a bowl of mush could not veil the ideal
of freedom" (Solzhenitsyn, quoted in Amis 2002, 264).

Despite its romantic popularity, however, the martyrological model
is not a proper way of understanding the notion of freedom in currency
among the Greeks, long before Christian times. In Classical Athens
there was no tyrant, no governor, no prefect to oppress the individual;
and without a Pontius Pilate, an Olibrius or yet a Stalin, there can be
no Christ, no St. Margaret, and no Solzhenitsyn. Prior to the development of Christian apologetic writings, and of the stoic literature that
similarly juxtaposed social position and personal freedom, the thinkers
of the fifth and fourth centuries B.C.E. did not explore the paradoxical
correlation between physical confinement or corporal punishment on
one hand and spiritual freedom on the other. No doubt, this is partly
due to the fact that incarceration was not a common practice in the
Greek world, and torture was largely reserved for slaves. For the class
of free men, from among whom came the literate élite, more common
sanctions were *atimia*—namely, a loss of citizen's rights, banishment,
or even death. Indeed, the only extensive "prison narrative" to come
to us from Classical Athens involves the philosopher Socrates, whose
execution has often been treated as an example of intellectual martyrdom. Certainly, to modern eyes, his trial and execution seem to fit the
very pattern of freedom internalized and confirmed through suffering.
According to such an interpretation, the Athenians could execute
Socrates but they could not silence him. But a closer examination of
Plato raises questions about whether any aspect of the Socrates myth,
from the trial in 399 B.C.E. to the hagiography produced by Plato in
the following generation, has had a deep or enduring impact on Greek
conceptions of freedom.

To begin with, it would be difficult to discover a statement in Plato's
work that explicitly connects Socrates' fate to the question of freedom.
Plato lived through the suspension of democracy at the end of the
Peloponnesian War and the reign of the Thirty, a pro-Spartan junta that
ruled Athens autocratically for nine months in 404–403 B.C.E. He then
witnessed the restoration of the Democracy and the trial of Socrates
shortly after. Referring to these events, Plato describes, in Letter VII,
how, as a young man, having assumed that he would go into a life
of politics, he was so disgusted by the prevailing wickedness of the

oligarchic regime that he abandoned the idea. And the Democracy's victory, in 403 B.C.E., did not improve matters, either. Socrates was tainted by association with the oligarchs—one of their leaders, Critias, had been his student. In 399 B.C.E., he was charged with impiety and with the corruption of the young. Once restored, the Democracy publicly vowed not to dwell on crimes committed during the rule of the Thirty. But the charges against Socrates, being clearly politically motivated, were not forgotten. The trial of Socrates, who, for Plato, was "the best man then living," would only add to Plato's disillusionment, precipitating his decision to go into self-imposed exile. In his words, "The corruption of written law and established custom was proceeding at an astonishing rate, so that I, who began by feeling full of enthusiasm for a political career, ended by growing dizzy at the spectacle of universal confusion. . . . I came to the conclusion that the condition of all existing states is bad" (Plato *Ep. VII* 325C–326A, trans. Hamilton).

The language here reveals a characteristically Greek way of seeing civil *stasis:* corruption and confusion are the enemies of harmony and good order, but nowhere does Plato complain of a loss of liberty. Nowhere does he characterize the coup of the Thirty Tyrants as an attack on democratic liberty, nor does he anywhere describe the trial of Socrates as an attack on an individual's liberty. Since Plato was closely connected both to the Thirty and to Socrates—the oligarchic leader Critias being a cousin of Plato's, and Socrates being a teacher of both Plato and Critias—it may be understandable why Plato was not too keen to untangle the skein of relations connecting Socrates and himself to the Thirty Tyrants. But Plato's own involvement aside, it is telling that freedom was not among the issues raised explicitly in Plato's treatment of Socrates' trial and execution.

In the *Apology*, Socrates eschews the role of martyr and, provocatively, even plays the role of the good citizen. He does this by *participating* actively in his own defense, right up to and into the sentencing phase—unlike most convicted defendants who, when facing execution, were more likely to flee than to risk the alternative. Also, Socrates bases his defense on a summation of his career, in which he argues that his questioning has always served the higher, nobler civic purpose of unmasking his fellow citizens' ignorance. It was a defense strategy that would prove as irritating as the behavior that had gotten him in trouble in the first place—and deliberately so. At no point does Socrates seek protection of his right to speak or complain that the very right to do just that is under attack. Rather, Socrates claims that his exposure of others' foolishness was in response to the Delphic oracle, which had confirmed that no one was wiser than Socrates—clearly thereby insinuating that his actions had been religiously sanctioned and also civically motivated. Yet, in the array of arguments that Socrates brings to his defense, freedom, whether of speech, of the individual, of conscience, or of even a loftier notion—the freedom of the democratic state—is always thoroughly absent.

Plato deals explicitly with the execution of Socrates in two dialogues: the *Crito* and the *Phaedo*. In the former, Socrates is portrayed as imagining the Laws of Athens to speak to him as a single voice in advising him on how to act, when faced with the condemnation of the court. In making the Laws of Athens Socrates' interlocutor, as it were, Plato liberates the first glimmerings of a concept of the State. But whereas a modern notion of the State would explore the state's formal responsibilities to the individual, and may contain an implicit tension between State and Individual, ancient Greeks were more inclined to think in terms of the individual's responsibility to the community. As Socrates suggests in the *Crito*, goodness and integrity, institutions and laws, are the most precious possessions of mankind. And so, the execution of Socrates raises problems about the question of order and the rule of law, but not the question of freedom. The dilemma Socrates faces concerns his obligations, not his freedoms. What transforms a martyr into a symbol of freedom, precisely because of her physical suffering and death, is the sense we can give to Socrates' fate, though it is not how Plato presents him.

In the *Phaedo*, Plato's Socrates tackles the question of how to face death. The underlying theme is that the search for goodness is a moral imperative and that death need not be feared, since it is no more than a release of the body from its mortal shell. Here, Socrates chooses to use the image of the shackled prisoner—familiar from the allegory of the cave in Book Seven of the *Republic*—to suggest the liberation offered by philosophy. Explains Socrates: "Every seeker after wisdom knows that up to the time philosophy takes it over the soul is a helpless prisoner, chained hand and foot in the body, compelled to view reality not directly but only through its prison bars, and wallowing in utter ignorance . . . . Well, philosophy takes over the soul in this condition and by gentle persuasion tries to set it free . . . . Now the soul of the true philosopher feels that it must not reject this opportunity for release, and so it abstains as far as possible from pleasures and desires and griefs" (Plato *Phaedo* 83A, trans. Tredennick).

The language used in both episodes—"bound," "released," "set free"—shows that enlightenment is envisaged as spiritual *liberation*, and yet this had little impact on how Plato's contemporaries understood freedom. What, however, both passages do address is not the *state* of freedom but the *process* of becoming free (see Hackney, chap. 11 in this book). Actually, Plato has little to say about what the ultimate state of philosophical freedom is like. It will be his successors, the Neo-Platonists, who will offer lyrical descriptions of the return of the Soul to God and the annihilation of self. Plato's philosophy is more about getting there than what one sees once one is there. The moment of release that Socrates imagines in death is like the setting free of a prisoner, or a slave. So the wise man, inspired by philosophy, turns his back on emotional attachments and physical appetites, becoming through that gesture the prisoner or slave who wins his freedom. Put differently, Plato's descriptions of enlightenment reflect very simply the otherwise conventional notion that, all in all, freedom is the most desirable status to which one can aspire.

The case of Socrates, therefore, is more complicated than we might expect. The Athenians came to regret their decision within a generation of executing the home-grown sophist. Twentieth-century C.E. appreciations of freedom being not conceivable to the Athenians of the fourth century B.C.E., however, the latter did not even attempt to fashion Socrates into their martyr to intellectual freedom. Indeed, the initiative would take much longer to arrive. Yet, if enlightenment had little impact on the ancient Greek conception of freedom, at least freedom did help to shape the ancient Greek understanding of enlightenment. In the third century B.C.E., the mode and mood of Socratic philosophical inquiry would grow both more systematic and more dogmatic, but many philosophers continued to share the belief that the key goal of philosophy was to free the mind of disturbance. For Epicurus this began with those natural desires that must be indulged "to free the body from troubles" (Epicurus *Diog. Laert.* 10.127). After accommodating his basic human needs, the wise man could "refer every choice to the health of the body and the freedom of the soul from disturbance" (Epicurus *Diog. Laert.* 10.128). In the hands of Epicurus and his followers, who turned away from active engagement with the outside world, preferring the ascetic pleasures of *the Garden*, freedom came to be the opposite of the emblem of the full member of the community, instead becoming the mark of one's interior life. "A free life cannot acquire great wealth, because the task is not easy without slavery to the mob or those in power" (Epicurus *Sent. Vat.* 67). Here the traditional usages of the free/slave opposition are inverted, or translated from the public realm to the private operations of morality and self-realization. Similarly, "[t]he greatest fruit of self-sufficiency is freedom" (Epicurus *Sent. Vat.* 77). This transference of freedom from the public realm to the private became a trope of philosophic self-fashioning. Thus, Seneca, one of the most wealthy and powerful men to live in Nero's Rome, could write without a hint of irony: "You ought to be a slave to philosophy in order to achieve true liberty" (Sen. *Ep.* 8.7).

Freedom and Status

The Greek conception of freedom was shaped by the conditions of the polis, a city-state in which all adult male citizens were expected to perform the role of the free man. Freedom was not regarded as a right, but rather as a privileged *status*—the final marker of *inclusion* (Kumar and Silver 2008). In Chariton's *Chaereas and Callirhoe*, a popular romance of the Hellenistic age, the heroine Callirhoe survives beating, burial, and kidnapping. She is sold as a slave, but her master, Dionysios, a well-born city councilor, sees her beauty and falls in love with her. When pressed to reveal her status, she blushes and says, "This is the first time I have ever been sold." Dionysios exclaims triumphantly, "I told you she was not a slave! And I'll bet she is of noble blood!" But she demurs, "I beg you to allow me to remain silent about my fortunes. My origins were but a fabulous dream. I am now what I have become, a slave and a foreigner" (Chariton *Chaereas and Callirhoe* 2.5.5–6). For the free man, that was the ultimate nightmare: to lose one's origins, to lose one's status, and to lose one's freedom. As cultures changed and civilizations diversified, so would the modes of citizenship and the moods of freedom, and the attending tone and tenor in their understanding and conduct would transform over time, in response, although sometimes also in reaction, to the new circumstances and imperatives of the evolution in the human condition. But then, this is a matter for Greg Urban to dwell on, in his chapter, with an eye to the future.

References

Amis, Martin (2002) *Koba the Dread: Laughter and the Twenty Million*, New York: Vintage.

Berlin, Isaiah (2002) "Two Concepts of Liberty," in Henry Hardy, Editor, *Liberty: Incorporating Four Essays on Liberty*, New York and Oxford: Oxford University Press.

Bynum, Caroline Walker (1995) *The Resurrection of the Body in Western Christianity, 200–1336*, New York: Columbia University Press.

Cartledge, Paul (1993) *The Greeks*, Oxford: Oxford University Press.

Davies, John Kenyon (1977–78) "Athenian Citizenship: The Descent Group and the Alternatives," *Classical Journal* 73:105–121.

de Romilly, Jacqueline (1989) *La Grèce antique à la découverte de la liberté*, Paris: Éditions de Fallois.

duBois, Page (1988) *Sowing the Body. Psychoanalysis and Ancient Representations of Women*, Chicago and London: University of Chicago Press.

———— (1991) *Torture and Truth*, New York: Routledge.

———— (2003) *Slaves and Other Objects*, Chicago and London: University of Chicago Press.

Finley, Moses I. (1983) "Between Slavery and Freedom," in Moses Finley, *Economy and Society in Ancient Greece*, edited with an introduction by Brent D. Shaw and Richard P. Saller, New York: Penguin.

Garlan, Yvon (1988) *Slavery in Ancient Greece*, J. Lloyd, Translator, Ithaca, NY: Cornell University Press.

Hansen, Mogens G. (1996) "The Ancient Athenian and the Modern Liberal View of Liberty as a Democratic Ideal," in Josiah Ober and Charles Hedrick, Editors, *Demokratia*, Princeton, NJ: Princeton University Press; pp. 91–104.

Kumar, Rahul, and David Silver (2008) "The Ethics of Exclusion," in Jose V. Ciprut, Editor, *The Future of Citizenship*, Cambridge, MA: The MIT Press.

Mathias Jr., Charles McC. (1995) "The Story of the Constitution," in *The Constitution of the United States of America*, pp. 85–112, New York: Barnes and Noble.

Mulhern, J. J. (2008) "Ethics, Morals, and the State: A Classical View," in Jose V. Ciprut, Editor (2008), *Ethics, Politics, and Democracy: From Primordial Principles to Prospective Practices*, Cambridge, MA: The MIT Press.

Ober, Josiah, and Charles Hedrick, Editors (1996) *Demokratia: A Conversation on Democracies Ancient and Modern*, Princeton, NJ: Princeton University Press.

Ostwald, Martin (1996) "Shares and Rights: 'Citizenship' Greek Style and American Style," in Josiah Ober and Charles Hedrick, Editors, *Demokratia: A Conversation on Democracies Ancient and Modern*, pp. 49–61, Princeton, NJ: Princeton University Press.

Parke, H. W. (1977) *Festivals of the Athenians*, Ithaca, NY: Cornell University Press.

Raaflaub, Kurt (1985) *Die Entdeckung der Freiheit*, Munich: Beck.

Strauss, Barry (1996) "The Athenian Trireme, School of Democracy," in Josiah Ober and Charles Hedrick, Editors, *Demokratia*, pp. 313–325, Princeton, NJ: Princeton University Press.

Thucydides (1996) *The Landmark Thucydides: A Comprehensive Guide to the Peloponnesian War*, edited by Robert B. Strassler, with an introduction by Victor Davis, Harrison, NY: Free Press.

Vidal-Naquet, Pierre (1995) *Politics Ancient and Modern*, Cambridge: Polity Press.

3   Boxed In, Boxed Out: Whither Freedom?

Elvira Arcenas

Nothing more effectively conveys a sense of diminishment of the self than the metaphor "confinement." When I admit to being "trapped, imprisoned, or boxed in," what in fact I am conveying is that "I am not, or do not feel, myself." Conversely, when I express deliverance from what I have regarded to be a physical, let alone a psychological, or moral entrapment, my suggestion is that—at long last—I was able to recover my "self" and to set it free: now, "I am finally myself." With natural ease, we tend to identify our self with "freedom"—that ethereal human capacity to think, feel, but also to enact "liberty" in the manner and in the direction of our choosing. "But what is this self of mine?" asks Kierkegaard. "If I were to speak of a first moment, a first expression for it, then my answer is this: It is the most abstract of all, and yet in itself it is also the most concrete of all—it is freedom" (Hong and Hong 2000, 80).

The self, essentially, is freedom; yet, to be "boxed in" is a fact of life. We are born into this world as a bundle of possibilities. These are framed, however loosely, by our biological heredity and our physical and social worlds. We come confected (or "thrown," as Williams and Barber put it in their chapter), endowed with definite physical and psychological features never completely identical even among twins, and always vulnerable to particular kinds of maladies. It was not for us to select the mix of chromosomes that make up our human self, or to elect the womb that safely delivered us into daylight. We are thrust into this world at a time and a place we have neither willed nor foreseen, to be entrusted into the hands of strangers from whom next we have to learn how to live a human life. Even our first bursts of recognition of the world around us are shaped by the peculiarities of our speech organs and by the very sounds that we are given to hear.

In short, we were delivered into this world like an unwrapped gift of both indeterminate and indeterminable potentialities (see Krippendorff 2008), to make of it what we can, as we wish. Our "being," initially a given, promptly demands to be transformed into a project of "becoming." We are chosen, and once "chosen," we are in turn expected to choose. If we paused even just briefly to review the life path we have traversed, we would hardly fail to recognize that birth—our very own "delivery" as a newborn—has been but a promise of freedom with a price tag. The new creature is sent forth to acquire "real" freedom, by being born anew in the never-ending exercise of free will, in an endless series of performances that are tested by the limits of the human condition.

Free choice, above and beyond its immediate or final object, is always a choice of one's self. Every act of choice is one that entails risks (Kleindorfer, chap. 6 in this book) and as such contributes to what makes us a person—what constructs our identity. Each act, in a more or less direct way, is tied to the initial conditions of our existence and is constantly shaped by the interactions of the self with its surroundings (Urban, chap. 10 in this book). The exercise of free choice is thus conditioned by the world that affects, infects, and sometimes rejects our actions. Moreover, the exercise itself has to be coaxed, oriented, and assisted in the initial stages of life, the length of which varies across cultures. The developmental stages of human growth depict an expanding awareness of personal autonomy, therefore of one's capacity to make free choices. As reason claims an ever-intrusive role in the exercise of free actions, careful deliberation increasingly informs the will. So do purposeful actions gradually supplant the instinctive act or the impulsive reaction by the pondered action. As we improve our ability to make categorical distinctions and to construct symbolic representations of things, particularly in linguistic usage, we also begin to discover both the blessing and the burden of free choices.

In a short animated cartoon produced by the National Film Board of Canada in 1968, director Elliot Noyes adroitly uses line drawings to depict the predicament of a person boxed in by life. Given the opportunity to be liberated from his confining "box" and to float in the ether of unbridled movement, the character prefers to return to the security and comfort of his shell, however cumbrous. After all, one can always find a modicum of freedom even within the hedges of a narrow life. This arguably is a better option than the barrierless situation conjuring up images of disorder, chaos, and meaninglessness. Yet, being smug about the present state of one's existence defeats the inherent dynamism of freedom. For freedom is not just about what is; it is also and particularly about what can be. Walls are not torn down merely for the sake of being freed of obstruction. Absent the reach of "freedom for," the safeguards of "freedom from" are meaningless.

The human quest for freedom—hence, for self-actualization—is continually thwarted and challenged, not only by the natural equipment of our human bodies, and by the world that harbors us, but also by the walls of our own handmade boxes, built from complex choices driven by such labyrinthine feelings as prejudice, hatred, and envy. Fettered by the necessities and contingencies of earthly life and by the very same actions that tie humans in a web of relationships, the self has to be released continuously from its bondage—through the exercise of the free will. What is peculiar about this task is that the self, as well, emerging and developing as it does always—in relation to the other—cannot disengage itself from that bondage without the other. Freedom, in other words, cannot but be relational.

The genuine path to freedom can be traversed through dialogue: that social matrix in which the human community emerges, sustains, and re-creates itself, that medium by which community can become communion. In communion, human beings are released from the entanglements of self-absorption; they experience each other as "presence." If truth sets us free, as so often we are told, it is because truth, which commits us to discern the kernel of meaning in human encounters, merges with interpretation in a horizon voluntarily shared by all the co-present.

This chapter examines the plight of human freedom—wo/man caught between indefinite boundedness and incessant desire for liberation—the better to expose the virtues of dialogical encounter, the latter which, at its most reflective, paves the path to liberating communion.

Boxed In/Boxed Out

The boundaries constraining human freedom are manifold. Some are built into our very fabric as embodied beings. Others, which we share with nonhuman creatures, are given by our spatial-temporal locations on earth. Then there are the social limits we create, such as customs and laws, in response to either the superabundance or the utter poverty of our earthly reality. Not least are the boundaries of thoughts, feelings, and behavior, which we impose upon ourselves and others either as a function of individual propensities and cultural habits, or in defense of our personal interests, or yet as a means to compete for power and scarce resources.

Paradoxically, to be free is to engage in a continuous process of breaking down walls that stand in our way while erecting new barriers that safeguard one's pursuit of the authentic self for which freedom is fought. Walls built to shut out potential threats to freedom often also can deprive those seeking such latitude of one of the most important prerequisites for durable liberty: inclusiveness in self-liberating diversity.

The Biological Box

Our first experience of limited freedom occurs when we come up against the cloak of natural limits with which we have been outfitted at birth. The most fixed of them is genetic inheritance. For the most part it serves us well, enabling us to do the things conducive to our goals. The fact is: we are not easily resigned to accepting it as is.

The history of medicine is replete with cases in which the barriers erected by physical abnormalities are proven to be far from impregnable. We have seen the successful "normalization" of people afflicted with physical anomalies, as in the surgical separation of the conjoined heads of the two-year-old Egyptian twin boys, to restore them to the autonomy they were entitled to in nature (Grady 2003). Medical drugs, human organ replacements, prostheses for all kinds of physical impairments, each and all, attest to the human determination to surmount physical limitations of natural or accidental origin.

Nor do physical repairs ever suffice to quell our thirst to experiment with freedom. We strive to improve on nature. We tamper with, and select certain unique properties of, living things—plants, animals, humans—to combine them in ways that will produce the new creatures of our dreams. We go on to choose the sex of our children, make test-tube babies, prolong and terminate human life at will. Pending some political decision, alter egos may soon cease to be metaphors in a clone-filled milieu. The future seems to bar no holds (see Pyeritz 2008).

Increasingly, our world is becoming artificial also in the ways that we technologically extend the reach and capacities of our biological heritage. We simulate and duplicate our characteristically most human function—intelligence—by constructing even higher speed computers and dexterous robots. We extend our ubiquity and sensorial range through cellular technology that accelerates the tempo of our already highly pressured workaday existence and allows prying eyes and ears to let no nook of our private life remain sacred. "Tethered by a high-tech leash," as one news title puts it, we impose upon ourselves extended working hours, without therefore even blaming our employers.

Aware of our subjection to necessity, whether of the body, or of the earth, we seek to reassert our freedom in quests of new worlds where we anticipate that our natural laws are not likely to obtain. We rise above the earth, far into the vast universe, in hopes of knowing (and therefore perchance subduing) the secrets of our own habitat, and perhaps also discovering among our planetary neighbors a "new earth" that may host the new "human" we are liberating. As Hannah Arendt (Arendt and Fackenheim 1971) has pointed out, we are no longer content to accept human existence as it was given, a free gift from nowhere, but we want to trade it, as it were, for something human-made.

As we endeavor to overcome the limits imposed by nature, we are also busily at work barricading ourselves within the sometimes more if other times less invisible walls of our own making. Embodied spirits or minds as we are, we appear superbly well qualified when it comes to constructing boundaries—geographical, political, social, or cultural. Try as we may, we seem unable to bring ourselves to live and to let live without some separation, division, exclusion, or enclosure. For no sooner do we find ourselves about to emerge from our shells, as a larva from its cocoon, than we find ourselves already spinning webs of entrapment as if to protect ourselves from total surrender to the very world that beckons us to freedom. Uncertain of what awaits us there even as we heed the call, we make provisions for a hostile reception.

Geopolitical Boundaries

Boundary-making is integral to our attempt to cope with the plenitude of life. It is a tool of survival. It affords our senses and our higher intellectual capacities a ground manageable enough for the selective satisfaction of our basic needs and desires. Unlimited space and overabundant variety intoxicate but also inhibit action.

Offered a piece of land, we build fences around it. We assign various parts of it to serve different hierarchies of needs. Within the bounded area, we choose a special space for our private dwelling large enough to meet real or perceived requirements and/or to make an implicit or a public statement about our image of our self. Material resources permitting, ordinarily we design our houses, our reception areas, in such a way that they express the kind and amount of freedom we consciously or unconsciously attribute to and want for ourselves.

Like most human projects, boundary-making, whether political, geographical, or social, cannot be performed in isolation, every wo/man a fort to oneself. Borders implicate all the entities situated on either side of them. Attempting to modify extant borders often threatens the equilibrium of relationships at the fulcrum of peaceful coexistence. Past and ongoing conflicts in many parts of the world exemplify the consequences of unilateral moves to redraw limits—by invaders, colonizers, "gerrymanderers," and others. And even when a boundary is somehow successfully imposed, when it is arbitrarily drawn by a stronger hand and not jointly agreed upon by the contending parties, its legitimacy remains questionable on the simple ground that it violates the "human condition of plurality" which Arendt (1971), for one, has considered to be the foundation of all political life.

In practice, being the victor of a bitter war does not always assure the sweet peace of freedom one has sought. When the bounded-out party resists, the victor can become its own prisoner of sorts while trying to hold the rebellious vanquished at bay. In Baghdad, allied occupation authorities and international workers barricaded themselves inside the Green Zone, a four-square-mile enclave protected by 15-foot concrete walls and rings of barbed wire, put together to shield the reformers from reactionary insurgent attacks.

Where freedom risks being curtailed by turmoil in limitrophic space, setting up a protective wall may well be the only defense under the circumstances. When the president of Georgia, Edward Shevardnadze, was ousted by the recent "revolution of roses," the leader of nearby virtually sovereign Adzharia reacted by closing in parts of that region's borders with the rest of the country. A precaution that the Adzharian leader, Aslan Abashidze, argued to be a sound way of preventing the outbreak of war, which, as wars in the Caucasus go, once triggered, are never ending (Baker 2003).

Humans, nevertheless, refuse to be daunted by geopolitical boundaries. They invent ever newer ways of circumventing or bridging them. In addition to the transportation channels that these days make physical boundaries look as imaginary as in fact they are, they find other creative ways of zipping together two separate countries—for example, by creating cross-border wildlife refuges and parks. In addition to the 150 border parks existing in the world today, new "peace parks" are being envisioned in the demilitarized zone between the two Koreas and between Russia and Japan. These peace projects face resistance not so much from the recalcitrant topology of physical geography as from the adamantine walls of suspicion and distrust that continue to divide peoples still fettered by memories of past wrongs.

Psycho-Social Borders

Beyond or underneath the physical and political delimitations that humans devise, there exist boundaries of attitudes, feelings, and behaviors that are consciously and unconsciously built into almost every psychosocial-cultural relationship.

First, there is the more evident deep-rooted tendency to view and judge others through our ethnocentric filters (see Riggs 2000). Ethnocentrism is a function of our bounded nature as embodied beings. We tend to see things only from *our* "standpoint" and to process the meaning of all that surrounds us in terms of that point of reference. We have been socialized early on—in our family, our neighborhood, and our social institutions—to believe that truthful and friendly are only those defined by proximity and similarity to our own principles and pursuits. What is strange, foreign, and distant to us is doomed to remain dubious and probably dangerous. Our myths, laws, traditions, and customs, for better or for worse, codify our ethnocentric views and values in broad strokes. Formed naturally and unconsciously, and therefore more likely to be left unchecked by reflexive thought, our ethnocentric views can become ultimately noxious, not only to self's "shut-out" other, but also and especially to self's very own freedom. Despite our natural tendency to move inside the limits of our ethnocentric box, we are fortunately accoutered to break through those very limits. Differences repel, but they also attract. They break the monotony and restrictions of homogeneous relationships.

The tendency to associate with similar others, or homophily, is natural and not to be scorned: "Every beast loveth its like: so also every man him that is nearest to himself" (Eccles. 13:19). "Tell me who your friends are, and I'll tell you who you are." We love what is like us, even when we have a private reason to dislike ourselves. The recent rise in the Internet of friendship forums, differentiated from matchmaking services, confirms humans' inveterate proclivity to seek out compatibility through like-mindedness. Some Web sites now promote chance encounters among friends of friends, the underlying assumption being the likelihood of transferability of likes and dislikes inside the expanded family of a close-knit group of individuals. "If friends are friends because they have something in common, there is a greater likelihood that the friends of your friends may have something in common with you" (Jamison 2003).

Homophily builds up, protects, and defends identity. Without the reassuring company of a similar other, the self is liable to break down (see Gergen 2000). Similar identities are mutually reinforcing and developing, albeit not always for the greater good. This in turn explains the mushrooming of racist chat-sites and subversive cliques.

A case can be built, nevertheless, for the necessity and the usefulness of heterophily, or the tendency to seek out "dissimilar" others. Without difference, identity cannot define and sustain itself. It is through the eyes of different others that the self is confirmed. A distinct identity calls for something apart and different from it. To consolidate its growth, the self needs the support and affirmation of similar others. But to define and to build its distinctiveness, the self needs contrast with dissimilar others. A person thus owes its own distinctiveness and wholeness to the continuous interaction with both similar and different others. One's need for similarity and difference may explain another emerging practice on some Internet sites—profuse provision of opportunities for "strangers" to meet and befriend each other along lines of activities: guitarists with other guitarists, and students preparing for an exam in a field teaming up with theretofore unknown comrades-at-arms in the same predicament, for joint review.

Prejudice—a by-product of an extreme form of homophily—cannot be tolerated as a natural or justifiable boundary between persons or groups of persons, precisely because it corrodes the integrity of self and other, as well as the malevolent relationship that links the two. Prejudice is built upon irrational fears feeding on antipathies of the unknown and on hasty condemnations of that which remains to be faced— whether different races, colors, creeds, social statuses, or the like. We also build walls of prejudice to protect us from "contamination" by what seems to threaten our identity as individuals or as a group. Such defensive solidarity with our like-minded others can, and often does, lead to legitimating practices that can in turn institutionalize and entrench prejudice even more deeply into group consciousness (see Spinner-Halev 2008).

In the name of national security, it is easy to translate an obdurate dislike for a certain bodily appearance or consonance of name typifying actual and potential enemies into exclusionary regulations and laws. Justifiable on grounds of threat of infiltration by dangerous foreigners, such laws are often also tinged with a sweeping distrust of people who appear merely different. And so we build our walls ever higher, in an attempt to spare ourselves the discomfort of discovering the possibility that perceived differences and dissimilarities may be in the eye of the beholder. Immigration laws that may seem too lenient in their capacity to rigidify the boundaries between citizens and foreigners sometimes have to be reworded to the extent of separating a permanent resident from one's own children. And, as in the case of the two teenage Ghanaian girls—daughters of a permanent resident in Hamburg, Germany— ordered to be deported back to their homeland Ghana (Bernstein 2003) by the terms of a coercive and nondiscretionary German law, innocent children, by a twist of misfortune, may well end up in one or the other deportable category of undesirable aliens.

In the United States, the new immigration laws enforced in the wake of September 11, 2001, have made the deportation of *personae non gratae* in general, and of "undesirable aliens" in particular, much easier. This would seem to have more particularly hit Cambodian-Americans who were admitted to the country after the war in Indochina, but whose lingering difficulties to adjust to the way of life of their country of adoption have made many of these refugees—most of them peasants in their native land—more susceptible to repatriation. Ironically, many of these refugees argued that the most they had expected from the United States was but an implicit promise of freedom (Sontag 2003).

Prejudice, pushed to its limits in hate crimes, cannot thrive without the support of a tight-knit group. Hilton (2003) reports on a study by Jessica Stern, which—in the case of religious militants who kill—found that each group believes itself to be uniquely favored by God, even though each individual follows his own trajectory. Feuds, more often than not, turn out to be struggles for land and resources, mediated by ideologies of identity as well (see Fetni 2008).

Lastly, there are, of course, boundaries of gender (Hirschmann, chap. 9 in this book), which sometimes support rationalizations of violence. During the conflicts in Liberia, which began in 1989, many women— often the same ones—were raped by armed men from all factions. In wars within or between nations, women often end up as spoils of conquest, "not unlike sacks of rice and four-wheel-drive vehicles" (Sengupta 2003).

In the Grips of Technology

Alongside individually erected or group-created walls injurious to freedom are those erected by institutional greed. Economic demands can create working conditions deleterious to human relationships, and that includes self's relationship with itself. An economy that aims at constantly higher profits treasures productivity so much that at times it can place the psychological and physical health of workers at risk. The fewer worker protection laws in the United States, compared with those in Europe, for instance, can drive employees, fearful of losing their jobs, to work even more and to take even fewer vacations (see Jones 2003).[1] The American obsession with work, undoubtedly, benefits the strongest economy in the world, but arguably, at the expense of the quality of family life. Ironically, under pressure from the expansion of U.S. businesses around the world, the hitherto seemingly more worker friendly European firms are starting globally and locally to adopt American work habits.

Even as they leave it to their workers to place their health at risk for the greater corporate good, businesses prefer to pursue self-enhancement by identifying with social causes. Thus, fashion tries to "ennoble" and sell its frivolity by association with social issues, such as cancer research, environmental protection, or medical care for disadvantaged communities. Examples are the initiative taken by Ralph Lauren companies to promote youth volunteerism through jean sales and the use by Giorgio Armani of some of its profits in a special edition Armani Barbie to battle youth AIDS (Trebay 2003). In a competitive and crowded market, where consumers are increasingly dazed by the numerous choices they have to make, the theme of good citizenship comes to the rescue, often by virtue of special-effects criteria for discriminating among brands. Aggressive profit-making puts on a jolly mien of freedom through altruistic gestures of corporate social responsibility staged principally to favor self-serving aims in the shorter and longer runs.

Universally considered to be a savior of humans' subjugation to labor, technology consistently has fomented and furthered utter obsession with work, instead of slowing it down (Bonné 2003; Schoen 2003). The 40-hour-week schedule is quickly becoming a thing of the past as

---

1. At the time of this writing, European workers typically take an average of thirty paid vacation days a year, while U.S. workers still take only sixteen such full days.

an increasing array of computers, mobile phones, pagers, and fax machines begin to blur the boundaries of home and office. Though no company rules expressly demand it, there seems to be a tacit expectation for workers to have Internet connection at home and access to e-mail and fax machines at all times. Because time and place no longer condition work, telecommuting has leashed us permanently to technology, which in turn serves to extend the reach of our gaze and thought but also our bodily availability, in all directions all of the time. We have accepted that we must trade the directness of eye-to-eye interactions for the convenient spontaneity of vicarious and virtual contacts through cellular-texting or wireless e-mailing. There is no going back to leisurely times, for our ever-faster self-depleting and self-replacing efficient technology is demanding, exacting greatest energy and highest commitment to work.

The barriers to freedom built by technology-assisted obsession with work complement the barricades set up by technologically managed images of the self. We surround ourselves with gadgets, imagining them to possess the magic to transform us into the self that they promise. Soon enough, we discover the flimsiness of the hard-pedaled imaginary connections linking product purchased to extant self, to aspired aura. Instead of bestowing empowerment, objects vainly sought to reflect the pretended self end up preventing personal freedoms from taking wings.

Another kind of boundary enhanced by technology can be seen in the increasing robotization, therefore depersonalization, of services in the marketplace. Customers now have the option of making purchases more efficiently through self-service machines, online ordering and payment, bypassing potentially frustrating interactions with service workers. The tendency to prefer robotic efficiency to thereby sadly suboptimized human interaction, though sometimes of undeniably high relief, can deprive the self of the vital processes and contexts that humanize our civic freedoms.

Globalization: Disabling and Enabling

Citizens of industrialized countries may be bearing the brunt of the drive by their highly advanced societies to sustain or to buttress economic abundance, but peoples in less modern countries continue to be hemmed in by walls of poverty upheld by asymmetries in institutional greed exercised by the dominant economies of the world, as also by the corrupt ineptness of their governing bodies at home, and their own lingering shortcomings in matters of health, education, nourishment, skills, and political will. Public pledges by rich countries to provide funds—for example, for the basic education of the world's children— often dissolve in hollow rhetoric. The Global Campaign for Education reported that in 2003 the US$1.4 billion contributed annually by the affluent countries fell far too short of achieving the goals of education. The estimated US$5.6 billion needed in additional aid is equivalent to just three days of global military spending, and, as Oliver Buston of Oxfam notes, is just one fifth the US$28 billion that ordinary Americans spend on pizza each year, and as much as half of the US$11.2 billion that Europeans spend annually on ice cream, on last count (see Reuters 2003).

Thanks to "globalization," territorial insularity may appear at long last to be giving way to cultural openness. And as the world grows friendlier, Western culture, too, seems to be shedding many of its self-styled trappings that have made it appear so different and so difficult to access for so long. A Chinese-American, all-Chinese looks and fluency in Mandarin Chinese to boot, only a decade earlier was met with urban curiosity in China. Now, even the rural Chinese take him for granted, without so much as a raised eyebrow. This attitudinal change, one comes to realize, has little to do with the visitor from abroad if much to do with how many among the 1.5 billion Chinese have changed their traditional selves and their set views, in the interim.

The other face of globalization, however, looks more menacing to national and cultural freedom. Wal-Mart—the biggest corporation in the United States—helps to brighten Mexico's grim economy by being that country's biggest private employer. Supermarket space in Mexico City now looks practically the same as in Kansas City, USA, or uptown Vancouver in Canada—in layout, range of service, and product variety, as well as in quality and price (Weiner 2003). But the nation's cultural integrity suffers under the veneer of commercial assimilation. Even a study by the Carnegie Endowment for International Peace questions the beneficial effects of trade liberalization. The North American Free Trade Agreement is reported to have failed to generate substantial job growth in Mexico, to have hurt hundreds of thousands of subsistence farmers there, and to have yielded "minuscule" net effects on jobs inside the United States (Dugger 2003).

Some U.S. trade practices are also taking their toll on AIDS victims in poor countries. Guatemala, with its 67,000 HIV-infected people, spends most of its scanty AIDS funds on proprietary drugs made by U.S. companies like Bristol-Myers Squibb, instead of using its meager budget for purchasing far lower priced generic antiretrovirals (Kristoff 2003). The fear of antagonizing the United States, seen by some to be enough reason to protect patents rather than to prolong lives, is one of the motives driving some governments in Central America to purchase brand names rather than the less costly generics. It is not surprising, therefore, that many citizens in some developing countries are opposing globalization as being synonymous with submission or self-denigration. In October 2003, several thousand Bolivian workers, mostly miners and coca growers, marched to protest their govern-ment's decision to export natural gas to the United States through a Chilean port (Rohter 2003). Disillusioned by their twenty-one-year experience with the free-market model, Bolivians now want to go it alone in solving their persistent problems of poverty and social exclu-sion. A tall order, indeed.

Symbolic Fences

So far, we have explored some of the more obvious boundaries to freedom, deriving from human action and from some of the corre-sponding attempts to overcome those constraints. However, comple-mentary to, and independent of—yet more often closely intertwined with—human action, language has proven to be a formidable tool both for suppressing and for releasing freedom at all levels of human rela-tionships, be they in the interpersonal, intercultural, or international sphere of exchanges. In fact, language is a special kind of action—that is, symbolic action (see Burke 1966)—capable of producing conse-quences as weighty, and at least as emotionally hurtful, as those of physical action.

Language can demarcate person-to-person and also group-to-group relationships. Such polar expressions as us-versus-them, enshrined in the daily lexicon of every living language, attest to the human propen-sity for creating spheres of inclusion and realms of exclusion (see Kumar and Silver 2008). Those two, supposedly innocent, words speak volumes of emotions that delineate those worthy of trust, loyalty, or love, and those who merit distrust, dissent, or hate. In many an Asian country, alongside common parlance, there exists an honorific language that is deferential to seniority and assigns one's interlocutor a recognizable place in the social hierarchy. The Japanese pronouns for I or you, for example, can be variably used to recognize age-qua-wisdom, gender-qua-fragility, status-qua-nobility, and role-qua-power, among others. The traditional emphasis on seniority, which used to place value on greater knowledge based on longer experience, is fast eroding, however, given the preeminence placed on economic efficiency by the far less wise if far more cunning among the many up-and-coming.

Social borders also take the form of speech or linguistic lines drawn by communities which embody a group of people sharing the same communication styles and meanings from which others are excluded (see McDaniel, Kuhn, and Deetz 2008). We can be recognized as belonging to this or that speech community, simply by whether or not we speak mainstream, marginal, or accented English, fashionably deliberate and politically loaded abuses of grammar aside. Men and women are also said to belong to different and separate (but "equal") linguistic communities, to explain away misunderstandings that sometimes occur owing to different gender styles of communicating and creating meaning (Tannen 1990).

Social space is bounded by linguistic fiat, as is territorial space by physical action. Social categories, whether based on economic status, age, gender, or ethnic origin, are all products of linguistic coercion. Words used to categorize people in this-or-that class force the so-labeled into attitudinal and behavioral pigeonholes. It follows that social borders created by language can be more resilient than the ones imposed physically. Ingrained habits of communicated thought, in general, and those crystallized into cultural customs, in particular, are resistant to change. To break down social borders requires no less than starting the categorization process all over again. This in turn demands that established relationships be reedited or recommenced. And these processes of renaming have been recognized, by feminist scholars in particular, to wield a potent force for social change. This is why inclusionary language has been invoked as an indispensable means for reconfiguring encrusted power and gender relations (see Merrill 1998).

The power of language to create walls of distrust and enmity in human relationships is constantly demonstrated in daily life. Words do hurt and can wound just as deeply as a piercing sword. Be they carefully or impulsively chosen, and uttered with a just-so inflection, words in one short instant can shatter the longest-standing happy relationships and alter life's course in unforeseen ways for all involved.

Even when the words do not carry the intentions and feelings that the recipient may mistakenly attribute to the speaker, a linguistic mediation always bears consequences that neither of the interlocutors could anticipate. It is the irreversibility of both real and symbolic action that in the final analysis constitutes the most formidable trap for human freedom.

And it is so that we find ourselves "boxed in," not by genetic inheritance or culture only, but most notably by our choices—whether spoken or enacted. Within the confines of the "box" we wear, we may rest complacent, oblivious to what or whom we may have excluded. Or we might wriggle out of our puny container and attempt to create greater spaces defined by newer borders, sensing somehow that the "box" we have been carrying around was not destined to be our prison forever. Unwilling to derive passive contentment from the givens of our initial conditions, many of us would allow ourselves to be led by a mysterious urge to seek ever greater freedom in the name of a higher good if only we knew what it is that we seek and why, and where to find it and how.

Whither Freedom?

The Self is freedom, but not quite, and not yet, until the last barrier that has shut it out from its every Other has been demolished.

To be trapped inside the limits set by nature and culture, or to be boxed out of opportunities to overcome them, always runs the risk of some degree of exclusion from social intercourse. What makes these forms of un-freedom oppressive is not so much a deprivation of access to resources or of potential accomplishments (serious though they may be) as the social cleft that they engender. Human freedom is to be won, then, not just in the sphere of corporeal phenomena such as thinking, feeling, and acting, or in one's acquisitive appetitions, but through self-transcendence. Put another way, not so much in "having" but in "being." And in "becoming," through that ideal fruit of all dialogical encounters—human communion—in virtue of which the self can at long last transcend itself and perchance attain full humanity.

The search for freedom is essentially a yearning for perfection in guise of completeness—for the attainment of what Burke (1950) has termed "consubstantiality," one's capacity to identify with others. According to Burke, human beings are divided because their individual substances do not overlap, let alone juxtapose. The sense of guilt, tension, and unease provoked by such ontological disjunction provides the propulsive force behind communication. We communicate in order to attain our fullest humanity. Kant, as well, saw in communication the indispensable condition of humanity (Jaspers 1962). Embedded in the infinite web of life's "unending conversation" (Burke 1941), humans participate wholly in this dialogue, investing their entire self in a discourse that "enters into the dialogic fabric of human life, into the world symposium" (Bakhtin 1984, 293). Society cannot exist, and community becomes unthinkable—for neither society, nor community, can maintain and renew themselves—absent the underlying social substrate of communication. In dialogue we exist. In and through communication, we find self-liberation. We are set free.

Dialogue in human life, although a given, remains problematic. Bakhtin's idea of dialogic plurality—polyglossia, heteroglossia, as in "two voices is the minimum for life, the minimum for existence"—is not an expectation or a presumption that the human arena displays always-harmonious interactive give-and-take. A struggle for a voice here, a plea for a hearing there, and the polyphony of voices quickly can turn monologic. Short of being dismissed by the undiscerning as a cacophony, the intricacies of dialogic practice—with its "entrances and exits, interferences, oppositions, gaps, silences, the arduous construction of common topics, passages, breaks and laughters," which only compound the complexity of the exercise (Gurevitch 2000)—do not lend themselves to easy de-codification. And experience all too often shows that dialogic encounters can be as enslaving as they can be liberating. Talks often break down, words can play into the hands of power, and dialogue can explode into a war of irreversible wordings.

The revival of the notion and method of dialogue in recent literature and social practice—Gergen et al.'s (2001) transformative dialogue and Isaac's (2001) action theory, to name just two—underscores the urgent need for novel methodological orientations. Even in the theoretical sources inspiring much of this revival—be it Habermas's (1984) stress on dialogue as a direct source of normative validity and, thus, as a mechanism for legitimating social rules, norms, and arrangements; or Gadamer's (1989) hermeneutic Socratic-style probing to bring about shared understandings; or yet Dewey's (1927) pragmatic approach to communication as social action necessary for democratic governance (see Linder 2001)—the underlying concern is how to come up with a suggestion of a dialogic strategy or approach that can help to accomplish the common goal of (dis)solving aged internecine conflicts.

The pressures of modern living, which tend to reinforce muted yearnings for "community," often allow such wishes to rise no higher than a prayer in passing for a conflict-free environment. Such wishes can demand immediate solutions in ready-canned dialogic techniques. Yet, if freedom is to aspire to fullness, it must look to dialogue not just as an easy fix, but as a field in which humanity far less incompletely can unfold in the experience of persons constituting a "presence" in the minds and hearts of each other—no longer as mere "strangers" but "guests," insofar as guests, in the best traditions of hospitality, are regarded with reverence and respect, and, in turn, do not forget what they are. Among "co-presences," welcome guests all, communion finds its nest.[2]

Communion, to be sure, is an experience resistant to purposeful crafting. It cannot be willed into existence solely by polishing one's dialogic skills. Some dialogic methods may have their impeccable uses for action and for community building, but important as they are, they cannot assure communion. In fact, ecstasy, which is the loftiest form of communion, occurs in the most unguarded moments of a person's life, as experienced by mystics, artists, thinkers, or persons deeply in love. But even ordinary experiences of communion have this sense of being "taken out" of oneself—a leap of sorts—into one's otherwise walled-in embodied other(s), whereby I and Thou become We, as in Buber (1966, 107), whose metaphor for such an encounter is "leaping fire."

We simply cannot produce communion by sheer dialogic exercise or even through conversation—the communicational form that comes the closest to experiencing "co-presences." But we can clear the ground for its advent, by cultivating a special quality basic to any genuine dialogue—a truly indispensable prerequisite often lost in procedural discussions. That quality is reflection, or better still, the habit of reflection.[3]

The verb "to reflect" means "to bend back" in Latin. As such it evokes a freezing action. To reflect on an experience is to keep it in

---

2. Communion should not be equated with homogenization, which often is a result of mind management. It is instead a seeking of common ground—intellectual, above all ontological—where individual diversity, otherwise called uniqueness, is recognized as the root of reciprocal autonomy. The very requirement that communion spring from self-awareness is therefore also its antidote to un-thinking and de-individuating social conformity.

3. Paulo Freire's (1970) method of "conscientization" in emancipatory dialogue has this reflective quality, though my approach to reflection here has less to do directly with definite political or social aims than with a general formative concern for intersubjectivity.

"pause" mode, so to speak, the better to enable the self to glean from it—as one does, in a mirror—the manner of its own implication. Reflection, thus, comports a double dynamic: a standing back from the experience that is objectified, and a delving deep into the self in its relation to the experience. The dichotomy between the experienced object and the experiencing subject is resolved when the self somehow appropriates responsibility for the very experience. Now revealed to itself through its confrontation with that experience, the self next can acquire a depth that it has not known before. Having become more self-aware, the self's newly gained self-awareness paves the way for recognition of—and reverence for—the uniqueness, and the mystery, of its other(s).

Let me illustrate a simple process of reflection, distilled from Marcel's (1950, 79–80) ideas, and try to relate it to what I mean by the expression dialogic encounter:[4] Reflection is rooted in the daily chain of life. This chain generally is sustained by the flow of habit, but at times it is interrupted by a break, as when a behavior of a friend disappoints us. When such a break occurs, it can jolt us and set us to thinking how it could have happened. Reflection is nothing but this "attention" to the disruptions in our routine. We never reflect on things that are not worthwhile, but on things that touch our living personal experience. Once we have paid attention, we cannot pretend that the disruptions never occurred. We may even be forced to call our own position into question and make some proper readjustments. Though this may leave us in a mood of anguish, there is also a sense of being let go, as if some formidable hold on us has been lifted. Only then do we come to realize that, having allowed our self to confront itself, not only can we now communicate more deeply with ourselves but henceforth we can also step into a far more serene breadth of communication with our other-become-mate-become-friend, if only because the hitherto inoperative drawbridge over the moat, which has kept us apart for so long, now has been lowered for full service.

Why is the habit of reflection so important? Because dialogic encounters are the stuff of life: they engage us daily and totally; we cannot afford simply to remain on their surface. In the habitually reflective human mind, words and all the nonverbal accouterments of dialogue

---

4. Marcel speaks of two kinds (or more properly, of two phases) of reflection: the first—or primary reflection—is objectifying and reductive, tending to dissolve the unity of experience first put before it; the second—or secondary reflection—is recuperative in that it reconquers the unity disrupted in primary reflection.

gradually lose their obstructive opacity, maybe by virtue of the utter intensity of self-awareness that the very act of reflection induces. They recover their magic, however, as they conjoin beyond their ordinary instrumental power, only just as extraordinarily to reconcile what previously were seemingly unbridgeable realities—the most important among which perhaps are the "self" and the "other."

Lived experience thence ceases to be a mere succession of images of actions and phenomena perceived as object. It becomes the encounter of the self with itself and with its other(s). And whence, the discovery of intersubjectivity. With habitual reflection comes depth. It is in depth that truth appears as the "intelligible setting or background," which Marcel (1950, 104) speaks about—a backdrop of sorts, against which minds are able to communicate with each other and with themselves. It is against that horizon of light that fractured humanity can be recomposed, as a sense of self-liberating truth takes over and entrusts it with an unprecedented experience of freedom.

Truth, here, refers neither to a perpetuated ideological verity nor to a congealed fact, or to a metaphysical doctrine meant to cement the like-minded into becoming true believers, or into joining cohesive action groups, or yet into transforming themselves in the way of postmodernist language-gamers celebrating fragmentation and difference. Rather, the term reaches out to Thought itself, much deeper and much further than the specific contingent products of thought ever could—in the sense that the humane experience being lived merges with the common ground of being first and foremost human, and to the extent that it becomes one with that self-liberating humanity.

As the intelligible background of intersubjectivity, truth (as authenticity)—so defined—enables dialogue across ideological and perspectival divides, to foster human communion. Truth is not there to service the prerogatives of dominant cliques—whether these are of the élitist, exclusivist, revanchist, catalytic, or domineering kind. Rather, understood and perceived to be the very source of inspiration for human solidarity, truth helps to bridge islands of dissent, to reconcile mutually exclusive clusters of hostility, and to illuminate the paths of the perplexed and the misguided.

Freedom, then, is best realized, not alone, but in communion—nurtured by genuine, thus self-emancipating and mutually liberating dialogic encounters. But the path to enlightening verity demands a constant effort of us all, once so often inviting us to pause, the more meaningfully to contemplate and to reflect during such salutary breaks in one's journey, that much the better to penetrate our sense of relation with our self and with our others. It is during such pauses that we will stand in awe at the significant "presences" that sincere reflective activity can reveal. Unless and until we as mortal humans—immersed as we are in worldly affairs and trapped as we find ourselves to be in self-made boxes—learn to be inspired by our actively generous, and voluntarily habitual "presence" to each other, our self-liberation through human communion can hardly ever add up to anything more than a pipe dream.

References

Arendt, Hannah, and Emil L. Fackenheim (1971) *The Human Condition After Auschwitz: A Jewish Testimony a Generation After*, Syracuse, NY: Syracuse University Press.

Baker, Peter (2003) "Regional Leader Decries Georgia's New Government," *Washington Post,* Foreign Service, Nov. 27, A14.

Bakhtin, Mikhail M. (1984) *Problems of Dostoevsky's Poetics,* Caryl Emerson, Editor and Translator, Minneapolis: University of Minnesota Press.

Bernstein, Richard (2003) "Hamburg Journal: Girls from Ghana Are Mired in a German City's Conflict," *The New York Times*, Nov. 18, A4/C3.

Bonné, Jon (2003) "Are We Done with the 40-Hour Week? How Technology, Productivity and Family Change the Way We Work," *MSNBC*, Aug. 25. Available at: http://www.msnbc.com/news/949259.asp?0cb=-118173784.

Buber, Martin (1966) *The Knowledge of Man: A Philosophy of the Interhuman*, New York: Harper Torchbooks.

Burke, Kenneth (1941) *The Philosophy of Literary Form: Studies in Symbolic Action*, Baton Rouge: Louisiana State University Press.

——— (1950) *A Rhetoric of Motives*, New York: Prentice-Hall.

——— (1966) *Language as Symbolic Action: Essays on Life, Literature, and Method,* Berkeley and Los Angeles: University of California Press.

Ciprut, Jose V., Editor (2008) *Democratizations: Comparisons, Confrontations, and Contrasts*, Cambridge, MA: The MIT Press.

——— (2008) *The Future of Citizenship*, Cambridge, MA: The MIT Press.

Dewey, John (1927) *The Public and Its Problems*, New York: Henry Holt.

Dugger, Celia W. (2003) "Report Finds Few Benefits for Mexico in NAFTA," *The New York Times*, Nov. 19, A8/C4.

Fetni, Hocine (2008) "Citizenship Divided: Muslim Subjects, Arab Citizens, Democratic Dilemmas," in Jose V. Ciprut, Editor, *The Future of Citizenship*, Cambridge, MA: The MIT Press.

Freire, Paulo (1970) *Cultural Action for Freedom*, Cambridge, MA: Harvard Educational Review and Center for the Study of Development and Social Change.

Gadamer, Hans-Georg (1989) *Truth and Method*, New York: Crossroad.

Gergen, Kenneth J. (2000) *The Saturated Self: Dilemmas of Identity in Contemporary Life*, New York: Basic Books.

Gergen, Kenneth J., Frank J. Barrett, and Sheila McNamee (2001) "Toward Transformative Dialogue," *International Journal of Public Administration* 24(7–8):679–708.

Grady, Denise (2003) "No Longer Joined, Boys Face Tough Journey," *The New York Times*, Nov. 18, F1/C3.

Gurevitch, Zali (2000) "Plurality in Dialogue: A Comment on Bakhtin," *Sociology* 34(2):243.

Habermas, Jürgen (1984) *The Theory of Communicative Action*, Boston: Beacon Press.

Hilton, Isabel (2003) " 'Terror in the Name of God': Everybody Hates Somebody Somewhere," Book Review, *The New York Times*, Nov. 16, sec. 7, P50/C1.

Hong, Edna H., and Howard V. Hong, Editors (2000) *The Essential Kierkegaard*, Princeton, NJ: Princeton University Press.

Isaacs, William N. (2001) "Toward an Action Theory of Dialogue," *International Journal of Public Administration* 24(7–8):709–748.

Jamison, S. Lee (2003) "The Links to Friendship; An Online Search for Fun, Without a Look for Love," *The New York Times*, Dec. 12, B1/C2.

Jaspers, Karl (1962) *Kant*, San Diego, CA: Harcourt Brace.

Jones, Roland (2003) "Which Side of the Atlantic Is Crazy? U.S. Enjoys Less Vacation than Europe, but the Economy Is Stronger," *MSNBC News*, Aug. 29. Available at: http://www.msnbc.com/news/952424.asp?0cb=-518173784.

Krippendorff, Klaus (2008) "Four (In)Determinabilities, Not One," in Jose V. Ciprut, Editor, *Indeterminacy: The Mapped, the Navigable, and the Uncharted*, Cambridge, MA: The MIT Press.

Kristof, Nicholas D. (2003) "Death by Dividend," *The New York Times*, Nov. 22, A15/C1.

Kumar, Rahul, and David Silver (2008) "The Ethics of Exclusion," in Jose V. Ciprut, Editor, *The Future of Citizenship*, Cambridge, MA: The MIT Press.

Linder, Stephen H. (2001) "An Inquiry into Dialogue, Its Challenges and Justification," *International Journal of Public Administration* 24(7–8):651–678.

Marcel, Gabriel (1950) *The Mystery of Being*, vol. 1, London: Regnery.

McDaniel, J. P., T. Kuhn, and S. Deetz (2008) "Voice, Participation, and the Globalization of Communication Systems," in Jose V. Ciprut, Editor, *Democratizations: Comparisons, Confrontations, and Contrasts*, Cambridge, MA: The MIT Press.

Merrill, Lisa J. (1998) *Untying the Tongue: Gender, Power, and the Word*, Westport, CT: Greenwood Press.

Pyeritz, Reed E. (2008) "The Future of Genetics in Medicine: Practices, Prospects, and Peril," in Jose V. Ciprut, Editor, *Ethics, Politics, and Democracy: From Primordial Principles to Prospective Practices*, Cambridge, MA: The MIT Press.

Reuters (2003) "Report: Rich Nations Flunk Test on Educating Poor," Nov. 18, 7:14 AM ET.

Riggs, Fred W. (2000) "The Para-Modern Context of Ethnic Nationalism," in Jose V. Ciprut, Editor, *Of Fears and Foes: Security and Insecurity in an Evolving Global Political Economy*. Westport, CT: Praeger.

Rohter, Larry (2003) "Bolivia's Poor Proclaim Abiding Distrust of Globalization," *The New York Times*, Foreign Desk, Oct. 17, A3/C1.

Schoen, John W. (2003) "Are We Working Smarter – Or Harder? The Darker Side of the Rise in U.S. Productivity," *MSNBC*, Aug. 28. Available at: http://www.msnbc.com/news/952422.asp?0cb=-418173784.

Sengupta, Somini (2003) "All Sides in Liberian Conflict Make Women Spoils of War," *The New York Times*, Nov. 20, A3/C1.

Sontag, Deborah (2003). "In a Homeland Far from Home," *The New York Times*, Nov. 16, sec. 6, 48, col. 1.

Spinner-Halev, Jeff (2008) "Exclusion, Fear, and Identity in Emerging Democracies," in Jose V. Ciprut, Editor, *Ethics, Politics, and Democracy: From Primordial Principles to Prospective Practices*, Cambridge, MA: The MIT Press.

Tannen, Deborah (1990) *You Just Don't Understand: Women and Men in Conversation*, New York: Morrow.

Trebay, Guy (2003) "I Came, I Bought and I Helped," *The New York Times*, Nov. 18, B10/C1.

Weiner, Tim (2003) "Wal-Mart Invades and Mexico Gladly Surrenders," *The New York Times*, Dec. 6, A1/C3.

4

Freedoms Lost, Freedoms Regained

David R. Williams and
Jacques P. Barber

The practice of psychotherapy is an art, as is the practice of any other profession. The psychotherapist's art is applied to the medium of human freedom—to the individual person's experience of voluntary behavior, cognitive as well as physical. Our goal in this chapter is to provide a sense of how psychotherapists generally regard the human freedom they encounter: not as a problematic of philosophy, science, or social theory, but as a widely recognized attribute of individual human experience.

The experience of freedom results most commonly from an exercise of what liberty allows,[1] and in this sense, psychopathology can be understood as a failure to take fullest advantage of opportunities available. We will focus on the loss of freedom that results from psychopathology and explore the types of treatment that are currently in use. Because neither the experience of freedom nor the origins of psychopathology are well understood, the psychotherapist's practical involvement with freedom issues can make a unique contribution to a general understanding of the concept. Therefore, we will begin by describing some essentials of the psychotherapist's outlook as it pertains to the issue of personal freedom.

About Those in Whom Freedom Resides

The experience of freedom happens only *in* individual human beings, each of whom differs from human others in many significant ways. Individual human beings are prized by psychotherapists for their

---

1. We think of "liberty" in the Oxford English Dictionary's (OED) sense of "The condition of being able to act in any desired way without hindrance or restraint." The psychological experience of freedom is distinct from the political foundation of liberty that often fosters it, and indeed can occur despite an absence of liberty.

differences, and psychotherapists honor these differences in their work. The psychologist's code of ethics[2] (American Psychological Association 2003) describes, in *Principle E*, how psychotherapists regard individuals: they "respect the dignity and worth of all people, and the rights of individuals to privacy, confidentiality, and self-determination." Even though not all psychotherapists are psychologists, all professional therapists belong to organizations that have similar stipulations. It is important to set this principle in place as a context for all that follows, because it establishes the therapist's limits of liberty.[3] Divergent as the formal approaches that distinguish psychotherapists may all be, at a practical level therapists speak a common "patois of freedom," an intuitive language about human experience. The patois derives from two remarkable characteristics of the human mind.

The first characteristic is known in cognitive science generally as *"Theory of Mind"* (Gopnik 1999), or "ToM"—an acronym worth using, because it tends to take attention off two misleading attributes of the fuller phrase:

• The term "theory" refers to one's *own* inborn beliefs about the existence and nature of mind, not to some kind of general theory based on evidence.

• The "mind" referred to is *not* one's own, but another person's whose outlook, thinking, or actions you are trying to take into account.

In sum, ToM acknowledges that one can know another's mind only inferentially, extrapolating from one's own experience. For each of us, it is a matter of belief—and not fact—that others have private inner experiences of their "minds," "desires," "expectations," and "beliefs,"

---

2. Not only are there many "mental health" professions, including psychologists, psychiatrists, social workers, and pastoral counselors, among others, but there are also widely divergent theoretical views within each. The commonsense mingling of their outlooks which we develop here is supported by the mammoth "Consumer Reports Study" (Seligman 1995) of responses by clients and patients, which shows, surprisingly, that although duration of therapy had an impact on consumer satisfaction, neither the professional affiliation nor the theoretical orientation of the therapist had an impact on the result reported as perceived by the "consumer." Whatever their often profound theoretical differences, psychotherapists in practice do share an ethical outlook that is well summarized in the Principle quoted here.

3. The limits of liberty are set by ethics rather than knowledge because practical problems are often immediate and cannot be postponed until all the necessary facts and a reliable theory are at hand. Practitioners are judged according to whatever "state of the art" standard is prevailing at the time interventions are made.

that they value the personal "meaningfulness" of their lives and the "voluntary" origins of their behavior. These and kindred terms arise from organized perceptions of our own experience and are used without difficulty in ordinary talk about ordinary things. ToM *represents* a human ability as universal as language, but it provides no explanation for the subjective phenomenon to which it refers.

The second remarkable characteristic is called "empathy,"[4] the ability to "take another's point of view." Empathy is a projection based on ToM and represents the very height of anthropomorphism, or as the vernacular would have it, mind-reading. We readily, but not necessarily accurately, sense each other's feelings and intentions. Empathy is a flaw-ridden process but unavoidable in practical terms because bits of behavior—isolated actions—do not point clearly to the reasons behind them. "Empathy" can be thought of as a schema that connects behavioral dots in ways that fit recognizable patterns which reflect ToM concepts. Empathic understanding is an inference based on a relatively small amount of behavioral information, much in the way elaborate outlines of mythic constellatory figures are sometimes derived from relations among the very few stars that "represent" the mythic figure. Clearly, the schema that connects behavioral dots must be chosen on the basis of something beyond the information given by the dots (Bruner 1973). Whether the schema is chosen solely from ToM, or incorporates a system borrowed from Freud (Strachey 1953–66), Skinner (1953, 1957), or Rogers (1951), the pattern read into the behavioral dots often provides useful clues about the thinking and likely future behavior of the one whose actions are empathically beginning to be understood.

The flaw in the projective process of empathy comes into play when one fails to recognize one's own organizing contribution to the pattern and attributes one assigns totally and solely to the person whose behavior is to be understood. Whenever we sense another's point of view empathically, we must keep in mind that what we sense in others is really what we find in ourselves.

Psychotherapists regard the experiencing individual as a person poised between two worlds—one outside, the other inside—and facing the responsibility of reconciling the sometimes conflicting demands

---

4. OED: "The power of projecting one's personality into (and so fully comprehending) the object of contemplation."

these worlds make. The world outside is a world of perceived things located in space and time; the world inside is a world of perceived meanings and significant relationships outside the flow of time. Aspects of the two subjectively perceived worlds converge on objects we value—meaningful objects we can deconstruct during moments of reflection into outer-world and inner-world constituents. This commonsense view of the individual as an "Experiencer" is diagrammed in figure 4.1, which focuses on the viewpoint of the experiencing individual.

Figure 4.1 represents a purely subjective viewpoint on personal experience. It separates the 'true source' of experience (the shaded box below the horizontal line) from its impact on the subjective awareness of an Experiencer (above the horizontal line). The unshaded elements of this map are products of cognition, of the mind at (computational) work. The diagram depicts the distinction between physical and spiritual reality as a product of the mind, imposed on the common underlying reality that gives rise to both.

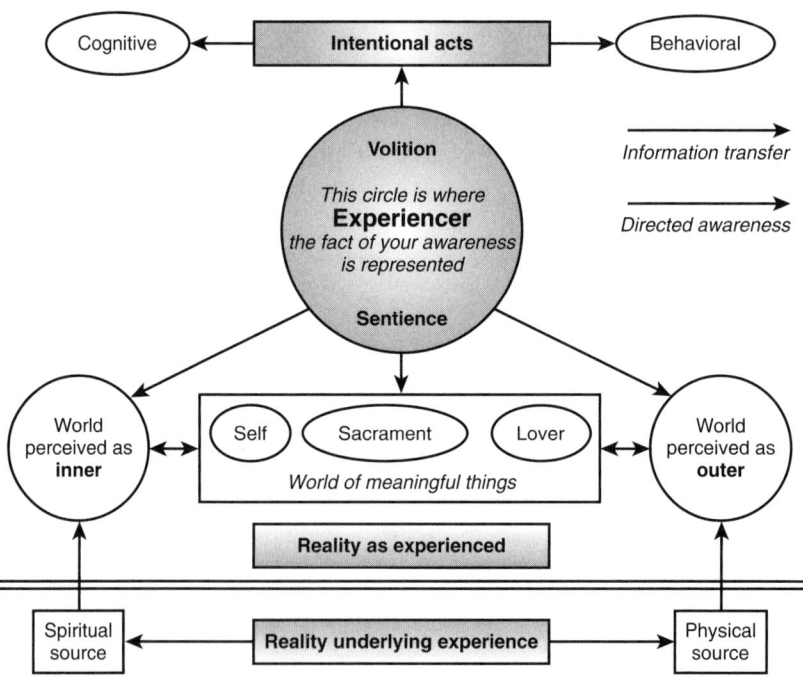

Figure 4.1
The Commonsense Experiencer's Point of View

Above the line, unshaded circles represent the perceived inner and outer worlds. The unshaded rectangle between them shows three important token examples of 'meaningful things'. Meaningful things appear in both perceived worlds of experience, and these worlds, in turn, confer properties on the tokens; hence the bidirectional arrows. Meaningful tokens incorporate information from both outer and inner worlds, and so bring them into alignment.

Sentience and volition—that is, awareness and the capacity to initiate action—are included as properties of the Experiencer, whose role as a source of chosen behavior is shown at the top of figure 4.1. All arrows point out from the Experiencer's circle because this commonsense parsing of everyday reflective awareness represents the viewpoint from which personal freedom is felt—the lack of constraint *from outside*[5] that the experience of freedom necessarily entails. The intentional acts that an Experiencer chooses are thus represented as truly voluntary, initiated from a place beyond the reach of either inner or outer world: from the timeless perspective of the Great Divide of Consciousness.[6] In reflective moments, a person is captive of neither world, and feels free to assign priorities to their various demands and opportunities. The Great Divide—a place of pure being—is the vantage point that permits a person to have a say in the way these two worlds interweave meaningfully.

From the Great Divide of Consciousness, a person can launch 'truly voluntary' intentional acts, based on a mix of considerations that is unique to the Experiencer and perhaps the moment as well. The cognitive and behavioral consequences of these intentional acts (Irwin 1971) will be experienced through their subsequent effects on outer and inner worlds, arguably also influencing new intentional acts. It is from the lonely viewpoint of the Experiencer, perched on the Great Divide, apparently outside of time and space, that people actively manage their lives and deal with the underlying reality—the "thrownness" or

---

5. See chapters in this book by McInerney (chap. 2), Urban (chap. 10), Hackney (chap. 11), and especially Hirschmann (chap. 9), on the inside/outside issue.

6. One's sense of the passage of time is often attenuated or even missing when perched on the Great Divide, giving rise to what is called the experience of the "eternal now." The mystery of "now," of the "specious present" (James 1890, 609), makes sense, whatever its phenomenological origin, because the cause-and-effect relations that constrain freedom all require *time*: causes must come before their effects, and so the experience of freedom may well require the experience of timelessness—almost of the sort experienced by self-abandonment in fervent prayer (see Haskelevich, chap. 7, Haight, chap. 8, and Arcenas, chap. 3, in this book).

"facticity" of their experience (Heidegger 1927)[7] and ongoingly "playing the hand they have been dealt." From this point of view, an Experiencer creates possibility, and experiences personal freedom. Psychotherapists influence the process of another individual's self-management by encouraging acceptance of the (thrown) things that cannot be changed and helping the development of a new line of play.

This generic, experience-based description of how people lead their lives as unique individuals shapes the practical outlook of psychotherapists as they work professionally in the medium of human freedom. The view of a person consciously engaged in the process of living, guided by information received from inner and outer worlds, requires an underlying ToM empathically deployed. If we are to profit from what psychotherapists have learned while working in the medium of freedom, we must interpret what they say in the context of their patois and their commonsense view of the Experiencer.

The Self-Management Spectrum

Psychotherapists have built a formal language of reference that supplements, but does not supplant, the clinical experience on which their practice rests. The formal language rises categorically above the chatter of the patois: it is codified in a compendium—*The Diagnostic and Statistical Manual of the American Psychoanalytic Association/Revision IV* (*DSM-IV*, 1994) issued by the American Psychiatric Association (APA)—that catalogs mental disorders and their pathognomic signs. The categories of the APA's *DSM-IV* are intended "to enable clinicians and investigators to diagnose, communicate about, study, and treat people with various mental disorders"[8] (*DSM-IV*, Introduction, xxvii). *DSM-IV* explicitly disavows the "common misconception that a classification of mental disorders classifies people, when actually what are being classified are disorders that people have" (xxii). It explicitly focuses on problems of self-management, while remaining silent on the origins and causes of disorder; it attempts to provide clinicians with a

---

7. The "thrown" metaphor mercifully sidesteps deeper questions when rendered from the more precise German *entworfen* into English, since in English the term equally well refers to *chance* as in a throw of the dice, and some kind of predisposition, as when a potter "throws" a pot, whereas the German word refers to projected *design*. I thank the editor for sensitizing me to this, otherwise ordinarily overlooked, fact.
8. In some ways, most importantly, the categories are also used for billing third-party insurers for services.

nonhistorical, nondevelopmental, atheoretical description of behavioral and psychological dysfunctions.

The psychotherapist, called upon to treat people in some domain of their living, typically thinks of a person's use of his liberty—or available freedom—as lying somewhere on a spectrum of self-management ranging from 'fully effective' through 'adequate' to 'disastrous'. Figure 4.2 represents the spectrum in "formal" language. Locating someone's primary problem in this spectrum is not a judgment made lightly. It depends on professional socialization, on personal morals, and on the very values of the community that supports the psychotherapist's work. In effect, the self-management spectrum provides a bridge between the patois of freedom and the formal language of disorder and well-being. Not surprisingly, the way a psychotherapist works with a person's liberty depends in part on where within this spectrum of effective self-management the person is thought to lie.

The spectrum of self-management possibilities covers a span from disastrous self-management on the left, to optimal self-management on the right. It is best regarded not as a continuum of pathological severity, but as a depiction of the uses of liberty—weak and strong. Axis I and Axis II refer to different types of diagnostic categories, as specified in *DSM-IV*, and in actual practice the categories often overlap in their implications for liberty. The examples are indicative, not exhaustive. The psychotherapist's task as a human 'freedom worker' is to shift, sustainably, a person's place in the spectrum as far as possible toward the right-hand or 'optimal' end of the continuum.

Formally, Axis I and Axis II refer to 'mental disorders'. But what, exactly, does this term mean?

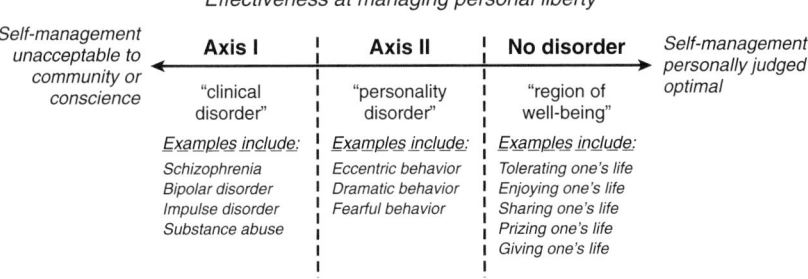

Figure 4.2
The Self-Management Spectrum

In DSM-IV, each of the mental disorders is conceptualized as a *clinically signifi-cant* behavioral or psychological syndrome or pattern that occurs in an individual and that is associated with *present distress* (e.g., a painful—often mental—symptom) or *disability* (i.e., impairment in one or more important areas of functioning) or with a significantly increased risk of suffering death, pain, disability, or *an important loss of freedom*. In addition, this syndrome or pattern must not be merely an expectable and culturally sanctioned response. . . . Whatever its cause, it must be currently considered a manifestation of a behavioral, psychological, or biological *dysfunction in the individual*. Neither deviant behavior (e.g., political, religious, or sexual) nor conflicts that are primarily between the individual and society are mental disorders unless the deviance or conflict is a symptom of a *dysfunction in the individual*, as described above. (American Psychiatric Association 1994, xxi–xxii; emphasis added)

This is an admirably clear description, but one that calls for considerable judgment as well: "clinically significant"? . . . "not culturally sanctioned"? . . . "distress"? . . . "behavioral, psychological, or biological dysfunction"? . . . These terms or phrases, among others in the definition, are meaningful but loose, and in their practical application must be interpreted according to the very values of the culture and the circumstances of the individual. *DSM-IV* cautions that: "The diagnostic categories, criteria, and textual descriptions are meant to be employed by individuals with appropriate clinical training and experience in diagnosis. It is important that DSM-IV not be applied mechanically by untrained individuals. The specific diagnostic criteria included in DSM-IV are *meant to serve as guidelines* to be informed by clinical judgment and are *not meant to be used in a cookbook fashion*" (American Psychiatric Association 1994, xxiii; emphasis added). In short, 'disorder' is a term of art rather than one of science.

Axis I disorders[9] provide a basis for restricting a person's liberty, at least until there is a remission of symptoms, on the grounds that the individual may present some kind of threat or danger to self or others. There is plenty of debate about the causes of Axis I disorders,[10] but within contemporary Western culture at least, there is broad consensus about the restriction of liberty in florid cases of individuals whose use of liberty places them in the most negative region of freedom management effectiveness.

---

9. Axis I includes schizophrenia, bipolar disorder, mood disorders, anxiety disorder, eating and sleep disorders, impulse and adjustment disorders, substance abuse, and sexual and gender disorders.
10. For example, see Szasz (1961).

Not so with the Axis II disorders of "personality." Here, we find controversy at every turn, from the specificity of patterns to the question of whether insurance should pay for their remedy when they are discovered. There is not even full agreement about whether Axis II disorders can be pallid precursors or even subclinical manifestations of Axis I disorders. But the definition is reasonably clear, and whether or not it defines "disorders" or "unfortunate proclivities," it seems reasonable to think of them as occupying a less-than-fully-adequate mid-range area on the spectrum of stewardship of personal freedom.

The characteristics of life in the mid-range region of the continuum are clearly identified as "An *enduring pattern of inner experience* and behavior that deviates *markedly* from the expectations of the individual's culture" (*DSM-IV*, 633; emphasis added). *DSM-IV* (p. 629) assigns patterns fitting these criteria to three clusters: the "odd or eccentric," the "dramatic, emotional, or erratic," and the "anxious or fearful." As is the case with Axis I disorders, clinical judgment is needed for a valid assessment of a person's inner experience and behavior, as to deviance from cultural norms, inflexibly and pervasively so, and sufficiently beyond the "normal" range to cause either inner distress or functional impairment that can be seen from the outside.[11] The formal categories are rather fuzzy in actual use.

The third major region of the freedom-management spectrum is the well-being end, and understandably, it is not covered by *DSM-IV*. Within this region, there is ample variation from "adequate" to "fully effective" enjoyment of liberty. Respecting the dignity and worth of the individual and the individual's right to self-determination—including, say, setting the priorities of inner- and outer-world demands—means that the therapeutic issue at this end of the continuum is not "what's wrong," but rather, "is this person's life the best it can be, by their own

---

11. An important issue of personal freedom arises when others find behavioral impairment but the individual is not distressed. If one is the perpetually lazy member of a family of strivers, is one Axis II disordered? Or as Maslow (1968, 7) put it: "I am deliberately rejecting our present easy distinction between sickness and health. . . . Does sickness mean having symptoms? I maintain now that sickness might consist of not having symptoms when you should. Does health mean being symptom-free? I deny it. Which of the Nazis at Auschwitz or Dachau were healthy? Those with stricken conscience or those with a nice, clear, happy conscience? Was it possible for a profoundly human person not to feel conflict, suffering, depression, rage, etc.? In a word, if you tell me you have a personality problem I am not certain until I know you better whether to say 'Good!' or 'I'm sorry.' It depends on the reasons. And these, it seems, may be bad reasons or good reasons."

standards." Helpfulness requires more and more personal humility from the therapist, who may not possess some of the strengths or depth of feeling[12] an individual shows while resolving the issue that occasioned the therapy. In the region of well-being, the balance an individual wishes to strike between inner and outer worlds is more a matter of personal preference than rationality.

Those who work with freedom in this fortunate region of well-being tend to accept two general principles, as expressed in the patois:

• The client seeks to give up needless self-limitations, even though these do not rise to Axis II level.

• The client seeks to incorporate into the personal process of living an expression of personal "actualizing potential"[13] (Maslow 1970, 150). The actualizing potential is sometimes referred to as an "inner guidance system"[14]—the sort of thing that in some people produces a "calling," and in most others provides a basis for constructing what is experienced as a "meaningful" life (see Arcenas, chap. 3 in this book).

These two concepts are intertwined: needless self-limitations are likely to interfere with full self-expression, and thus limit the meaningfulness of personal endeavor.

Ways of Working with Human Freedom

Now that the lens of freedom has been used to characterize some attributes of the broad range of individuals with whose perceived liberty and sense of freedom psychotherapists work, it is appropriate to consider the kinds of interventions psychotherapists make. There are three types, each modestly associated with a particular region on the self-management continuum, sometimes in combination. The types are depicted in figure 4.3, which emphasizes a key fact: all three types focus on the person at the center of the intervention.

---

12. This is the *Equus* problem (Shaffer 1973): How does a therapist deal with a patient who brings to "treatment" a greater, perhaps more admirable, sensitivity to the thrill of living, or the possibility of living meaningfully, than the therapist possesses?

13. Horney (1950, 17) describes the Actualizing Potential intuitively and well: "You need not, and in fact cannot, teach an acorn to grow into an oak tree, but when given a chance, its intrinsic potentialities will develop. . . . Similarly, the human individual . . . will grow, substantially undiverted, toward self-realization."

14. This is a generic phrase psychotherapists of many persuasions use because patients quickly grasp what it means.

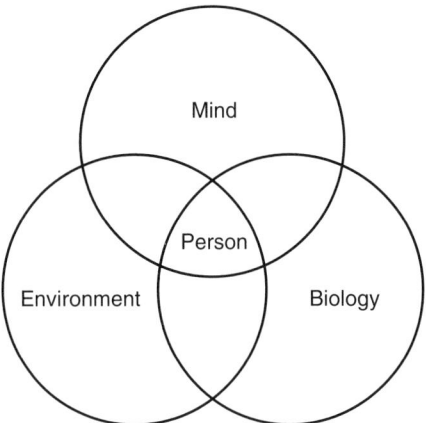

Figure 4.3
The Domains of Intervention

Changing the Environment

Institutionalization as a tool of psychotherapy is built on the idea of restricting liberty, so it is a serious tool of great personal significance and social concern as well: although it restricts the normal range of opportunities that liberty provides, its rationale is to establish a "safe and supportive" environment within which the individual can function advantageously. The therapeutic environment takes over some of the functions of self-management so that the remaining capacity can be exercised fully.

Patient's rights groups and lawyers have created a legal climate that prevents, among other things, families from using mental hospitals for indefinite periods of time, to hide away "troublesome" or "disobedient" members. Their efforts have often been supported by theories of mental illness—especially schizophrenia—that explained disorder as a mind-warp arising from unfortunate child-rearing practices (e.g., Bateson et al. 1963; Berne 1961; Laing 1972; Schiff 1969). The idea of unwarping the mind by experiences that might include both talking and occupational therapy as well as psychodrama provided the therapeutic rationale of mental "hospitals," which were established to create a safe and supportive environment for new learning to take place and supplant old, dysfunctional, learned patterns of thought and behavior. As implemented, however, many institutions fulfilled the practical demands of institutional care but neglected their ostensive therapeutic purpose, primarily because they lacked the wealth required to mount a full therapeutic program. They provided only a "maintenance" or, less charitably, a "warehouse" environment. The argument that an environmental warp is the source of serious disorder, with its implication that a corrective therapeutic environment provides the key to remediation, has not survived the ravages of time and evidence. Full hospitalization today is almost exclusively short-term, and arranged primarily for the purpose of immediate protection and medication of those with Axis I disorders.

Structured therapeutic environments (partial hospitalization and sheltered workshops, for example), sometimes successful in providing institutional support, permit a considerable restoration of liberty. Contemporary therapeutic environments are frequently successful in supporting the individual's functioning and (especially) quality of life, but often fail to produce the kind of learning that permits full self-management. Whether fully successful or not, the net effect of institutionalized therapeutic environments is to increase the patient's ability to have a say in the management of some part of the personal process of living, thus providing the patient with a greater role in self-management and a stronger experience of freedom.

Many of those with Axis I disorders are unwilling to participate in supportive programs; these individuals—often against clinicians' advice—claim their right to full liberty and disdain the discipline and routine that supportive programs provide. This often leads to social problems like homelessness, a complex phenomenon due in part to the lack of willingness of current institutions and governmental agencies to restrict liberty.

Distinguishing between an acceptable exercise of liberty and its possible abuse is among the most difficult professional decisions a psychotherapist is called upon to make, even as a practical matter. At bottom, denial of liberty is a question for society as a whole. This is why the negative end of the self-management continuum is labeled "unacceptable" rather than "erroneous."

Changing the Biology

The attribution of mental disorder to "chemical imbalance" is a widely used justification for prescribing medication, and relief is often attributed to a correction of the condition by chemical means. However, the issue of whether psychotropic medications actually work by restoring chemical balance is far from resolved: the mechanism of their action is largely speculative, even though their symptomatic effectiveness for the most part can be empirically demonstrated. When a medication seems effective, it might well be that it has produced a "chemical imbalance" of its own, making the individual feel happy and compliant by quelling those inner processes that normally would produce discomfort and provide an impetus for change. Whether the commonly used psychotropic medications operate by influencing "behavioral, psychological, or biological dysfunction" as *DSM-IV* requires, is open to question: medication might be entirely palliative, like aspirin for a toothache, cloaking or concealing an underlying disorder without touching its cause at all.

Whether medication is palliative or curative is central to the question of psychotherapy and freedom. While institutional treatment is directed at maximizing the liberty an individual can acceptably handle, the matter is not so clear in the case of pharmacological treatment. The example of depression illustrates the problem. When we consider medication for individuals who are depressed, as determined by professional standards, how are we to assess whether the person is suffering from a "chemical imbalance," or happens to be in the wrong environment? The conventional answer is statistical: if most people are or would be content with this individual's circumstances, it is assumed that the individual should be as well. This statistical norm is surely not always appropriate, because individuals can experience the same circumstances quite differently. The question of permissible liberty becomes acute when people live in comfortable circumstances where radical change would risk bringing on immediate stress via loss of material advantage, perhaps putting prized relationships at risk as well. It is for the individual to decide whether to risk a radical redirection in personal life, such as a change of career or of a significant relationship, or to seek palliative chemical treatment; but the evidence normally offered to support a possibly indefinite program of medication for symptomatic relief is neither adequate nor relevant.

There is mounting evidence (Hollon, Thase, and Markowitz 2002; Scott et al. 2003; among others) that, in contrast to psychotherapy, the use of medication for psychological problems does not by itself resolve the underlying problem and thus, when medication is stopped, a relapse often occurs. In the last twenty years, data has emerged to indicate that "cognitive therapy"—a form of psychotherapy for "rectifying" depressed patients' way of thinking—does tend to prevent relapse in depression better than short-term medication (e.g., Barber and DeRubeis 1989). The response of the medical establishment to these findings has been "creative": these days, depressed patients much too often are maintained on antidepressant medications—such as the selective serotonin re-uptake inhibitors—for extended periods of time. This reduces the relapse rate, if only by postponement of its resurgence until the time when medication is discontinued. Whereas, in the past, patients were kept medicated for a few months, it is not uncommon today for a patient to remain medicated for a few years or even indefinitely. It is perhaps coincidental that extended periods of medication result not just in lower remission rates for the patients (at least while medicated), but in greater profits for large pharmaceutical companies as well.

A similar case arises with the burgeoning disorder called Attention-Deficit/Hyperactivity Disorder (ADHD), currently diagnosed and treated in a remarkably high percentage of children and young adults. The treatment of choice is Ritalin, and it has a calmative effect. Both the biology underlying the disorder and the mechanism of drug action are unknown. *DSM-IV* appropriately cautions about the difficulty of diagnosis: clinicians must find reason to infer a problem in the individual, and not merely as to the fit between the individual and the environment. While one can reasonably argue that one's management of liberty is enhanced when one is assisted by medication to pay attention and to perform diligently, is it less reasonable in the case of ADHD to locate the problem in the fit of the individual to the standardized, assembly-line curricula that so many schools provide for practical reasons? If even 10 percent of students do not adjust well, and there is some kind of conflict between their environmental needs and the system's demands, is medicating them to make the system acceptable a clinically responsible use of this tool? Are personal dignity and worth being respected under this account? The answers to these questions would not be clarified if the brains of the 10 percent of the population were found to differ in some way from those of 90 percent of the people whose needs somehow do seem to fit more readily into the system. A difference from the norm is not grounds for inferring a disorder.

The abundant prescription of medication, based on evidence that is not necessarily relevant to the cause of an individual's manifest dysfunction, may well distract a person from other avenues to change, avenues that would actually address the underlying problem instead of masking it. Prescription medications, when they divert attention from modes of therapy aimed at an underlying cause, and treat the symptom instead, are at risk of providing support for the serene acceptance of a self-limiting status quo that might otherwise be fundamentally changed if it were addressed with sufficient courage and wisdom. The difference is a treatment favoring the satisfaction of a life well lived—in preference to the gratifications of a life lived without much psychic discomfort. One might argue that a willingness to allow medication to take away discomfort without addressing the actual cause is itself a dysfunction that deserves treatment rather than medical suppression. SOMA[15] is not the answer!

True, medication is a powerful practical tool of therapeutic management, but it is difficult to be certain whether it supports or inhibits the experience of freedom by providing the maximum liberty that can be advantageously accessed. Whether or not to change an individual's biology through pharmacology is, from the standpoint of liberty and freedom, a much subtler problem than the one posed by the question of institutional control, because therapists cannot be sure why the treatment works; and if it does, then at what personal cost.

Changing the Mind

The third type of intervention available to the psychotherapist is cognitive, a matter of using "talk" to induce an individual to understand, experience, or believe something new about self or, yes, circumstance, perhaps even adopting a new outlook on personal life as a whole. Change is typically brought about by a conversation with a psychotherapist regarding the individual's experience as witnessed from the Great Divide of Consciousness—a conversation that takes account of both worlds of awareness and of the ways they appear in the meaningful objects that connect them. There is wide variation in the ground rules for carrying out therapeutic conversations, covering both the topics to be explored and the manner of speaking about them. Despite the broad array of means, the common goal of mind-changing therapies is to develop new ways for individuals, somehow caught in dysfunctional or suboptimal cognitive patterns, to construe the experience

---

15. The drug, in the novel *Brave New World* (Huxley 1932), that promotes happiness at the expense of vitality and personal growth. Of course, in Huxley's novel the drug was widely accepted, and perhaps even today it would be a viable option for some if not all of us.

of living and, as a consequence, to find new ways of being within the worlds of their experience.

It is an axiom of the mind-changing psychotherapies that people react not to events but to the meanings they create from them. To a surprising extent, the experience of living is a product of the way one chooses to map it, and so one's ability to choose among mappings is the most powerful source of the personal freedom one perceives. Psychotherapy changes minds primarily by providing new interpretive possibilities and then encouraging reflection on the differences in personal experience that the new ways of understanding provide. Whenever there is a preference for the new ways, there and then a step forward in the therapeutic journey has been taken.

Michelangelo is reputed to have said that "God put a statue within every slab of marble and it is my job to remove what isn't part of the statue." Analogously, a therapeutic conversation is aimed at unconcealing capacities and attributes that a person has not seen before, or has allowed to become hidden. As the positive end of the self-management continuum is approached, the psychotherapist becomes neither a manager nor a mentor, but a facilitator of the experience of *voluntary* living—of living according to one's apparent free choices— among possibilities framed with due regard for features of inner and outer worlds over which one appears to have no say. The psychotherapist works by keeping a therapeutic conversation on track at the boundary between folly and freedom, questioning erroneous thoughts and illogical conclusions. Mind-changing therapies enhance an Experiencer's capacity to create and choose the best possibilities that the world of subjective reality can provide.

For talk therapies aimed at changing minds, persuasion is not intellectual but experiential: the new way of interpreting events, the new frame of reference for making sense of experience, must produce favorable subjective consequences at the Experiencer's level if it is to be adopted.

The Price of Personal Freedom

For the Individual in Therapy

When the positive end of the self-management continuum is at play, the work of mind-changing therapy may well lead an individual to new views from the Great Divide. Encountering new views is a hollow exercise unless the individual decides to test them beyond the safety of the consulting room. However, there is a price to using new viewpoints because, for reasonably well-functioning people at the positive end of the spectrum of self-management possibilities, the old viewpoints are likely to have been comfortable and in certain ways advantageous: for example, seeing less fully from the Great Divide can mean avoiding the anxiety attendant on the risks of intimacy, or fostering self-esteem by seeking the approval of others at the expense of one's inner beliefs and values. In addition, one's immediate community may have adjusted to one's old style of self-management, or to one's previous commitments, and may respond unsupportively when attempts to change threaten to destabilize other's customary patterns of behavior. In parallel with Urban's argument (chap. 10 in this book) that freedom serves as "a giant lever redirecting the flow of history, from a determination of present by past to a determination of present by present," the psychotherapist, as a freedom worker encouraging a fuller view from the Great Divide, acts to redirect an Experiencer's style of self-management from a matter of habit to a matter of choice. Choice is a phenomenon of the present: it cannot happen in the past or the future. And just as redirection of the flow of culture can produce social disturbance on the way to a new tradition, so can divorcing an outgrown life story be envisaged and/or experienced as painful and costly.

Sometimes the cost of living by a new view can far outstrip the cost of the treatment that revealed it, yet the benefit is ultimately experienced as worthwhile in light of the ensuing quality of life. Deciding whether the benefit is worth the cost requires real-life testing, and only a well-functioning individual involved in exploring a new view can make the judgment: overall, it is a personal and subjective matter, and the essence of an Experiencer's freedom.

For the Psychotherapist

The psychotherapist, working with freedom, faces costs as well. One cost can arise while attempting to assist the individual under treatment toward fuller voluntary living. Was Joan of Arc, voices and all, on a mistaken path? Were some or all of the prophets? Would restraining Joan, medicating her, using all of the conscientious psychotherapist's legitimate wiles to dissuade her from following her calling, have been consistent with respecting her dignity and worth as a human being? Should a psychotherapist disparage a deeply felt calling, even if it exacts a high price from the individual who heeds it? Are there no exceptions to a narrow but reasonable standard of normalcy? The therapist sometimes feels like the proverbial character with one foot on the dock of professional customs, the other on the canoe of respect for the patient's individuality: something has to give, lest the therapist fall into the lake, neither staying dry nor retrieving the canoe. The commitment to do no harm can be agonizing in such cases.

A second cost is akin to the first, albeit arising from the therapist's own human frailty, not from the enigma of another human's dignity. "Managing the counter-transference"[16] was originally a technical psychodynamic term, but it has entered the therapeutic *argot* because it refers to a common experience among therapists: sometimes the issues a patient is addressing—legitimate issues of living, whether about friendships, marriage, or divorce, about a career, or about life's purpose—are not satisfactorily resolved in the therapist's own life. When a therapist uses a technique that demands the empathic projection that all psychotherapy requires, the therapy takes the therapist to views from the therapist's own Great Divide—and these views are sometimes troublesome and conflicted, because the therapist, too, is a human being. But the therapist must somehow, for professional and ethical reasons, avoid the pitfalls that arise when the blind lead the blind. It is poor practice, and poor service, to encourage someone to explore regions of their intimate being that correspond to regions which you as a therapist are afraid of entering yourself. Work on the therapist's own view is called for, and that is rarely easy.

The Value of Therapeutic Liberation

The idea of liberation underlies practically all the procedures psychotherapists use when they work in the medium of human freedom. Freedom is the exercise of liberty and, in our view, liberation is the process that enhances it. Our assumption is that, for people in the positive region of the self-management spectrum, their willing commitments to plans and beliefs—choices—are best made when all elements of the view from the Great Divide of Consciousness are taken into account. Hirschmann's theorizing of freedom (chap. 9 in this book) makes the point that shifting "the central goal of freedom from 'doing

---

16. "Counter-transference" refers to projection onto the patient of the therapist's own unresolved conflicts.

what I want'—or 'making choices'—to 'defining what the choices are' . . . means that freedom cannot be simply about making choices within existing contexts; freedom has to be about having a say in defining that very context in the first place." Hirschmann's argument goes to the heart of what an Experiencer's view from the Great Divide, and the therapist's efforts to support it, is all about. Hirschmann's argument shows the way to settle Barry Schwartz's (2004) paradoxical claim that too many alternatives inhibit freedom: Schwartz does not take into account a chooser's ability to define alternatives. Her position also helps make sense of Kleindorfer's (chap. 6 in this book) finding that, in the purchase of automobile insurance, people are likely to select "default" coverage *because* it is the default, and not on the more rational basis of its costs and benefits. Heuristics like "choose the default" reduce the overhead of liberation—the work of (thoughtfully) developing alternatives available on the Great Divide. The liberation by the psychotherapy session lies in a consideration—of the fit between outer and inner worlds of experience—that is both guided and time-limited, so that the individual is not left forever buried in thought. Liberation in psychotherapy is valuable because it is disciplined and finite.

By focusing on the formulation as well as on the availability of alternatives for choice, the boxes and boundaries Arcenas describes (chap. 3 in this book) can be restructured to allow better room for growth and self-expression. As beneficiary of many journeys at the border between folly and freedom, and veteran of many trails blazed along it, the psychotherapist has a broader practical experience with the exercise of liberty than most observers of the human condition. In the course of therapy, a psychotherapist persuades by influencing the flow of another's awareness during moments of self-reflection, grappling directly with the human experience of freedom, rather than acting on its scientific, political, or spiritual foundations. And not only with the flow of the experience of others, either: a benefit of the counter-transference experience is the benefit of the "psychic scrubbing" it provides. A psychotherapist's projective empathy sometimes may take him into heretofore neglected regions of his own experience—regions normally overlooked or avoided in the therapist's own active engagement in the process of living beyond the consulting room. Like anyone else, the psychotherapist is likely to be excited, and even uplifted, by a newly experienced and unexpected view from the Great Divide. The fruit of the therapist's expanded view returns to the patient through the renewed energy and confidence that arise now from the therapist's own newly augmented perspective. The journey to the Great Divide falls in the category of the productive partnership that Arcenas advocates.

Freedom from the Subjective Point of View

Does the psychotherapist, as a person who works in the medium of other's freedom, have anything to contribute to "reassessments and rephrasings" of "Freedom"? We offer the following thoughts to represent that possibility:

Reassessments

• People know and value freedom as an experience, even though its source is a mystery that cannot be understood within a concrete explanatory framework of cause-and-effect.

• Those who work with others' freedom find that the human capacity for voluntary living is strength, and not a danger, unless clinical disorder is present. For those at the positive end of the self-management spectrum, the actualizing potential is much more influential than unconscious destructive urges, and something it is potentially devastating to ignore (cf. Frankl 1955).

• Subjective experience depends far more profoundly on the interpretation of events than on the raw fact of their occurrence. Accordingly, the psychotherapist's professional task is to bring to mind advantageous interpretations that are, on their merit, preferred by the person in treatment.

Rephrasings

• Freedom is regarded as taking place *inside* the "Experiencer," the subjective aspect of a person where sentience and volition, the attributes of awareness, occur.

• Psychotherapy is a matter of liberation aimed at providing the greatest responsible experience of personal freedom to each individual treated.

• Taking account of the individual's place in the spectrum of effective self-management, psychotherapists use the experience of freedom as a beacon that guides their work.

In Conclusion

Within the framework of individual subjectivity developed here, freedom resides in an Experiencer's ability to confront and resolve conflicting demands that arise from perceptions of the outer and inner worlds. Freedom is lost when this ability is impaired, and regained when biological, environmental, or cognitive repair takes place. The experience of freedom occurs in the course of creating and choosing realistic possibilities for self-management from the vantage point of the Great Divide of Consciousness. Freedom arises from the way circumstances are faced; it is not something inherent in those circumstances themselves.

Whatever the ultimate source and purpose of the subjective experience of freedom, it provides the individual with an inner beacon, a signal that gets stronger as Experiencer awareness becomes more complete. That an everyday, subjectively salient beacon would send out false signals makes no biological sense. Even though the source of this beacon is not understood, it is often used in psychotherapy to guide the course of treatment across the self-management spectrum, helping patients and clients learn to make the most of their apparent free choices among possibilities framed by salient features of the inner and outer worlds of experience.

The closer to the well-being end a person's position on the self-management spectrum lies, the more likely it is that his or her therapist will be working to support the capacity to bring outer and inner worlds together in personally meaningful representations of such things as self, sacrament, and lover. Search and encounter with meaningful things is a phenomenon of the Experiencer, produced by directing the mind's assimilation of information from outer and inner worlds under guidance from the actualizing potential, and evaluated by the experience of the result.

Psychotherapy is merely one way to contribute to the fullness of Experiencer awareness. Relationships outside psychotherapy can make a similar contribution, as Arcenas's chapter suggests. Conversations that people carry on from the Experiencer level, frequently touching on meaningful things, are the stuff of fully effective partnerships between Experiencers who have an agreed purpose—they are the stuff of intimacy when that purpose also includes developing the fullest representation possible of each other's point of view. Associated as it is with psychological well-being, the beacon of inner freedom can be accessed anywhere, and used to guide important relationships as well as individual lives.

References

American Psychiatric Association (1994) *Diagnostic and Statistical Manual of Mental Disorders*, 4th ed., Washington, DC: American Psychiatric Association.

American Psychological Association (2003) *Ethical Principles of Psychologists and Code of Conduct*, Washington, DC: American Psychological Association.

Barber, Jacques P., and Robert J. DeRubeis (1989) "On Second Thought: Where the Action Is in Cognitive Therapy for Depression," *Cognitive Therapy and Research* 13:441–457.

Bateson, Gregory, Donald D. Jackson, Jay Haley, and John H. Weakland (1963) "A Note on the Double Bind," *Family Process* 2:154–161.

Berne, Eric (1961) *Transactional Analysis in Psychotherapy*, New York: Grove Press.

Bruner, Jerome (1973) *Beyond the Information Given: Studies in the Psychology of Knowing*, Oxford: Norton.

Frankl, Victor (1955) *The Doctor and the Soul*, New York: Knopf.

Gopnik, Alison (1999) "Theory of Mind," in R. Wilson and F. Keil, Editors, *The MIT Encyclopedia of the Cognitive Sciences*, Cambridge, MA: The MIT Press.

Heidegger, Martin ([1927] 1962) *Being and Time*, J. Macquarrie and E. Robinson, Translators, New York: Harper.

Hollon, Steven D., Michael E. Thase, and John C. Markowitz (2002) "Treatment and Prevention of Depression," *Psychological Science in the Public Interest* 3:39–77.

Horney, Karen (1950) *Neurosis and Human Growth: The Struggle Toward Self-Realization*, New York: Norton.

Huxley, Aldous (1932) *Brave New World*, London: Chatto and Windus/Garden City, NY: Doubleday, Doran.

Irwin, Francis W. (1971) *Intentional Behavior and Motivation*, Philadelphia: J. B. Lippincott.

James, William (1890) *Principles of Psychology*, vol. 1, London: Macmillan.

Laing, Ronald D. (1972) *The Politics of the Family and Other Essays*, New York: Vintage Books.

Maslow, Abraham H. (1968) *Toward a Psychology of Being*, 2nd ed., New York: Van Nostrand Reinhold.

——— (1970) *Motivation and Personality*, 2nd ed., New York: Harper and Row.

Rogers, Carl R. (1951) *Client-Centered Therapy: Its Current Practice, Implications, and Theory*, Boston: Houghton Mifflin.

Schiff, Jacqui (1969) "Reparenting in Schizophrenia," *Transactional Analysis Bulletin*, 8:47–62.

Schwartz, Barry (2004) *The Paradox of Choice: Why More Is Less*, New York: ECCO.

Scott, Jan, Stephen Palmer, Eugene Paykel, John Teasdale, and Hazel Hayhurst (2003) "Use of Cognitive Therapy for Relapse Prevention in Chronic Depression: Cost-Effectiveness Study," *British Journal of Psychiatry* 182:221–227.

Seligman, Martin (1995) "The Effectiveness of Psychotherapy: The Consumer Reports Study," *American Psychologist* 50:965–974.

Shaffer, Peter (1973) *Equus: A Play*, London: Deutsch.

Skinner, B. F. (1953) *Science and Human Behavior*, New York: Macmillan.

——— (1957) *Verbal Behavior*, New York: Appleton-Century-Crofts.

Strachey, James (1953–66) *The Standard Edition of the Complete Psychological Works of Sigmund Freud*, London: Hogarth Press.

Szasz, Thomas S. (1961) *The Myth of Mental Illness: Foundations of a Theory of Personal Conduct*, Oxford: Harper and Row.

5

Degrees of Freedom: Jazz and the Art of Improvisation

William Parberry

Throughout the history of Western music, Classical music has been documented on paper. The composer, usually after numerous drafts over weeks, months, or sometimes years of labor, finally puts his *Deo gratias* on the last page and sends the work to his publisher. Such a creative process would represent the opposite of spontaneity or freedom. Improvisation, on the other hand, is the ultimate expression of freedom in music, and only in jazz is the art of improvisation the central means by which the performer communicates his music.

A recording of Beethoven's Fifth Symphony by the Boston Symphony Orchestra is not particularly different from a recording of the same composition performed by the Philadelphia Orchestra, because both ensembles are *trying*[1] to interpret the symphony "exactly" as Beethoven wrote it. The 1939 recording of Coleman Hawkins's inspired sax solo on Johnny Green's "Body and Soul," however, is unique, never to be performed the same way again. Had his solo not been recorded, the improvisation that he created, undocumented, would never have reached our ears. In jazz, the performer (Hawkins), not the composer (Green), determines the quality of the music.

The only style of jazz that does not involve improvisation is ragtime, and it is the earliest style that can be documented for that very reason. Written examples of ragtime and piano rolls predate the first documented example of improvised jazz—recorded in 1917 by the ODJB

---

1. For an excellent discussion of the complexities involved in this seemingly simple matter-of-fact assertion, see Jay Reise, "Context, Choice, and Issues of Perceived Determinism in Music," in Jose V. Ciprut, Editor, *Indeterminacy: The Mapped, The Navigable, and the Uncharted* (MIT Press, 2008).

(Original Dixieland Jazz Band) at the RCA Victor studio in New York.[2] Once improvisation was captured on vinyl, music scholars and critics began to evaluate the jazz artists, and recordings served as a teaching tool for young performers who were eager to learn the very difficult discipline of improvising jazz.

As different styles of jazz emerged in the twentieth century, the degree of freedom in improvisation changed from one period to the next. While one might assume that every jazz artist approached improvisation with the same amount of musical freedom, this was not the case. During certain periods, the jazz musician had to follow underlying rules in the process of improvisation that were dictated by the audience for which he was playing and by the general musical conventions of the time. And sometimes, the artist's approach to improvisation would change during the same evening. While playing with the Jay McShann band in the early 1940s, Charlie Parker, in order to accommodate the dancers, would improvise in a rhythmically restricted style. After the big band's performance was over, Parker would join Dizzy Gillespie and a select group of Beboppers in a late-night jam session at Monroe's in Harlem, where, as a small combo, they would experiment with a much freer approach to improvisation, both rhythmically and harmonically. The function of the dance band was to help, not to hinder, the dancer; so Parker, in the context of the band's arrangement, would accent his improvised melody in a manner that would support the beat. In contrast, at the late-night jam session, his accents would be irregularly spaced off the beat, unpredictable, and hardly suitable for dancing. At Monroe's, the audience was there to listen, not dance. Parker and his progressive cohorts were there to break free from the musical formulae of the dance bands.

Jazz evolved as a hybrid of African and Euro-American musical characteristics. African music contains improvisation, complex rhythmic accentuation, the blues scale, and call-and-response melodic phrasing. Euro-American music contains harmony, proportional rhythm (meter), the diatonic major and minor scales, and symmetric form.

Jazz has all of the above musical characteristics, merged together over many decades, from the advent of slavery in America to the latter

---

2. "The Original Dixieland Jass Band One-Step" is the earliest recording that uses the word "Jazz" or "Jass." Somewhat earlier recordings in the jazz style were produced by the Gennett Record Company of Richmond, Indiana, but they lack the term "jazz." Regardless of "who was first," the recordings of the ODJB and other New Orleans groups in New York and Chicago led to the jazz craze.

part of the nineteenth century, when the first inklings of a jazz style arose in New Orleans. For an African, music is part of daily life, whether celebrating the birth of a child or accompanying a mundane task, such as washing clothes by the river. As a slave in America, the African was not allowed to practice his musical customs with the same freedom that he had in Africa. African slaves and their descendents were prohibited from drumming, throughout the South, until the post–Civil War era. A notable exception to this rule was *Place Congo* in New Orleans, where drumming, dancing, and singing were permitted. The complex rhythmic patterns of African music may have been preserved at this location, and, in turn, this may have contributed to the development of the syncopated rhythmic approach that we hear in the earliest recordings of New Orleans jazz musicians. While the musical practice in *Place Congo* represented a relatively uncontaminated style of African music, elsewhere in New Orleans and wherever slavery was practiced, the African learned that by incorporating Euro-American musical characteristics with those of his own culture, his music became more readily accepted by the white man, and even encouraged. Work songs, field hollers, spirituals, and the country blues show evidence of this amalgamation of musical elements even before a pure jazz style emerges.

Ragtime, which lacks improvisation and qualifies as jazz only because of its frequent use of syncopation, was popular at the end of the nineteenth century and into the beginning of the twentieth century. At the same time, the style of improvised jazz that would be recorded in 1917, namely Dixieland, or Classic jazz, was being performed in the red light district of New Orleans—Storyville. Prostitution, restricted to this one area of New Orleans, was legalized there in 1897. The numerous brothels provided employment for many black and Creole musicians who were eager to make a living playing the music that they loved. White jazz musicians, while in the minority, also saw the economic rewards; several formed combos playing in the sporting houses, bars, and surrounding nightclubs of the Crescent City. When the construction of a naval base in New Orleans closed Storyville in 1917,[3] in addition to many prostitutes being out of work, many jazz musicians who had jobs in the brothels likewise found themselves unemployed. The ensuing migration of New Orleans jazz musicians up the Mississippi River to Chicago, west to California, and east to New York, led to the first recorded performances of Classic jazz. Given the prejudices of the

---

3. A federal law prohibited prostitution within five miles of a military establishment.

established record companies, the first group ever to be recorded was not the best if the best-known all-white ensemble—the Original Dixieland Jazz Band. Black groups such as King Oliver's Creole Jazz Band and Jelly Roll Morton's Red Hot Peppers found employment in the clubs and speakeasies of cities like Chicago, San Francisco, and New York, but they were not recorded until 1922, five years after the ODJB.

New Orleans Classic jazz, often called Dixieland jazz because of its origins in the South, became the musical rage of "the roaring twenties," mixing black and white New Orleans musicians with musicians in Chicago and New York. While jazz was not new to the northern cities, the type of jazz played in nightclubs, vaudeville theaters, and ballrooms prior to 1917 was not the combo style of Dixieland, but ragtime, mildly syncopated dance arrangements, and in the black cabarets—the blues. What most distinguishes Dixieland from all other styles of jazz is ensemble improvisation. Solo improvisation is also present, but the distinctive sound of New Orleans Classic jazz is heard when three or four members of the group improvise at the same time. Each of the front line melody instruments in the combo—called front line because they were positioned in front of the rhythm section (back line)—has a specific role in the exciting counterpoint of collective improvisation. The trumpet syncopates the melody in the mid-register, the clarinet improvises a faster countermelody in the high register, and the trombone improvises yet another countermelody below the trumpet. With a tacit understanding among the performers as to their respective roles, the front line players create different rhythmic and melodic ideas that result in a spirited interplay between skilled musicians. Each artist follows the chord progression that accompanies the melody, the more effectively to keep the various melodic lines in agreement; yet, within the prescribed structure there remains a good deal of freedom. Simultaneously, the players communicate and compete, each imaginative phrase played by one performer challenging the other to respond in kind, without disturbing the delicate balance of the tri-linear polyphony.

Solo improvisation in early jazz meant embellishing the melody: a few ornamental pitches and syncopation were added to the theme during a typical solo. When discussing his playing in 1917, the clarinetist Buster Bailey describes what he and most jazz musicians of that period considered improvisation: "At the time I wouldn't have known what they meant by improvisation. But embellishment was a phrase I understood" (Hentoff and Shapiro 1957, 78). This ornamental approach to the main melody was the same process that the lead trumpet used in the context of ensemble improvisation. Here, however, the lively countermelodies improvised by the clarinet and trombone enhanced the relatively simple line of the trumpet part, making the overall effect sound more musically complex. This is one reason why the early Dixieland groups eschewed solo improvisation in favor of ensemble improvisation. Most early jazz instrumentalists were accustomed to working as a team during ensemble improvisation, but few had the experience or imagination to sustain the interest of the listener with a lengthy solo that was little more than a decorated version of the theme. In the early 1920s, and probably during the pre-recording days of New Orleans jazz, the musicians experienced more freedom when improvising collectively than when thrown into the spotlight as individual soloists. By the middle of the decade, largely through the example of the great Louis Armstrong, solo improvisation itself becomes freer and less chained to the melody.

During the early '20s, Armstrong played second trumpet to his mentor King Oliver in Oliver's Creole Jazz Band. Since Oliver was the leader of the group, and the arrangements focused on ensemble improvisation, Armstrong had little opportunity to perform as a soloist. As second trumpet, Armstrong would improvise a countermelody to Oliver's lead. In other words, while Oliver was extemporizing a variation on the main melody, Armstrong would have to create new melodic phrases that were different from the central tune, but that followed the chords in the accompaniment. As a result, Armstrong discovered early on that he could improvise creatively without using the theme as a skeletal framework for his melodic ideas. Armstrong's freedom as a soloist was certainly restricted during his youthful years in Oliver's combo, yet the method he learned while playing second trumpet— extemporizing original melodic phrases based solely on the chord progression—paid dividends when he applied the same approach to his solos after he left Oliver. We first hear this in 1924, when Armstrong departs for New York to play with Fletcher Henderson's band as lead trumpet in the brass section. Armstrong's solo on the band's recording of Irving Berlin's "Mandy, Make Up Your Mind" is completely divorced from the original melody. Released from the predictable four-square rhythm of the tune, Armstrong also improvises with much greater rhythmic freedom and sophistication, at one point even throwing off the rhythm section, which barely holds on to the beat against his complex syncopations. After one year with Henderson, Armstrong returns to Chicago and forms his own small combo, the Hot Five. While, ostensibly, the Hot Five seemed to be yet another of many Dixieland combos on the proliferating jazz scene in the late '20s, in reality, Armstrong's approach to improvisation redefined the standard roles of the Dixie combo. With his unmatched technique on trumpet, Armstrong would not confine himself to the mid-register, as was customary for the lead trumpet in the context of ensemble improvisation. Instead, he would rise into the upper register of his instrument, his volume overpowering the other members of the ensemble. Collective improvisation no longer sounded "collective," and Armstrong's dominance in the texture produced a constantly soloistic sonority. Soon, other members of his group, like clarinetist Johnny Dodds and pianist Earl "Fatha" Hines, began to emulate in their own solos Armstrong's disregard for the theme. By the end of the '20s, jazz had become so popular that there was a massive increase in the number of skilled musicians mastering the art of improvisation. Unlike earlier jazz artists, many had the prodigious technique required to craft musical phrases spontaneously on a given harmonic sequence. The degree of freedom in solo improvisation had progressed from its nadir in the thematic variation of the early '20s to the newly melodic approach based on chord changes that would become standard practice in traditional jazz.

Largely, the meteoric rise in the popularity of jazz resulted from its function as dance music. In the Jazz Age of the '20s, Dixieland combos provided the accompaniment for the Charleston and the Black Bottom. Dancing to jazz, an activity enjoyed with abandon during the prosperous decade prior to the depression, was to become a nostalgic escape from troubled times following the crash of 1929. From the Lindy Hop to the Jitterbug, dances of the Swing era brought jazz to the forefront of popular music in the '30s, where it remained through the end of World War II. From 1930 to 1945, dancing to jazz was America's principal form of entertainment, and musically, the consequent growth in the number of listeners and dancers led to major stylistic changes. With radio and recordings spreading the sound of jazz throughout the country, its audience exploded in the '30s, and the volume produced by a small Dixieland combo became insufficient for the larger venues. High school gymnasiums and large auditoriums were required to accommodate the many dancers, and, as a result, the combo expanded into a much larger ensemble in order to generate enough sound to be heard by everyone moving their feet to the beat. Along with the growth of the jazz audience came a corollary increase in the number of musicians wanting to acquire the skills of a jazz artist. Not all of these would-be jazz musicians had the natural talents of a soloist, but even the less-proficient found homes as sidemen in the brass or reed sections of the new bands. Never called upon to play solos, these journeymen of the Swing bands provided an indispensable cog in the wheel of the style until the passing of the dance bands, in the '50s, made them obsolete. Instead of the trumpet/clarinet/trombone trio of a standard Dixieland front line, the new big bands had three or four of each in the brass and reed sections, making ensemble improvisation altogether impractical. Music scored for sections or for the full band had to be written out or memorized. These arranged passages would alternate with improvised solo choruses by lead musicians who fronted each section. A reduced instrumentation played background chords or riffs[4] behind the soloist while the rhythm section continued to lay down the beat for the dancers. Even the soloist was expected to help the dancer feel the beat rhythmically; consequently, his accentuation often reinforced the accents of the rhythm section. Except for mild syncopation, the rhythmic style of the Swing band soloist rarely deviated from slapping the beat. Were he to venture into a more sophisticated rhythmic style, he would undermine the function of the music, and the average dancer might lose his way. The lively counterpoint of ensemble improvisation and the rhythmic freedom enjoyed by Dixieland soloists in the late '20s were both lost in the subsequent Swing era. As early as 1926, the transition was in progress. In that year, Fletcher Henderson recorded "The Stampede" with an eleven-piece band grouped into sections. The arrangement lacked collective improvisation, and every soloist accented the beat.

Ten years after Henderson's "The Stampede," the general approach to improvisation in the Swing bands had changed very little. Most of the players in the bands that played and recorded in large cities like New York were musically educated and could read music. Arranged passages for these "National" bands were no problem for such musicians. In the rural areas of the country, however, the so-called Territory bands, or "Kansas City style" bands, were made up of musically uneducated players who were adept at improvising, but who often could not read music.[5] Since ensemble improvisation was no longer practical

---

4. A riff is a short, simple, repeated phrase.
5. Count Basie, a major arranger and band director in the Kansas City style, never learned to read music. Even in the 1950s, when most of his players were reading musicians, he taught his own arrangements to the band by rote from the piano.

in big-band arrangements, any passages played by a section or by the full band in the Kansas City style had to be simple enough to memorize. Arrangements composed of riffs were the standard for these bands, since both riff-tunes and the chords that accompanied them were easy to remember. In the National band style, with arrangers like Henderson and Benny Goodman, the focus was on the arrangement, and the solos were brief and few. The opposite was the case in the Kansas City style, in which solos were profuse, and arranged passages were often limited to the opening chorus and a final, driving "out" chorus. In both styles, the soloist improvised in predictable rhythms and symmetric phrases, with little melodic freedom. Even Goodman, a virtuoso clarinetist, limited his melodic approach to embellishing the theme or executing fast arpeggios and scales that were reminiscent of musical exercises. To no small degree, the Swing soloist had regressed in terms of his freedom, when compared with the likes of Armstrong and the best of the Dixieland soloists.[6]

Although Kansas City style musicians conformed to the same musical conventions as their counterparts in the National bands, their emphasis on improvisation, the blues, and riff-tunes, rather than intricate arrangements, was more in touch with the African roots of jazz. Kansas City style soloists had more freedom to air out their melodic ideas in lengthy improvisations. National band soloists were usually limited to one chorus or less. It should come as no surprise, then, that the three major forerunners of a new, more sophisticated approach to improvisation should come from the Southwest: Coleman Hawkins (Kansas), Lester Young (Mississippi), and Charlie Christian (Texas) grew up listening to Kansas City style bands—arrangements that focused on solo improvisation. While all three made their livings playing in Swing bands, their individual approaches to improvisation broke free from the predictable rhythmic and melodic approach that had been the norm for the past decade. Coleman Hawkins, originally lead tenor sax with the Henderson band, formed his own nine-piece band in 1939 and made an historic recording of Johnny Green's "Body and Soul," in which, after playing only the opening phrase of the melody, he then improvises without any reference to the theme, fashioning a completely original solo based on the chord changes. With total disregard for the original melody, Hawkins extemporizes on his own tune over the

6. Armstrong continued to perform into and beyond the Swing era, but he, too, began to conform to the conventions of the time, never again surpassing the level of his playing with the Hot Five.

chord progression that Green composed to accompany his famous standard. Moreover, Hawkins expands the given harmonic sequence, implying more sophisticated versions of the fundamental chords through upper partials[7] which are introduced into his improvised melody. By the same means, he inserts additional, passing harmonies, crafting an elaborate variation on the original progression. Contrary to the traditional Swing practice of paraphrasing the melody and sticking to a specified chord progression, Hawkins frees himself melodically, and for the first time, a jazz artist views the harmonic progression as a malleable source for improvisation. Hawkins anticipated harmonic, structural, and melodic advances that would form the musical syntax of the Beboppers in the '40s. His rhythmic approach, however, remained conservative, and he never shed the slap-the-beat accentuation of Swing.

Another tenor sax player, Lester Young, also discarded the melody as the source for his solos, instead improvising motivically. Young, with his understated tone that became the signature sound of the "cool school" of the '50s, would improvise a short musical phrase (motive) that generated another phrase, and another, and so forth, constructing his solo like a musical story. His 1939 performance in "Lester Leaps In" with Count Basie's Swing combo illustrates this motivic approach, which, unlike the typical Swing solo, develops in asymmetric phrases. While Young's performance on this recording maintains a regular Swing accentuation, his solo in Basie's big band arrangement of "Doggin' Around" is rhythmically unpredictable. In contrast to every other soloist, Young accents his pulses irregularly, frequently off the beat, leaving the dancer to depend on background riffs and the rhythm section for metric guidance. Young's asymmetric phrasing, his structuring of his solos motivically, and his occasional forays into unpredictable accentuation began to free the soloist from the rhythmic function of dance music.

Charlie Christian, the brilliant guitar player who joined the Benny Goodman band in 1939, played as a soloist in Goodman's Swing combos until Christian's premature death from tuberculosis in 1942. During these years, while Goodman's band was located in New York, Christian often jammed at Minton's after hours. Dubbed the "Father of Bebop," Christian combined Hawkins's harmonic advances, and Young's movitic phrasing, with his own intricate rhythmic

---

7. Partials are notes added to a basic chord that make it more harmonically complex.

accentuation, providing a model for the progressive musicians who
would benefit from his legacy. Christian's improvisation on "I Found
a New Baby," recorded in 1941 with Benny Goodman's sextet, goes in
a completely different direction than the leader's clarinet solo. Goodman
plays a stylization of the melody, grouped in symmetric phrases and
foot-tapping rhythms that support the dancer. Christian's solo rides
above the beat in asymmetric phrasing that subtly develops internal
motives not derived from the tune. His additive rhythmic approach,
grouping pulses through irregular accents in cross-rhythmic[8] cells of
twos and threes, is an atavistic hearkening back to his African heritage,
making him a pivotal figure in the transition from Swing to Bebop.
Liberating himself from the melodic and rhythmic constraints of Swing,
Charlie Christian, with just three years of active performing, introduced the freest style of improvisation to date.

  During the '40s, jazz divided into two branches: Swing and Bebop,
each with its own audience. Swing might have succumbed to the progressive Bebop movement were it not for the war, which kept dancing
to big bands booming through 1945. In the second half of that decade,
some bands, such as those led by Woody Herman and Stan Kenton,
tried to accommodate their soloists by extending to them greater
freedom to improvise at length in a Boplike style. Bebop, however, was
a combo style, in which the soloist, not the arrangement, was the sole
focus of the performance. While Swing bands continued to thrive
during the war years, Bebop evolved in the after-hours clubs of New
York—Minton's and Monroe's in Harlem, and the many jazz clubs on
52nd Street in Manhattan. The civil war between Bebop and Swing was
initiated by the likes of Hawkins, Young, and Christian, but the com-
manders-in-chief of the bop army were Charlie Parker (alto sax) and
Dizzy Gillespie (trumpet). While both Parker and Gillespie played in
big bands to support themselves, they were at the same time perfecting
a very different approach to improvising in the small combos of the
nightclubs, where they were lucky if they received union wage. Having
heard Charlie Christian both live and on the recordings of his sessions
at Minton's and Monroe's, Parker first absorbed the guitarist's musical
advances and then went even further, particularly in Parker's own
rhythmic and harmonic innovations. As early as 1939, while working
with the guitarist Biddy Fleet, Parker discovered the process of impro-

---

8. The simultaneous use of strikingly contrasting rhythms in different parts—in this case,
Christian's accents against the regular beat of the rhythm section.

vising on the upper partials of chords. His revelation is documented in an article from *Down Beat* magazine: "At the time, Charlie says, he was bored with the stereotyped changes being used then. 'I kept thinking there's bound to be something else,' he recalls. 'I could hear it sometimes but I couldn't play it.' Working over Cherokee [a jazz standard written by band leader Charlie Barnett] with Fleet, Charlie suddenly found that by using the higher intervals of a chord as a melody line and backing them with the appropriately related changes, he could play this thing he had been 'hearing'. Fleet picked it up behind him and bop was born" (Levin and Wilson 1949, 12). Parker became aware of advanced chord structures through the harmonic voicing of Fleet's guitar, and he constructed his improvised sax melody around the upper partials in those chords. This approach is more advanced than that of an earlier innovator like Armstrong, who based the melodic phrasing in his improvisations on the fundamental notes in chords.

Rhythmically, Parker was without peer. His dynamic articulation of the pulse, in a constant state of flux, created polyrhythmic phrasing at breakneck tempos through accentuation off, on, and between the beat. "Ghost notes," underplayed dynamically to act as pick-ups to the pitch that follows, are scattered throughout, adding a subtle dynamic means of shifting the pattern of accents. Even Bebop's co-founder, Dizzy Gillespie, acknowledged his debt to Parker when it came to rhythm: "I think I was a little more advanced, harmonically, than he was. But rhythmically, he was quite advanced, with setting up the phrase and how you got from one note to another. How you get from one note to another really makes the difference. Charlie Parker heard rhythms and rhythmic patterns differently, and after we started playing together, I began to play, rhythmically, more like him" (Gillespie, with Fraser, 1979, 177). By 1945, Parker and Gillespie were recognized masters, and their collaboration on several recordings in that year represents the epitome of Bebop, setting them apart from all other musicians. Their performance of "Shaw 'Nuff," a Gillespie tune based on the chord changes of George Gershwin's "I Got Rhythm," is so fast that the listener can hardly keep track of the beat.[9] Their ensemble on the unison theme is remarkable for the precision of the synchronized inflections at such a blistering tempo. They play as if they were of one mind, and

---

9. Rebelling against the standard tunes of Swing, the Beboppers would often replace these famous melodies with Bop-like tunes of their own while retaining the original chord progressions—a practical necessity, since the jam sessions that generated the style required that any newcomer wishing to join in would be familiar with the harmonies.

their solos set a new standard of virtuosity combined with melodic and rhythmic invention.

Only the marquee big bands survived into the '50s, soon to be replaced completely by groups playing and singing a perplexing new generation's dance music—Rock and Roll. As many Swing bands faded into obscurity, sidemen were out of work, and big-band soloists who learned to navigate the treacherous waters of Bebop formed their own combos. From 1917 to 1945, jazz listeners were also dancers, and most improvisation was contoured to accommodate that function. Always aware that his rhythmic and harmonic role had to adhere to well-accepted conventions, the improviser was never completely free to play as he wished. The arrival of Bebop ushered in the modern era of jazz, and skilled musicians capable of playing the demanding style considered themselves artists more than entertainers. Improvisation became a means of expression with no constraints, rhythmically or melodically. Harmony, while still a governing factor in the improvising process, was open to exploration and embellishment. Along with greater freedom for the improvising musician, however, there came a smaller audience that could understand the music. True, jazz still had many fans in the 1950s, but younger listeners were following Chuck Berry and Elvis Presley, while many older jazz fans, unwilling or unable to appreciate the unusual intricacies of Bebop, continued to buy the latest Goodman and Basie recordings. The big band, however, was a dinosaur drawing its last breath, and the small combo would forever more be the medium for jazz improvisation. Jazz had become a chamber art, and much like chamber music in the Classical genre, it had a relatively small coterie of musically astute devotees.

The '50s saw many new Bebop combos, but with not enough audience to go around. Musicians, as might be expected, were quicker to learn the style than listeners were to appreciate it. Jazz was at a peak of musical complexity, if still within the traditional format of improvisation over a chord progression. Groups seeking to distinguish themselves from other combos created a signature sound with the hope of attracting their own following. Cool jazz, one attempt to separate from the pack, underscored musical complexity, while also minimizing expression. Miles Davis (trumpet), Stan Getz (tenor sax), and Lenny Tristano (piano), all leaders in the Cool school, had been trained in Bebop, but by stripping Bop of its emotional content—timbral effects, expressive tone, wide dynamic range, an active drummer, the blues—they believed that the listener would be forced to focus on, and hence understand better, the purely musical elements of jazz. Improvisation was neither more "free" nor more sophisticated than it had been in Bebop, but the Cool jazz artists assumed a cerebral posture that brought jazz closer to Classical music in atmosphere. As a consequence of this intellectualization of jazz, a reaction by musicians who saw Cool jazz as a further alienation of the average listener led to an opposing style: Hard-bop. It featured black musicians such as Horace Silver (piano) and Art Blakey (drums), who were offended by the shedding of musical characteristics derived from the African side of jazz's origins. Aroused by both social and commercial concerns, the Hard-boppers now proclaimed a back-to-the-roots movement, returning jazz improvisation to an elementary level, together with a soulful, almost gospel-like tone. It was their hope that the funky sound, the riff-laden solos, and the slap-the-beat rhythms of Hard-bop would catch the ear of many listeners who had become disinterested in the urbane sonority of progressive jazz. However, by courting the public with such a musically regressive style, the Hard-bop improviser lost much of the freedom that he had gained in Bebop. Easier to play and a lot more accessible, Hard-bop had a fleeting popularity, but it passed in historical importance as many musicians tired of confining their solos to predictable rhythms and obvious clichés.

Although Hard-bop was a step backward in the progressive art of improvisation, the acute social awareness that it raised among black musicians remained a force in the avant-garde styles of the '60s. The social unrest throughout that decade led many black performers and listeners to view freedom in jazz as a socio-musical double entendre. By removing traditional harmony, a regular beat, and standard forms, the socially concerned black artist attempted to free jazz of its "white" elements, while also seeking to free himself as an improviser. Until the end of the '50s, improvising on a composer's chord progression was standard practice. In Bebop and Cool jazz the musician might enhance or augment the basic harmony, but the original set of chords was still the source for the artist's improvisation. Functional harmony, or music in a key, was the one remaining characteristic that prevented absolute freedom in the process of improvisation. Miles Davis, always at the vanguard of jazz, is credited with the initial foray into the uncharted waters of improvising without a chord progression.

In the spring of 1959, Miles, with Bill Evans and Wynton Kelly (pianists), John Coltrane (tenor sax), Cannonball Adderley (alto sax), Paul Chambers (bass), and Jimmy Cobb (drums) recorded the album *Kind of*

Blue, pioneering the first modal approach to jazz improvisation. Instead of writing themes with chord changes, Miles and Bill Evans composed melodies in modes, or scales that were akin to the modes of medieval music, for example, the Dorian and Lydian scales of ancient chant. After playing the theme, soloists improvised freely within one mode, or modes—as displayed in the track "Flamenco Sketches," which has five different scales. In place of a chordal pattern underpinning the melody, a stationary vamp that creates a drone and a walking bass line in the mode were used to accompany, respectively, the theme and subsequent solo. Since the chorus principle (a chord progression repeated at regular intervals) no longer applied, solos were open-ended: an improviser played as long as he wished, after which the next soloist would have the same freedom to express himself at length. In theory, the group was rhythmically free as well. No steady beat was necessary, since, without a chord progression, no counting of measures between chord changes was in play. The measure, or meter, was not required, freeing the rhythm section from its metronomic role. In spite of the musical implications with regard to the beat in this new style, Miles the progressive, who was also an astute judge of his audience, felt that even his more open minded fans, not to mention his fellow musicians, might not be ready for a complete break with tradition. "So What," the best-known track on the album, exhibits his carefully calculated mix of the familiar and new. A riff, accompanied by a vamp, is played over an eight-measure phrase, which is repeated, then repeated again with the mode shifting up a half tone; finally, shifting back to its original pitch, the phrase is repeated once more. Formally, Miles creates the familiar sound of pop song form via a modal shift in the third phrase (A-A-B-A in sequence, wherein each phrase lasts eight measures), yet he fabricates this impression without an actual chord progression. The vamp produces a steady beat, and Miles retains the familiar characteristic of meter so that everyone knows when to shift the modal scale. The procedural form is also traditional. The riff and vamp are stated in the beginning and recapitulated at the end, between which, instead of playing open-ended solos, the performers improvise over a walking bass line, following the A-A-B-A pattern with a modal shift every third phrase. Miles introduces a major change in harmonic theory, but softens the blow by preserving a steady beat, meter, and the appearance of a chorus principle, assuring continuity alongside the transformation.

Improvisation in a mode hence freed the jazz musician from the obligation of shaping his melody around a chord structure that for so long had dictated *when* he ought to change pitch sets in order to match each chord in the progression. While confining one's improvisation to a single mode would seem limiting, too, in reality it gave the creative artist more freedom. Miles explained this approach in an interview with Nat Hentoff (1958, 11–12): "When you go this way, you can go on forever. You don't have to worry about changes and you can do more with the line. It becomes a challenge to see how melodically inventive you can be. When you're based on chords, you know at the end of 32 bars that the chords have run out and there's nothing to do but repeat what you've just done—with variations."

The solos from "So What" that best exemplify the new freedom are those by Coltrane and Evans. Evans, who wrote the track "Blue and Green" and had a hand in every setting, essentially functioned as a co-arranger on the album. In his standard role as an accompanist, Evans was accustomed to laying down chord changes, a practice that was no longer required in Modal jazz. When backing up the other soloists in "So What," Evans creates a new sonority by playing mildly dissonant simultaneities rather than functionally related chords. In his own solo, he uses the keyboard to negate the expected chordal sonority of the instrument: instead of playing triads (chords built in notes that are a third apart), he plays dissonant diads (adjacent pitches) and quartal patterns, introducing a nonchordal technique that became the standard method of many post-Bop pianists.

Coltrane's solo on the same track is remarkable for the ease with which he improvises in the new modality. All of the soloists perform well, but Coltrane seems particularly adept, as if he had found his voice. Rather than structuring his solo in traditional melodic phrasing, he develops melodic cells, using a small set of pitches within the mode to generate ever-expanding phrases that grow in intensity until he arrives at an eloquent conclusion. Prior to *Kind of Blue*, Coltrane had explored a similar approach when playing chord changes, but the harmonic process suppressed his melodic expression. Describing Coltrane's playing over a chord progression, Miles said: "What he does, for example, is to play five notes of a chord and then keep changing it around, trying to see how many different ways it can sound. It's like explaining something five different ways" (Hentoff 1959). On his own playing at that time, however, Coltrane hints at the intense frustration that he was experiencing: "I feel like I can't hear but so much in the ordinary chords we usually have going in the accompaniment. I just have to have more of a blueprint. It may be that sometimes I've been trying to force all those extra progressions into a structure where they don't fit" (Hentoff 1959). Modal jazz liberated Coltrane from the constraints of chord changes. He would go on to become the standard-bearer for the style well into the '60s, until his untimely death in 1967. After leaving Miles, who soon abandoned the modal style for new explorations, Coltrane investigated and deliberately imitated the modal music of India in his own jazz arrangements. Miles had retained certain traditional sounds to make Modal jazz more accessible, but Coltrane felt no such obligation, often having his rhythm section play freely without a steady beat, moving further away from the Euro-American in jazz. To many Afro-Americans, Coltrane's highly charged improvisations during his rise to prominence in the '60s symbolized their cry for freedom (see Hackney, chap 11 in this book) and their struggle for civil rights.

Only one step remained on the path to complete freedom for the improvising artist—the removal of all pre-set conditions, including modes or scales. In 1959, the same year that *Kind of Blue* was released, the saxophonist Ornette Coleman took that step, playing to a packed house at the Five Spot in New York City. Appropriately, the style he played was called Free jazz, and there were no rules.

Historically, Lenny Tristano and his combo recorded two isolated examples of this style in 1949: "Intuition" and "Digression." They were free, collective improvisations, in which, to avoid musical anarchy, members of the group communicated by responding to each other's ideas. Tristano's experiment was short lived, however, and today he is remembered more for his contributions to Cool jazz. Coleman was the first musician to perform Free jazz consistently, introducing a second branch of the avant-garde that ran in tandem with Modal jazz throughout the '60s. Prior to immersing himself in free improvisation, Coleman had played mainly rhythm and blues. Unlike Miles or Coltrane, he had never played Bebop or any sophisticated style of traditional jazz. Consequently, most jazz musicians felt that he had not "paid his dues," and many were offended by the amount of praise he received from notable music critics. His "Congeniality," from the 1959 album *The Shape of Jazz to Come*, substantiates the accusations about his technical limitations. After a Bop-like theme for unison sax and trumpet (Don Cherry), Coleman proceeds to improvise—supported by a rhythm section of bass and drums. But, since his improvisations use neither drones nor chords, chording instruments like the piano are absent from his ensembles. Although original in its avoidance of tonality,

Coleman's improvising remains hence melodically unimaginative and rhythmically predictable. Drawing on his rhythm and blues background, he slaps the beat in relatively symmetric phrases, never structuring his melodic lines with any direction. There is none of the motivic development or driving intensity that one finds in a solo by Coltrane. However, credit is due Coleman for having the courage to forge ahead, embracing a style that was not likely to have a large following. While not a highly skilled improviser, he opened the doors for more accomplished jazz artists like Cecil Taylor (piano) and Eric Dolphy (sax, bass clarinet), who brought free improvisation to its fruition in the 1960s with their expressive, technically brilliant solos.

Once Free jazz liberated the improviser from all conventions and rules, his creative talent was the sole determining factor in a successful performance. He was no longer aided by the familiar goal-directed motion of functional harmony, which in and of itself could hold a listener's attention. Free and Modal jazz alienated many jazz fans who had neither the musical acuity nor the desire to comprehend styles that lacked both harmony and meter. Conservative jazz musicians were still playing Bebop, Hard-bop, or Cool jazz, and some listeners confined their experience to these traditional styles, eschewing the avant-garde. Disillusioned by the increasing complexity of both traditional and avant-garde jazz, many former listeners had already abandoned jazz for more popular genres. After a long history as America's music, jazz had fallen to its nadir in popularity during the 1960s, raising the question of whether greater freedom was a positive development in the art of improvisation.

Jazz would need a new sound if it was to attract new listeners, sensed Miles Davis, after exploring Free jazz in the mid-'60s. Rather than attempting to woo back older jazz fans by returning to a more accessible tonal approach, he sought to court a younger audience that would accept jazz improvisation on his terms, if placed in a familiar medium. Wisely, instead of relying on veteran sidemen, Miles managed to surround himself with young talents like Wayne Shorter (tenor sax) and Chick Corea (acoustic and electric piano), who—attuned to the tastes of a younger generation—could offer advice on his musical direction. Jazz had always been played on acoustic instruments,[10] but the most popular music of the '60s, Hard-rock, was performed in the electric

---

10. The few exceptions would be the vibraphone, organ, and amplified guitar of an earlier vintage, used for example, by Charlie Christian, not by Jimi Hendricks.

medium. In a move that shocked the jazz community—musicians, fans, and critics—Miles switched to the electric sonority of Rock, partially in 1968 with *Filles de Kilimanjaro*, and completely in the 1969 albums *In a Silent Way* and *Bitches Brew*. In addition to electric keyboards, guitar, and bass, Miles used studio amplification of his trumpet, and he had Shorter play soprano sax, which penetrated the electronic sonority better than tenor. Not wanting to compromise the process of improvising, Miles insisted that all solos be melodically free, and without chord changes. However, the improvisations were played over the sonority of a Rock rhythm section, with a steady beat and frequent vamps that created the effect of a tonic or drone. Above the vamp, soloists would improvise as they wished—modally, atonally, or in the blues scale. *Bitches Brew* has sold better than any album to date in the history of jazz. Many young listeners, then, were eager to explore a musical style that challenged them, but they were not ready to give up the familiar sonority of Rock. These new fans, along with more open minded supporters of modern jazz, became a base of listeners that saw this hybrid of Jazz-rock, or Fusion, as the future trend.

More recently, in the music of trumpet player and arranger Wynton Marsalis, the concept of improvisatory freedom has acquired new meaning. Marsalis spurns Fusion, or any incorporation of elements that are foreign to the original Afro-American characteristics of jazz. He feels that jazz is a fertile ground for experimentation without the introduction of devices or characteristics that are outside the native rubrics of the genre, such as the electric medium of Rock or imitation of Indian music. He suggests that musicians celebrate, rather than reject, the past, honoring and learning about former jazz greats and their styles. Marsalis, who can play in many different styles, sees in the process of improvisation freedom of choice. Like Miles in *Bitches Brew*, Marsalis, too, installs a background that creates a stylistic expectation; but his improvisation develops independently, divorced from the customary rules of that style. In a single evening's performance, Marsalis might present a Bebop standard, a Modal piece, and a Free jazz original, each endowed with a different tonal syntax. Regardless of which style he employs, Marsalis improvises in a melodic approach that is purely linear in conception. Hence, in a piece with chord changes, any vertical relationship between his pitches and those of the bass or piano is secondary to the horizontal motion of his melody. In his performance of Charlie Parker's Bebop tune "Au privave" (from the CD *Live at Blues Alley*), Marsalis plays the original theme in the standard Bop style, and his rhythm section continues in a similar fashion, playing the chord progression in the chorus format. Marsalis, however, does not *improvise* in the Bebop style, nor does he derive his improvised melody from the chord changes. Instead, his improvisation pays homage to Parker's theme by extracting motives from the tune and developing them into new melodic ideas that both relate to and expand on the original. One phrase links logically to the next in a continuous flow of seamless melody. Harmonic tension is created by his moving away from the scale of the key when he ventures into more elaborate lines, at times even improvising dissonantly against the underlying chord progression. The process of thematic reference—improvisation that is structured on motives taken from the melody—is the common thread that runs through his solos in any style, tonal or atonal. With a myriad of past styles from which to choose, Marsalis rejects none that is purely acoustic, but he gives each a reinterpretation through the strictly thematic orientation of his improvisation.

Charlie Parker was so revered that his disregard for the theme as a source of improvisation became the accepted attitude in modern jazz, even when the alternative source, the chord progression, was later discarded. Those who varied from this thinking were few, but they anticipated a need on the part of the listener. During the '50s, in the waning years of traditional jazz, Sonny Rollins (tenor sax) and Thelonious Monk (piano), still playing chord changes, were the only two major artists who stood apart from the mainstream in their theme and variations technique of improvisation. Miles Davis, influenced by his young sideman Wayne Shorter, experimented with Free jazz in the sixties using a thematic-referential approach to improvisation. On Shorter's "Dolores," from the 1966 album *Mile Smiles*, they improvise in open-ended solos that are built around motives taken from the theme. Shorter also brings back the theme between solos, creating a rondolike structure that refreshes the listener's memory. Shorter and Miles use thematic reference as a substitute for the absent, familiar sound of functional tonality, giving their audience a melodic thread to follow. They, like Marsalis, realized that the more jazz removed itself from traditional harmony, the more its listeners needed a return to thematically based improvisation. While jazz seemed to have come full circle, hearkening back to early improvisations that were thematic embellishments, the modern approach was not simple ornamentation, but motivic development—a much more complex method of extemporizing melody.

Completely free improvisation, absent conventional harmony and thematic reference, is so personal an expression that the performer's ideas are at risk of appearing arbitrary and lacking in melodic logic. Sometimes the smallest gesture toward tradition will be enough to guide the listener through the challenging path of an avant-garde solo. The modal album *Kind of Blue* offered the world some of the most sophisticated improvisations in jazz. Though the music theory employed on the album was considered avant-garde in 1959, today *Kind of Blue* is the largest-selling jazz recording of all time—surpassing *Bitches Brew*. The solos by Coltrane, Miles, and Evans are no less complex than many, often brilliant improvisations by more radical artists from the '60s and '70s. What separates *Kind of Blue* from other worthy, yet overlooked, albums is not simply the quality of improvisation, but the comfortable sonority that belies the underlying complexity. In his liner notes to *Kind of Blue*, Bill Evans (1959) hints at the difficult task confronting the performers: "Although it is not uncommon for a jazz musician to be expected to improvise on new material at a recording session, the character of these pieces represents a particular challenge." And, unaware that the album would achieve legendary status, Evans (1959) also strikes on the salient point that explains the album's success: "Aside from the weighty technical problem of collective coherent thinking, there is the very human, even social need for sympathy from all members to bend for the common result. This most difficult problem, I think, is beautifully met and solved on this recording. . . . Miles Davis presents here frameworks which are exquisite in their simplicity and yet contain all that is necessary to stimulate performance with a sure reference to the primary conception."

Communication between performers blossoms when they learn a new musical language that at the same time retains a connection to their past experience. The steady beat, vamps, riff tunes, and formal settings do not interfere with the execution of the modal concept, but they give the performers confidence to interact skillfully and excel individually in a style of improvisation that offers them more melodic freedom with an accompanying sonority that is accessible to most listeners. Whether through the thematically derived approach of Marsalis or through Miles's merging of the familiar and the complex, the jazz artist will communicate with his audience most successfully when his improvisation contains a guideline that, though it may limit freedom, will help to clarify the thrust of his message.

References

Evans, Bill (1959) "Kind of Blue," liner notes for *Kind of Blue*, Columbia Records CL 1355. LP.

Gillespie, Dizzy, with Al Fraser (1979) *To Be, or Not to Bop*, Garden City, NY: Doubleday.

Hentoff, Nat (1958) "An Afternoon with Miles Davis," *The Jazz Review* (December):11–12.

——— (1959) "Giant Steps," liner notes for *Giant Steps*, Atlantic Records 1311. LP.

Hentoff, Nat, and Nat Shapiro, Editors (1957) *Hear Me Talkin' to Ya*, New York: Horizon Press.

Levin, Michael, and John Wilson (1949) "No Bop Roots in Jazz: Parker," *Down Beat* (September):12.

Reise, Jay (2008) "Context, Choice, and Issues of Perceived Determinism in Music," in Jose V. Ciprut, Editor, *Indeterminacy: The Mapped, the Navigable, and the Uncharted*, Cambridge, MA: The MIT Press.

6   Freedom and Risk

Paul R. Kleindorfer

Rationale

Freedom is quintessentially associated with choice. We think of a free person as someone who, within prescribed bounds of law and social norms, can choose actions and dispositions of owned resources as he or she sees fit. This apparently simple and transparent notion of freedom as "freedom to choose" entails nonetheless many issues that at first lie hidden from view. In this chapter, I seek to uncover these and to explore their implications for choice when outcomes are uncertain. I do so primarily for "economic risks" and individual choice in which outcomes can be expressed in monetary terms, though I will also discuss personal risks, such as the loss of life, which cannot easily be monetized.

My basic thesis can be summarized as follows. Risk in situations involving individual choice clouds both the constraints and predictability of outcomes; and because society imposes certain restrictions on allowed outcomes, the presence of risk inherently precludes a clear delineation of situations in which choice will be or should be "free," that is, unconstrained. For example, in situations involving personal bankruptcy, society may deem it unacceptable to allow an individual or his dependents to be required to meet obligations that may be so large as to imply long-term penury if these obligations are honored. These social constraints on the outcomes of free choice under uncertainty are further complicated by behavioral biases that represent systematic departures of human choice from certain rational ideals. The central issue that then arises is whether the state, the family, or others acting as surrogates of the state or family should be given the power to constrain such choices in a manner that is intended to de-bias individual choices—protecting the individual from herself as it were. If de-biasing individual choices is considered a desirable option, then a whole range of social and personal interventions come into view. In one sense, such de-biasing arises naturally if society is required to bear the burden of poor choices of its members. At the same time, however, the nature and extent of constraints imposed in the name of correcting individual decision biases may affect the scope and nature of freedom that individuals have in specific contexts.

In order to provide some concrete points of reference for the discussion that follows, let me begin with two examples to whet the reader's appetite for the problem we wish to discuss.

Choosing an Insurance Policy—The Importance of Default Options

Johnson et al. (1993) noted that, following the introduction of no-fault automobile insurance options in New Jersey and Pennsylvania in the early 1990s, automobile owners in both states could buy one of two (types of) policies:

• Full Rights: A more expensive policy that maintains the right to sue in the event of injuries related to an accident.

• Limited Rights: A cheaper policy that restricts the right to sue.

There was, however, a difference in the way these options were presented to potential insurance purchasers: in New Jersey, the default option was presented as "Limited Rights"; in Pennsylvania, the default option was presented as "Full Rights." Otherwise, the insurance choice problem was identical in both states. Thus, the risky choice problem confronted by the potentially insured was:

• In New Jersey, Limited Rights as the default option, but any insured could acquire the Full Rights policy at a price higher than the default option.

• In Pennsylvania, Full Rights as the default option, but any insured could opt for the cheaper Limited Rights policy.

Table 6.1 shows the outcome of this process for the first calendar year (1990) following enactment of the enabling legislation. The conclusion is striking: merely specifying the default option has the consequence of tilting choice fundamentally in the direction of the indicated default. Lest the reader think this is the result of something strange, specific to New Jersey and Pennsylvania drivers, let me note right away that this

Table 6.1

Default Option	Percent of Insured Retaining Full Rights
Full rights (PA)	75
Limited rights (NJ)	20

"endowment" or "status quo" effect is a very robust finding, in numerous studies, in experimental economics as in many other applications, including such important personal choice areas as pension planning and health insurance (Madrian and Shea 2001).

From the perspective of this chapter, the existence of such a status quo or default option bias is interesting since it implies that the designer of insurance options, pension options, and many other personal choice policies has an important role to play in the choice of the default option offered. There is no escaping this fact, as it is the direct result of the way in which humans appear to be "wired." In the spirit of "freedom to choose," the simple act of designating one of the feasible options as a default option will confer upon this option a special status in the minds of many. This implies (as other related decision bias effects seem to do) a special responsibility for the designer of choice consideration sets that are intended to allow "free choice" to a set of informed individuals.[1]

Mitigation and Catastrophes—Myopia and Wishful Thinking

Empirical studies in hazard-prone areas of the United States suggest that individuals are not willing to invest in mitigation measures even after observing large damages from recent disasters. For example, after Hurricane Andrew in Florida in 1992, in terms of economic losses the

---

1. Political economists and legal scholars, such as Cass Sunstein and Richard Thaler (forthcoming), have argued that this type of problem should be addressed in the framework of libertarian paternalism, within which the paternalistic designer of the choice situation carefully analyzes the context to determine what is likely to be the best alternative for the typical decision maker, denoting that very alternative as the default. However—and this is essential to the preservation of the notion of freedom of choice—the decision maker is encouraged to consider why the default option is appropriate or inappropriate and, if desired, to choose an alternative different than the default. This design process recognizes the propensity of the decision maker to choose the default, and lays a special responsibility on the designer to propose a default option that recognizes this propensity. More on this subject, below.

most severe natural disaster in the United States, most residents in hurricane-prone areas appear not to have made improvements to existing dwellings that could reduce the amount of damage from another storm. In a July 1994 telephone survey of 1,241 residents in six hurricane-prone areas along the Atlantic and Gulf Coasts, 62 percent of respondents admitted they had not installed hurricane shutters, used laminated glass in windows, installed roof bracing and/or made sure that sidewalls were bolted to the foundation either before or after Hurricane Andrew (Kleindorfer and Kunreuther 1999).

In seismically active areas like California, measures such as strapping a water heater cost relatively little (e.g., US$75) and can significantly reduce damage by preventing the heater from toppling during an earthquake and causing a fire. The expected benefits from such a measure greatly exceed the costs in quake-prone regions and yet these and other loss reduction investments are not being adopted. Based on laboratory and field studies over the years, the basic reason for this lack of interest appears to be that homeowners do not believe that investing in mitigation will increase their residence's property value sufficiently to warrant the investment. Also, individuals facing such decisions appear to be quite myopic in that they act as if the time horizons for recovering their investment is a matter of months, and not years; accordingly, their perceived net benefits from mitigation do not counterbalance the upfront investment costs of such measures.

These findings on natural hazard mitigation are also consistent with studies of the reluctance of individuals to incur the higher immediate cost of energy-efficient appliances in return for reduced electricity charges over time. For example, Kempton and Neiman (1987) and others imputed relatively high discount rates (on the order of 150 percent per year) for individuals who had the option to purchase energy-efficient consumer durables such as air conditioners and refrigerators.

What is the point? The point is that regulations on building codes, insurance coverage available, and required emergency response infrastructure by communities would not need to be imposed by the state if citizens and homeowners could be assumed to weigh carefully the choices available to them, and to choose some option that was arguably in their best interest. Such regulations are, after all, restrictions on the freedom of choice of individuals and communities to deal with the risks of natural hazards in a manner that suits them best. Consequently, if property owners were forced to cover their own disaster losses, then one might contend that they should be left to their own designs, "free to choose" as it were, since they would have only themselves to blame for not insuring themselves or undertaking cost-effective mitigation measures. However, this is not the way the social contract is set up in most countries. Rather, all taxpayers bear some of the costs of restoring damaged property through disaster assistance, low-interest loans, and grants. Hence, there is an economic justification for all citizens to design structures to be safer, and this is a fortiori the case when property owners, because of decision biases or strategic free-riding, fail to undertake appropriate action when confronted with the risks of natural hazards.[2]

This example illustrates further aspects of "freedom to risk" when choices made by some citizens or economic agents affect the well-being of others. Many studies have shown that individuals tend to be myopic and to exhibit other biases when confronted with choices such as housing location or retrofitting investments to make their homes safer against natural hazards. But if the state assumes a large measure of responsibility for decisions relating to these matters, then citizens will naturally tend to abdicate any responsibility at an individual level for preparedness and planning for such hazards. Thus, there must be a balance between the amount of "rescue" undertaken ex post and the level of intervention and regulation ex ante. Given the social and political complexities of achieving this balance, the problem of assuring the adoption of cost-effective mitigation in hazard-prone areas has been largely intractable in the developed world, and even more so in the developing world.[3]

---

2. Cohen and Noll (1981) provide an additional rationale for building codes beyond decision process imperfections. When a building collapses, it may create negative externalities in the form of economic dislocations and other social costs that are beyond the economic loss suffered by the owners. These extras may not be taken into account when the owners evaluate the importance of adopting a specific mitigation measure. For example, if a building topples off its foundation after an earthquake, it could break a pipeline and cause a major fire, which would damage other homes that were not affected by the earthquake in the first place. In other words, there may be an additional annual expected benefit from mitigation over and above the reduction in losses to the specific structure adopting the mitigation. All of the financial institutions and insurers who are responsible for these other properties at risk would favor building codes to protect their investments and/or to reduce the insurance premiums they charge for fire following earthquake.

3. For example, Kleindorfer and Sertel (2001) provide an overview of some of the efforts to assess and to regulate mitigation issues for seismic risks in emerging economies. It is in emerging economies that natural hazards cause the overwhelming number of fatalities, and it is there that disruptions from natural hazards can leave economic scars for years thereafter.

These two examples illustrate the interaction of several factors that condition our notions of freedom of choice under risk. First is the overtone of decision biases—can the decision maker determine reasonable outcomes on her own? Second is the issue of externalities—causing losses to others while pursuing one's own gain. Third are the issues of personal responsibility and of self-sufficiency, the very foundations of freedom, and those of the social compact in which citizens participate, and which assures them some minimal safety net. Just how these features determine a balance of freedom to choose, and enable paternalistic interventions to correct individual decision biases, is fundamental in the determination of the relationship of individuals to their social context and of their ability freely to put themselves and their futures at risk. In what follows, we shall examine each of these in turn, beginning with the foundations of decision biases as essential elements of humanly free decision making.

Decision Sciences and Decision Biases

As noted in a decision sciences survey book—Kleindorfer, Kunreuther, and Schoemaker (1993)—decision making enjoys a long history of interest in philosophy, economics, and the social sciences. The modern view of decision sciences is shaped by a concern for three different but related perspectives—(1) descriptive: theories and evidence on how humans and their organizations and institutions actually make decisions; (2) normative: theories on how decisions should be made, typically based on principles such as consistency and rationality; and (3) prescriptive: theories, evidence, and methods for improving decision making in specific contexts, which typically rely on removing biases or limitations identified in descriptive theories.

Research in particular decision making contexts, such as insurance or natural hazard mitigation, begins with descriptive theory to understand the problems and current approaches used. This is followed by the development of normative theory to identify idealized approaches to the decision problems identified. Finally, prescriptive approaches are developed to attempt to improve decision making through mitigating decision biases or providing decision support tools. Beyond these theoretical perspectives, decision sciences also distinguish among theories at various levels of social aggregation, including the individual, group, organizational, and societal levels.

The key research findings from decision sciences, for decision making under risk, relate to what Simon (1957) has referred to as "bounded rationality," which captures the idea that human decision makers are rational in intention, but that information processing limits on memory, perception, and judgment bound their abilities to evaluate complex choices and to act completely consistently over time. A consequence of bounded rationality is that individuals, groups, and organizations adopt heuristics (rules of thumb) for all phases of problem identification and problem solving. These heuristics give rise to systematic departures from what might be expected under a normative rationality framework.

Systematic departures from normative rationality often are called "biases." Researchers have catalogued a large number of such biases (see Kleindorfer, Kunreuther, and Schoemaker 1993 for further details). These include the facts that individuals tend to evaluate only a very few alternatives and that these are usually close to the status quo alternative. In terms of choices under risk or uncertainty, human decision makers are poor statisticians who tend to overweight concrete data, rely on biased models of likelihood estimation, and exhibit sizeable overconfidence in the results of their judgment and choice processes. A typical example of the consequences of such biased statistical reasoning is for a homeowner in the 100-year flood plain to believe, following a severe flood, that there is more than a 50–50 chance that a flood will come again next year or, alternatively, that she is safe from another flood for 99 years. The results of such biased reasoning can strongly affect the decisions this homeowner takes in rebuilding and insuring her home after the flood. And, in addition to biases in statistical reasoning, individuals also show a remarkable sensitivity to the framing of problems, as first explored in detail by Tversky and Kahneman (2000). Consider the example in table 6.2, according to Quattrone and Tversky (1988).

Framing Example

Imagine you are faced with the decision of adopting one of two economic policies. Which would you prefer? (Respondents are shown either problem 1 or problem 2; the experimental results are shown in the final column of table 6.2.)

Programs J, K are identical to programs L, M, with the sole "framing" difference that one comparison is stated in terms of unemployment and

Table 6.2
Problem 1

Economic Program	Workforce Unemployed (%)	Rate of Inflation (%)	Preferred by (%)
J	10	12	36
K	5	17	64

Problem 2

Economic Program	Workforce Employed (%)	Rate of Inflation (%)	Preferred by (%)
L	90	12	54
M	95	17	46

the other in terms of employment, but with very different results (as evident from the final column). Many similar choice anomalies have been formulated since the original work of Tversky and Kahneman. Some of the various effects, including framing, noted in these experimental results, include the following (see Frey 1992 and Kleindorfer, Kunreuther, and Schoemaker 1993, for further discussion).

Framing Effects

The way a decision problem is formulated and information presented has a strong effect on decision maker preferences, as in problems 1 and 2.

Reference Point Effect

Alternatives are evaluated by individuals not in terms of total wealth but relative to a reference point, often the status quo. The reference point (and thereby preferences) can be affected by the way the problem is formulated (see the insurance example offered in the introduction).

Sunk Cost Effect

People tend to take past costs into account even when these do not have any effect on the future consequences of decisions.

Endowment Effect

Goods currently owned or controlled by an individual are valued more than goods not owned or controlled by an individual (even when the goods are otherwise identical).

Availability Bias

More recent or more vivid and personally experienced events are over-weighted when people estimate probabilities or make decisions.

Opportunity Cost Effect

Out-of-pocket monetary costs are given higher weight in decisions than are opportunity costs (e.g., foregone benefits from not choosing a given alternative) of the same magnitude.

Aversion to Trade-offs

Individuals find trade-offs across multiple attributes to be difficult; the larger the number of attributes, the more difficult the choice problem becomes.

Myopia

Individuals discount the future heavily and weigh near-term costs and benefits much higher than the "cost of money" over time would dictate.[4]

The above decision anomalies appear to hold up across many different problem contexts and decision makers. Taken together, these research findings suggest that, even in seemingly simple and repeated situations, predicting individuals' preferences or decisions requires careful descriptive analysis, perhaps also followed by prescriptive interventions to reframe the problem, to present accurate information, or to explain why such "irrational effects" as sunk costs or chance endowments should be disregarded by decision makers. Does not the art of decision consist in making use of effects such as those catalogued

---

4. A typical example of myopia is that investments in energy-efficient appliances are hard to sell to consumers, who focus primarily on the upfront cost of an appliance and not on its long-term benefits (Kunreuther, Öncüler, and Slovic 1997).

above? in a manner to help decision makers and policy makers understand more fully how preferences are formed in particular problem contexts? and in how framing, and changes in experience and information employed to evaluate these problems, affect decision outcomes? On occasion, the deeper understanding attained can lead to better decisions; on other occasions, the decision anomalies are an essential part of the policy context and simply cannot be removed, be it by better information or by better discussion. In these instances, the framing of the problem itself (e.g., see problems 1 and 2 in table 6.2) is an essential element of policy, which will significantly affect citizen/consumer preferences and choices.

Toward a Taxonomy of Risky Decisions and Freedom of Choice

Building on the above discussion, let us note four classes of risky choices or problem types (see table 6.3). Easy problems are those for which decision complexity is low and where there is a good alignment between individual costs and benefits. For easy problems, the "market" should be relied on—that is, complete freedom of choice should obtain. When decision complexity is low but there is poor alignment between individual costs and benefits, "commons dilemma" problems result.[5] In the classical case of the "commons dilemma," regulation and standards, coupled with appeals to individual ethics, are required to motivate individuals to constrain their choices to a set that allows both efficient collective action and a monitoring of compliance with the collective action standard. But when decision complexity is high, improved decision making requires informational interventions, and possibly incentives for performance as well.

Consider the alignment of individual costs and benefits. Where there are relatively low individual costs and benefits, the problem is not likely to demand attention unless it is regulated. In the case where costs are high and perceived benefits are low, however, we have the classic

---

5. A commons dilemma problem exists when the incentives in the problem context tend to motivate individuals to behave in a manner that serves them well, but at a clear cost to society. The prototypical example is that of a group of villagers sharing a commons that can be used for grazing of sheep. There may be strong individual incentives for any member of the village to put more sheep in the commons, but overgrazing could lead to a reduction in the overall wool and meat that could be harvested if more sheep are allowed into the commons. The conflict between individual and social outcomes discussed here in a perspective of freedom is explored in detail elsewhere, albeit in the context of transactional ethics (Kleindorfer 2008).

"commons dilemma" problem. Solutions here require both regulation and a strong appeal to ethics, a point to which we return below. In the case where costs are low and benefits are high (e.g., household radon detection or smoking), the real problem is to ensure that individuals in fact understand the magnitude of the benefits, immediately and over time. If they do not, they will not act in their own interest.

Finally, in the case where both perceived costs and benefits are high, individuals must be convinced that the status quo is unacceptable and that there is some feasible alternative, the pursuit of which will be desirable and will lead to a fair apportionment of costs to them. Cost-benefit analysis is important for such decisions in validating both the acceptability of the status quo and the desirability of the alternative. Building on such cost-benefit analysis, default options (as in our earlier insurance example) can be designed and promoted to assist individuals in their choice process. Following the principles of "libertarian paternalism" per Sunstein and Thaler (2003), such default options are meant not to constrain the ultimate choice of individuals, but rather to provide a focal point for the start of their evaluation process.

The final case in table 6.3 illustrates a real dilemma as there is poor alignment between individual costs and benefits, and the problems are difficult to understand in the first place. Problems of global development, global warming, and the population explosion are just of this type. If individuals cannot put the costs and benefits on the same scale or if there are significant long-term effects somehow associated with personal decisions, individuals will find it difficult to make any informed choice, and hence they will resort to various heuristics, such as saliency of attributes, myopia (just considering current period costs

Table 6.3
Four Classes of Decisions under Risk

	Good Alignment between Individual Costs and Benefits	Poor Alignment between Individual Costs and Benefits
Low complexity in decision making	*Easy Problems* Rely on the "market" or on simple regulation	*Commons Dilemma Problems* Regulation and standards Appeals for ethical behavior
High complexity in decision making	*Information Problems* Participation and consensus Provide needed information	*Tough Problems* Regulation, standards, enforcement, incentives, subsidies, etc.

and benefits), and so forth. These heuristics may result in actions that lead to both bad individual outcomes and bad social outcomes. In particular, if scientific knowledge is lacking and/or individuals do not see the relationship between their actions and the outcomes of these, they may even fail to register the problem at all. In sum, table 6.3 suggests a far richer fabric of interventions and default options, or regulations and public information to guide individual decisions, than what would arise if another route were taken—the road of the much simpler metaphor, that of "free and unfettered choice."

Individual Freedom to Risk and Social Safety Nets

Consider the classic problem of social choice—designing social safety nets to provide recovery funds to individuals who may suffer negative outcomes from risky behavior. An example of such a safety net is a program of emergency loans and disaster recovery assistance for homeowners who suffer losses because they did not insure their homes or did not undertake preventive mitigation. Another example is family assistance and other social assistance programs that help people whose means fall below a socially specified subsistence level. Let us examine a simple model illustrating the problem and its direct relationship to freedom and risk.

Consider a society of N individuals, each of whom can make a choice to lead either a conservative (cautious) lifestyle (denoted C in table 6.4) or a risky lifestyle (denoted R in table 6.4). For each individual, independent of others in society, the outcome of the personal choice can be either "good" or "bad," where the probability of the "good" state is p and the probability of the "bad" state is $(1 - p)$. The payoffs for the C and R individuals in a society with no social safety net are depicted in table 6.4. The cautious lifestyle leads to the same outcome, with a payoff of c no matter what the state of the world is. On the other hand,

Table 6.4
Payoffs to Various Lifestyles without a Social Safety Net

	Good State Occurs	Bad State Occurs
Cautious lifestyle (C)	$c > 0$	$c > 0$
Risky lifestyle (R)	$g > 0$	$-b < 0$
Probability of state	p	$1 - p$

the risky lifestyle leads to an outcome g if the "good" state occurs, and b if the "bad" state occurs. We assume that $g > c > 0$, but $b < 0$, where 0 is the "subsistence level."

Now consider the case in which a social safety net is put in place such that those individuals who choose the risky lifestyle R are paid b if the "bad" state occurs, which just brings them back up to the subsistence level, 0. The costs of the social safety net are supported by a general tax on everyone who can pay the tax. This tax is levied against both those who choose "cautious lifestyle" C and those who choose "risky lifestyle" R and who experience the "good" state. The tax rate t is set before the fact. The payoffs for the C and R individuals in a society with such a safety net are depicted in table 6.5.

One can analyze a number of issues arising from this specific arrangement. We are primarily interested in two. First, what is the expected aggregate output resulting from this arrangement? Second, is the arrangement feasible in the sense that the society in question generates enough wealth to pay for those who are promised the various benefits of the safety net?

We can compute the answer to the first question rather easily if we assume that we know how many individuals will choose the risky lifestyle (as we note below, this choice is actually endogenous to the setup and hence one must "solve" for this number): Let $n < N$ individuals choose the risky lifestyle, so that $N - n$ choose the cautious lifestyle. Of the n individuals who choose the risky lifestyle, the expected number who will experience the "good" and the "bad" state is $n(p)$ and $n(1-p)$, respectively. Thus, from table 6.4, the expected aggregate benefits generated by the society are:

$$E\{B\} = (N-n)c + npg - n(1-p)b = Nc + n[pg - (1-p)b] \qquad (1)$$

From this we can see that expected benefits are increasing in the number of individuals who choose the risky lifestyle as long as the coefficient

Table 6.5
Payoffs to Various Lifestyles with a Social Safety Net

	Good State Occurs	Bad State Occurs
Cautious lifestyle (C)	$(1-t)c > 0$	$(1-t)c > 0$
Risky lifestyle (R)	$(1-t)g > 0$	0
Probability of state	p	$1-p$

$[pg - (1 - p)b]$ is positive. We will consider only cases in which this is so.

Concerning the second question—if n individuals choose the risky lifestyle, then the number of those who experience a "good" outcome is a random variable. In fact, the actual distribution of this random variable is the well-known binomial distribution, with parameters (n, p). Denote this random variable by N_G, so that $n - N_G$ is the number of those who choose the risky lifestyle and experience the "bad" outcome. Then the probability that society can meet its commitments is just the probability that tax revenues collected are sufficient to support those who choose the risky lifestyle and then experience the "bad" state. From table 6.5, the total tax revenues collected are $N_G tg + (N - n)tc$ and the total required payments to those requiring assistance are $(n - N_G)b$. Thus, we can express this probability—that our model society is sustainable—as follows:

$$\Pr\{S\} = \Pr\{(n - N_G)b < N_G tg + (N - n)tc\}$$

which, with a little algebra, is equivalent to

$$\Pr\{S\} = \Pr\left\{N_G > \frac{n(b + tc) - Ntc}{b + tg}\right\} \tag{2}$$

We now show that there is a trade-off between the expected benefits society can generate, as measured by $E\{B\}$ in equation 1, and the probability that (our model) society actually can meet the commitments it makes, as expressed by the probability $\Pr\{S\}$ computed in equation 2. To illustrate this trade-off, consider the "base case" values of the parameters of this model (table 6.6). For these parameters, one can compute the level of expected benefits $E\{B\}$, and the sustainability probability $\Pr\{S\}$ in equation 2, for various values of n. We show the results in table 6.7 for several values of p.

As expected, as n increases, so do expected social benefits $E\{B\}$. But the probability that (our model) society will be able to meet its social net commitments, as measured by $\Pr\{S\}$, clearly decreases as n increases (for any given value of p). Thus, for our base case values, a trade-off

Table 6.6
Parameters for Base Case Model Outcomes

N	c	g	B	t
100	20	100	20	0.15

Table 6.7
Results for Base Case Values for $p = 0.3$ and $p = 0.5$

p	N	E{B}	Pr{S}
0.3	20	2320	0.893
0.3	$n* = 26$	2416	0.540
0.3	40	2640	0.063
0.3	60	2960	0.001
0.5	20	2800	0.999
0.5	40	3600	0.866
0.5	60	4400	0.551
0.5	$n* = 77$	5080	0.247

exists between the expected aggregate benefits produced by society and the security of the safety net provided. As the number of individuals choosing the risky lifestyle increases, the expected benefits to society increase, but so do the expected number of such individuals who will require rescuing via the safety net when their risky lifestyle leads to bankruptcy (the "bad" state).

The rows labeled $n*$ in table 6.7 are especially interesting. I computed these by assuming a standard risk preference relationship for individuals in this society and by allowing each individual then to choose the optimal lifestyle (C or R) given that individual's risk preferences. The risk preferences were assumed to be heterogeneous, with some individuals very risk averse and others much less so.[6] Allowing individuals to choose their own lifestyle, given the parameters of the problem (essentially the payoffs in table 6.5), allows n to be endogenously determined. The rows $n*$ indicate the number of individuals who choose the risky lifestyle, given the base case values of table 6.6, and the indicated probability of success p (the probability of the "good" state) for individuals choosing R. It can be noted that as the environment becomes more "friendly" (i.e., the probability p of the "good" state increases),

---

6. The actual risk preferences assumed were of the Constant Absolute Risk Aversion family, represented by the von Neumann-Morgenstern cardinal utility function $U_i(w) = -\exp(-a_i x)$ for individual $i = 1, 2, \ldots, N$, where the Arrow-Pratt constant risk aversion parameter a_i for individual i was assumed given by $a_i = aHi$, where $a > 0$ is fixed. For the examples in table 6.7, we assumed $a = 0.0005$, so that $a_1 = 0.0005$ while $a_{100} = 0.05$.

more individuals elect the riskier lifestyle. For example, when $p = 0.3$, $n^* = 26$, but when $p = 0.5$ (so that the world becomes a friendlier place for individuals choosing the risky lifestyle), then $n^* = 77$, as more individuals will want to choose the risky lifestyle.

Note from table 6.7 also that the social safety net commitments become less secure as n increases. The interaction of the parameters in this case is quite interesting in that for $p = 0.3$, $n^* = 26$, and $\Pr\{S\} = 0.54$. When the world becomes a more friendly place for those choosing the risky lifestyle (i.e., because p increases), one might expect the outcome to be that the social safety net becomes more secure. However, for the base case values, as the world becomes more hospitable to risk takers, more individuals choose the risky lifestyle (n^* increases to 77), with the consequence that society becomes much less likely to be able to meet the commitments embodied in the social contract, with $\Pr\{S\}$ decreasing to 0.25.

Just to explore one more aspect of this problem, suppose that we consider the following "alternative case" values in table 6.8, in which b is increased from 20 to 40 relative to the base case, while g is increased from 100 to 400.

Table 6.9 provides the outcomes for this alternative case. The base of the inhospitable world ($p = 0.3$) is quite similar to those of the base case in table 6.7, with E{B} increasing as n increases and with a social contract that is quite unreliable ($\Pr\{S\} = 0.259$ at $n^* = 42$).

But note the impact of increasing g from 100 to 400 when $p = 0.5$. In this case, $\Pr\{S\}$ remains relatively constant as n increases. And the reason for this is that as more and more individuals choose the risky lifestyle, about half of them on average strike it rich and provide significant tax revenues to support those of their number who are not so lucky. The consequence is that society's commitment through its social contract remains relatively viable over a broad range. Of course, if those who choose the risky lifestyle argue to lower tax rates ($t = 0.15$ has been kept constant throughout these examples), then the problem of the unreliable social contract would reemerge.

Table 6.8
Parameters for Alternative Case Model Outcomes

N	c	g	b	t
100	20	200	40	0.15

Table 6.9
Results for Alternative Case Values for $p = 0.3$ and $p = 0.5$

p	N	$E\{B\}$	$Pr\{S\}$
0.3	20	3840	0.762
0.3	40	5680	0.297
0.3	$n^* = 42$	5864	0.259
0.3	60	7520	0.162
0.5	20	5600	0.994
0.5	40	9200	0.981
0.5	60	12800	0.986
0.5	$n^* = 81$	16580	0.987

While a number of other interesting implications could be derived from this simple framework, now we have come far enough to recapitulate the basic point that arises from this analysis. Freedom to choose is encouraged by the existence of social safety nets. This can have important positive effects for a society: for example, it can promote entrepreneurship and innovation (riskier lifestyles) with the assurance that failure will not lead to dire consequences. However, maintaining the security of such a social safety net requires taxes and social assistance that allows riskier lifestyles to coexist with other more cautious lifestyles. Absent such a safety net, a much less risky behavior will be the rule of the day. And while this may appear to be of no loss at all to society, the true loss in overall societal benefits can be considerable as we can see from this simple example—(note how $E\{B\}$ increases as n increases). In real life, the social contract allows individuals to invest in risky undertakings, leading to greater innovation and economic output as a result.

The notion of a social contract is clearly far from a pure "freedom to choose" paradigm. The very fabric of the arrangement described here is woven to insure risk-taking individuals, if only by guaranteeing them at least subsistence outcomes, even if they should experience the misfortune of failure (a "bad" state). To do so in a sustainable manner, a balance must be struck between the tax burden of securing the social safety net and the number of individuals who are encouraged to choose a risky lifestyle, however. If incentives are too great, too many individuals will choose the risky lifestyle and the social contract will become unsustainable. If incentives are not sufficient, then too many will choose the cautious lifestyle and society will have thereby sacrificed the many benefits of innovation.

In concluding our discussion here, one might naturally raise the question as to why it is that society has to bear the burden of rescuing failed risky behavior. Why not let private insurance do the trick? This is, of course, the very question that is being asked around the world by many conservatives, who recommend replacing state-supported social safety nets with privatized social security or other private insurance arrangements. In principle, these would work at least as well as the social safety arrangements modeled above. For example, in the context of the payoffs shown in table 6.2, those who choose the risky lifestyle could insure themselves through a private insurer for something close to actuarial rates of $(1 - p)b$, namely, the expected value of the loss resulting when the "bad" state occurs. As long as $pg > (1 - p)b$, we have a condition recognized in the foregoing as being necessary for risk taking to be deemed socially beneficial; here, the expected payoffs in the "good" state would be sufficient to pay the related insurance costs. If there were enough individuals who chose the risky lifestyle,[7] then private insurance could be set up to insure all risk takers, thereby replacing the social safety net with this private network. No taxes would be needed and no governmental intervention whatsoever.

What is wrong with this kind of private arrangement? Why are governments in advanced economies worldwide involved in the funding of safety nets like social security and disaster relief payments? The answer lies in the continuing historical record that individuals, left to their own designs, do not undertake actions like insuring and investing for the long run. Some may do this, but the large majority of us seem to be afflicted with an insistent myopia that impedes our long-term vision. The basic motto that seems to govern our perception of whether misfortune can strike us when we get into risk-taking behavior is, "It cannot happen to me!" Given the sorry consequences of this motto in the long run, and the many risks that each of us faces in our lives, providing a social safety net has been the nearly uniformly preferred

---

7. Insurance is a pooling arrangement that works well only when there are a sufficient number of individuals covered by the arrangement: the Law of Large Numbers allows premiums adjacent to the expected value of the loss covered to be adequate for the coverage of all claims, with very high probability.

method of providing protection against outcomes that menace a citizenry's subsistence levels. This is to assure the well-being of the risk-taking individuals themselves as well as the dependents of these risk takers. Rather than openly embracing the notion of freedom to choose, with risk takers then fully confronting the choices of their actions, a more constrained and paternalistic alternative—the solution by way of an assured, publicly provided, safety net—has been the practice of modern society since Bismarck's first reforms of the state's social functions in the nineteenth century.

Conclusions: Legitimation and Moral Obligation

Legitimation is the process by which a decision maker explains to himself, and to other stakeholders in a given decision problem, why both the choice made and the decision process pursued were reasonable. Since the seminal work of Henri Bergson (1932) and Jürgen Habermas (1972), it has been understood that decisions under risk, especially decisions affecting parties other than the decision maker, must be assessed against the backdrop of the legitimation process which the decision maker believes will be used to determine whether she has or has not acted reasonably. It is here, in the domain of legitimation, that a number of the factors explored in this chapter come together. The decision maker's anticipation of required legitimation forces her attention, ex ante, on constraints and values of individuals who may be affected by, or have a say in, her choice of certain alternatives. Framing of problems, information available to the decision maker, and the general social ethic or sense of moral obligation associated with particular problems, can all be important components of how decision makers view the requirements of legitimation. And the anticipation of these requirements can, in turn, have a fundamental impact on decision processes and outcomes.

In this sense, a legitimation process embraces both the final stage of decision making and the anticipatory ones that condition the very decision making to begin with. The key elements of legitimation include the perceived need preemptively to make sense of one's choice to oneself, as if to the judges—and to all the stakeholders who may observe the choice and/or may want independently to evaluate it—and hence they themselves affect choice. Frameworks have been developed for understanding the impact of legitimation on decision processes. Kleindorfer, Kunreuther, and Schoemaker (1993), for example, explore in detail two sets of requirements. The first set of requirements applies to the outcome of the decision process—is it fair, efficient, safe? etc. The second set applies to the decision process itself—is it transparent, logically defensible, based on good science? etc. Depending on which of the stakeholders are viewed by the decision maker as central to a particular decision, different criteria for process and for outcome will be considered and prejudged for appropriateness. For example, a decision viewed by its maker as affecting only herself, and as involving clearly measurable economic costs and benefits, may well become a problem "solved" by a cost-benefit calculus, whereas a decision deemed likely to impact a decision maker's relevant others—multiple stockholders/stakeholders from whom one's livelihood might depend, for instance—may come to require difficult qualitative trade-offs (such as siting a hazardous waste facility, "there" rather than "here") and may come to require an open, participative community process if it is to be deemed and thus accepted to be legitimate (see Tomazinis 2008).

Legitimation is central to our theme of freedom and risk. Let me illustrate this in the context of a social choice problem of whether a community should accept a new risk—say, the location of a highly hazardous facility. Frey and Oberholzer-Gee (1997) explored in several Swiss communities the level of compensation required for citizens in these communities to accept the location of a low-risk and mid-level nuclear waste facility in their jurisdiction. When the issue was posed as an economic pricing problem (the compensation required to "offset" the potential hazard the facility represented), most citizens were not prepared to accept the facility at any price. However, when the issue was posed without compensation (because the facility was viewed as a problem of fulfilling the community's civic duty to dispose of the hazardous wastes produced by their region), a significant increase was noted in the number of citizens now willing to accept the facility. The former framing of the same problem may be viewed as having allowed the citizens of each community the "freedom to choose," with compensation as part of the choice bundle. The latter framing imbues the choice problem with morality, as fulfilling the social responsibilities associated with using new technologies.

Frey and Oberholzer-Gee suggest that framing the problem as an issue of *getting the price right*, in a freedom of choice perspective, "crowds out" the intrinsic values many citizens see to be inherent in the fulfillment of their civic duty. This rejection of compensation has been observed frequently in other contexts as well (e.g., Kunreuther and Easterling 1995). This same idea is inherent in Bergson (1932). Bergson argues that each society has a sense of "moral obligation" which citizens recognize as characterizing normal and reasonable behavior. When an issue is presented as a mere fulfillment of the citizenry's responsibility to society's code of ethics, many "commons problems" (see table 6.1) that otherwise would be tough to resolve now become couched in a sense of collective moral obligation which every law-abiding citizen would feel to be integral to one's individual civic duty. However, when such problems are framed within the framework of a calculus of self-interest (as a matter of costs and benefits, for instance), the results are often quite different.

Posed in this manner, a central challenge to the balancing of freedom and risk is to provide a better sense of where one is truly free to risk without consequences to others, and in a manner that is sufficiently informed as to make one's risk-taking behavior an utmost responsible act. In the case of "commons problems" and social safety nets, freedom to act—without advice or without consideration for the consequences of one's actions on others—would be condemnably selfish and foolhardy. The paradox in such cases is that treating constraints on one's individual actions as issues of individual cost and benefit evokes precisely the wrong mind-set, leading to a never-ending maze of public regulations and incentives seeking to measure fallouts and to motivate persons through the murky veil of their boundedly rational decision processes.

The choice of which problems will be left completely in the hands of individuals and which will be dealt with as integral to the fabric of social responsibility—and as determining of social safety nets—is itself a key political and societal public policy challenge. It can be alleviated only through continuing education and in open discussions of social ethics capable of enhancing a deep appreciation of the duties that befall democratic citizenries pursuing individual and collective freedoms. What modern decision sciences have indicated so far is that this complex challenge will not be easily resolved. To the extent that action by individual citizen consumers is essential in a particular domain necessitating collective decision, developing appropriate programs and policies to address challenges and to resolve problems will require more discerning understandings of self-adaptive processes in dynamic contexts; new theories and newer methods to test the direction, intensity, and magnitude of the interests at play and interplay; and new units of measurement for the impacts of framing, the inputs of regulatory incentives, and the constantly reconfiguring complexity of the decision processes per se. Simply acting as if freedom to choose in situations of risk is a matter to be left to the individual alone is bound to fail to detect the biases that always condition individual choices and that burden societies as a whole; and it may also lead to losing track of the central issues—the evocation of social responsibility in the framing of a problem, the requisite preconditioning of choices through the integration of the individual within the broader duties of citizenship, essential to a functioning free society. As I hope this chapter has demonstrated, determining which decision contexts should be left entirely for individuals to determine, and which should engage us in social trade-offs, remains the central issue for the framing of freedom in the years ahead and also for redefining risk in modern society as the freedom to choose.

References

Bergson, Henri (1932) *The Two Sources of Morality and Religion*, Notre Dame, IN: University of Notre Dame Press.

Cohen, Linda, and Roger Noll (1981) "The Economics of Building Codes to Resist Seismic Structures," *Public Policy* (Winter):1–29.

Frey, Bruno S. (1992) *Economics as a Science of Human Behavior*, Boston: Kluwer Academic.

Frey, Bruno S., and Felix Oberholzer-Gee (1997) "The Cost of Price Incentives: An Empirical Analysis of Motivation Crowding-Out," *American Economic Review* 87(4):746–755.

Habermas, Jürgen (1972) *The Legitimation Crisis*, Boston: Beacon Press.

Johnson, Eric, Jack Hershey, Jacqueline Meszaros, and Howard Kunreuther (1993) "Framing, Probability Distortions and Insurance Decisions," *Journal of Risk and Uncertainty*, 7:35–51.

Kempton, Willett, and Max Neiman, Editors (1987) *Energy Efficiency: Perspectives on Individual Behavior*, Washington, DC: American Council for an Energy Efficient Economy.

Kleindorfer, Paul R. (2008) "Trust, Ethics, and Markets," in Jose V. Ciprut, Editor, *Ethics, Politics, and Democracy: From Primordial Principles to Prospective Practices*, Cambridge, MA: The MIT Press.

Kleindorfer, Paul R., and Howard C. Kunreuther (1999) "The Complementary Roles of Mitigation and Insurance in Managing Catastrophic Risks," *Risk Analysis* 19(4): 727–738.

Kleindorfer, Paul R., Howard C. Kunreuther, and Paul J. H. Schoemaker (1993) *Decision Sciences: An Integrative Perspective*, New York: Cambridge University Press.

Kleindorfer, Paul R., and Murat R. Sertel (2001) *Managing Seismic Risks in Turkey and Internationally*, Boston: Kluwer Academic.

Kunreuther, Howard C., and David Easterling (1995) *The Dilemma of Siting a High-Level Nuclear Waste Repository*, Boston: Kluwer Academic.

Kunreuther, Howard C., Ahmet Öncüler, and Paul Slovic (1997) "Time Insensitivity for Protective Investments," Working paper, Wharton Center for Risk Management and Decision Processes, Philadelphia: University of Pennsylvania.

Madrian, Brigitte, and Dennis Shea (2001) "The Power of Suggestion: Inertia in 401(k) Participation and Savings Behavior," *Quarterly Journal of Economics* 116(4):1149–1186.

Quattrone, George A., and Amos Tversky (1988) "Contrasting Rational and Psychological Analyses of Political Choice," *American Political Science Review* 82(3):719–736.

Simon, Herbert A. (1957) *Models of Man*, New York: Wiley.

Sunstein, Cass R., and Richard H. Thaler (2003) "Libertarian Paternalism Is Not an Oxymoron," *University of Chicago Law Review*, 70(4) (Fall):1159–1202.

Tomazinis, Anthony (2008) "Adaptive Planning in Dynamic Societies: Giving Sense to Futures Conditional," in Jose V. Ciprut, Editor, *Indeterminacy: The Mapped, the Navigable, and the Uncharted*, Cambridge, MA: The MIT Press.

Tversky, Amos, and Daniel Kahneman (2000) *Choices, Values and Frames*, New York: Cambridge University Press.

7

Liberation and Freedom in Jewish Liturgy and Practice

Levi Y. Haskelevich

Liberation and the Birth of a Nation

The eighteenth-century French revolutionaries, who put "Freedom" at the head of their famous motto *"Liberté, Égalité, Fraternité,"* were not the first to come up with this fundamental three-in-one formulation.

The *liberation* of the ancient Hebrews[1] from Egyptian slavery is described in the book of Exodus (1–16) and has been celebrated for generations as the holiday of Passover. This is the first biblical holiday, celebrating the birth of ancient Israel as an independent nation (see Ezek. 16:4; Schneur-Zalman 1836, 109). The "Men of the Great Assembly,"[2] who composed the basic Jewish liturgy, defined Passover as *zman herutenu*—"the season of our freedom" or "the festival of our liberation."[3]

The concept of judicial *equality* is expressed in Leviticus (25:39–40): "And if thy brother be waxen poor with thee, and sell himself unto

---

1. In the Bible, Israelites are called Hebrews (*'Ivrim*) usually only when speaking to aliens or when aliens refer to Israelites in the third person. *Bene Israel*, Children of Israel, or Israelites are the proper terms favored by the people redeemed from Egypt. The late designation *Yehudim*, Judeans or Jews, common also in Aramaic and in Arabic, dates from the times of Babylonian or Persian domination. According to the Talmud (*Megillah*, 13a), *Yehudi* (sing.) is one who rejects idolatry/polytheism, or one who is connected to YHWH, G-d's ineffable Name—the Tetragrammaton (*Esther-Rabba*, 6). These are the designations the scriptures use. Other identifications, proposed in archeological theories (*Apiru, Habiru, Hyksos,* among others), are not substantiated or corroborated by the Jewish sources.

2. The 120 "Men of the Great Assembly"—a body of great authority for Jewish law, functional under the leadership of Ezra during the establishment of the Second Temple (fifth to fourth century B.C.E.)—introduced the daily prayer *Amidah* (while standing), the *18 Benedictions,* and the *Kiddush* (Sanctification of the holiday) and *Havdallah* (the Separation concluding the holiday).

3. "The Passover *Haggadah*," *Kiddush* (in *The Birnbaum Haggadah,* 1976, 57). "*Amidah* for the Three Festivals" (in Mangel 1978, 253).

thee, thou shalt not make him to serve as a bondservant. As a hired servant, and as a settler, he shall be with thee." Whether it is working the fields or housework, the so-called *slave* must be the *equal* of a contracted worker. Even if he is being sold into slavery by a *Beth Din* (Jewish Court of Law) in order to repay a theft that he has committed, his bondage cannot exceed six years: he must be set free at the approach of the seventh year (Exod. 22:2; *Rashi*, on Exod. 22:2). Many authorities see in the biblical association of a Hebrew slave with a hired worker the legal implication that a hired worker is entitled to the same benefits that the Torah has established for a Hebrew slave (*Ha-hinuch*, 1982, 482). When the servant completes the period of his servitude, his master (or employer) is supposed to furnish the "freedman" with a parcel of the wealth that G-d has bestowed on the master: "And when thou lettest him go free from thee, thou shalt not let him go empty; thou shalt furnish him liberally out of thy flock, and out of thy threshing-floor, and out of thy winepress; of that wherewith G-d . . . hath blessed thee thou shalt give unto him" (Deut. 15:13–15).

The concept of *brotherhood* is sanctioned in Judaism's precept of brotherly love: "Thou shalt not hate thy brother in thy heart . . . thou shalt love thy neighbor as thyself" (Lev. 19:17–18). For Hillel the Elder (first century B.C.E.), "this is the whole Torah, the rest is commentary."[4]

Liberation in Every Generation

"In every generation a man must demonstrate as if he himself came out from Egypt, as it is written: 'And thou shalt tell thy son in that day, saying: It is because of that which G-d did for me when I came forth out of Egypt' (Exod. 13:8)."[5]

The Passover supper (the *Seder*) is an occasion for participants to celebrate freedom. Paradoxically, this celebration of freedom is mandatory even during the harshest times of repression. Prisoners, who could not get the necessary supplies (Matzoth and wine) in their cells,

---

4. Talmud, *Shabbat*, 31a. See also Tzemach-Tzedek 1911, 55–58, on why "this is the whole Torah." In brief: The ultimate goal and inner meaning of the commandment of brotherly love is to establish unity of the opposites in the "lower world," as a prerequisite for the revelation of the Higher Unity of the One G-d. This is also the inner meaning and the inner mechanism of the 613 commandments of the Torah as vehicles of monotheism.

5. Maimonides (ca. 1171), *Laws of Passover*, "The Haggadah Liturgy," 36. The quote in Maimonides differs slightly from the Talmud: "A man must see himself as if he himself came out from Egypt" (Talmud, *Pesakhim*, 116b).

observed the *Seder* by reclining (a symbolic manifestation of freedom) and reciting the *Haggadah*.

The earliest known extrabiblical record of Passover celebration is from Egypt, noted in the Elephantine papyri of the fifth century B.C.E. In a letter (Cowley 1923, letter no. 21), a Persian king named *Deryawesh* (Darius) orders, or permits, the Jewish soldiers stationed in Egypt to celebrate Passover in accordance with all the requirements of the Jewish Law.

A famous painting[6] depicts a Spanish Marrano[7] family celebrating the Passover Seder, while the watchdogs of the Inquisition break into their home to arrest them. Under such circumstances, what meaning could the symbolic celebration of "the season of freedom" have?

The paradoxical inconsistency of celebrating freedom in a state of physical bondage (in prison, at the mercy of the Persian monarch, under the Inquisition, or in tsarist or Stalinist Russia) is intoned at the very beginning of the Passover story. The father, as the head of the family, who must conduct the *Seder*, tells the children and the adults assembled around the table: "[We are] here this year, in the Land of Israel next year. [We are] slaves this year, [we will be] free next year" (*Haggadah*, 1976, 61).

We still are not completely free, we still are in comparative slavery, declares the Redemption story, but we know, we are assured, that freedom—the ultimate deliverance—is coming. It is like the assurance of a physician to a suffering ill person: "You are diagnosed with such and such disease and here is your remedy, so you will begin recuperating." The celebration and the manifestation of freedom cherished is a taste of freedom in itself.

Freedom's Reason to Be

Like life itself, freedom must have a meaning. Without meaning life becomes unworthy—and so with freedom, for being a purpose-laden

---

6. Moisey Maimon's "The Marranos and the Spanish Inquisition" (St. Petersburg, ca. 1893) was painted in reaction to an incident during the *Seder* celebration, when the tsarist gendarmes came to arrest his host allegedly for residing in St. Petersburg without a valid permit. The painting was originally ordered by the Museum of Alexander III of St. Petersburg (the modern Russian Museum), but subsequently canceled because of its "anti-Christian content."

7. Editor's note: Marranos were Jews forced to convert to Christianity in medieval Spain, but who secretly continued to keep their Jewish customs, and who—for this—were harassed and persecuted by the Inquisition of the Catholic Church.

meaningful exercise of liberty (Williams and Barber, chap. 4 in this book).

In a Passover address, the Lubavitcher Rebbe[8] writes: "A plant, when all the necessary components needed for its growth (soil, water, air . . .) are supplied, is 'liberated' from all 'concerns' and disturbances. Although it cannot move from its location, for having been 'sentenced' to stay put in one place for its entire life, being only a plant, it is truly 'free'."

In contrast, even when it receives everything essential to its livelihood, an animal condemned to stand motionless in one place would be in a state of harsh captivity.

Now, if a human being, as a rational individual, were accorded total freedom of movement but deprived of intelligent life, would he be anything more than a prisoner denied his very essence?

Within the realm of intelligence there reside many levels of selfhood. Treated as if he were a child, a person capable of reaching even higher levels of intellect would sense a suffering inflicted by the severest suppression of his emancipated Self. And when an adult restricts his natural reservoir of liberty, say, by wasting his years, intelligence, and capabilities, or by limiting these to attend to his daily sustenance, such self-imprisonment becomes the worst kind of enslavement and carries with it much graver consequences.

In Judaism, for having been created in "the Image and likeness of G-d," a human being worthy of his Maker embodies a "spark" (Image) from G-d and, as such, is the bearer of a Heavenly Soul, which, though entrapped in a body and imbibed in animal instincts (the Animal Soul), never severs its link with the Creator. The Creator is *Ein Sof* (Infinite); hence, the Divine Soul of the human being strives to become one with Him. This is the Soul's freedom—its *true* Self. But the limits of the Body, the Animal Soul,[9] being the prison of the Soul, the latter's struggle to free itself from the bondage of bodily and animal desires in order to fulfill its mission in this "lower" world is a fight at all levels—intellectual, emotional, and practical. This struggle is symbolized in

---

8. Rabbi Menachem Mendel Schneerson (1902–94), the seventh spiritual leader of the Chabad-Lubavitch Chassidic movement.

9. The biblical verse uses the terms "Spirit of man" (*Ruach ha-adam*) and "Spirit of the beast" (*Ruach ha-behema*). Chassidic literature uses *Nefesh ha-bahamit* (Animal Soul) with the explicit explanation that this soul, although animal, possesses *Sekhel* (reason). The biblical verse apparently speaks of animal, *behema*, as the beast that does not possess a soul the same way humans do. I follow this uniformity in the text.

the Exodus—the liberation of the Children of Israel from the Egyptian "house of bondage."[10]

Freedom and the Soul

Even though some contemporary philosophers define freedom as the "absence of obstacles to the realization of desires" (Russell 1940), "probably no serious philosophical or social thinker has defended freedom in the sense of absence of obstacles to the satisfaction of *any* desire; what has been defended, and what freedom has been identified with, is the absence of obstacles to the exercise and satisfaction of specific interests and forms of activity which are accepted as possessing especial moral and social significance" (cf. Hirschmann, chap. 9 in this book; Partridge 1967, 223). For example, in America, a person trying to jump off a tower or a bridge inevitably will attract scores of police officers, firefighters, and psychologists, all trying to stop him from "exercising his freedom" to satisfy his desire: suicide.

Speaking of "desires," a human being is born with them. The cry of a baby in need is an expression that becomes the baby's very own, once it is physically separated from its mother. Not accidentally is the Hebrew word *Nefesh* (soul, life) used also to denote "desire" (see Jer. 15:1; *Rashi* on Gen. 23:8)—a yearning deeply rooted in the Soul, in quasi-synonymous symbiosis with it, as such preceding the autonomous advent of reason.

Ironically, although man can be liberated from the oppression of a hostile power, he may remain subjugated to the dominion of wicked and destructive forces in himself—elements that may compel him to lose control of himself and even of his life. This, too, is bondage, since liberty is not being exercised here, and freedom is absent, in the very sense intuited by Williams and Barber in this book.

This idea is alive in the theoretical and practical foundations of Jewish Law. Maimonides, in his *Laws of Divorce*, discusses a case in which, required by the Torah to set his wife free by virtue of a *Get* (bill of divorce), a husband refuses to do so willingly. Jewish Law requires the consent of the husband for the *Get* to be legally valid. Maimonides comments that, where the case warrants that the law *require* the husband to divorce his wife, the man *may* be coerced into verbally agreeing to the divorce. This is based on the fundamental

---

10. Schneerson 1992, II, 20. (Quotations cited are free translations from Hebrew.)

belief that a person's inner "true" Self is essentially good, that he is willing to do good as preordained by the Divine Law, and therefore inherently predisposed to distance himself from evil . . . if it were not for his "evil consciousness," *da'ato hara'a* in Maimonides' own words, which is external to man's inner Self, and yet stands in the way of performing a *mitzvah*.[11] If "under compulsion" (but only when the Law determines that to do so would be a *mitzvah*) the husband ultimately agrees to divorce, it is his *true Self* that finally speaks out. The compulsion is viewed as a means of expulsing the exogenous forces of the "evil consciousness," which do not belong in his true Self—all in a lawful effort to help him to "liberate" himself from the alien wickedness, and to consent to divorce . . . out of his own true, endogenous *free will* (Maimonides ca. 1171, *Laws of Divorce*, Book 2, 20).

Maimonides' explanation that the "evil consciousness" of man is exogenous—thus often in contradiction with the true Self (which is rooted much deeper in the Soul than one's state of awareness)—is in perfect harmony with the Jewish mystical tradition. In the Kabbalah, and especially in Chabad Chassidism, the Rational Soul (*Nefesh ha-Sikhlit*) is wholly external to the Unconscious Mind of the Divine Soul (*Nefesh Elohit*). As part of the Natural Soul (*Nefesh ha-Tiv'it*)—synonymous with the Animal Soul (*Nefesh ha-Bahamit*), also known as the *Nefesh ha-Khiyunit* (Life Force)—the Rational Soul comprises both Intellect (*Sekhel*) and Emotions (*Middot*), each of worldly nature. The Animal Soul is the source of "beastly" (base) passions such as anger, pride, lust, frivolity, boasting, idle talk, sloth, and melancholy (Schneur-Zalman 1796, I, 1). Its rational part serves as a tool with which a person satisfies the desires or necessities of the body. The Rational Soul can excel in arts and sciences and engage in the most advanced abstract philosophical thinking.

Like the Natural Soul, the Divine Soul itself consists of both Intellect and Emotions, but is a "portion of G-d, from above" (Job 31:2). The Emotions of the Divine Soul are directed "towards G-d": Love of G-d, the deep desire to become one with Him, and Fear of G-d, awe and reverence, among them—as the Divine Soul is modeled on the arrangement of the ten *Sefirot* (Divine attributes): ten "powers" of the human soul—of which only three are intellectual, and seven are emotional (Schneur-Zalman 1796, I, 2).

---

11. A *mitzvah* is a Divine commandment, a good deed.

The ten powers of the Divine Soul, "inserted" into the powers of the Natural Soul, rule the body in a conjoint mode. The "Divine Image"—mentioned in the Bible's Story of Creation—is the Divine Soul, but the term "Likeness" applies to the Natural Soul, which was conceived in correspondence with the powers of the Divine Soul. Additionally, scripture sometimes uses the terms "Spirit of man" and "Spirit of the beast": "Who knoweth the spirit of the man whether it goeth upward and the spirit of the beast whether it goeth downward to earth?" (Eccles. 3:21). These two spirits, which represent diametrically opposed cravings, are in perpetual struggle: the Animal Soul's desires are of "earthly" essence; the Divine Soul is the source for high morality, religious feelings, and the awareness of how empty earthly life is.

In many ways, the psychology in the Kabbalah and Chabad can be compared with twentieth-century Freudian psychoanalysis, where the Id, the Ego, and the Superego are strikingly reminiscent of the idea of the multilayered substance of the human soul in Chabad Chassidism. The *Guf* (Body) and *Nefesh ha-Bahamit* (the Animal Soul, which encompasses the Rational Soul) may be seen to correspond to the Id and to the Ego in Freudian psychology, whereas *Nefesh Ha-Elohit* (the Divine Soul) may be seen to correspond to the Superego. Psychoanalyst David Bakan (1990) has argued that Freud, perhaps indirectly, was influenced by the Kabbalah. More recently, Schneider and Berke (2000) studied the hypothesis that discussions held between the fifth Lubavitcher Rebbe Sholom B. Schneersohn and Sigmund Freud, in Vienna during the winter of 1902–1903, may have provided the latter with the rudiments of his theory. Whether this may be true or not, the Chassidic concept of tension and struggle between the intellectual Divine Soul and the instinctual Animal Soul, also of the need to subjugate the latter to the former, was developed by Rabbi Schneur-Zalman of Lyady[12] in his major work, *The Tanya* (1796), in ways reflected by Freud's own views of dialectic tensions between Ego and Id, and between the Conscious and the Unconscious, and akin to Freud's belief of the Ego's ability to render Conscious what had been Unconscious. Let us allow ourselves to use such ideational comparisons for illustrative purposes only.

Caution is appropriate here, however: contrary to Freudian ideas that the human inner Self is associated with animal desires, such as the

---

12. The founder of the *Chabad* Chassidic movement (1745–1812).

libido or man's craving for power,[13] Judaism's outlook always has been that the inner Self of a human being was created in the Divine Image (Gen. 1:27, 9:6; Psalms 39:7), and therefore is morally of good origin as it is also of higher substance.

Keeping in mind what represents the *true Self* of man in Judaism, we should be able to define next the meaning of freedom, at personal, collective, and national levels of analysis. After all, is liberation not the long road taken by the Israelites upon leaving Egypt, and is the basic meaning of freedom not that which continues to permeate all facets of Jewish life still so very intensely today?

Liberation and Its Meaning

At the sight of the Burning Bush, Moses knows he is being called by G-d to liberate the nation from the shackles of slavery in Egypt. For he is provided with the meaning for liberation: "When thou hast brought forth the people out of Egypt, *ye shall serve the Almighty* upon this mountain" (Exod. 3:12; emphasis added). And when Moses approaches Pharaoh with the request "Thus saith . . . G-d of the Hebrews: Let My people go," he adds the meaning: "that they may serve Me" (Exod. 9:1). The meaning, the purpose, of liberation from Egyptian slavery, is in the very "Service of G-d."

Every Generation, Every Year, Every Day . . .

"In every generation *and every day* a person is obliged to regard himself as if *that day* he had come out of Egypt" (Schneur-Zalman 1796, I, 47).

---

13. The idea that sexual impulses repressed since infancy are behind mental and/or physical symptoms of neurosis is Freudian (Freud 1905). Freud's foremost disciple, and later rival, C. G. Jung would disagree with his erstwhile mentor's emphasis on sexuality as the sole or dominant factor in unconscious motivation. Jung, a devout Christian with a penchant for archetypes, chose to define neurosis rather as "the suffering of the soul which has not discovered its meaning" (Jung 1912). Another prominent associate of Freud, the Austrian psychiatrist A. Adler, repudiated the causal effects of infantile sexuality, preferring to trace character and neurosis to the desire for power. And still another prominent Austrian psychiatrist, Viktor Frankl, would agree with Nietzsche that "[h]e who has a why to live for can bear with almost any how" (Nietzsche, quoted in Frankl 1963, 121). Among prisoners in the Nazi concentration camps, Frankl's studies concluded, those with faith in G-d and in the meaning in life had a much higher chance of survival under the severest circumstances than those who had no faith to cling to. Frankl's focus on healing through faith in G-d and in meaningful life (Logotherapy) is the path to follow under distress, according to the Lubavitcher Rebbe (Gotfryd 2003, 356–357; Schneerson 1990, 22, 227).

Rabbi Schneur-Zalman uses this quote from the Talmud,[14] adding the words "and every day" and . . . "that day." For the Exodus is not only an event that takes place once in every generation—it still is a daily occurrence in the spiritual life of every Jew. And R. Schneur-Zalman continues: "This refers to the release of the Divine Soul from the confinement of the body, 'the Serpent's skin'" (I, 47).[15]

The body is a source of confinement for the Divine Soul, since it derives its life-force from kelipat nogah[16]—the Serpent's skin.[17] It is from this exile that the Divine Soul escapes: "In order to be absorbed into the unity of the Light of the *Ein Sof*,[18] blessed be He, through engaging in the Torah and commandments in general, and in particular through accepting the Kingdom of Heaven during the recital of the *Shema*,[19] wherein the faithful explicitly accept and draw upon themselves G-d's unity, when they say: 'G-d, our G-d, G-d is One'." The term "our G-d" should be understood in the same manner as "G-d of Abraham," in the sense: Abraham nullified his Self before G-d and became absorbed into the sublime Unity of the Light of the blessed *Ein Sof*.

---

14. *Mishnah, Pesakhim* 10:5. See also footnote 5.

15. *Mashkha de-Hivya* (Aramaic: Serpent's skin) in Kabbalah should not be confused with similar legendary terms in ancient cultures and mythologies where "serpent's skin" symbolizes renewal/reincarnation (as in Buddhism), or with snakes and serpents worshiped as deities (in ancient Egypt). The Serpent in the Torah is evil and cursed (Gen. 3:14–15). Aaron's Rod turning into a serpent (Exod. 7:8–10) was meant to demonstrate to the Egyptians that even those evil forces that they worship are derived and are an extension (as a "rod") from holiness (Schneur-Zalman 1836, 113). Pharaoh himself is compared to a Serpent (Ezek. 29:3). The heretical Gnostic sect of the Naasene (from Hebrew *Nahash:* serpent) even identified Jesus with the biblical Serpent as the Antagonist of the biblical Creator-Lawgiver, who "freed" mankind from the shackles of the Law. All these pagan mythological terms have little in common with the biblical images or Kabbalistic terms of "serpents" or "serpent's skin."

16. *Kelipah*, pl. *Kelipot* (literally, "husk," "peel," "nutshell")—a Kabbalistic term denoting "outer skin" (the physical world) that is covering the "fruit" (the spiritual goodness and holiness). Three of the existing *kelipot* are "impure," forbidden, and cannot be used in Divine service, but the fourth, *kelipat nogah* (the shining husk), is a mixture of "good and evil" and is permitted; therefore, it can be used for holy purposes and converted into holiness.

17. "The Serpent's skin" is a Kabbalistic term denoting impurity of the body. The physical body is said to derive its vitality from *kelipat nogah*, and is thus the "skin"—"outer shell" of the "Serpent." The term "Serpent" refers to three utterly impure *kelipot*, while the skin, after it is shed, can be used for good purposes. The Body by itself is not evil, unless possessed by the Serpent (source of evil). The subject is treated at length by R. Menachem Mendel of Lyubavitch (Tzemach-Tzedek 1843–56, 136).

18. *Ein Sof* (The Infinite): in Kabbalistic literature the term "the Light of *Ein Sof*" is employed to denote Emanation—a coming from G-d, the Infinite One.

19. The *Shema* prayer: "Hear, o Israel, G-d, our G-d, G-d is One," and the text that follows from Deuteronomy (6:4–9), is a twice-daily mandatory recitation for a Jew.

The ultimate desire of the Divine Soul is to return and to unite with its Source: "the dust returneth to the earth as it was, and the spirit returneth unto G-d Who gave it" (Eccles. 12:7). Thus, Divine service is not bondage but *true* freedom. If the limitations of the "dust" (the mortal body) contradict the realization of the Soul's strivings, exodus from these limitations is true liberation of the Self.

The idea of an *every day* Exodus from Egyptian bondage through the liberating work in the Divine is a "service of the heart"—*prayer*—as unambiguously expressed in many Kabbalistic and Chassidic works. This interpretation is based on a verse from the prophet Micah: "As in the days of thy coming forth out of the land of Egypt will I show unto him marvelous things" (Mic. 7:15). Why is the prophet referring to the *days* (plural) of the Exodus from Egypt, when the Torah speaks about a single day: "That thou mayest remember the *day* of thy exodus from the land of Egypt all the days of thy life" (Deut. 15:3; emphasis added)? The Exodus was completed in one day, the fifteenth of Nisan; the other "days" were those spent wandering in the desert.

The explanation found in Kabbalistic and Chassidic sources is that both the Exodus and the liberation are ever-ongoing processes, continuing every generation, every year, and every day (Schneersohn 1957, 159–165; *Zohar* 1970, III, 176a). The *duty* to remember the Exodus—the liberation from Egypt—"all the days of thy life" is in itself the very mode of worshiping G-d. Through remembrance, a person is supposed to live and relive the event, again and again, as if one were only just liberated from slavery. Reliving the event in its spiritual content is *liberating*, ever again enabling one to unburden oneself.

Bondage as Self-Enslavement

Slavery, as a state of mind, could not be thoroughly shed by the Israelites upon leaving Egypt, if only because they were miraculously *brought out*—by "a mighty Hand and an outstretched Arm" (Deut. 26:8). In their own spiritual capacities, however, they were neither ready nor capable of rejecting bondage, as of yet: "And had not the Holy One, blessed be He, brought our fathers out of Egypt, then we, our children and our children's children would still be enslaved to Pharaoh in Egypt" (Haggadah, 1976, 64–65).

For a journey that began at the borders of Egypt, Exodus was but a first step—the beginning of a Redemptory Process—which would make possible all future liberations. If G-d had not made that deliverance possible in the first instance, none of the subsequent stages in the still-ongoing liberation process would have been possible. The level of impurity and evil, absorbed during the sojourn in Egypt by the Hebrews, was never wholly successfully shed off by their descendents (Schneur-Zalman 1796, chap. 31; 1973, 143–144). This is why the remembrance and celebration of the original Exodus must take place once a year, every year, around the Seder table. However, no sooner would the Israelites attain success, or falter to secure their gains, than they would find themselves under siege or occupation, or in exile, again, and again: whether into Assyria, in Persia, conquered by the Greeks, or occupied by the Romans.

Worship and Self-Perfection through Prayer

Because meaningful freedom is to be found in the attainment of the cravings of the true Self, in the fulfillment of the Divine Soul's innermost desire to be liberated from the bonds and limits of the spiritual *Mizraim*, and in becoming one with G-d the Infinite, through prayer, a more detailed understanding of Jewish prayer may prove helpful here.

The entire structure of the Jewish Liturgy is built around the *Shema* prayer. It proclaims the Absolute Unity and Love of G-d (the inner strivings of the Divine Soul to re-unite with its Creator). Exodus from Egyptian bondage is mentioned in passing at the end of the *Shema* prayer: "I am . . . your G-d, Who brought you out of the land of Egypt, to be your God: I am . . . your G-d" (Num. 15:41).

"[There is] a positive commandment to pray every day, as is written: 'And ye shall serve G-d, your G-d' (Exodus 23:25). This 'service', the *Tefillah* (prayer), is meant to: 'Serve Him with your whole heart' (Deuteronomy 11:13). Remark the Sages: 'Which service is with the heart? *Tefillah*'" (Maimonides ca. 1171, *Laws of Prayer*, Book 1, 1; Talmud, *Ta'anit*, 2a).

"Service of the heart" is one of the three pillars on which Judaism's world is firmly established: "Simon the Just," one of the remaining members of the "Great Assembly,"[20] used to say: "The universe stands on three [principal] things: on Torah, on Worship [of G-d] and on Acts of kindness" (*Mishna*, *Avoth*, 1, 2). Worship is *Tefillah*, namely, prayer— "service of the heart."

---

20. See footnote 2.

On the primitive level, praying is merely *soliciting* G-d for the fulfillment of one's needs or desires. This has an educational merit: when
one acknowledges that the fulfillment of all of the wants comes from
G-d and not as a result of one's own strength or worldly wisdom, one
is committed to adopt the ways of G-d: "Trust in G-d with all thy heart,
and lean not upon thine own understanding. In all thy ways acknowledge Him, and He will direct thy paths" (Prov. 3:5–6). On a more
profound level, however, *Tefillah* is deemed to offer a means to *unite*
with G-d. The *Torah* alludes to both kinds of prayer: "And ye shall
serve . . . G-d, and He will bless thy bread, and thy water; and I will
take sickness away from the midst of thee" (Exod. 23:25), but also
"Serve Him with all your heart" (Deut. 11:13). The first verse speaks of
the utilitarian necessity of praying daily to G-d, for one's needs—for
just as food is a daily necessity so too is prayer a daily requirement.
And while the former mode of prayer may sound self-serving, the
latter is totally devotional.

Although it might seem impossible for these two opposite modes to
be simultaneously present in the same prayer, one of the founding
fathers of Chassidism, Rabbi Dov-Ber of Mezhirichi,[21] lends some
insight into how such duality in prayer may be reconciled: he refers to
the Kabbalistic concept of "parallel worlds." According to this approach,
we see failure or shortcomings in our physical existence only after
falling behind in our higher spiritual pursuits. We may describe this
metaphorically, by suggesting that the cause of human affliction is the
suffering of the *Shekhinah* (Divine Presence): just as there is suffering
when physical needs are unmet, so is there Divine suffering when
forces of evil are allowed to dominate this world (Schneerson 1972, 23,
217 note 41; Schochat 1990, 73–78). Thus, the needs of Heaven become
one's very own.

The Talmud refers to the "pious of old" (*Chassidim ha-rishonim*) that
would "wait" one hour before each *Tefillah* (Talmud, *Berakhot*, 5, 1). What
was the purpose of this "hour of waiting"? Kabbalistic sources refer to
it as a way of meditating: "They would shed all their worldly thoughts,
concentrate their mind on the Infinite, blessed be He, for a long hour,
become completely absorbed by the Light emanating from Him, while
their heart was consumed with the fire of the selfless love of G-d and
awe" (Hurwitz 1689, *Yoma* [Day of Atonement], Laws of Repentance).

---

21. Known as the *Maggid* (Preacher) of Mezhirichi (1710–72), Rabbi Dov-Ber was first a
disciple of, then successor to, the founding Head of the Chassidic movement—Rabbi
Israel, the *Baal Shem Tov*.

This mode of worship corresponds to the order of the *Shema:* "Hear, O Israel: G-d, our Lord, G-d is one. . . . And thou shalt love G-d, thy Lord, with all thy heart, and with all thy soul, and with all thy might" (Deut. 6:4–5). *Shema* (hear) means also "comprehend," "be aware of" (meditate on, and contemplate) G-d's infinite greatness, over His being, at once, *Elohenu,* "our Lord," "our Life-Source," and still, our "G-d is One." Reflecting on these philosophical ideas will lead to the uncovering of the natural resources of emotional energy of the Divine Soul: "And thou shalt love G-d thy Lord with all thy heart." Another possible translation from the Hebrew of this phrase reads "And thou *willst* [emphasis added] love G-d thy Lord [YHVH] with all thy heart," implying that the supreme love for G-d will come naturally through contemplation, through elevating oneself during *Tefillah* worship, a practice that leaves its mark on the worshiper for the entire day.

Mandatory daily prayers were instituted by the sages and prophets of antiquity to replace the daily sacrifices at the Temple. In that new mode of worship, duties shift from the priest to the worshiper: the animals once offered on the altar embodied man's animal desires (e.g., profane love) and animal emotions, which are drawn into the fierce fire of emotions of the Divine Soul, aflame in the heart as if on the Temple's altar. By contrast, in a mode of self-enlightening worship through prayer, the Divine Soul, by being liberated daily from its earthly "bonds"—the desires of the Body and of the Natural Soul—reenacts the Exodus periodically, as liberation from bondage, along one's long journey to one's final and ultimate Redemption. The biblical name for Egypt, *Mizraim,* comes from the singular noun *Meizar* (limit, or boundary).[22] *Mizraim* therefore translates as *boundaries,* and thus, "flight from Egypt" as *escape from bounds.* Worshiping the Infinite One, blessed be He, is to have one's soul strive to unite with Him, by being released from the shackles and limitations of one's lowly bodily cravings. This mode of self-liberating service—by which the Divine Soul breaks free of its bondage within the Body and the Animal Soul—is analogous to the Exodus from Egyptian bondage, of which it is written that 'the people escaped' (Exodus 14:5) (Schneur-Zalman 1796, I, 31).

---

22. The designation *Mizraim,* although not attested in extant Egyptian monuments, is known also in Aramaic; and the Arabic name for Egypt is *Misr,* from the same root as *Mizraim.* Since *Meizar* means "boundary," "limit," "strait," or "isthmus," the plural form, *Mizraim,* may be analogous to the Hebrew designation for Mesopotamia: *Naharaim* (Two Rivers). The entire land of Egypt in ancient times consisted of a narrow strip comprising two banks divided by the Nile. The remainder was desert. Hence, the Chassidic interpretation of *Mizraim* is in harmony with its likely literal meaning.

The Talmudic notion of *Chassidim ha-rishonim* observing "waiting periods" may refer to an ancient tradition of meditation in prayer as practiced in biblical times by adepts of prophecy—who practiced or prepared to receive such (Maimonides ca.1171, *Laws of Foundations of the Torah*, Book 7, 4–5). The ancient practice of meditation in prayer has been kept alive, first in the secrecy of Kabbalistic circles, later among the modern Chassidim in general,[23] and by Chabad in particular.

Ultimate Freedom or Eternal Liberation?

Since spiritual Exodus means liberation of the Soul from earthly limitations to union with the Infinite, is there a sense to 'eternal exodus from exile'? Does the Soul ever achieve 'a state of Nirvana'?

An oft-cited anecdote about Rabbi Schneur-Zalman exemplifies the distinction. Engrossed in prayer, the Rebbe could be heard to say: "I don't desire anything. I do not seek [the high spiritual delight of] Thy Paradise; I do not want [the spiritual rewards of] Thy 'World to come'; all I want is *Thou* alone" (Tzemach-Tzedek 1911, 148a). Rabbi Schneur-Zalman hence viewed even a concern for spiritual benefit to be obstructive for genuine prayer: "Whom have I in Heaven but Thee? And beside Thee I desire none upon earth" (Psalms 73:25)—one "should not desire the [spiritual rewards of the] Lower Paradise or [those of the] Higher Paradise, [but instead] strive to unite with His Essence" (Schneur-Zalman 1836, I, 9a).

The Lubavitcher Rebbe compared the flight of the Heavenly Soul in prayer to the flight of a space shuttle into outer space.[24] Through burning and discharging fuel, a rocket flies ever higher into space, breaking free of the forces of gravity. As does the Soul in prayer: by burning and discharging our animal desires one by one, our Soul can make its way "upward." Upon reaching the state of weightlessness, the shuttle no longer needs the burning fuel. The Soul, too, after completing its transformation of the bodily animal desires, continues its endless flight to Infinity, by interaction with its "opposite"—*Sefirot* (e.g., Love

---

23. The designation *Chassidim*, for the eighteenth-century pietistic movement in Eastern Europe, was coined by their opponents—most likely because of their ostentatious devotion and profound meditation in prayer.

24. In December 1968, as American astronauts were orbiting the moon, the officially unpublished talk, offered to college students spending their midwinter vacation in Lubavitch HQs in Brooklyn, NY, was based on the teachings of the Baal Shem Tov. It intimated that all a person sees or hears must serve as guidance in his worship of the Creator.

and Awe). That is precisely what Rabbi Hiya bar Ashi meant when he said in the name of Rav: "Students of the Sages do not know rest, not in this world and not [even] in the world to come, as is written: 'They go from strength to strength . . . to appear before G-d in Zion' (Psalms 84:8)" (Talmud, *Berakhot*, 64a).

Freedom through Torah

While self-perfection through prayer is the road to personal and universal liberations envisioned in the Torah, there is a path to freedom through the Torah itself. Rabbi Joshua ben Levi has said "It is written: 'And the tablets were the handiwork of the Almighty, and the writing was the writing of the Almighty, engraved [*harut*] on the tablets' (Exodus 32:16). Read not *harut* (engraved), but *herut* (freedom), because no one is free except one who occupies himself with the Torah" (*Mishna, Avoth* 6:2).

This saying is quoted numerous times in *Aggada*[25] and Chassidic literature to convey that only those whose main occupation is Torah are truly free. The entire interpretation is based on a simple play of two seemingly unrelated Hebrew words: *harut* (engraved) and *herut* (freedom), spelled with identical consonants (without vowels). The *Masoretic* (textus receptus) reading is *harut* (engraved), but if we substitute *herut* (as Rabbi Joshua has suggested), the verse would read: ". . . and the writing was the writing of the Almighty, *freedom* on the tablets." Why would Rabbi Joshua substitute the reading of the received text with a word that does not make much sense in this context?

There is a basic rule that whenever the sages say "read not . . . but . . ." they do not mean to deny the received reading; they just add another dimension to the obvious meaning of the written text (Zevin 1974– , 2, 1). The word *harut* ("engraved," in the textus receptus) can be found nowhere else in the Hebrew Bible (Ibn-Ezra, Exod. 32:16). But the great eleventh-century Spanish-Hebrew grammarian and lexicographer Jonah Ibn Janāh (1896, 173) does connect *harut* with *harusha* (graven) in the words of Jeremiah (17:1): "The sin of Judah is written with a pen of iron, and with the point of a diamond; it is graven (*harusha*) upon the tablet of their heart."

The association with Jeremiah's words comes in handy: ". . . it is graven upon the tablet of their heart." When does a student of the

---

25. The *Aggada* is a homiletic interpretation of Torah passages by ancient rabbis.

Torah become free? When the Torah is *engraved upon the tablets of his heart*. Note that Rabbi Joshua did not say: "no one is free, except one who *studies* the Torah," but "one who *occupies himself* (*'oseq*) with the Torah."

The terms *'oseq* (occupies himself) and *'eseq* (business) are fungible. Unlike a hired worker, a businessperson is not employed for a limited amount of hours. When a customer arrives a few minutes before closing time, unlike a salaried worker who would rather be home enjoying his freedom, a business owner is happy because a good customer is what his business is all about: business *occupies* his thoughts day and night. So, too, a Torah scholar may be exercising a profession to support himself and his family, but his principal occupation is the *Torah*: "When thou walkest, she shall lead thee, when thou liest down, she shall watch over thee, and when thou awakest, she will talk with thee" (Prov. 6:22).

According to the rules of Torah study, a person is supposed to make regular Torah study his permanent occupation. In contrast, one's business/professional "occupation" should be viewed as "temporary" (Maimonides ca. 1171, *Laws of Torah Study*, Book 3, 7). No matter how many hours a day a scholar devotes to work or to business, his main occupation is still the Torah, since Torah is the ultimate "purpose" of his life.

When the Torah is engraved upon the tablets of one's heart, one is free. There are two modes of writing that are used for the Torah: writing (on parchment) and engraving (on tablets). The difference? In writing, ink is applied on the parchment; in engraving, letters are cut into stone. Ink and parchment are different substances. In the case of engraving, the letters are not imparted to the stone but embodied from the stone itself. The letters and the stone are not two substances but one and the same (Schneur-Zalman 1848, II, 45a, 46b). When a person acquires the Torah, such that the words of Torah are "incised on the tablets of one's heart," heart and Torah become one as an inseparable entity, whereby such a person achieves the highest form of freedom for his Heavenly Soul.

The expression "heart" in Hebrew is a homonym, figuratively applied to express "the middle part of a thing," as "unto the midst (*lev*, or heart) of heaven" (Deut. 4:11). It also signifies thought, desire, will, the innermost traits of the Soul (Maimonides ca. 1190, I, 39). Accordingly, when the words of the Torah are incised on the "tablets of the heart," the Torah is not knowledge "applied" to the Soul, like ink on parchment, but rather an act become one with the substance of the Soul. The Soul's thoughts, the ideas, letters, and units of thought, become the "letters" of the Torah.

The basic difference between Torah and general science is that Torah is Law, as more or less correctly translated into European languages. The word "Torah" means "instruction." It comes from the verb *le-horot* [to instruct] (Loew, *Gur Aryeh*; Gen. 1:1; *Zohar* 3, 53). Although the Torah holds a wide range of knowledge, from cosmogony to jurisprudence, it is not studied as a general subject. A student of any science does not necessarily identify with the subject of his study, if because knowledge acquired is not necessarily lived. A Torah scholar is held in legal bond with the teaching *and* the practice of the Torah. Every utterance in the Torah, even words in the simplest Bible stories, are studied as Divine Law: they are read and heeded as an instruction in the intimate life of each individual, as a law for all of Israel or a source for universal law for humankind freely to follow. The Torah is conceived both as Divine Wisdom and as G-d's Will—the Law of the Supreme Ruling Lawgiver of the Universe. By becoming one with the Creator's Infinite Wisdom and Will, a person may reach the highest spiritual level of human existence, and the ultimate desire of the true Self—the Divine Soul, called "Freedom."

A Roadmap to Freedom

According to the teachings of the esoteric—Kabbalistic—part of the Torah, and of some medieval Jewish philosophers, the downfall of Man began when Adam and Eve "ate" from the forbidden fruit of the mythical "Tree of Knowledge of Good and Evil." Created by G-d in His Image, Man was perfect in his super intelligence of knowing the Creator, and could not have had any evil inclinations. What G-d had withheld from Man, for Man's own good, was Wisdom in judgment—of *Good and Evil*—not cunning for preference, or intelligence of choice. The precept of "good versus evil" was an abstract principle that had, so far, nothing to do with the nature of the human race. The Soul was in complete harmony with the Body, since the latter was created in the likeness of the former. The Body was in complete control of the Intellect and in command of the "Divine Image," so evil or shameful erotic inclinations were out of the question. The Body was innocent, as the body of a child that knows of "no good or evil," so even garments were not necessary. The temptation to taste the fruit of the seemingly "superior" knowledge from the "Tree of Knowledge of *Good and Evil*"

destroyed the virtuousness of the Body *and* the primordial harmony in
G-d's creation. When the once-abstract "knowledge of Good and Evil"
became concrete upon being "ingested," Good and Evil, both, "became
an integral part of human nature, whence the struggle between the
Heavenly Soul and the earthly bodily desires" (ca. 1190, I, 2).

The disobedience of Man[26] resulted in the expulsion from Paradise
(*Gan Eden*, Garden of Delight). Filled with Evil (disobedience of G-d),
the earth quickly became a place of suffering. Evil produced more evil,
until the Deluge[27] cleansed the world. After the Flood, during the building of the Tower of Babel, the struggle among peoples precipitated the
collapse of unity in the Family of Nations. Since then, humankind has
remained divided, and bloody wars between nations have plagued
almost every generation: So much for "freedom."

According to the esoteric teachings of the Kabbalah, it is through
actions of Goodness and Kindness (concordant with the precepts of the
Torah) that the profane can become holier, by approaching the spiritual
realm of the Creator, whereby immanence can reestablish the harmony
and unity between the Universal Soul and the Body of the material
world: Matter becomes less impure, more receptive to the Sublime. At
the horizon of this path, the Hebrew prophets envisioned an almost
utopian idea—an ideal: a messianic universe in which G-d's Law would
rule without compulsion, where the nations of the world "shall beat
their swords into plowshares . . . nation shall not lift up sword against
nation, neither shall they learn war any more" (Isa. 2:4), and "shall not
hurt nor destroy in all My holy mound; for the earth shall be full of the
knowledge of G-d, as the waters cover the sea" (Isa. 11:9).

The development and diffusion of scientific knowledge were long
predicted by the esoteric book the *Zohar*, which augured the world's
preparation for a Messianic future—a "universe filled with Knowledge
of G-d": "And in the Sixth century of the sixth millennium [of the Creation Era[28]] the gates of Wisdom from above [mystical Wisdom of
Torah, Knowledge of G-d] will open and the wellsprings of wisdom

---

26. When the Universe is understood as an Organized Body, disobedience of the Brain
by any of the organs can be seen to ruin the harmony of that Body. The reach for the
Forbidden Fruit constituted, therefore, an act of insubordination by the Heart (Emotions)
to the Brain (Intellect), altogether debasing Man into man.

27. The Destruction by Flood came as a result of *Hamas* (violence) and of sexual promis-
cuity. Having learned nothing from their Fall from Eden, humans may have ruined the
Harmony of Creation by their worldly lawlessness, turning celestial lawful order into
terrestrial chaos, once again.

28. The Creation Era begins in 3761 B.C.E., thus the sixth century of the sixth millennium
begins in 1739.

from below [worldly sciences, human knowledge] . . . the world will prepare itself to come into the seventh [millennium], as a person on the Sixth day [of the week] prepares himself . . . to enter the Sabbath" (*Zohar* I, 116b).

The spread of Information Age technology, the burgeoning freedom of information, the peaceful collapse of oppressive totalitarian states, the efforts by newly independent nations aspiring to the rule of justice and democracy, the treaties between superpowers declaring the end of the Cold War, the annulment of the arsenals of weapons of mass destruction, the remaking of "swords into plowshares" (tanks into tractors), the insistence on letting International Law, not force, rule relations between nations, the helping hand stretched out by the rich nations to the poor ones, the freedom that the Jewish people could come to enjoy in almost all the countries of the world—are just a few of the signs of the Dawn of the Messianic Age, of the possibility of "Redemption" and of the promise of freedom for all.

This ultimate meaningful Freedom is envisioned in the concluding chapter of Maimonides' Code of Law: "The Sages and the prophets did not desire the Messianic era in order to rule the whole world or conquer the nations, or that the nations of the world should extol them . . . but to be free for the Torah and Wisdom without any oppressor or obstacle. . . . In those times there will be no hunger, nor war, no envy, nor strife, there will be an abundance of grace, precious things will be in abundance like dust . . . and the whole world will be occupied with knowledge of G-d, as is written: '. . . For the earth shall be full of the knowledge of G-d, as the waters cover the sea' (Isaiah 11:9)" (Maimonides ca. 1171, *Laws of Kings*, Book 12, 4–5).

References

1. Bible

The Holy Scriptures according to the Masoretic Text, a New Translation (1917), Philadelphia: The Jewish Publication Society of America. [Genesis, Exodus, Leviticus, Numbers, Deuteronomy, Isaiah, Ezekiel, Mica, Psalms, Ecclesiastes, Proverbs, Job]

2. Biblical Commentaries

Esther-Rabba [5th century?] (1878), Jerusalem: Buber.

Rashi, Rabbi Shlomo Yarkhi [1040–1105] (5743/1983) *Perushey Rashi al Ha-Torah* (Commentaries of Rashi on the Torah), Jerusalem: Mosad Harav Kook.

Ibn Ezra, Abraham [1089–1164] (5725/1965), in *Mikraot Gedolot*, NewYork: A. I. Friedman.

Loew, Rabbi Judah, Maharal of Prague [1525–1609] (1578), *Gur Aryeh*, in *Mizrahi* (1862), Warsaw.

3. Mishnah [earliest Talmudic Codex, 2nd century CE] (1970), Jerusalem: Tora la'Am

———— *Avoth* (Fathers, basic maxims of Torah and ethics).

———— *Pesakhim* (Paschal offerings).

4. Talmud [The Babylonian Talmud, completed in 499 CE] (1990), Jerusalem: Israel Institute for Talmudic Publications

———— *Berakhot* (Benedictions).

———— *Pesakhim* (Paschal offerings).

———— *Shabbat* (Sabbath).

———— *Ta'anit* (Fasts).

———— *Megillah* (Scroll [of Esther]).

5. Miscellaneous Sources (Jewish)

Dov-Ber, *Maggid* (Preacher) of Mezhirichi [1710–72] (1973) *Ohr Torah*, Brooklyn, NY: Kehot Publication Society.

Haggadah (1976) *The Birnbaum Haggadah* (with English translation), New York: Hebrew Publishing.

Ha-hinuch (1982) ("Book of Education"—Anonymous *Halachic* work, end of 13th century), Jerusalem: Mosad Harav Kook.

Hurwitz, Rabbi Isaiah (1689) *Shene Lukhot Ha-Berit* (Two Tablets of the Covenant), Amsterdam.

Ibn Janāh, Jonah (1896) *Sepher Haschoraschim*, Berlin.

Maimonides, Moses [1135–1204] (ca. 1171, 1887) *Mishne Torah* (Code of Jewish Law), 14 books, Jerusalem: Mosad Harav Kook.

———— (ca. 1190, 1881) *The Guide for the Perplexed*, M. Friedlander, Translator, New York: Dover.

Mangel, Nissen (1978) *Siddur Tehillat Hashem* (Praise of G-d, Prayerbook with English translation), Brooklyn, NY: Merkos L'inyonei Chinuch.

Schneersohn, Joseph-Isaac [1880–1950] (1957) *Sefer Hamaamarim—5708* (Book of Sermons—5708), Brooklyn, NY: Kehot Publication Society.

Schneerson, Rabbi Menachem Mendel [1902–94] (1992) *Torath Menachem* (The Teaching of Menachem), Kfar Chabad, Israel: Kehot Publication Society.

——— (1972) *Likute Sichot*, Brooklyn, NY: Kehot Publication Society.

——— (1990) *Igrot Kodesh*, Brooklyn, NY: Kehot Publication Society.

——— (1992) *Igrot Melech* (King's letters), Kfar Chabad, Israel: Kehot Publication Society.

Schneur-Zalman, Rabbi of Lyady [1745–1812] (1796) *The Tanya*, Slavuta, Russia. [Bilingual edition 1973, Brooklyn, NY: Kehot Publication Society.]

——— (1836) *Torah Ohr*, Kopyst, Russia. [New edition 1996, Brooklyn, NY: Kehot Publication Society.]

——— (1848) *Likkute Torah* (Selected Teachings), Zhitomir, Russia. [New edition 1996, Brooklyn, NY: Kehot Publication Society.]

Schochat, Rabbi Immanuel (1990, 1995) *Deep Calling Unto Deep*, Brooklyn, NY: Kehot Publication Society.

Tzemach-Tzedek, Rabbi Menachem Mendel of Lyubavitch (1843–56) *Sefer Ha-Chakirah* (Book of Philosophy). [1st edition 1912, Poltava, Russia; 2nd edition, 1913, Berdichev, Russia; new edition 1955, Brooklyn, NY: Kehot Publication Society.]

——— (1814–1828) *Derech Mitzvotecha* (The Path of Thy Commandments). [1st edition 1911; new edition 1991, Brooklyn, NY: Kehot Publication Society.]

Zevin, R. Shlomo Yosef, Editor (1974–) *Talmudic Encyclopedia*, Jerusalem: Talmudic Encyclopedia Publications.

Zohar (Splendor) (1970) Jerusalem: Mosad Harav Kook. [A highly authoritative and widely quoted Kabbalistic commentary on the Torah (Pentateuch) and some biblical books, of unknown authorship, expounding the mystical teachings by 2nd-century sage R. Shimeon bar Yochai, circulated in manuscripts since the 13th century.]

6. Miscellaneous Sources (General)

Bakan, D. (1990) *Sigmund Freud and the Jewish Mystical Tradition*, London: Free Association Books.

Cowley, A. E. (1923) *Aramaic Papyri of the 5th Century BC*, Oxford: Oxford University Press.

Frankl, V. E. (1963) *Man's Search for Meaning: An Introduction to Logotherapy*. New York: Washington Square Press.

Freud, Sigmund (1905) *Drei Abhandlungen zur Sexualtheorie*, Leipzig and Vienna: Franz Deuticke.

Gotfryd, Arnie (2003) *Mind Over Matter*, Jerusalem: Shamir.

Jung, C. G. (1912) *Symbols of Transformation*, Vienna.

Partridge, P. H. (1967) "Freedom," in Paul Edwards, Editor, *The Encyclopedia of Philosophy*, New York: Macmillan.

Russell, Bertrand (1940) "Freedom and Government," in Ruth N. Anshen, Editor, *Freedom: Its Meaning*, New York: Harcourt.

Schneider, S., and J. H. Berke (2000) "Sigmund Freud and the Lubavitcher Rebbe," in *Psychoanalytic Review*, 87(1), Martin Schulman, Editor, New York: National Psychological Association for Psychoanalysis (NPAP), available at: http://www.jhberke.com/Freud _Lub_Rebbe.htm.

8

Human Freedom:
A Christian Understanding
of Salvation as Liberation

Roger Haight

The language of salvation expresses the core of Christian faith and the believer's self-understanding. For Christians, Jesus is the savior. How should the process of such a salvation be understood? If human existence is understood fundamentally as a form of freedom, it is this very freedom that is saved. This chapter will begin with that premise and discuss the meaning of salvation from the perspective of its relationship to human freedom and human liberation. It will unfold in two parts: the first will lay out a number of attendant problems that set the context of the question that is engaged and the method of approach used to address it; the second will outline a theological interpretation of the Christian meaning of salvation that also responds to the problems or issues. The result will be a holistic interpretation of the Christian idea of freedom and salvation formulated into a relatively concise outline.

Framing the Discussion

Flourishing in the late eleventh and early twelfth centuries, Anselm of Bec in Normandy, and then Canterbury, following Augustine of Hippo in North Africa in the fourth and fifth centuries C.E., proposed that the discipline of theology be conceived as "faith seeking understanding." The phrase stuck in the West, and most Christian theologians can appropriate it. It involves a generative ambiguity in the tension between faith and reason, what the believer receives from what he or she takes as an ultimately transcendent authority and what the corporate human mind can critically discern with all the tools of observation and logic. Theological conviction lies somewhere between fideistic assertion of incomprehensible mystery and reduction of mystery to psychological, sociological, or rational mechanism. If it is to be genuine theology, it must preserve the two languages of transcendent mystery and natural explanation in tension: one truth in two languages (Schillebeeckx 1990, 110).

Various different styles and methods dot the theological landscape, and it makes some difference which method is employed. Since theology unfolds as a hermeneutical discipline, the method of the interpretation, with its premises and suppositions, largely controls the content of the interpretation itself. But different methods suit different problems; taking a wrench to the class on water colors will not help. I shall begin, then, with a set of issues that define the concerns operating behind this essay before turning to an outline of a suitable theological method.

The discussion is set within a framework shaped by four problems. Each one seems to call into question the intelligibility of the Christian language of salvation. The perspective from which they arise originates in present-day late modern or postmodern intellectual culture. From this perspective several Christian teachings connected with salvation seem archaic and surely complicate communication of this profound reality for those looking to learn about it.

One problem that arises with the Christian language of salvation concerns a background conception that stipulates a division between two spheres of human existence—natural and supernatural—that accompany Christianity as a religion based on revelation. Early on, perhaps in the course of the development of christology in the second century, Christians became convinced that something happened in Jesus that not only changed history but altered human nature itself. The event of Jesus Christ set up a new human order of reality. Although his context was limited, Cyprian of Carthage asserted in the mid-third century that no salvation was available outside the church. Augustine could not conceive of people outside the historical influence of Jesus being saved, because if they were, the whole point of the divine drama in Jesus would be voided. In the theology of the schools in the Middle Ages the appropriation of Aristotle's philosophy of nature facilitated the conception of two distinct spheres of God's interaction with the world and human history, the one natural and the other supernatural, each with its distinct economy and teleology. "Human nature" was that which constituted the human as such, and it provided a basis for specifically human activity that led to the goal of human existence, its ultimate happiness or fulfillment. But since human beings in Christ were called to the higher goal of intimate personal communion in God's own life, this required a higher supernature to generate

the proper actions of faith, hope, and love to achieve the higher pro-
portionate goal (Aquinas 1990, I–II, 109, 2; 112, 1). In a variety of ways,
in theological thought and ecclesial society, this distinction risks separating Christian identity from the rest of the world, often setting itself
above or against the world. Yet human beings do have experiences of
contingency, gratuity, and gift that signal a transcendence that breaks
into the natural order. The language of spirituality portrays both a
depth and a height in human existence, neither of which is fully
accounted for by a historical causality or a flat two-dimensional worldview. The question of the two orders of reality plays a major role in the
Christian conception of salvation, and it faces major challenges from
contemporary conceptions of the continuous character of all finite
reality.

Another problem lies in the basic story that as children Christians
learn of creation, sin, the need for redemption, the saving appearance
of Jesus Christ, and the promise of everlasting life. One of the factors
of this story, the conception of an original sin and a fall of humankind,
portrays a pervasive negativity; Christians are taught to have a consciousness of sin. Most educated Christians accept the mythic character
of the story of Adam and Eve, and surely it has more power understood
as such than as a literal narrative. The same is true of the event of a
fall. Once people begin to appreciate the human race as a product of
evolution, they simultaneously put aside the idea of a human fall portrayed in terms of a comic-book narrative. The story in the end does
not, and is not meant to, explain; as a symbolic narrative it expresses
the sense of guilt of the religious person before the holy God (Ricoeur
1960, 242–243). This doctrine is often defended as the one with the most
empirical evidence: a dark side does seem intrinsic to human freedom.
The symbol effectively places in full view not only the whole range of
human depravities but also tendencies inside us. Such a consciousness
need not be disordered; it can reflect a proper internalization of the
Greek maxim, "know thyself." But Christian realism can also mediate
a heavy, negative view of human existence that cripples freedom and
is almost as destructive as the evil it portrays. The Christian religious
symbol of salvation has to preserve the power of the ancient symbol in
a credible way, but without a simplistic or destructive residue; an
account of this doctrine should also energize and not diminish human
freedom.

A third problem area emerges with the idea of a redemption occurring at a precise moment, as if it were a historical transaction. Almost

immediately, disciples of Jesus who were caught up in the Jesus movement and who confessed Jesus as savior asked themselves exactly what Jesus had done for their salvation. The New Testament contains many answers to that question, but some have become standardized in Christian language: Jesus Christ is a sacrifice or a ransom victim for human sin. Athanasius of Alexandria comes close to affirming that human nature itself was altered by the incarnation of the divine Son. In the mid-fourth century, he wrote: "the incorruptible Son of God, being conjoined with all by a like nature, naturally clothed all with incorruption, by the promise of resurrection" (Athanasius 1954, 63). Augustine developed the idea that Jesus' death was a sacrifice to God, atoning for human sin, thus winning salvation for all who would accept it (Augustine 1963, 144–164). He also developed a theory of Christ's death as a ransom in a negotiation with Satan (384–404). Anselm, again borrowing from Augustine, developed the most influential of all theories: Jesus the God-man, by his free self-offering of his life to God, satisfied for the injury done to God by the sins of humankind (Anselm 1970, 156–164). True, educated Christians today recognize that these descriptions of a metaphysical transaction between Jesus and God in a point of time are symbolic representations and not to be taken literally; and they also see God's salvation as available across the whole range of history, however that may be explained. But at the same time Christians consistently look back to Jesus of Nazareth as the one who provides the answer to the religious question of ultimate meaning. Something happened in him; something raises him above the horizon and commands attention as mediator of God's saving grace. Christian theology has to give an account of this pervasive Christian attitude.

A fourth issue concerns freedom itself. In the second half of the twentieth century, a number of analogous liberation theologies arose across churches and continents and interpreted Christian salvation in terms of liberation. By and large, what was meant was some form of social liberation for large groups of people who were marginalized and oppressed. Liberation theology in Latin America and beyond focused on the poor; black liberation theology fought racism with Christian symbols of saving, of resistance, and of construction; feminist liberation theology brought forward new meaning of Paul's dictum: "There is neither Jew nor Greek, there is neither slave nor free, there is neither male nor female; for you are all one in Christ Jesus" (Gal. 3:28). But the secular citizen questions whether one needs God or religion to settle social problems (see Cameron, chap. 13 in this book), and many people of faith seem to agree: What have God and God's salvation to do with politics? But if human freedom is socially constituted, one will have to find the connection between salvation and the public order lest religion be reduced to an individual and private sphere. If personal religion entails privatization, the loss of all public relevance, then religion also surrenders all claim to truth.

The central issue that these cumulative questions pose to Christians and also to those who inquire from outside the circle of Christian faith regards the intelligibility of this salvation in a period marked by a heightened sense of historicity, by the social construction of consciousness, and by the sheer diversity of religious beliefs. Historicity means that all human ideas and values are particular to the specific time and culture of their expression. Social consciousness recognizes the social component of all individual thought and behavior. Both convey forcefully the relative dimension of human thought and largely explain the multiplicity of religions and religious beliefs. This means that a view of salvation that claims universal relevance to human freedom must be explained in a way that takes account of this pluralism and the intellectual culture that it has generated. Theology has to widen its scope and present a view that can be appreciated universally.

I turn now to a discussion of an appropriate theological method for addressing the meaning of salvation in the context of these issues. One can no longer just start "talking theology" and expect to be understood, not even in the context of a close-knit array of multidisciplinary essays; let alone in the vast context of Christian theology itself, so pluralistic has that field become. In the arts and sciences, it has become customary constantly to recall that method shapes the logic and affects the intelligibility of any discourse dealing with theoretical issues. In theology the situation becomes infinitely more complicated because, to many, theology appears to be "data-free" analysis. Explanation of exactly what one is talking about is crucial, and this is a question of method. In what follows, then, I shall propose brief statements about, first, the nature of theological language as intrinsically symbolic but not "merely" so and, second, the method of theology that is employed here.

On the Nature of Theological Language

Theology is often transliterated as talk about God. But if God is really God, God must be utterly transcendent, and thus not available to human knowledge as it is ordinarily understood. Since God can only be reached or contacted by faith (see also Haskelevich, chap. 7 in this book), theology has to be viewed as having its base in some form of religious experience resulting in religious faith. Actually the idea of "talk about God" is far too restricted in its object to be adequate to actual theological discourse whose range is, practically speaking, unrestricted. A more adequate description of theology might take a cue from Thomas Aquinas, who defines the object of what he called "sacred doctrine" as the whole range of reality from the perspective of Christian doctrine (Aquinas 1990, I, 1, 7). Adapting that point of view, theology is understood here as interpretation of reality, the same reality as is mediated by any other discipline (cf. Urban, chap. 10, Hackney, chap. 11, Hirschmann, chap. 9, and Cameron, chap 13, in this book, for instance), but through the lens of the symbols used by Christians to express their faith. Theology is a hermeneutical discipline. It interprets reality out of faith experience. It employs symbolic language.

Innumerable theologians across the span of Christian history discuss the symbolic character of religious language. But no one explains the logic of the religious symbol better than a mysterious Greek writer, probably a Syrian monk, of the late fifth and early sixth centuries, who wrote pseudonymously as Dionysius the Areopagite, the name of a disciple whom Paul is said to have won over in Athens (Acts 17:34). His thought influenced the theology of the icon of Eastern Christianity and the theological epistemology of Medieval Western theology. For Dionysius this world is interpenetrated by a divine sphere which can only be perceived through symbols. A Platonic distinction between above and below, the divine and the creaturely (see Haskelevich, chap. 7 in this book), is bridged by the symbolic. Because the world is suffused with God's creative power, the "below" participates in the "above" and symbols are mystagogic; that is, they lead or draw human consciousness into divine mystery. Symbols are perceptible images by which human beings "are uplifted as far as we can be to the contemplation of what is divine" (Dionysius 1987, 197). The reference of religious symbols is transcendent reality; thus they do not yield a kind of knowledge that can be translated into objective data or information. They mediate a kind of transcendent consciousness and participatory or contemplative knowledge that, indeed, exceeds the empirical or the literal. The mechanics of symbols unfold in a manner analogous to symbols in the spheres of other disciplines. A symbol mediates access to something other than itself, and is especially significant when that other thing can be reached in no other way. Symbols play a major role in areas ranging from psychoanalysis (see Williams and Barber, chap 4, and Cameron, chap. 13, both in this book), to literature (as in McInerney, chap. 2), and to the social sciences as well (Urban and Hackney, chaps. 10 and 11 in this book, for instance). And as in all disciplines, when the reality that is disclosed by symbols cannot be known in any other way, the realism of symbols cannot be demonstrated outside of the very experience that they mediate.

On Method in Theology

What theological method will be appropriate for the interpretation of the symbols that constitute the language by which Christians interpret salvation? For this chapter, I have elected a method that owes a debt to hermeneutical theorists such as Hans-Georg Gadamer (1982), Paul Ricoeur (1974), and David Tracy (1984). It operates under three imperatives. First, the interpretation tries to be faithful to the tradition that defines the symbols of the Christian community's language. It must be especially attentive to the New Testament, and to the Bible generally, as the normative source for Christian theology. But in attending to past symbols, attention focuses—to the extent possible—on the experience that is contained within them, that generated them, and to which they give expression. Second, in order to be intelligible in today's world, interpretation must attend to the common human experience and knowledge that defines present-day culture. Absent such a correlation with contemporary thought and experience, theology would be unintelligible. These two, traditional symbols as they were established in the past and present human experience, are the two principal sources of theology. The first source makes the language of theology Christian, the second makes it credible. These two sources for reflection are brought into conjunction with each other, each criticizing and illumining the other, often under considerable tension, thereby generating an interpretive discussion.

But these two criteria are also modified or controlled by a third, the imperative that theology open up to those who pursue, read, or study it as a certain way of viewing the world, and of living and behaving, too. Not only the past and the present have a bearing on theology, but also the future makes a demand for a distinct praxis. Religion can hardly be reduced to a system of understanding; as elements in an autonomous cultural system, religious communities incorporate a way of life. Theology thus implicitly bears an intimate relationship with ethics, so that the vision of reality contained in religious texts opens up a possible way of acting in the world. An appeal to or empowerment for a certain set of values or mode of living implicitly directs theological discourse.

Salvation as Liberation of Human Freedom

I turn now to a constructive interpretation of salvation as liberation—of innate human freedom. This interpretation unfolds in four stages. Each of these stages takes a classical Christian symbol and elicits its symbolic meaning through a brief phenomenology of human experience. The four are: creation, sin, salvation, and heaven. The intent is to be faithful to the essential dimensions of what is revealed by the symbol. When the theologian fails in this, the community he or she represents will not accept the interpretation. But the interpretation has to make sense to people who live in the world today, for we live in no other world. The description of experience thus implicitly or overtly appeals to common dimensions of meaning and value that guide human life in today's world. In other words, I shall use Christian symbols here, to construe what is going on in the human realm as such. The theological affirmation "Jesus saves" has to be a statement referring to what is going on universally if it is to be considered a universally relevant (cf. Cameron, chap. 13 in this book) statement. The appeal to common human experience therefore ironically becomes intrinsic to unpacking the meaning of specifically Christian theological statements.

Creation

I begin with the symbol of creation because it is an absolutely primal religious understanding of reality. The Christian creed begins: "We believe in God . . . creator of heaven and earth." The point in treating these foundational Christian symbols, however, cannot be to unfold fully the doctrines contained in them but only to make one or two relatively fundamental points that help advance a fuller understanding of salvation relative to human freedom. With respect to creation, three points seem important: the meaning of creation, what God has fashioned in the human, and God's presence to the human.

The symbol of creation refers primarily not to something that God did "in the beginning" but to the permanent power of being that holds finitude in existence and on which all things are absolutely dependent.

The Christian concept of creation contrasts with some Deist views that God built the world system and left it to run on its own, so to speak. Such a distant and uninvolved God is not the object of Jewish and Christian faith or discourse in the Bible. Rather, God "creator" means God always actually "creating." But at the same time, that which God creates is other than God. Creation is not some form of emanation of the divine that ultimately entails pantheism. Various concepts have been adopted to distinguish and relate the influence of God's causality to intraworldly causality, such as the primary causality of God as distinct from the whole system of secondary causes that are observable. But the coherence of such distinctions is less important than the fundamental experience and conviction that God must be the power behind all powers—the power of being itself that holds reality off from the void of non-being.

What is it that God was wrought in the creation of the human? Before providing an answer to that question in a paragraph, let me explain how one might attempt such a thing. I presume that ultimately the human is a mystery just short of the mystery of God. The mystery of human existence provides much more workable data, but it still remains impenetrable in its ultimate why and wherefore. As a product of history, the meaning of the human will not be complete until the end. The arena within which this history unfolds and in which the human is to be understood has so vastly expanded in terms of time and space that humanity seems dwarfed in the cosmos; the many sciences that study the human continually reveal new dimensions. It can only be with a sense of absolute humility that one points to what God through time has created in the human: namely, spirit, whose very nature is freedom. This idea is consistent in the Christian theological tradition of the West and finds a clear modern proponent in Karl Rahner (1978, 26–39).

The symbol "spirit" points negatively to non-matter; this is manifested primarily to human existence itself as self-consciousness. That which distinguishes the human is the power of reflection, the ability to bend back upon the self and know the self as knower. The human "knows it knows." The grounding meaning of freedom, then, is not choice (cf. Kleindorfer, chap. 6 in this book) or even existential commitment, although these important dimensions do help define it more fully. Rather, I use freedom here as a symbol that runs parallel with spirit and points to the defining characteristic of the human: self-transcendence. Far from being separable from matter or the physical in which it is embedded, human spirit—freedom—is the self-transcendence of matter itself, or matter transcending itself as self-conscious knowing and willing.

The doctrine that God creates reality implies that there is no "space" between God and the physical world. This conception spills over into anthropology: God is a direct and immediate presence to human existence. For Edward Schillebeeckx, finitude and contingency are the inherent characteristics of creation. They are not negativities to be transcended: ". . . we do not need altogether to transcend our contingent or finite nature and to escape from it or regard it as a flaw" (Schillebeeckx 1983, 93). God is present to finitude; creation is creation out of nothing, and this means that nothing lies between creation and the Creator. God is totally present to creation: "From a Christian perspective, the world and man are totally other than God, but within the presence of the creator God" (93). The view of the God–world relationship depicted here could be called "panentheism," signifying that all creation subsists within the power and personal presence of God who sustains it, while remaining other than God. This provides the radical ontological basis for the symbol and language of God as Spirit at work in the world. The fuller doctrine of God represents God as personal, benevolent, and loving, the active lover of what God has created out of love. No other divine motive can account for creation except self-transcending or altruistic love. God is present not only in power but also in love, a personal love that is appropriate to personal creatures. The doctrine of creation by a loving creator entails a divine will for human flourishing and fulfillment.

To conclude: this symbol of creation can overcome the various dichotomies between the so-called different orders of creation and redemption, or the natural and the supernatural, that have so plagued the Christian imagination over the centuries. The meaning of God as lover of humanity, or savior, or redeemer are all entailed in the conception of God as loving creator. No reason necessarily demands a distinction between a natural and a supernatural relation of God to humanity, as many theologians today deny such a distinction as affirm it. This does not mean that such a distinction is incoherent and yet useful at some points. We may regard these as alternative theoretical frameworks, each of which has a coherent logic highlighting different particular aspects of the God–human relationship. But given the very history of how such a distinction has narrowed the Christian vision, the expansive power of the doctrine of God as creating Spirit, by contrast, seems to promise a world of new meaning.

Sin

Despite the positive creative power of the Creator, creation is marked by finitude and headed toward death. More will be said in response to those features further on. What is of concern here is that human existence also seems intrinsically marked by an inability to "get it right." One cannot avoid the doctrine of sin. This symbol, too, points to ultimate mystery, but I want only to draw two points forward: sin infects freedom itself on a personal level; but even more powerfully, sin as social wraps individual human freedom in a near total bondage.

The symbol of sin refers not to objective evil; rather, as Augustine and more recently Paul Ricoeur have shown, it points to a condition of human freedom itself prior to the exercise of choice and decision. The term "original" has several specific references, but let it stand here for this a priori character which I will discuss broadly on a personal and then on a social level, although these two dimensions of human freedom cannot be separated.

In the course of his life, Augustine developed a full-blown doctrine of sin, especially in his controversies with Pelagius and the Pelagians in the last twenty years of his life. But earlier, in the late 390s C.E., when he was engaged in writing his Confessions, one can observe him wrestling with the mystery of sin's manifestation in the will itself. The spiritual will can move the body; the will commands and the hand obeys. But the will cannot will itself; spirit does not obey but resists itself (Augustine 1991, VIII, 8, 10). Paul's words struck home: "I do not understand my own actions. For I do not do what I want, but I do the very thing that I hate" (Rom. 7:15). Augustine's introspective phenomenology of the mechanism showed that this inability to transcend the self affected the will itself: spirit, or will so to speak, curved back and in on itself, unable to transcend a clinging self-interest. Over time, the inner self buttressed itself with the muscle of habit, and custom, and reflexive response. The self continued to enjoy freedom of choice, for this is the elemental self-transcendence that is constituted with the human as such: the human as spirit is a freedom that can self-consciously choose. But it lacked what Augustine called liberty, the desire for truth and value outside and above the self (cf. Williams and Barber, chap. 4, and Cameron, chap. 13, both in this book) and requiring self-transcendence of a different sort: transcendence of a concern for the self. Spirit was thus trapped within the prison of self-interest. Freud and the discipline of psychology have given us a fuller language to characterize what Augustine referred to on a psychological level. Yet for Augustine himself, the distinction of freedom from liberty was a matter of putting the human self in a right relationship with ultimate reality.

But an even higher wall confines the human spirit. It may be called, paradoxically, social sin. Social sin consists in an arrangement of a society or culture in which one or more groups of people are systemically excluded, oppressed, or violated in their humanity. Such a situation is evil because it diminishes or destroys human being as measured against the intrinsic value of the human person. It is sin because we know that ultimately the arrangement of society depends on human freedom and can be changed. In other words, human beings are responsible for this situation. But, precisely, this responsibility is social and not individual. The paradox consists in sharing some measure of responsibility for a social situation, as a member of a society, while not having any individual freedom or power relative to the same situation. Frequently, this intrinsic tension is either not experienced or simply denied in highly individualistic cultures.

How can such social sin be diagnosed since moral and ethical standards are precisely socially determined? One such way is through a negative experience of contrast, a corporate moral perception borrowed from social theorists and described by Schillebeeckx (1990, 5–6). Such an experience is like a corporate intuition in which a person, but more importantly a group, comes to the intuitive realization that a certain situation is simply wrong because it appears implicitly against the background of something like a Platonic idea or ideal of what can and should be. Such experiences can be quite powerful, as in the reaction against the Holocaust, against racism in the United States, against systemic poverty in much of the Third World, against a system that discriminates against women (see Hirschmann, chap. 9 in this book), and so on. Although such systems rest on the stuff of socially organized freedom, not an individual's freedom, still the individual person is through and through socially constructed and thus becomes part of the system. The helplessness of the individual before various groups and society at large indicates how society and culture can constitute structures constricting human freedom and closing off transcendence in the person's disposal of the self (cf. Cameron, chap, 13). This analysis of sin helps to provide a context within which the notion of salvation can be meaningful.

Salvation

The symbol of salvation refers to the flourishing wholeness that the doctrine of creation affirms is the will of the creator. It seems thwarted on two levels: in this world, human freedom seems to be held in a bondage of sin and self-interest that prevents both personal and social fulfillment. On a broader scale, finitude and death threaten existence itself with final annihilation and senseless insignificance. I deal with these two aspects under the two symbols "salvation" and "heaven," the latter being an aspect and projection of the former. The meaning of salvation has been portrayed as liberation: liberation in this world, discussed in this section, and final or eschatological liberation, discussed in the next section.

The Christian symbol of salvation draws its meaning from the basic religious questions of why human existence is at all and what it is for. So dense and illusive are these questions that more and more people are simply surrendering to their mystery and giving up any attempt at an answer. Yet because of their basic and comprehensive character, they continue to press in and call our own existence into question. In fact, one cannot avoid answering to such questions because human behavior itself carries a conscious or unconscious response. Christians are unanimous in looking to Jesus of Nazareth for an answer. But no single construal of that answer rules the rest. What follows is one interpretation among several. It attempts to be responsive to the problems raised in the first part of the discussion.

I had begun with the principle that if Jesus is to be considered as relevant for all, he must reveal something that is going on universally in the world. Application of this premise to the question of what Jesus did for human salvation militates against reading that salvation as a transaction that Jesus negotiated with God in a point of time to the advantage of his disciples. It can also shift the way one conceives the relevance of Jesus. Instead of considering his earthly career as a particular transaction with God, one may regard it as a concrete symbol revealing the intrinsic character of the primal relation between God and human existence. From this perspective one would read in the actual teaching, ministry, and final outcome of Jesus a pattern revelatory of God, human existence, and the relationship between them. Jesus saves by revealing what is going on generally in the world and in history, from the beginning. This outlook in broad terms is found in John's gospel where Jesus is presented as revealer of God; this perspective serves well to open up the revelatory power of Jesus and his message. It provides a palpable possibility for all people to read in them, as in a classic, a direct relevance to their own actual experience. The task of Christian theology in such a framework would be to analyze how Jesus reveals salvation going on within human freedom itself on both the personal and social levels.

On the level of individual persons, salvation may be construed as liberation of human freedom from internal bondage of various forms of egoism and the release of freedom toward altruistic values. Jesus reveals that God as Spirit is at work in human hearts opening up freedom closed in upon itself through self-transcending love. I turn once again to Augustine for an analysis of this phenomenon because he addresses it at a primal level. No one analyzed more minutely or brilliantly the logic of grace than the dour theologian of sin. Most people are partially scandalized when they ask the question: Why is there evil in the world? Why, especially, do human beings prey upon each other? Augustine reversed the question: "From what source is there in people the love of God and of one's neighbor" (Augustine 1948, 763)? Given the sin of the world, one has to marvel at the phenomenon of genuine self-transcending love. Where does it come from?

In the light of this second question, he analyzed the human condition in the following way: everyone has the power to choose freely. But from where comes the liberty that allows one to break out of self-enclosure in a delight for what is of transcendent value or truth? For Augustine, this could be only from the power of God as Spirit at work within the human spirit, illumining the mind with attraction and empowering the will to action. "It is certain that it is we that will when we will, but it is He who makes us will what is good. . . . It is certain that it is we that act when we act; but it is He who makes us act, by applying efficacious powers to our will" (1948, 759–760). For Augustine the first time this happens marks the beginning of an "ascent" toward absolute truth, goodness, and being. What is absolutely crucial for our times, however, is that we be more faithful to Augustine's primitive intuition than he was. For Augustine, the drama of salvific grace was relatively rare, and where it seemed to occur outside the Christian sphere, he considered it a mere illusion. The virtues of the pagans only appeared to be such. In effect, he underestimated the universal scope of the revelation in Jesus Christ. On the basis of the universal relevance of Jesus Christ, one should be open to seeing the power of God's grace more abundantly, indeed universally, in individual human life.

On the social level, salvation is no less real and can be discerned as operative within or through various forms of human solidarity that enhance the freedom of groups, and support a common good. In other words, social grace or social salvation is the negative image of social sin: it negates the negation. In themselves, social structures appear as inanimate things, as routinized patterns of human behavior. But they rest on freedom and they canalize it in specific directions. They act as a kind of second material nature that materializes, or concretizes, action of the human spirit and will. In the measure in which these structures build up and nourish the common good, they bear the marks of gratuity and come as gift; as such the religious imagination construes them as grace, as salvation. In this view of salvation, Jesus of Nazareth is not considered as its efficient cause but as its revealer or exemplary cause, a view that among others is supported by the New Testament. Jesus promised that the power of God's Spirit would work in groups and communities. The kingdom of God that Jesus preached is precisely a symbol for social grace and social salvation. The kingdom of God is also that for which Christians pray with the prayer that Jesus taught his disciples. It is an object of prayer because ultimately peace and reconciliation in justice in this world is a gift that transcends human ability. Few leaders in the world today would fail to recognize that every breakthrough of reconciliation and peace is a "blessing" which has to be embraced in gratitude. All who long for social grace and salvation and accept it in gratitude when it appears in fragments are implicitly praying.

How did Jesus save? As revealer, Jesus preached and actually mediated in his ministry the kingdom of God. This means that Jesus is an invitation to look for this process going on within the whole of human life and history. Movements aimed at advancing justice, reconciliation, and peace in the world, at resisting social suffering, have a sacrality marked with religious depth. They can hardly be taken for granted.

Heaven

The second aspect of salvation points to an ultimate or final salvation in an end time. It is symbolized by "heaven" and its equivalents. As an eschatological symbol, heaven expresses and appeals to hope. Heaven is not a place, since the sphere of God—whatever it may be— precisely transcends this finite place. People do not spend time in heaven, because eternity precisely transcends time. Rather, heaven is a symbol for the sphere of God into which Jesus was raised; it gives direction to human conscience, mediates openness to an absolute future, and offers an "object" of hope.

It is important that there be clarity about the epistemology of faith and hope. Neither faith nor hope is the equivalent of knowledge; although both have cognitive aspects. William James has documented a certain cognitive immediacy to religious experience that is self-validating (James 1963, 55–74). Hope is that same religious experience reaching into the future. Although the future remains absolutely unknown, it is imagined or constructed on the basis of a projection of faith experience in the present. Hope for the future can only have meaning that is based on faith that is rooted in contemporary religious experience. Although hope lacks the clarity of the religious experience of faith in the present, it lives off the latter's conviction and shares in its realism. For historical beings, in fact, some form of hope is just as necessary for human existence as is faith; one cannot live without some form of faith and hope, for each is integral to the elemental self-transcendence that defines human existence as such. All human beings live on the basis of some faith into some future hoped for, even when that faith is unknown to them and only betrayed by their actions (see Cameron, chap. 13, on Kierkegaard and Abraham's seemingly paradoxical—unquestioning—faith).

On this logic, heaven and its equivalents—the kingdom of God, for example—have two functions, and both are essential to the salvation of human freedom. The one has to do with the eschatological future, the other with the role of that future in life today.

The first function is to express the final fulfillment of human freedom in the absolute future. That meaning includes but ultimately transcends the fulfillment of my personal freedom. Since we are social creatures whose existence and fulfillment are unimaginable outside of social relationships, our ultimate salvation must be a social reality. It must also be real and comprehensive, drawing the whole of human life up into itself. Lacking either reality or comprehensiveness, it would not be ultimate salvation. Salvation in the absolute future, in order to be such, must draw the present and the past into a wider horizon of meaning that promises to redeem the negation of life, the innocent suffering, the evil of the whole past, present, and temporal future into absolute meaning. The alternative? Total meaninglessness, and only the fool hopes for the death of meaning.

But hope in heaven and the ultimate kingdom of God has another function without which it would be an opiate. Jesus' life and ministry did not sedate. Rather, this utopian symbol and vision of resurrection bends back from the absolute future to criticize life in this world, life in its sinful actuality. Jesus Christ saves by being the catalyst for the negative experience of contrast that simultaneously unmasks sin and reveals what can and should be. The absolute future of heaven measures finitude as finitude, not as an absolute in any of its forms; it deabsolutizes the finite and the relative and unmasks idolatry in all its many guises. It also judges sin as sin; not as what ought, or has, to be. And, finally, it empowers resistance to evil with the promise of coherent meaning which, in the measure in which it is absolute by the promise and power of God, is also saving.

God entrusts history to human creativity. The Christian humanist asks why God would have created human freedom if God did not trust it. Jesus is an expression of God's trust and the proper human response. And Jesus' resurrection is testimony that God's trust will not be put to shame: "In Jesus, both God's trust in man and man's response of trust in God take on their definitive historical form" (Schillebeeckx 1981, 109). In Jesus, one sees God's entrustment to human freedom of the struggle against evil. Jesus is to be interpreted as "the man in whom the task of creation has been successfully accomplished, albeit in conditions of the history of suffering. The consequence of this is that trust in this man is the specific form of belief in God, creator of heaven and earth, who reposes unconditional trust in man through his active creation[: w]ithout this divine trust in man, creation would in fact make no sense" (111).

In sum, these four symbols are interlocking, and when they are construed as they have been presented here, they meet the four challenges to their credibility. Setting the Christian story of salvation firmly within the framework of a theology of creation overcomes the various possible and actual dichotomies that people have set up between a natural and a supernatural order. Such a distinction, while surely possible, is not at all necessary. A unitary, theocentric framework of the creator God bent in love on human salvation conveys more clearly the power and the universal relevance of the Christian story of salvation. It is true that sin pervades the whole of human history from the beginning: there is no break between a before and an after and no ultimate explanation for its existence. But in no way does sin become the focus of the Christian imagination. Sin is the pervasive background, the context, the situation in which human existence must make its way, but the nature and goal of this existence is the freeing of freedom from the bonds of sin for creativity. Creation means that God is in God's world and human existence unfolds in this one—ours. Resisting and overcoming suffering in this world is the human task: "It is not a matter for God, except that this task is performed in his absolute presence and therefore is a human concern which also is close to his heart" (Schillebeeckx 1983, 96). Salvation, then, is not an event that happened all at once, but a process that has been going on with the dawn of creation and the appearance of the human species. God as Spirit is the within of cosmogenesis, the immanent power of being in the development of the human, and the personal presence of God to a human self-transcendence that can respond to God's presence by responding to the suffering of God's creatures. This is the potentially universal dialogue which is revealed in the life and ministry of Jesus. Salvation, which symbolizes the fulfillment of human existence, is no private reserve of any religion but the inner telos of creation itself, in Christian language called the eschaton and designated by Jesus the kingdom of God.

The question of whether this salvation should be the public language of a society cannot be answered in the abstract. There is simply no formula that can regulate the relation of all religions to all societies. But it is just as sure that the energy released by the Christian symbol of salvation is not private and that in its authentic form necessarily it has a bearing on the way society works. The problem arises not with religion but with hegemony in a pluralistic society. But the Christian view of salvation offered here clearly indicates that the power of salvation is going on in religions other than the various forms of Christianity and that in principle they have an equal voice on public affairs. Centering Christian salvation in creation makes its representation in different religions, again in principle, noncompetitive.

The four symbols of creation, sin, salvation, and heaven form the spine of the Christian vision of reality. Albeit their ultimate credibility depends on the degree to which the whole body of ordinary Christians actually redeem ultimate meaning for human freedom from an alternative of sheer contingency by the way they live.

References

Anselm (1970) "Why God Became Man?" in Eugene R. Fairweather, Editor and Translator, *A Scholastic Miscellany: Anselm to Ockham*, New York: Macmillan.

Aquinas, Thomas (1990) *The Summa Theologica*, Chicago: Encyclopedia Britannica. (References by part, question, and article.)

Athanasius (1954) "On the Incarnation of the Word," in Edward R. Hardy, Editor, in collaboration with Cyril C. Richardson, *Christology of the Later Fathers*, Philadelphia: Westminster Press.

Augustine (1948) "On Grace and Free Will," in Whitney Oats, *Basic Writings of Saint Augustine*, vol. 1, New York: Random House.

——— (1963) *The Trinity*, Washington, DC: Catholic University of America Press.

——— (1991) *Confessions*, Introduction by Henry Chadwick, Translator, New York and Oxford: Oxford University Press. (Reference by book and chapter.)

Dionysius the Areopagite (1987) "The Ecclesiastical Hierarchy," in Colm Luibheid, Editor, *Pseudo-Dionysius: The Complete Works*, New York: Paulist Press.

Gadamer, Hans-Georg (1982) *Truth and Method*, New York: Crossroad.

James, William (1963) *The Varieties of Religious Experience: A Study in Human Nature*, New York: Vintage Books/Library of America.

Rahner, Karl (1978) *Foundations of Christian Faith: An Introduction to the Idea of Christianity*, New York: Seabury Press.

Ricoeur, Paul (1960) *The Symbolism of Evil*, Boston: Beacon Press.

——— (1974) *The Conflict of Interpretations*, Evanston, IL: Northwestern University Press.

Schillebeeckx, Edward (1981) *Interim Report on the Books Jesus & Christ*, New York: Crossroad.

——— (1983) *God Among Us: The Gospel Proclaimed*, New York: Crossroad.

——— (1990) *Church: The Human Story of God*, New York: Crossroad.

Tracy, David (1984) "Part II," in Robert Grant with David Tracey, *A Short History of the Interpretation of the Bible*, pp. 149–187, Philadelphia: Fortress Press.

9

Theorizing Freedom

Nancy J. Hirschmann

Any question about the political, ethical, aesthetic, or moral significance of freedom must start with what the term means. Within my own field of political theory, the definition of freedom has been under serious and protracted contention. At least since C. B. Macpherson's (1962) creative Marxist reading of Enlightenment social contract theory was published, many political theorists have been skeptical of Enlightenment claims of the natural freedom and equality supposedly sitting at the heart of liberal and democratic theory. Macpherson argued that Enlightenment theorists such as Locke in essence defined freedom for the propertied classes at the expense of oppression for the poor. This economic freedom was put in terms of the political language of rights; indeed, some of those rights were to intangible ideals such as freedom of religion. But as scholars of the eighteenth century have maintained, property was always linked to such less tangible ideals. In England, for instance, freedom of religion was tied to fear that a Catholic monarch would confiscate private property (Ashcraft 1986; Schochet 2000).

Feminists, Marxists, and critical race theorists have created parallel arguments to assert that "freedom" is defined within dominant discourses specifically for economically privileged heterosexual white men. They seek an extension and even a refiguring of the concept to apply to their experiences of exclusion and oppression (Brown 1995; Cohen 1995). The tension such arguments suggest between theoretical understandings of freedom and the political reality of unfreedom suggests that the importance of defining freedom extends across the political and intellectual spectrum. How freedom is conceptualized, as well as how its conceptualizations are deployed, is a core question of political theory and theoretical politics. It is a core goal of all historically excluded groups, who identify themselves as victims of "oppression" (ending which, by definition, requires some form of "liberation"). It may also be significant that such groups (notwithstanding popular misreadings of some feminist work as urging women's superiority over men) advocate equality and democracy as preconditions for that freedom. It is important to remember the dynamics of such political struggles and theoretical debates as we theorize freedom.

Defining Freedom

The most common definition of freedom was articulated by Isaiah Berlin, as "negative liberty," which consists in an absence of external constraints. The individual is free to the extent that she is not restrained by external forces, primarily viewed as law, physical force, and other overt coercion. For instance, if I decided to change my mind about contributing to this volume and our editor locked me in my office until I wrote my chapter, he would be restricting my freedom. As Berlin puts it, "By being free in this sense I mean not being interfered with by others. . . . The wider the area of non-interference, the wider my freedom." On this conception of freedom, restraints come from outside the self, they are "other"; other people's participation in "frustrating my wishes" is the relevant criterion in determining restraint (Berlin 1971, 123).

Furthermore, these wishes which I must be allowed to pursue are seen as coming from me and from me alone. Desires may be reactions to external stimuli, of course; I may not want to write the essay because someone offered me money not to or because of a sudden anxiety about my writing. But the source of my desire does not matter to negative liberty. Rather, the important fact is that I can identify a desire as mine, regardless of why I have it. Negative liberty draws clear-cut lines between inner and outer, self and other, subject and object: desires come from within, restraints from without; desires are formed by subjects, by selves, they are thwarted by objects, by others.

This may pretty much seem to cover what is commonly understood as freedom: not being prevented from doing what we want. And it is this major conception of freedom that underwrites Enlightenment political thought. Seventeenth-century British thinker Thomas Hobbes, for one—despite his authoritarian solution to the philosophical dangers posed by the very real political dangers of civil war—is often cited as the classic proponent of negative liberty: "By liberty, is understood, according to the proper signification of the word, the absence of external impediments: which impediments, may oft take away part of man's power to do what he would" (Hobbes 1985, 189). And in chapter 21 of *Leviathan*, again: "Liberty, or freedom, signifieth (properly) the absence of Opposition; (by Opposition, I mean external Impediments of motion)" (261). Hobbes's definition of freedom as the absence of "external impediments" started from a founding assumption of radically individualist beings, each of whom seek their continual motion, fulfilling "a perpetuall and restlesse desire of Power after power, that ceaseth onely in Death" (161). The problem with the state of nature, in Hobbes's view, was precisely that others could obstruct your motion; what the social contract did was to impose its own obstacles to prevent people from interfering with other people's motion and thereby facilitate free movement in particular directions.

To many modern eyes, Hobbes presented a somewhat convoluted understanding of freedom—fear was not considered an impediment, for instance, so that giving a thief my wallet when he is holding a gun to my head is done "freely"—which is why some tend to argue that negative liberty has gotten, unfairly, a bad rap through its direct association with Hobbes.[1] But others, such as Richard Flathman (1987), fiercely hang onto the Hobbesean legacy and rightly point out that the fundamental principles of negative liberty and the basic understanding of liberty as being left alone by other people, have their clearest articulation in Hobbes's formulation.

Locke's somewhat more familiar, even esoteric, ideal of freedom, based on rights and equal respect for rights founded in the laws of nature, tempered Hobbes's extremist philosophy. Locke recognized that fear could inhibit freedom, so he posited a less chaotic and less conflicting natural state for mankind. Moreover, whereas Hobbes suggested that government was the solution to the problem of freedom, since it reigned in the unruly appetites of one's fellows, Locke envisioned the ideal of freedom as a realm protected not only by government from the interference of others but from government as well. Writing at the time of the Exclusion Crisis controversy,[2] Locke wrote

---

1. My discussion of the modern canonical theorists' relationship to the typology of negative and positive liberty borrows from, and is further elaborated in, *Gender, Class, and Freedom in Modern Political Theory* (Hirschmann 2008).
2. The Exclusion Crisis refers to a bill sponsored by Locke's patron, the Earl of Shaftsbury, to exclude the Catholic James II (the brother of the sitting Charles II) from the line of succession to the throne of England. A Catholic monarchy was feared for, among other things, its presumed allegiance to Rome, including potential confiscation of property, and its tendency to absolutism, following on the model of France's Louis XIV. See Ashcraft (1986) for a complete account of the political intrigue surrounding this bill.

against the danger of absolute monarchy; for him the biggest threat to freedom was "Absolute, Arbitrary Power" (Locke 1963, 324), namely, the power of an authoritarian government. The social contract and rule of law were seen to protect against such power; though they limited our freedom to some extent, they ended up enlarging it much more significantly, through more effectively practicable liberty.

But Locke nevertheless similarly defined liberty by means of the notion of leaving other people alone to do what they want; "To understand Political Power right," he maintained, "we must consider what State all Men are naturally in, and that is *a State of perfect Freedom* to order their Actions, and dispose of their Possessions, and Persons as they think fit, within the bounds of the Law of Nature, without asking leave, or depending upon the Will of any other Man" (Locke 1963, 309). The conditional phrase, "within the bounds of the laws of nature," is, of course, significant, as this proviso restricted individuals' freedom to kill or injure others, except in self-defense; to take more than one could use; or to violate the dictates of reason. The ostensible reason for such limitations was to prevent people from injuring others in their enjoyment of life, liberty, and the pursuit of property, these three things being so entwined with each other for Locke that they are difficult to conceptualize independently: property was necessary to life, and hence was the most important liberty that humans had a right to pursue, since it involved expressing the essence of humanity in the form of labor, or "property in the person." Locke suggests a more social understanding of human nature and of freedom, within a framework of negative liberty. The idea of "equal liberty" assumed that, if everyone were to be free, then the only way to avoid Hobbes's anarchic state of nature, and the absolutist social contract that it called for, would require introducing into human culture a greater understanding of the fundamental need for human association and of the paradoxical need to get along with others if one is to be left alone to do what one wants.

John Stuart Mill, of course, demonstrated the culmination of this principle of "equal liberty." He stated explicitly that only harm to others, specifically to their liberty, could ever justify interference—whether by other individuals or by the state—with my freedom to do what I want. Like Hobbes and Locke, Mill often is considered to offer the classic notion of negative liberty; Berlin, in fact, draws on him explicitly several times when formulating this conception, much more than the social contract theorists have. One of the key themes in Mill's *On Liberty* is the importance placed on the ability of people to pursue their desires and to act as they wish, without interference from other people or by the government. "The struggle between Liberty and Authority" and "the nature and limits of the power which can be legitimately exercised by society over the individual" constitute the central theme of this book (Mill 1992, 5). By focusing on conscience, thought, and speech as the essential dimensions of human freedom, Mill operates from an exceedingly individualist notion of the subject and individual desire. The essence of the individual lies in the mind, in the private realm of thought and conscience, which no other person is entitled to—or, indeed, even *can*—affect or restrict.[3]

Furthermore, this means that we are all different and have different ideas. We therefore must be allowed to explore and express those ideas, which are the essence of our difference and uniqueness. Mill valorizes the "eccentric" simply because difference is so vital to the productive confluence and interaction of ideas, an interaction that in turn stimulates individual mental processes. Similarly, he loathes the mediocre masses who conform to common opinion and fail to think for themselves, for this gives way to the antithesis of individual liberty, the tyranny of the majority. "The danger which threatens human nature," he writes, "is not the excess but the deficiency, of personal impulses and preferences" (Mill 1992, 68). The need to be independent and different, to think for oneself, is for Mill the essence of human liberty, suggesting an extreme liberal individualism: "The only freedom which deserves the name, is that of pursuing our own good in our own way, so long as we do not attempt to deprive others of theirs" (17).

Not being prevented from doing what I want by intentional agents may seem a straightforward conception of freedom. But it masks deeper complexities about the nature of desire and of what constitutes prevention. Certainly desires change in different social and political contexts. For example, two hundred years ago, nobody could have desired to be a bio-informaticist because no such field existed. But the meaning of "restraint" can also alter. The disability rights movement, the feminist movement, and the civil rights movement have identified certain physical customs like stairs, or social practices like segregation, which were previously seen as natural or inevitable parts of the social landscape but are now seen as "barriers" to freedom. The idea that freedom

---

3. This includes "The liberty of expressing and publishing opinions" which is "almost of as much importance as the liberty of thought itself, and resting in great part on the same reasons, as practically inseparable from it" (Mill 1992, 16–17).

means being able to do what I want is thus complex, socially located, and historically specific.

Such complexity suggests that negative liberty is not the only conception of freedom that underwrites liberal democracy. Another strand of freedom, what Berlin called "positive liberty," also plays a significant role. Positive liberty is a controversial concept. Some theorists have gone so far as to maintain that positive liberty is not a conception of liberty at all (Flathman 1987). Such objections sacrifice accuracy for the sake of false clarity, however, as if ruling out the messy complications of human desire by definitional fiat is the only meaningful way of dealing with them.

Positive liberty expands on negative liberty in three ways. First, as its name implies, it requires positive provision of the conditions necessary to take advantage of negative liberties, such as providing wheelchair access to buildings, or offering scholarships for education. Adopting a more contextual and communal notion of the self, positive liberty views individual conditions such as disability, or social conditions such as poverty, as barriers to freedom that can be overcome by positive action, or through the provision of appropriate conditions that the individual cannot accomplish on her own.

I think this is also in keeping with everyday understandings of freedom; for instance, many people would agree that the freedom to get an education is rather hollow if you cannot afford tuition or get into the classroom. But positive liberty also focuses on what might be called "internal barriers": fears, addictions, compulsions, or disabilities can inhibit my freedom because they are at odds with my "true" self. This introduces difficult psychological questions that involve qualitative evaluation about our desires, which can be higher or lower, genuine or false. Because of this, it is once again not enough to experience an absence of external restraints, since the immediate desires I have may frustrate my true will. For instance, if I am trying to quit smoking, but an argument with a colleague makes me crave a cigarette, positive libertarians maintain that by giving in to that spontaneous urge, I violate my true desire and make myself unfree.

Of course, this also involves the strong possibility that others may know my true will better than I do, particularly when I am in the grip of these self-destructive desires: as you snatch the cigarette from my mouth, you preserve me from my false desire and enhance my liberty. This is often called the "second guessing" problem, because others claim to know what you want better than you do yourself (Taylor 1979).

It is the most troubling aspect of positive liberty: the determination of my will by others and particularly by the state. The classic example is Rousseau's notion of "general will"; since the laws embody my true will, he says, when I am forced to obey the law I am only "forced to be free"(Rousseau 1973, 177). His concept of moral freedom, "obedience to a law we prescribe to ourselves" (178), distinguishes "true freedom" from the idea of "natural liberty" that characterizes Berlin's negative conception. And it has been the source of much Rousseau-bashing in the name of antitotalitarianism. Rousseau's vision of moral liberty and idea of forcing us to be free may too easily be taken to foreshadow the double-speak of communist dictatorship that Berlin's critique of positive liberty harshly attacks. What critics of positive liberty miss, however, is the more important idea of an individual's capacity for conflicting desires and a divided will: I may want one thing as a citizen who has to obey the law, but quite another as a law-making member of the polity. That, clearly, is the sentiment behind the conclusion that the addicted smoker is "unfree." I really want to quit smoking, but the stress is pushing me to cheat. I really want Social Security to be around when I retire, but I do not want to pay higher taxes now to make it solvent.

Such a notion is hardly totalitarian, as critics often charge. In liberal democracy, values like the rule of law and due process often "force" us to acknowledge that adherence to rules and procedures is sometimes in our true long-term interest even when doing so undermines our immediate or apparent interests. Preserving the architectural structure of democracy in which freedom is possible sometimes must supersede doing what you want.[4] The notion that desires can conflict, that this conflict of desires betokens multiple selves contained within us, is key to Rousseau's theory, which posits a highly malleable theory of human nature. His *Émile* is unabashedly concerned with the production of a young boy into a man, who will be a virtuous citizen. Émile is carefully taught many different kinds of lessons by his tutor, who continually seeks to manipulate his pupil into adopting the values that the tutor promotes, while thinking they are his own. Thus, although it might appear that the virtuous man is naturally good, he is, in fact, a very careful product of education and character formation: today we might say that he is "socially constructed."

---

4. Indeed, some theorists interpret Rousseau's infamous phrase as meaning no more than that (Mostov 1992; Pateman 1985). In my view such a position is just as blindfolded, for ignoring Rousseau's conception of a divided will, as does Berlin's own somewhat facile dismissal of Rousseau as totalitarian.

Similarly, although Rousseau is frequently excoriated by feminists for his rather perverse account of women's "nature," he takes a social constructivist approach to women as well: in Paris, where women truss their children and pass them off to nurses, so they can flirt with men in the salons, vice runs rampant. The environment in which they live, with its bawdy theaters, immodest dress fanning men's passions, and the free intermingling of men and women in the salons, is bound to produce women who are corrupt, incapable of doing their one true civic duty, which is raising children and being good wives. By contrast, in the pure, uncorrupted country, women are more virtuous. They are not "naturally" so, however; just as Parisian women are corrupt in response to the environment in which they live, so is the young woman Sophie virtuous because her parents have done such a good job bringing her up. As Sophie herself puts it, "O my mother, why have you made virtue too loveable for me? If I can love nothing but virtue, the fault is less mine than yours" (Rousseau 1979, 405). Men and women have multiple possibilities inherent in their nature, Rousseau suggests, some good, some bad. Different inclinations will be developed in different contexts. So, he says, you had better be careful about the social context that you create if you want virtuous citizens. The point of virtuous social institutions is to encourage the good qualities and repress the bad ones. That is what his social contract tries to do, create a particular political and social context for the creation and sustenance of citizens.

This social constructivist theme is evident in other canonical thinkers, even those traditionally allied with classic negative liberty, such as Hobbes and Locke, who pay considerable attention to the workings of the inner self and the construction of desire, even though they may not explicitly acknowledge that. Locke's writings on education as the construction of character, for instance, are quite similar to Rousseau's, as the production of gentlemen citizens depends vitally on the tutors' and parents' ability to impart, to the "white sheet" that children's minds and lives are, the "proper marks." As Tarcov (1984) notes, Locke's *Education* is concerned with character more than with scholarly subjects: children should eat little if any fruit or flesh, but only bread, water gruel, and flummery (a bland custard made from oatmeal); they should wear shoes that leak, to accustom them to wet feet; and obstinate children should be beaten "only" to the end of breaking their will and thereby saving them from themselves (Locke 1996). As harsh, if not bizarre, as many of Locke's recommendations sound to twenty-first-century ears, the point of such recommendations in Locke's view is not punitive, but rather to build health, mental discipline, reason, and strength of character. Locke repeatedly argues that attributes that we commonly ascribe to nature are really the result of habit; hence the goal of education, Locke argues, is to instill the correct habits in children so that their reason will develop properly. In subscribing to the "white paper" theory of mental development, Locke seems to be suggesting that preparing the canvas is at least as important as the paints one uses, if not more so.

In his more overtly political writings, particularly the *Two Treatises*, Locke similarly demonstrates the social constructivist elements of positive liberty. As a number of commentators have argued, Locke's theory of tacit consent seems to "guide" citizens into "choosing" things that are good for them, most specifically the social contract that he prescribes. Freedom is to do what I want "within the bounds of the law of nature"; but what about the many who do not understand what the law of nature requires? His arguments about the importance of "Right Reason," which the majority of the population do not have, pose serious problems for a theory of government based on consent. Tacit consent is Locke's way around this difficulty: by using the roads and living within the geographical boundaries of a government's jurisdiction, we tacitly consent to its authority. This is the way in which the unfree, unequal, and irrational majority—laborers, the poor, women—are ensured of making the right choices, more specifically, of having choices made for them, which they would agree were the right ones if they could only have the rationality to know it (Hirschmann 1992; Pateman 1985). Furthermore, in Locke's account of law, we can see the operation of what McClure (1996) refers to as his "architecture of order." As Locke puts it, "Law, in its true Notion, is not so much the Limitation as the direction of a free and intelligent Agent to his proper Interest, and prescribes no farther than is for the general Good of those under that Law. Could they be happier without it, the Law, as a useless thing would of itself vanish; and that ill deserves the Name of Confinement which hedges us in only from Bogs and Precipices. So that, however it may be mistaken, the end of Law is not to abolish or restrain but to preserve and enlarge Freedom . . . where there is no law there is no Freedom" (Locke 1963, 347–348).

The point of the social contract is to create a structure wherein those with "right reason"—the educated, certainly, who were often also those with property and at least fairly exclusively white males—would be empowered to make laws that the rest of the population were to obey. By and through this obedience, most people realize their true interests and thereby express their true freedom. In keeping with the worst aspects of positive liberty, Locke is concerned to make sure that people make the right choices, whether or not they realize what they are (cf. Haskelevich, this volume).

Similarly, Mill is seen by many as the paragon of liberal, negative liberty, with a very strong individualism; the freedom to pursue your own good in your own way. And yet, in *The Subjection of Women*, he explicitly acknowledges that theories of human nature are so much bunk. "What is now called the nature of women is an eminently artificial thing," he notes, "the result of forced repression in some directions, unnatural stimulation in others" (Mill 1992, 493): women are how they are because of a patriarchal culture that made them. Hence, if women are denied education on the basis that they are irrational, do not be surprised if they are not skilled at rational thinking; ideology (Cameron, this volume) determines the material conditions for choice, which produce the very effects usually claimed to found it (532). At the same time, however, Mill is not averse to some social construction himself, particularly in his theory of utility, where higher pleasures have greater utility than lower ones. And since not everyone is equally qualified to say which pleasures are higher and lower, society must be structured to give to those qualified more of a say in determining our choices, namely, to the better educated, who will be given additional votes in the electoral system; "better to be a human being dissatisfied than a pig satisfied; better to be Socrates dissatisfied than a fool satisfied" (140), Mill suggests, because some kinds of desires and preferences are more valuable than others. But the problem, as it was for Locke, is how to convince those fools that their satisfaction is inferior, that what they want is not really in their true interest. Here, too, education is one answer; in *On Liberty*, Mill proposed a state examination system that all children would take, with fines assessed against the fathers of children who did not score well. And in *On Representative Government*, Mill proposed a system of plural voting, where everyone received one vote, but some received more than one, based on an examination to determine levels of education.

Mill's own childhood education was extremely intense. Tutored at home by his father, he learned Greek, Latin, and mathematics at a very young age. He also had a nervous breakdown when he was sixteen years old, but this apparently did not shake his faith in extraordinary education; on the contrary, he believed that his father somehow had left out an essential aspect of education, namely, "sentiment" (Di Stefano 1991; Mill 1971). Mill saw in his own education nothing remarkable, neither an indication of any particular talents, nor a proof of high intelligence on his part: "what I could do could assuredly be done by any boy or girl of average capacity and healthy physical constitutions." Rather, the credit was to go to the time and attention his father took to bestow this education on him (Mill 1971, 65). Hence, an important point in Mill's *Autobiography* was to show "how much more than is commonly supposed" can be achieved through a more demanding education (41). Social construction did not simply reveal how some, such as women, were artificially stunted, but also suggested how many of them could be better than they are.

Of all the canonical freedom theorists, Hobbes would probably seem the most unlikely candidate for this social constructivist reading, for Hobbes seems to take a very strong, and harsh, view of human nature. For Hobbes, as Macpherson argues, men are "appetitive machines" seeking their perpetual motion. And yet Hobbes also maintains that in order for the sovereign to preserve his rights of dominion, he must educate his subjects so that they understand these rights, as well as understand why they are in their own interests. Law in and of itself is not enough to maintain the grounds of these rights; understanding those grounds is vital. For instance, Hobbes says, if I do not understand the logic of prohibitions against rebellion as necessary to my primary interest in peace and security, then I will seek to rebel whenever an opportunity presents itself. Accordingly, citizens are to be taught not to prefer a neighboring country's form of government; indeed, not "to desire change" of any kind; surely not to challenge or dispute the sovereign's power, and legalistic variations of the Ten Commandments in which God is not portrayed as a superior power to the sovereign (Hobbes 1985, 377, 380, 381).

Despite the apparent individualism of Hobbes's theory, and the importance to his understandings of freedom of being left alone to pursue what you want, Hobbes is as concerned as Locke and Rousseau with the substance of what people consent *to*, with the *content* of the choices that people make, and seeks to ensure that people make "the right choices." Like Locke's theory of tacit consent, which ensured that only good governments would be chosen by the majority of citizens whether they realize they are choosing it or not, Hobbes similarly structures his theory such that consent to government (preferably absolute monarchy) is logically compelled. Precisely because the state of nature is so "nasty, brutish, and short" (Hobbes, 1985, 186), Hobbes wants to make sure that the social contract is relatively airtight; accordingly, "as well he that *Voted for it*, as he that *Voted against it*" gives consent to the compact (229). I believe that this is because he, too, is concerned with the social construction of the choosing subject, of creating individuals who will choose what they "should" choose.

Hobbes's emphasis on law dovetails with this social constructivism, and demonstrates a jarring affinity with positive liberty. Hobbes sometimes characterizes law as a restriction on liberty, so that liberty "depend[s] on the silence of the law. . . . In cases where the Sovereign has prescribed no rule, there the Subject hath the liberty to do, or forbeare, according to his own discretion" (Hobbes, 1985, 271). At the same time, however, Hobbes seems to suggest that law is not a limitation on freedom at all, but rather the condition under which freedom is possible; "the use of Lawes . . . is not to bind the People from all Voluntary actions; but to direct and keep them in such a motion, as not to hurt themselves by their own impetuous desires, rashnesse, or indiscretion as Hedges are set, not to stop Travellers, but to keep them in the way" (388). Indeed, so consonant with liberty is law that Hobbes seems to reject outright the idea that law restricts liberty: "if we take Liberty, for an exemption from Lawes, it is no lesse absurd, for men to demand as they doe, that Liberty, by which all other men may be masters of their lives" (264); without law, Hobbes says, we would not in fact be free, but rather subject to the unpredictable wills of others.

In order for men to understand this, of course, they must be appropriately educated: Hobbes likens education to agriculture, "the labour bestowed on the earth is called culture; and the education of children, a culture of their minds" (Hobbes, 1985, 399). As any suburban homeowner knows, though, once pernicious weeds like kudzu get into the soil, they are difficult to eradicate; and if left alone, will destroy the flowers one wishes to grow. Thus the key task facing the Sovereign "is the rooting out from the consciences of men all those opinions which seem to justify, and give pretence of right to rebellious actions"—conscientious objection, civil disobedience, or holding the Sovereign to the law—ideas that contemporary Westerners associate with the freedoms granted by liberal democracy. But Hobbes derides these: they "have delivered nothing concerning morality and policy demonstratively; but being passionately addicted to popular government, have insinuated their opinions, by eloquent sophistry" (Hobbes 1994, 218).

"Unlearning" erroneous beliefs is a difficult task; "opinions which are gotten by education, and in length of time are made habitual, cannot be taken away by force, and upon the sudden: they must therefore be taken away also, by time and education." The challenge of unlearning pernicious education is to be met by the provision of proper education; "there is no doubt, if the true doctrine concerning the law of nature, and the properties of a body politic, and the nature of law in general, were perspicuously set down, and taught in the Universities, but that young men, who come thither void of prejudice, and whose minds are yet as white paper, capable of any instruction, would more easily receive the same, and afterward teach it to the people, both in books and otherwise, than now they do the contrary" (Hobbes 1994, 218). In other words, they should read Hobbes's own works.

The Social Construction of Freedom

Why is it important that these canonical freedom theorists employ social constructivist arguments? The notion of social construction is the third way in which positive liberty challenges negative liberty; its presence in these theories suggests that the way we have thought of freedom in the modern era as emerging from the Enlightenment is not as straightforward as we commonly think.[5] Social construction is the most important contribution that positive liberty makes to our very understanding of the concept, even though it is an aspect of freedom that largely goes unrecognized by political theory. It suggests that desire, will, and identity formation are so deeply social that the dichotomy between internal and external pervading Berlin's typology is itself challenged. It thereby moves the inquiry from asking *what* I want to *why* I want it; why do I have the desires I have? Why do I make the choices I do? If it is possible to say that we can have conflicting desires, and if it is possible to rank these desires as better or worse, then the issue of "who I am" comes into play: what *is* my true will, what *do* I really want? Social construction says that who I am and what I want are not natural, but the product of social, cultural, and historical forces and contexts. Even the "state of nature," these theories suggest, is a construction of theory that serves a particular historical, political, and cultural understanding of social relations. The desires and preferences we

5. My discussion here of social construction, and particularly how it relates to gender, borrows from and is further elaborated in *The Subject of Liberty: Toward a Feminist Theory of Freedom* (Hirschmann 2003).

have, our beliefs and values, our way of defining the world, and of conceiving ourselves as individuals are all shaped by the personal, institutional, and social relationships that constitute our individual and collective histories.

The question that social constructivism raises for freedom is, "where do desires come from?" Like the theory of adaptive preference formation, it acknowledges that desires are shaped by factors external to the self (Elster 1983). For instance, if women are forbidden to attend medical school, I might decide to be a nurse: my preference is shaped by available options, according to the theory of adaptive preferences. Social construction pushes on this a bit further, however, to consider the ways in which such preference adaptation impacts on the selfhood, identity, and subjectivity of the chooser. For instance, admissions policies barring women from medical school, by pushing them into nursing school, manage to construct a particular understanding of femininity. This understanding generates and complements social and cultural norms of gendered behavior that become as effective as the admissions policies themselves in keeping women out of medical school. So, changing policies—social constructivism suggests—would not in itself be enough to change women's desires. Patriarchy would already have done too good a job of colonizing women's desires, of convincing them that being doctors is not something that they can competently accomplish.

True, my example is overly simplified. Where would the impetus to change policy come from, if at least some women did not want to gain admission to medical school? Social constructions like gender are never completely determinative; as Urban and Hackney each suggest in this volume, desires can be constructed by agents themselves, against social forces. But at the same time, such large social forces, lacking clearly identifiable sources, are difficult to resist on the personal level: that a few women go to medical school does not necessarily alter the social definition of "woman." Even significant numbers of women in medical school might not affect categories of gender; after all, the majority of nurses are still women, and the majority of women medical students select pediatrics and "family medicine"—branches that are more compatible with family life than high-powered specialty branches such as cardiology or neurosurgery. Finally, the increased number of women doctors, and even the small and increasing influx of small numbers of men into nursing, have not changed the differential social evaluation of nurses as less important and less well paid than physicians, because—despite the slowly changing nature of the bodies occupying these positions—subject professions do retain their gender categorization coded as male and female. That some men "effeminate" themselves by becoming nurses, or that some of the women doctors thereby become "masculinized," does not alter the basics conducive to the underlying stereotypical configuration.

Social construction thus cannot be conceptualized in a direct cause and effect relationship, or as something that has clearly identifiable sources. But the larger point here is that social construction involves three different aspects of freedom. First, it sets the parameters for what choices are available: are women allowed to go to medical school or not? And why is it that scientists can fertilize an ovum in a test tube and select an embryo for implantation that has a specific genetic composition, even as millions of women worldwide are forced to bear unwanted children because of the lack of effective birth control and safe abortion? Why is it that we can go and explore Mars, at a time when diabetes, cancer, multiple sclerosis, and Alzheimer's disease still ravage the lives of millions? Oftentimes, we tend to accept the options that are available, without much questioning, as if we deemed the limitations we face to be a function of nature or of the inevitable limits of knowledge. Therefore we adapt our preferences according to what we think is available to us. But social construction requires us to consider "why" these, and not others, are available; and often, the answer is located in power.

Second, the social construction of choice involves the literal construction of desire. For instance, a woman's husband, mother, and friends can affect her interest in becoming a doctor, by displaying disapproval and guilt-invoking blame ("children need their mother," "who will cook dinner?"), or fear and anxiety about her competence ("you'll never make it through gross anatomy, it's so gory, you'll faint dead away"), not to mention the ways in which medical training is based on gendered assumptions of a male breadwinner (do not the rather arbitrary assignment of 36-hour residency shifts make childcare difficult?). None of these challenges can be seen as manipulation or coercion; they are simply the customary expression of gendered values, expectations, and assumptions that shape and formulate desire along the lines of gendered identity. Gender is the most obvious difference here—men are constructed to be agents, to be assertive and make decisions, whereas women are constructed as passive, unassertive, and deferential. But race and class are also relevant; as Liebow (1967) has shown, the effects of racism and poverty construct black men into individuals who fit the very stereotype that supposedly justifies racism and class discrimination. For instance, if contracting bosses pay their black employees only half the worth of their labor on the assumption that these employees steal the other half, is it surprising that the very employees will be forced to steal? Or if economic advancement is the likely payoff for a boring job, then it makes sense to stick with it; but if such a payoff is unlikely, the motivation to keep plugging away is severely reduced. What we desire will always be influenced and shaped by our social context. Desire itself is socially constructed. Understanding the social context for choice, and how individual history can shape personal desires, are important to evaluating the "freedom of choices" made (see Kleindorfer, chap. 6 in this book). It is not less important, however, also to understand the meaning of the desires that motivate the choices in the first place.

Third, social construction affects the understanding of what can count as choice. The concrete options that are available must be seen, interpreted, and understood in the way that power systems require it in order for those systems to be effective. Hence, the dynamic interaction between individuals and society—between self-understandings and social perceptions and cultural beliefs, between individual preferences and social practices or institutions—is key to the social constructivist dimension of freedom, for it affects the meaning of choice, and hence of freedom, at the level of language itself. Different contexts affect not just the choices or options available, nor merely what different individuals want, but the very meaning of the concept of "choice" itself.

Accordingly, some things, although actually chosen, may be seen as the products of coercion: not a free choice at all. For instance, many Westerners, who see Afghani "religious police" beating up local women for showing their ankles may assume that Muslim women veil themselves because they are oppressed; that given a free choice, no woman would choose to be covered in such a manner. Such external assumptions negate the agency of those women who do actively choose the veil as a symbol of cultural identity or a means of political protest. The variability and specificity of the practice from nation to nation, and context to context, is denied. Conversely, people may be perceived to implement a choice when forced in a particular direction, such as when politicians characterize single mothers on public assistance as "welfare queens" ripping off taxpayers, or when it is assumed that a battered woman who stays with her abuser because she has no money must not mind getting beaten up (Hirschmann 2003).

The fact that I keep focusing on women in my examples might seem to present the problem in a skewed way: when a woman is beaten up by her husband, or forced by welfare reform to drop out of school in order to take a minimum-wage job, it might be fairly clear that the social forces of patriarchy limit women's freedom. But the logic of social construction belies such simplistic readings. If social construction theory is right, then men must be socially constructed as well as women. For instance, studies show that being abused as a child, or having to watch one's mother being abused, are strong indicators that a man may become abusive himself. Even when men exert direct force or power over women, they play into social constructions of their own masculinity. For example, the lessons that men learn about the ideals of romantic masculinity—about strength and possessiveness as the expression of love—dovetail with the power and control of abusive behavior. This does not mean that all men will become abusive—since clearly, the majority of men are not—nor that men who do abuse women have no choice about their actions. But it does suggest that abuse is an extreme on the continuum of normal masculine idealization, arguably an extreme that some men find attractive to access. That may be why domestic violence is so difficult to eradicate: even for men who would never dream of hitting their wives, or for women who would "walk out that door if he ever laid a finger on me," this kind of violence is tacitly accepted as normal gendered behavior. If it were not, then abusers would be in jail, shelters would be more plentiful and better funded, and police would be trained in the specific problems of domestic violence calls (Hirschmann 2003, chap. 5).

Both men and women are constructed by patriarchy. Nobody has the extent of control over social forces that the notion of "social *construction*" connotes. But if men are as socially constructed as women, whites as well as blacks, rich as well as poor, then what kind of purchase does "social construction" accomplish for us in terms of freedom? Because none of us has autonomous control over our lives, and we are all the victims of social forces, it may lead to the conclusion that freedom is an impossibility. Or it may lead to quite the opposite conclusion—if everyone is socially constructed, then we should accept that to be just a fact of human nature, and move on: no harm, no foul.

But that glosses over an important step: that we all are socially constructed does not mean that we are constructed in the same way, nor that we entertain the same relationship with all of the processes of social construction. While recognizing that social construction is a phenomenon or process that happens to everyone, it is also the case that some groups of people systematically and structurally have more power and freedom than others (McInerney, chap 2. and Williams and Barber, chap. 4, in this book). Not everyone is equally placed within society, and that means that both desire and choice are constructed differentially. Women, for instance, arguably are more restricted in their freedom than men, as are people of color more than whites, and the poor far more than the wealthy—in the three ways that I just articulated, in which social construction works. That is, first, Western social systems are structured to give men, whites, and the wealthy more choices than white women, men and women of color, and the poor;[6] the range of options from which the former can choose is wider than it is for their latter counterparts. Second, the options tend to feed into themselves, creating expectations of choice for men, limitations for women, and penalties for those who violate the gender code. Finally, the way we see, define, and evaluate choice and freedom is itself constructed from perspectives of inequality. For instance, poverty discourses that blame the poor for being "lazy" are constructed from the perspective of class power and privilege, and are made possible only by blinding ourselves to the reality of poverty: the deplorable conditions of inner-city public schools, for instance, which produce poorly educated children too ill-equipped to compete in the labor market (Kozol 1991).

If choice is key to freedom, then what is necessary to theorizing freedom is an examination not only of the conditions in which choices are made but also of the construction of choice itself: what options are available, and why; what counts as a "choice," who counts as a "chooser," how the choosing subject is created and shaped by social relations and practices. The discursive requirements of choice thus entail the recognition that the apparently negative liberty emphasis on individual choice necessarily involves positive liberty elements of community and social relationships, because the processes of choice making must be situated in a larger social and discursive context in order for choices to have meaning. Such contexts are necessary in order to make choices possible; they are the logical precondition for choice. Choices

---

6. Non-Western systems similarly privilege masculinity and wealth, but obviously may favor different racial constructions over others.

must be made by individuals for themselves; nobody can push battered women to leave their abusers, or pull closeted gays "out" of their closets, without grossly violating their freedom. But because "choosing selves" are located in particular contexts of relationships in which power and production occur, the activity of choice making itself is a social process.

What I have suggested here indicates that "theorizing freedom" entails theorizing such things as social identity, historical context, culture, gender, and so forth, which at first glance may not appear directly relevant. I said earlier that social construction shifts the focus of freedom theory from what we want, to why we want it—what are the social forces and structures that shape and feed many different kinds of desires in many different kinds of people? In shifting the central question from "what do I want" to "why do I want it," social construction shifts the central goal of freedom from "doing what I want" or "making choices" to "defining what the choices are." Choice is undeniably central to freedom; but choice is a complex process, involving negotiation of external factors that negative liberty focuses on, and consideration of internal factors that it tends to ignore, but which positive liberty does highlight. That is, choice involves a recon-ciliation of desire and will on the one hand, and the social conditions that enable or restrain them, on the other, and these two elements need to be theorized in an interactive dynamic. What we want and why we want it are influenced and shaped by social factors that affect what desires are conceivable and what choices are possible. And this means that freedom cannot be simply about making choices within existing contexts; it has to be about having a say in defining the context in the first place.

This is why we, in the West, believe that we are freer than those in other countries. We often assume that this is so because of specific freedoms: freedom of speech, of the press, religion, or conscience. But are not those actually expressions, even by-products, of the fact that democracy equalizes access to the points of power that shape the very conditions in which we live, and as such define the terms of choice? That is something that seems to have eroded since September 11, 2001, because Americans have allowed fear to overcome them. While not willing to give up on freedom per se, they have yielded their participation in the structures, which determine their choices (cf. Dinh, this volume). For instance, new airport security measures prob-ably appear to most people as inconveniences rather than intrusions on their freedom. But it is not the fact that we have to take our shoes off in the airport that makes us less free; it is the top-down determination of a policy that, if subject to democratic scrutiny, debate, and participation, would probably be seen as absurd and ineffective. It is the way in which government, under the guise of freedom of information, passes on vague and unsubstantiated threats of terrorist attacks by changing the color on the terror alert system, without providing meaningful data or information upon which individuals can base intelligent choices. It is the use of national security to hide a plethora of actions and hasty decisions that should be talked about and decided upon collectively. As Benjamin Franklin (1759) once put it, "They that can give up essential liberty to obtain a little temporary safety deserve neither liberty nor safety." Franklin's meaning here was not to criticize individuals (say, for not refusing to remove their shoes) but rather to criticize a collective failure to recognize the importance of democratic process in setting policy that determines what our choices are. For is it not in such participation that freedom truly lies?

References

Ashcraft, Richard (1986) *Revolutionary Politics and Locke's Two Treatises of Government*, Princeton, NJ: Princeton University Press.

Berlin, Isaiah (1971) "Two Concepts of Liberty," in Isaiah Berlin, Editor, *Four Essays on Liberty*, New York: Oxford University Press.

Brown, Wendy (1995) *States of Injury: Power and Freedom in Late Modernity*, Princeton, NJ: Princeton University Press.

Cohen, Gerald Allen (1995) *Self-Ownership, Freedom, and Equality*, Cambridge: Cambridge University Press.

Di Stefano, Christine (1991) *Configurations of Masculinity*, Ithaca, NY: Cornell University Press.

Elster, Jon (1983) *Sour Grapes*, New York: Cambridge University Press.

Flathman, Richard E. (1987) *The Philosophy and Politics of Freedom*, Chicago: University of Chicago Press.

Franklin, Benjamin (1759) *An Historical Review of the Constitution and Government of Pennsylvania, from Its Origin*, Richard Jackson, Editor, London: Arno Press.

Hirschmann, Nancy J. (1992) *Rethinking Obligation: A Feminist Method for Political Theory*, Ithaca, NY: Cornell University Press.

——— (2003) *The Subject of Liberty: Toward a Feminist Theory of Freedom*, Princeton, NJ: Princeton University Press.

——— (2008) *Gender, Class, and Freedom in Modern Political Theory*, Princeton, NJ: Princeton University Press.

Hobbes, Thomas (1985) *Leviathan*, C. B. Macpherson, Editor, New York: Penguin.

——— (1994) *Human Nature, or, the Fundamental Elements of Policy; De Corpore Politico, or, The Elements of Law*, with a new introduction by G. A. J. Rogers, Editor, Bristol, UK: Thoemmes Press.

Kozol, Jonathan (1991) *Savage Inequalities: Children in America's Schools*, New York: Crown.

Liebow, Elliot (1967) *Tally's Corner: A Study of Negro Streetcorner Men*, Boston: Little, Brown.

Locke, John (1963) *Two Treatises of Government*, Peter Laslett, Editor, New York: New American Library.

——— (1996) *Some Thoughts Concerning Education and of the Conduct of the Understanding*, Ruth W. Grant and Nathan Tarcov, Editors, Indianapolis, IN: Hacket.

Macpherson, Crawford Brough (1962) *Political Theory of Possessive Individualism: Hobbes to Locke*, New York: Oxford University Press.

McClure, Kirstie M. (1996) *Judging Rights: Lockean Politics and the Limits of Consent*, Ithaca, NY: Cornell University Press.

Mill, John Stuart (1971) *The Autobiography, in John Stuart Mill on Education*, Francis W. Garforth, Editor, New York: Teachers College Press, Columbia University.

——— (1992) *On Liberty and Other Essays*, John Gray, Editor, New York: Oxford University Press.

Mostov, Julie (1992) *Power, Process, and Popular Sovereignty*, Philadelphia: Temple University Press.

Pateman, Carole (1985) *The Problem of Political Obligation: A Critique of Liberal Theory*, Berkeley and Los Angeles: University of California Press.

Rousseau, Jean Jacques (1973) *The Social Contract and Discourses*, G. D. H. Cole, Editor, London: J. M. Dent and Sons.

——— (1979) *Émile: Or, On Education*, Allan Bloom, Translator, New York: Basic Books.

Schochet, Gordon J. (2000) "'Guards and Fences': Property and Obligation in Locke's Political Thought," *History of Political Thought* 21(3):365–389.

Tarcov, Nathan (1984) *Locke's Education for Liberty*, Chicago: University of Chicago Press.

Taylor, Charles (1979) "What's Wrong with Negative Liberty," in Alan Ryan, Editor, *The Idea of Freedom: Essays in Honor of Isaiah Berlin*, New York: Oxford University Press.

10 Freedom and Culture

Greg Urban

The premise of my chapter is that, reassessed in perspective and rephrased in context, freedom reveals itself to be a peculiar kind of cultural concept—a metacultural one. As an idea and as an embodiment in a specific linguistic form, "freedom" is a part *of* culture; it is socially learned and socially transmitted. But simultaneously, it is also *about* culture—about processes and products of social learning and social transmission.

And as metaculture, freedom is not merely of and about culture; it, moreover, has a practical effect *on* the movement of culture through the world: between people, across space, and over time. But I make an even stronger empirical claim: that the specific effect of freedom as metaculture is to block certain forms of cultural flows through the world the better to facilitate others.

The most obvious examples of this metacultural deployment of the concept of freedom are found in its opposition to subservience, as in the American Revolution or the antislavery movement or yet the Civil Rights movement. Just how is this concept about the flow of culture? By happening in the form of command(s) within an authority structure.

Many readers will not be used to conceptualizing freedom in the way they think of traditional forms of cultural motion—for example, as in learning to speak a given language by growing up in a family. And, indeed, freedom does differ from the latter kind of motion in a key respect: the acquisition of culture by children in the process of growing up inside their family is in large measure *inertial*. Children acquire the culture because it is there to be acquired. In the case of command, culture is there to be *accelerated*. The command acts to impel the movement of culture by getting individuals to do what they would not otherwise be doing—as when parents tell children to clean up their room. Cleaning up one's room is culture; but typically, it does not just happen: the culture does not perpetuate itself simply for being there as in the case of domestic language learning. Rather, it requires an outside force to help it move through the world. That force is the command— the imperative that is a parcel of metaculture. When the freedom concept is used in connection with command in an authority structure, it is being used metaculturally.

The effect of the metacultural usage of freedom in connection with command and authority is to block the very flow of that culture. The flow of culture is resisted through the commands that make up the authority structure. But in what does that resistance consist? That is what I propose to explore in this chapter.

Freedom and Self-Conscious Action

In the *Metaphysics of Morals*, Kant develops the notion of freedom as the basis for self-reflective conduct in the world (1991). If human beings are "free," this means that they are agents—able to determine their own conduct.

The Kantian notion was taken up by Max Weber (1978), for whom action was behavior "insofar as the acting individual attaches a subjective meaning" to it. As in the case of Kant, the idea here is that the meaning plays a causal role in relationship to the behavior. The behavior is not something that is simply determined independently, and then "rationalized"—to be explained away, as it were—by the subjective meaning. No, the subjective meaning impels the behavior.

Reconsidered from the point of view of action, therefore, Kant's freedom might be regarded as a concept introduced to account for the meaningful control of conduct—for the ability of ideas to affect and effect behaviors.

But Kantian freedom is more than that: freedom means not merely that acting subjects ascribe meaning to their behavior, but that the meaning ensues from processes of ratiocination internal to a subject.

While Kant does not make key distinctions in regard to internal ratiocination, Weber does: he distinguishes types of action—for our present purposes, the key distinction being between "traditional" and "rational" action. In traditional action, behavior and its attendant meanings are determined by the past: "traditional action" comes close to what anthropologists have classically called "culture"—socially learned and socially transmitted action. By contrast, rational action involves deliberation—an internal deliberation by the subject—as in Kant's notion of freedom with its attendant ratiocination.

Because of the distinction between meaning that flows from the past (via tradition) and meaning that derives from subjects' internal thought processes (via rationality), and the alignment of tradition with the classical concept of culture, it appears that rationality is something other than culture; hence, that freedom results in a break with culture. Internal reasoning means that subjects do not simply accept meanings that have been passed down to them, but come up with their own—by cogitating (see Cameron, chap. 13 in this book).

Kantian freedom is the essential condition that enables this severing of ties with tradition. But, for being socially learned and socially transmitted, freedom as a concept is a part of culture. Yet, if for defining a condition opposed to the traditional determination of meaning and hence of action, freedom is an element of metaculture, as well. Also, on closer look, the role of the freedom concept here reveals that the purpose of its deployment in discourse is to affect the motion of traditional culture—in particular, to stem or stop its flow across subjects—thereby necessitating that a subject's action, if free, be determined only by processes of reasoning internal to the very subject. The metaculture of freedom is deployed so as to cut the flow of traditional culture.

How, as metaculture, the freedom concept contributes to blocking certain forms of cultural flow in a manner to facilitate others becomes evident in Kant's treatment of the freedom concept in the *Metaphysics of Morals*. Having positioned freedom as the condition in which action can be guided by subjective meanings—and, in particular, by meanings that result from reasoning processes—Kant formulates an imperative from which he seeks to derive the principles that ought to govern the conduct of any and all reasoning beings—namely, the "categorical imperative"—the idea that reasoning subjects ought to choose to act such that maxims (rules) regulating their own conduct could equally well apply to every other reasoning being: here, Kant deploys freedom not only to argue for blocking the flow of traditional culture but also to facilitate the flow of a new form of culture—the categorical imperative and what can be derived from it.

I can take the metacultural analysis of Kantian freedom further, since Kant's arguments apply a propulsive force not only behind the categorical imperative but also behind the range of rights and duties that he sees to follow from the categorical imperative. The fact that those rights and duties—say, as to marital relations and property—happen to correspond closely to the laws and customs of his time only makes the point stronger that freedom, as a metacultural construct, is about cutting ties with certain forms of cultural flow in order to facilitate others.

Kantianism, especially via Weber's distinctions between rational versus traditional action, became the cornerstone of modernity theory— wherein the microflows of culture through individual subjects, and the interruptions of those flows, provide the basis for understanding large-scale historical processes: the movement from traditional forms of society to modern ones. In the traditional forms, the subject's actions are determined by meanings that are themselves determined by earlier meanings. Kant employs the freedom concept to argue against such determination by the past: in the grand scheme of things, it becomes an argument for the replacement of traditional forms of organization of society with modern, rational design. Freedom as metaculture, in this way, plays the role of a giant lever redirecting the flow of history, from a determination of present by past to a determination of present by present. Insofar as the Kantian project has succeeded, the freedom concept itself has been successful in blocking certain forms of cultural flow in order to let move others.

Freedom and Communicative Rationality

There is a paradox of sorts in Kant's notion of freedom as self-conscious control of conduct by processes of internal ratiocination. On the side of input to the subject, so to speak, freedom demands rupture: the subject's meaning cannot be simply what the subject has received from the past—it cannot be the result solely of culture as classically con-strued, as inheritance from the past. Subjects must reject determination by the past, to effect their own determination of conduct in the world. On the output side, however, the reasoning subject (in this case, Kant) produces an argument that, if successful, will be accepted as input by other subjects. But those other subjects are then being determined in their subjective meaning by something outside of them. Hence, they are unfree, acting in accord with traditional rather than with rational meanings.

The solution to the apparent paradox can be found in the claim to universality of the cultural product—in this case, the argument itself: the paradox dissolves since, were they truly free, subjects reason-ing independently would come to the same conclusion. There is no contradiction between freedom and universal conformity; quite the contrary: if internal reasoning produces truth and truth is singular, then every subject should gain access to it through Kant's methods. As a product of metaculture, the freedom concept hence provides a way to transcend culture: the cutting of traditional culture goes along with the rise of internally discovered universal truth.

But this is not the way Kant's deployment of freedom actually worked. In freedom there was a key component of an argument designed to persuade. It supplied part of the acceleration of that argument, as a piece of culture, through the world.

Here we glimpse a more contemporary view of culture, not just as what is received from the past by inertia (the classical concept of culture, from the mid-1950s), but what is metaculturally accelerated through the world in the present—in this case, an argument: one that still is culture for being socially learned and socially transmitted, but now also a form of culture made possible by acceleration. From this point of view, freedom in Kantianism, and as translated through Weber, is a lever for blocking the flow of inertial forms of culture, in order to facilitate the motion of accelerative culture.

Moreover, freedom exerts on subjects a pressure to differentiate their own productions (whether arguments, stories, or other forms of culture) from those inherited or received. In that sense, the test of freedom becomes the difference between the meanings (more generally, the culture) that come 'into' from the meanings and culture that come 'out of' the subject: as metaculture, the freedom concept pressures subjects to refract culture rather than simply to transmit it. The refraction becomes the demonstration to the subject, as well as to others, of the existence of freedom. This means that freedom is manifested through evidence of agency.

Cultural motion is not the framework in which Jürgen Habermas developed his theory of communicative action (1984): Habermas was working in the Kantian tradition, especially as taken up by Weber, with distinct influences also from Frankfurt school Marxism. But it is possible to understand Habermas's theory from both points of view: that of motion but (especially) also that of Kant's seemingly paradoxical notion of freedom, which requires rejecting external (cultural) determinations of subjective meaning while simultaneously demanding that both, these determinations *and* the conclusions drawn from them, be taken up by others as the determinants of their own subjective meaning.

Habermas interprets rational action in the Weberian scheme—as communicatively rational action: the rationality is to be found in the intersubjective realm of arguments, and in the mutual convincing of one another of the validity of arguments, such that the best ones (e.g., the most truthful) are those that come to be most widely held in communities. This, of course, necessarily involves a conception of cultural motion (circulation) in the special form of accelerative culture described.

Interactive communities move toward a consensus, or partake of culture, within this understanding—if because some arguments outpace and some cultural elements overtake others. In the context of free communication, arguments—and, more generally, cultural elements—that are more truthful, or useful, or aesthetically appealing will tend to be the most widely accepted.

This is not Kantian universalism, since the claim is not about a subject freely reasoning about conduct. It is Kantianism taken in the direction of cultural motion, of cultural circulation. Also, there is no notion that the circulating arguments (or culture) at one moment will remain valid for all time: conditions of the community, relative to knowledge, and to culture more generally, can change. It can approach universalism if the interactive community does come to encompass the entire globe. But the Habermasian perspective is more compatible with ideas about cultural motion—especially so when culture is understood as accelerative instead of, or in addition to, being viewed as inertial.

Freedom continues to play a key metacultural role in Habermasian thinking: a principal condition for rational communicative action in a Habermasian framework, it is also the very condition that makes possible internal ratiocination in the Kantian scheme. From the perspective of cultural motion, too, Habermas's meaning of freedom is strikingly similar to Kant's: In Kant, freedom is the rejection of a determination by the past of the subjective meaning; in Habermas, it is the rejection of influences from the past on subjective meaning—including especially power relations that have congealed over time, and economic influences as well, since these inhibit just appraisals of arguments and adequate assessments of culture by individual subjects.

Habermasian freedom means the absence of distorting influences that prevent the refraction of cultural motion as the culture moves through the subject, in accord with the subject's own nature. The influences of power and money mean that refraction is at the behest of motives other than the intrinsic worth of the culture itself. Where communicative freedom is absent, the culture that comes to be widely accepted can never adequately express the nature of the community and its individual members.

Most obviously in the case of power, Habermas's freedom concept, as in the Kantian case, reflects a desire to block a cultural flow—for the purpose of facilitating another flow. In this case, the other flow is accelerative culture, better attuned to the nature of the individuals through whom it flows, and more genuinely able to express it. Habermas's notion of power as distorting does not necessarily oppose traditional-versus-rational domination, as in Weber's scheme. Were we to imagine that it does, freedom would still refer to cutting the flow of traditional culture as a basis for determining subjective meanings, and to substituting accelerative culture in better accord with the nature of the individuals in question.

But why is traditional culture—even in the guise of traditional forms of domination—necessarily out of accord with the individuals through whom it passes? This question allows us to refine further our thinking: it is not the specific content, let alone the specific commands, of a given traditional domination relationship to which—following Weber—Habermas might object; rather, it is the very basis on which the traditional commands and the domination is accepted. Freedom requires that such acceptance result from processes of internal ratiocination linked, in Habermas's case, to public debate over what is best: what is opposed by freedom here is not traditional culture as such but the very basis on which that culture is accepted. If it is accepted because 'it has always been done that way', then one cannot be certain it is the best expression of the individuals currently at play. If it is accepted because, by internal thought processes and public debate, people have decided that it is best to do so, then—though passed down across generations—the culture is in conformity with freedom.

It becomes apparent here that Habermasian freedom as metaculture does not oppose tradition as such, but only tradition as metaculture. What is problematic from a Habermasian perspective of freedom is not necessarily culture transmitted between people across generations. Tradition is a form of metaculture pressing the point that the reason we should accept these meanings and this conduct is because we have always done things that way: by contrast, Habermasian freedom demands active justification for culture.

In this sense, Habermasian freedom does not entail the rejection of traditional culture in the way that the most extreme variant of Kantianism does, whereby all subjective meaning attached to behavior is the result of processes of internal ratiocination. In Kant, reason becomes opposed to culture. In Habermas, there is clear recognition that socially transmitted meanings and manners are compatible with freedom. What is incompatible is the metacultural justification of these meanings and behaviors on the sole grounds that they were once applicable.

Caveat: the metaculture of tradition can be heard to argue that the culture in question is compatible with the people through whom it is passing. Proven endurance over time justifies the superiority of inertial culture. The propulsive thrust of an accelerative culture grounded on the freedom argument must be justified, however, not on tradition only, but also on the basis of arguments not tested over time. From this vantage point, one can appreciate—at least in some measure—the power of a metaculture of tradition that is distinct from one of freedom. This is something that tends to be forgotten in the context of discussions of freedom. As I shall argue later, there are cultural reasons why a metaculture of freedom is so powerful and so able to move readily through the world. Likewise, I shall point to the reasons why metacultures of tradition have been historically so very successful.

Freedom and Economics

In Habermas's view, money, like power, plays a distorting role with respect to judgments about arguments and, more generally, about elements of culture. If one produces or accepts an argument or other cultural element not for what it is, but rather for what money it can bring, then the question is not about the intrinsic value of the argument or element itself. Since the principle of freedom, indeed, a metaculture of freedom, requires that the element be assessed on its own terms, independently of other considerations, then money, like power, has the potential to distort or to subvert the operation of communicative rationality.

But Habermas's argument here is not perfectly in accord with the perspective on freedom from cultural motion. Looked at in terms of motion, money provides a means of measuring the force of motion, so to speak. Since the goods and services bought and sold are bearers of culture, their movement through the world tracks the movement of the culture they carry. And what is the force that impels that culture? It is the desire for that culture of those who purchase. They are using the goods and services—extracting the culture contained in them—for their own local purposes, not those necessarily foreseen by the producers. So money—price, in particular—reflects the interest of the individual recipients of the disseminated culture.

From the perspective of a metaculture of freedom, individuals surely are free to choose from available alternatives. The capitalist system is one such finely tuned mechanism for disseminating culture—brilliant both in design and subtlety of operation, it permits a new element of culture to gain a popular interest greater than that for elements already available and, if so, with some probability, to come to dominate over those elements. Individuals express their preference by purchases that are not determined by the forces of production or supply only. Far from inhibiting individual preference for cultural elements, money facilitates the coordination of preferences on a global scale.

One may still argue whether the consumer is acting in accord with freedom when expressing a preference through a purchase. From a Kantian angle, one might ask: when expressing a preference, does the individual employ subjective meanings derived from internal processes of reasoning or are those meanings simply accepted from the outside? If the latter applies, then Kantian freedom is not present. Likewise from a Habermasian perspective, if there is no unconstrained public debate over the acceptance of an element affecting the collectivity, then freedom has not been truly exercised.

The irony in either case is that freedom appears not simply as the absence of constraint, but as a positive duty toward the use of private and/or public processes of ratiocination. Ironically, freedom itself appears as unfree, as something that must come to us from the outside in some kind of constraint.

Correspondingly, from the angle of the positive duty to reason, to assess, and to use critical judgment, instead of simply expressing a passing preference through an impulsive purchase, the subject can appear to be unfree if the real determinants of her choice stem from baser motives or desires, for instance. The capitalist system is maximally "free," in one sense, because it allows such desires to be expressed. It is unfree, however, because preference is determined by those desires and not by reason and debate.

The Secret of Freedom

Freedom thus presents a paradoxical quality: it appears as the absence of constraint while appearing also as a positive duty toward ratiocination that must oppose the forces of indolence. How can this be? I submit that, viewed from the angle of metaculture, these two opposing impressions not only make sense, they also reveal the magic of freedom: the very force that impels its motion through the world.

As metaculture, I have been arguing that freedom has a specific meaning—the absence of constraint. But freedom is also more than a meaning-bearing linguistic form. It possesses also a worldly efficacy—when blocking the flow of certain forms of culture, especially the meta-cultures of tradition—that facilitates the flow of other forms, specifically, critical reflection upon culture (in Kant's terms, the application of reason) in judgment of competing cultural elements.

Concomitantly, however, freedom is a part of culture. Not only does it reflect upon culture, it must also move through processes of social transmission in the way that any culture does. And, evidently, it does not circulate or move by virtue of inertia alone. Unlike a mother tongue, it does not travel through time simply because it was there to be learned. It is out there, in worldwide contestation with other elements. It must, therefore, have a force behind it that results in its own accelera-tion. What is the nature of the force behind freedom? What gets freedom to move?

From this perspective, it may be noted that part of the problem is that freedom fights against itself, so to speak. Since it opposes the acceptance of elements for no better reason than that they were there to be accepted, freedom in some ways fights against the possibility that it might move that way itself. Even in the United States, freedom moves along as inertial culture—for example, in phrases glossing the United States as "the land of the free and the home of the brave" in the national anthem. But the meaning of freedom as metaculture is to fight against the uptake of culture purely on the basis of this kind of tradition. As metacultural concept, freedom forces us toward reasoned positions as to why this form of culture (the freedom concept) is a good or valuable one. Thus, in opposing the apparent indolence of tradition, freedom is, in fact, fighting against its own traditionalism.

So whence does freedom derive its motive force? The secret is in the relation between freedom as metaculture and freedom as culture. I want to propose that what gets freedom as culture to move through the world is precisely the fact that freedom as metaculture can be used to block the motion of other forms of culture. People can embrace the freedom concept while rejecting other concepts that come to them from the outside, even though the freedom concept itself is being imported, if only because freedom helps them in their rejection of other cultural elements: paradoxically, freedom as culture receives momentum and wields a force imparted to it in commensurate proportion to its ability as metaculture to stop the flow of other cultures.

If one thinks back to the deployment of the freedom concept in the eighteenth and nineteenth centuries—notwithstanding that it has much older roots—the concept was used to resist other forms of accelerative culture, namely, commands coming from aristocratically constituted governmental regimes. The basis for the claim to legitimacy for those who ruled was traditional. Those in power justified their positions by reference to hereditary entitlement. But commands issued by aristocratic governments did more than carry traditional culture forward through the world. They also effected changes in the cultures of those who were commanded, as in the case of taxation. An increase in taxation by the British, for example, would effect changes in the culture of its colonies where those taxes applied.

As we know, the freedom concept took root in large part as a way to articulate opposition to imposed culture, although also to effect opposition to it. As in Patrick Henry's celebrated line ("give me liberty or give me death"), freedom served as a rallying cry in efforts to block other forms of cultural motion. And one can see the prominence of this cultural element, not long afterward, in the French Revolution: the phrase "liberté, egalité, fraternité" remains with us today. The notion of "liberation" spread in the nineteenth century throughout Latin America, but did not then vanish as an active force of resistance against other forms of cultural motion: in the twentieth century, it appeared as a rallying cry in decolonization movements in Africa and in the Indian subcontinent. South Africa now celebrates "freedom day." The autobiography of Jawaharlal Nehru, the first prime minister of India following its independence from Britain, is titled *Toward Freedom* (1958).

As a metacultural device for blocking the flow of certain forms of culture, in order to facilitate the flow of others, freedom gains momentum as culture by virtue of its ability to decrease the momentum of other forms of culture. The paradoxical quality of freedom and, simultaneously, of its motive force derives from its dual roles as culture and metaculture. To be useful as metaculture, the freedom concept has to be widely accepted as culture. Otherwise it lacks efficacy. To be widely accepted as culture, it must be useful as metaculture. Otherwise it lacks momentum. It cannot have metacultural force without acceptance, and it gains acceptance because of its metacultural force.

Freedom and Cultural Diversity

The formulation of freedom as culture and metaculture given here is largely compatible with Habermasian freedom in relation to communicative action. But there is a key point of divergence over the question of universality, carrying over from the Kantian foundations. For Kant, the dictates of internal ratiocination are the basis for universal law. Freedom leads to the categorical imperative, which itself leads to the specification of rights and duties. The matter is different in Habermas: communicative rationality aspires toward generalizable human interest and toward the common good.

The notion of freedom as metaculture takes us some distance into the worldview of another great eighteenth-century thinker, Adam Smith, who is not normally associated with anthropological ideas about culture, but whose work in many respects is prophetical—especially in its formulation of human differences as the key to understanding society, including the foundations of the economy—as in this passage from *The Theory of Moral Sentiments:*

The man of system . . . is often so enamoured with the supposed beauty of his own ideal plan of government, that he cannot suffer the smallest deviation from any part of it. He goes on to establish it completely and in all its parts, without any regard either to the great interests, or to the strong prejudices which may oppose it. He seems to imagine that he can arrange the different members of a great society with as much ease as the hand arranges the different pieces upon a chess-board. He does not consider that the pieces upon the chess-board have no other principle of motion besides that which the hand impresses upon them; but that, in the great chess-board of human society, every single piece has a principle of motion of its own, altogether different from that which the legislature might chuse to impress upon it. If those two principles coincide and act in the same direction, the game of human society will go on easily and harmoniously, and is very likely to be happy and successful. If they are opposite or different, the game will go on miserably, and the society must be at all times in the highest degree of disorder. (Smith 2000, 342–343)

Smith formulates here the central problem—from the point of view of cultural diversity—with the Kantian deductive scheme: any individual deduction of the organization of society from first principles is bound to meet up with resistance from other individuals or groups, whose own view of just order is incompatible with this one. If modernity has run aground in recent history, it is on the jagged shore of deductive difference.

Hence, Habermas's view appears as a way to set the ship back on its course: displace reason from the individual brain onto the collective interactions of society. But questions still remain: can generalizable rules, extendable to all of humanity, arise from such dialogicical processes? And, on a global scale, where more than six billion individuals are involved, can dialogue serve even as model for how global social order is achieved?

From the point of view of cultural motion, the issue may not be dialogue as such but the different kinds of cultural flows I have mentioned. When culture moves over time in a given population, it tends to undergo small changes that cumulate into larger ones. Language is the type case here: if speakers of the same language are isolated from one another, over time their language will change, and, after a couple of thousand years, they will no longer be able to understand one another. The same is true of culture more generally. It changes by processes of drift.

As Fredrik Barth (1969) astutely observed, culture also changes in response to the desire for difference. Two societies brought into social interaction may exaggerate the differences between themselves. This is something that the sociolinguist William Labov (1972) has demonstrated for even the microprocesses of sound change within language. In his study of the now tourist-saturated island of Martha's Vineyard, off the coast of Massachusetts, he measured differences in accent between the native islanders and the mainland vacationers. He found that, over time, rather than converging, the accents (in particular, certain vowel qualities) were actually diverging. The two groups were becoming less, rather than more, like each other as a result of interaction.

At the same time, as Smith observed, productive differences in the economy (in the division of labor) result in a form of mutual coordination. This is not the coordination of an imposed direct rule (as in Smith's "man of system"). Rather, it is the coordination of mutual interest. *The Wealth of Nations* was published in 1776 (1994). At the time, Smith was searching for means to reduce the influence of a strong central government on the coordination of society. Among anthropologists and others concerned with cultural diversity, that is not incompatible with desire—the rights of "peoples" to their cultural heritages.

But these forms of motion do not exhaust what culture is all about. We discussed the motion of culture within a population in a given locale as undergoing drift over time, and we examined adjacent populations desiring to differentiate themselves. But there are also flows of culture across the boundaries of populations that—by drift or by desire—have become distinct. This is what is known these days as "globalization."

What I have been suggesting is that, as a metacultural concept, freedom operates in the latter realm. It is a kind of metaculture that acts to instate cultural difference. But as culture, it acquires a globalizing force—seized upon, by population after population, and thereby producing a global culture, precisely because it can be of such help to those wishing to preserve their own culture, to stop the importation of other culture. Hence, freedom as metaculture produces a kind of common global culture, albeit by aiding those who desire the distinctiveness of their own culture patterns. In achieving cultural distinctiveness through freedom, the individuals and groups in question participate in the potentially universal culture of freedom.

Freedom: Hollow at the Core?

One question arising from the above account of freedom as a metacultural device for blocking the flow of other cultures is this: Does the freedom concept, if taken up by people, have no consequences for how they organize their lives internally? Does freedom allow one group of people, say, a "society," to organize itself internally in any way it pleases, and—freedom being merely a device for resisting outside influence—to maintain whatever external relations they choose with the outside world?

I have argued that, as metaculture, freedom provides a kind of charter for cultural diversity, and also for at least some measure of self-determination by "peoples": Does a commitment to freedom mean a commitment to complete cultural and ethical relativity, such that it provides no standpoint from which to criticize other people? Is it essentially a negative notion with no positive content?

As metaculture, freedom is essentially a negative concept—the absence of external constraints, the rejection of those constraints. But it is negative only when examined from the point of view of its specific meaning and deployment as a term. Taken in the context of the motion of culture more generally, it may also have normative implications. This is, of course, the view of Habermas and even of Kant, though neither man explicitly placed the concept in relation to cultural motion in the way I have here.

In the "Declaration of Independence," we see the canonical metacultural use of the freedom concept in lines such as: "That these United

Colonies are, and of Right ought to be Free and Independent States." The same document stressing freedom places emphasis on the "consent of the governed." One might ask: Does any society using freedom to inhibit the flow of culture into it from the outside also have to provide an internal metacultural conception that any government established within it must be based upon consent? The answer would seem to be "yes," that the freedom concept is not hollow at the core, when taken in the context of a broader understanding of cultural circulation.

Yet, a broader notion of cultural motion does complicate the meaning of "consent." If, from their time of birth, individuals are immersed in cultural institutions that shape their worldviews and sensibilities, what does it mean to speak of their "consent" to be governed in a particular way? This issue is raised in the chapter by Nancy Hirschmann (chap. 9). One can think of the extreme form of culture as a sort of brainwashing, so that the issue of free will and consent is far from clear. The notion of freedom as metaculture is in some sense directly opposed to the Kantian ideal (as is also part of the processes of cultural motion more generally) and poses challenges also to Habermasian communicative freedom.

For Kant, freedom means stripping away all external cultural influences in trying to adopt the point of view of reason (Cameron, chap. 13 in this book). From the point of view of cultural motion, however, the issue may not be stripping away cultural influences, but immersing oneself fully in them. For how can you know abstractly whether you would choose this way of governance or that, unless you have grown up in that system and know 'what it feels like' (how you would reason about it) from the inside. Free choice, in this case, means knowing the two cultural patterns equally well and opting for the one over the other without any other influence. This is not stripping away culture; on the contrary, it is saturating oneself with it—indeed, with different cultural patterns.

Anthropologists have spent their time endeavoring to reveal the value of other ways of life and worldviews. Consent here is relative and varied. But this does not mean that there is no cross-cultural content to the idea of consent. People do make choices if in no other way than with their feet; and if consent is to have cross-cultural content, part of that content must be the right to leave behind a situation that the individuals in question consider intolerable. If they are forced to stay under such circumstances, the idea of consent and the notion of freedom from which it derives have little content.

It is one thing for outsiders to come into a community and tell its members that they are oppressed, or unfree—the outsiders may be wrong; they may not understand what it is like to grow up in that cultural context. It is quite another for the members themselves to conclude that the system by which they are governed is one that is unacceptable to them. They have an insider's cultural perspective— even when they cannot yet imagine what life would be in a *different* cultural environment.

To be in conformity with a cross-cultural principle of consent grounded in freedom, any form of governance minimally would have to allow a dissenting minority to leave its sphere of jurisdiction and take up membership in some other community. It could not hold people against their will on the basis of a cultural argument, since those wills were formed in the environment of the culture they would be rejecting by choosing to leave.

For this reason, migration, and the cross-cultural rights of migrants, must be a key component of freedom. Similarly, a condition of formal slavery would be incompatible with consent, hence with freedom, since the enslaved individuals would not be able to opt out of their station if they so chose. Understood in terms of cultural motion, therefore, the Confederacy's argument for freedom during the American Civil War was consistent with the metacultural function of blocking the flow of culture from the Union, although inconsistent with the principle of freedom as consent applied to the internal organization of their proposed society.

There exists a way in which the freedom concept can be made compatible with slavery: by denying certain individuals their very humanity. But as discussed, since the freedom concept derives its force from the extent of its dissemination, the force of freedom is undercut by interpretations of it likely to limit the scope of its dissemination. Excluding some individuals from the category of those to whom freedom applies undercuts the scope of its dissemination: the circulatory principle of freedom impels the freedom concept in the direction of greater, not lesser, inclusiveness precisely because greater inclusiveness produces greater metacultural force.

Freedom as Traditional Culture

It is possible to deduce from the idea of freedom more of the shape of social organizations potentially compatible or incompatible with it. But

this exercise cannot be adequately accomplished through Kantian isolated ratiocination, alas, if because freedom is not fully stable as an
abstract concept. Being metaculture, freedom is part of culture as well,
and hence subject to the gradual change or drift in meaning just as any
other aspect of culture.

An excellent example of cultural difference facing "the freedom
concept" is Jeremy McInerney's account of ancient Greek conceptions
of freedom: in ancient Greece, freedom was not a "right" of all, but
rather a status of certain individuals, one that could be lost as well as
acquired. The notion of freedom as an inherent condition of human
beings is something that developed only gradually in Europe in the
seventeenth and eighteenth centuries. It continued to expand the scope
of its inclusiveness throughout the nineteenth century in the United
States and throughout the twentieth century elsewhere in the world.

Since the metacultural effects of the freedom concept depend in some
measure on the shape of that concept, whose shape is subject to the
flux of culture, the metacultural effects also are not completely stable
and universal. But, as argued, the freedom concept does appear to be
headed on a detectable albeit not inexorable trajectory toward greater
inclusiveness.

Freedom as Totemic Emblem

As metaculture, freedom operates by creating in us an awareness of
separation from the past, from the outside world, and from the emotions as well. By creating a consciousness of separation, it facilitates the
denial of determination of the self by emotion, tradition, or authority.
And because it can be used selectively, it can deny one cultural flow
even as it favors another. This is what provides it with a propulsive
force in the world. People want to take it up because it is useful to them
in denying other culture(s) that they do not want, and because it is
useful to them in enabling the motion of culture they do want. In the
process, ironically, freedom acquires a force over them.

Such an awareness or consciousness of separation is not confined to
the freedom concept. Probably at least for some tens of thousands of
years, people have been interested in group boundary delimitation
and in creating a consciousness of distinction between in-group and
out-groups. Such boundary making has been described countless times
in the anthropological literature in connection with the phenomenon
of "totemism"—the use of animal (or other) names to distinguish one

group from the next—for example, sports team differentiations by reference to "bears," "eagles," and "cowboys," among others.

The group appropriates a sense of its own identity by reference to its distinctiveness with respect to other groups. In identifying with one group, one simultaneously sees one's own separateness from others: in a way analogous to freedom as metaculture, therefore, group identification creates an awareness of separation that shuts down cultural influence from groups of which one is not a member while enabling flows from one's own group.

With totemism, there is no built-in impetus to move the totemic symbol beyond the bounds of the group, however. An "Eagles" fan might want others to become Eagles supporters, but surely not the "Bears" (given their status as a separate group) to adopt the Eagle as their totemic emblem. The very idea of totemism works against the lateral movement of the totemic emblem beyond the bounds of the group.

Totemism and the contemporary freedom concept are opposed in this way. Although both of them are metacultural—referring back to culture and designed to inhibit or cut cultural flows in order to facilitate others—unlike the freedom concept, the specific totemic emblem is not propelled beyond the bounds of the group: it cannot, lest it lose its differentiating property.

This is a key feature of the contemporary freedom concept. It generalizes the boundary-delimiting ability of the totemic symbol, while simultaneously enabling it to be used in more targeted ways, without having to characterize one group as distinct from another.

The Greek concept of *eleutheria*, described by McInerney, seems to reside somewhere between the totemic symbol and the contemporary freedom concept. Like the totemic symbol, it characterizes the whole group. If, like the contemporary freedom concept, more than one group could claim to be characterized by it, quite unlike the contemporary freedom concept, its metacultural deployment cannot be targeted to cutting certain cultural flows in order to facilitate others. It serves exclusively to facilitate the flow of culture *inside* the group characterized by it and to cut any flows from the *outside* that would result in the subjugation of that group.

From this perspective, it is possible to view certain attempts at equating freedom and the United States in quasi-totemic terms, for tending to inhibit the flow of the "freedom" concept beyond the U.S. border. The decision to name the buildings being planned to replace the destroyed World Trade Center in New York "Freedom Towers," with a construction height of 1,776 feet, designed to be both the tallest structure in the world and to symbolize the birth date of the United States as an independent nation, tends to inhibit the taking up of the freedom concept by countries opposed to the United States. Hence, this deployment tends to inhibit the motion of the concept. In this respect, the usage is reminiscent of the ancient Greek usage of the term *eleutheria*.

True, there is nothing especially new in this deployment. The United States has long associated itself with freedom in a quasi-totemic way. Even the words to the national anthem, "The Star Spangled Banner," date from a battle with the British in 1814. The anthem, like the totem, marks the United States as a distinctive social grouping. It concludes with the phrase: "the land of the free and the home of the brave." So, it is hard to predict whether any new totemic development—such as "Freedom Towers"—will represent a significant inhibition to the movement of the freedom concept around the planet.

It is possible to foresee how these kinds of inhibition to the globalization of the freedom concept might be responded to by others seeking simultaneously to assert their own distinctiveness vis-à-vis the totemically construed social grouping and to appropriate the metacultural term "freedom": the response would take the form of a denial that the totemically appropriate freedom concept is the true one. We see this, for example, in accruing statements that American freedom—where you can choose between ten types of breakfast cereal—is not freedom at all (Schwartz 2004). The same can be found in Islamic discourses about freedom,[1] or even in pro-Castro Cuba, where the claim is often made that "freedom" means access to health care and to jobs, something seen as lacking in the United States.

Such debates focus on the nature of "freedom" as a cultural concept. Yet, depending on how freedom is construed culturally, its metacultural role will be different, especially regarding the ability to deduce a specific form of social organization from it. The idea of a "universal" social organization derivable from the freedom concept is dependent on the commonalities in the concept of freedom as part of culture. Totemic appropriation of this concept tends to sharpen differences on the cultural plane, suggesting that a universal social organization would be derivable at best only in broad outline, with the specificities to be worked out locally remaining susceptible to change over time.

---

1. See the essay "Islam, Freedom and Justice," by Sayyid Mujtaba Musavi Lari, available at: http://home.swipenet.se/islam/articles/freedom.htm.

Freedom and Indolence

The concept of globalizing freedom, as distinct from its totemic refractions, demands constant input of conscious reflection from both individuals and collectivities. Insofar as freedom is construed as choice, choice ought to be one not determined exogenously, whether by affect, tradition, or authority, or by the metacultural efficacy of advertising. Understood in this manner, freedom requires unceasing vigilance over and constant input of energy into choosing.

From the angle of freedom's requiring the input of conscious effort—consciousness implying a force that affects cultural motion—there is truth to the criticism that "free market" capitalism is not necessarily free (Cameron, chap. 13 in this book). Concern here is that choice may degenerate into (1) succumbing to one's emotions and feelings or (2) falling prey to metacultural manipulation that typically involves some marshalling of emotions and feelings: free market capitalism is not necessarily evidence for the operation of a metacultural concept of freedom.

Even if this conclusion were true, it provides no evidence that a metaculture of freedom is therefore absent. It might be that some individuals are, in fact, exercising conscious judgments rather than succumbing to other forces.

At the same time, it seems obvious that there are many more choices available to an individual in the present world than they could possibly make through conscious study. Paul Kleindorfer's study in this book (chap. 6) of the default auto insurance in Pennsylvania and New Jersey suggests as much: the same percentage (ca. 80 percent) of the sample population chose the default, despite the fact that default coverage in the two cases was dramatically different—one minimal, the other maximal.

The Future of Freedom

The force impelling the lateral motion of the freedom concept around the globe would seem to be lodged in its peculiar metacultural quality. By bringing consciousness to bear on cultural flows, this force is able to cut certain flows in a manner to facilitate others. Owing to this capacity of freedom as metaculture, people want to take it up, make it their own. The freedom concept circulates through the world precisely because, as metaculture, it enables difference.

Paradoxically, if there were no cultural differences on the planet, if everyone had precisely the same culture, there would be no need for the freedom concept. Traditional culture inherited from the past would not require the cutting of lateral cultural flows from the outside, since the culture brought in from the outside would be no different from the culture already present inside—whereby the very force impelling freedom around the globe would be extinguished.

Correspondingly, the role of volition would be diminished. And if there were no cultural differences, the Kantian idea of freedom as internal ratiocination, the stripping away of emotional/traditional determinations of action, would make no sense. The ratiocinator needs choice only insofar as there is difference to choose from. And just as seemingly paradoxically, if Kant were right that universal laws of moral conduct could be derived from freedom by way of the categorical imperative, the role of conscious rational volition in the assessment of those laws would be diminished: for each new individual, volition would consist in little more than accepting what has been received from the past—the deductions made by previous generations. In short, freedom would lead to traditional culture.

One question about the future of freedom is whether, especially after such great expansion over the past 250 years, it is likely to retreat into traditional culture—a possible trajectory suggested by a metacultural analysis of freedom.

But this is not the only possible trajectory. Even though the lateral force of the freedom concept as metaculture may diminish as the concept spreads around the globe, the internal workings of the concept, understood in relation to cultural motion, suggest yet another possibility: universality may not be attainable on a cultural plane precisely because it is achievable on the metacultural plane. So, while it may be true that the freedom concept did propagate as metaculture because it facilitated the expression of difference via its role in cutting cultural flows, the metaculture of freedom—once established around the globe—may come to furnish a stimulus to the creation of difference.

It is likely that, where freedom is firmly established—say, in such places as the contemporary United States—the concept will encourage or promote the creation of new differences, and that the new differences will in turn assure the survival of freedom as metaculture, were it because it is the articulation or because it is the assertion of freedom that helps to protect the created differences.

This suggests that the freedom concept, rather than receding, may well be able to self-perpetuate. If, indeed, it does stimulate the development of difference even as it enables the discontinuation of cultural flows, then its two roles will reinforce one another. By stimulating differences, the freedom concept will create conditions favorable to promoting its own maintenance and spread—to sustaining demand for a metacultural device that eases the severance of cultural flows. If it did not encourage the creation of difference, freedom as shared metaculture would have no reason to be.

When viewed in terms of culture–metaculture interactions, the paradoxes surrounding freedom are not paradoxes at all. There can be, at least in theory, universal acceptance of freedom as metaculture precisely because that universal layer both enables and requires differences on the cultural plane.

One can detect a similarity between freedom as metaculture and the Hobbesean idea of the sovereign (1991): for Thomas Hobbes, in order to avoid the war of all against all, people agree to give up one of their natural rights; they turn over adjudication to an absolute ruler, the better to preserve their other individual rights. In the case of freedom, in order not to share the culture of others, one has to share their metaculture. The universality of freedom is thinkable only because it subsists at two levels simultaneously: the cultural and the metacultural. Sharing at the metacultural is made possible by difference at the cultural.

So, while a retreat from freedom might be foreseen—were there to be a universally deducible set of moral laws as Kant supposed and as Habermas in some measure still imagines—this is only one of the possible trajectories for freedom; and, at the time of this writing, it is perhaps not the most plausible one. Precisely because freedom requires the existence of cultural differences for its own propulsion and even survival, it may—if challenged—show far greater tenacity than the monolithic outcome of deductive reasoning.

References

Barth, Fredrik, Editor (1969) Introduction to *Ethnic Groups and Boundaries: The Social Organization of Cultural Differences*, pp. 9–38, London: Allen and Unwin.

Habermas, Jürgen (1984) *The Theory of Communicative Action*, vol. 1, Boston: Beacon Press.

Hobbes, Thomas ([1651], 1991) *Leviathan*, Richard Tuck, Editor, New York: Cambridge University Press.

Kant, Immanuel ([1785], 1991) *The Metaphysics of Morals*, Mary Gregor, Translator, New York: Cambridge University Press.

Labov, William (1972) "The Social Motivation of a Sound Change," in William Labov, Editor, *Sociolinguistic Patterns*, pp. 1–42, Philadelphia: University of Pennsylvania Press.

Nehru, Jawaharlal ([1941], 1958) *Toward Freedom: The Autobiography of Jawaharlal Nehru*, Boston: Beacon Press.

Schwartz, Barry (2004) *The Paradox of Choice: Why More Is Less*, New York: ECCO.

Smith, Adam ([1776], 1994) *The Wealth of Nations*, Edwin Cannan, Editor, New York: Modern Library.

——— ([1759], 2000) *The Theory of Moral Sentiments*, Amherst, NY: Prometheus Books.

Weber, Max (1978) *Economy and Society*, vol. 1, Berkeley and Los Angeles: University of California Press.

11

Shades of Freedom in America

Sheldon Hackney

Like other Americans, my understandings of the world have been challenged by the events of September 11, 2001. On that fateful day, after I had absorbed the stark horror of the event, and noted with pride the amazing responses of Americans both far and near, and also pondered the sort of fanaticism that employs terrorism, I began to wonder why al Qaeda had chosen those particular targets. The two planes that crashed into the towers of the World Trade Center flew right by the Statue of Liberty. The plane that struck the Pentagon might as easily have hit the Capitol or the White House. We do not know the target assigned to the fourth plane that went down in Pennsylvania, beyond the surmise that it was headed for Washington, D.C.

It seems clear that the targets were carefully chosen for symbolic purposes. The World Trade Center and the Pentagon represented America's economic and military power. Conspicuously not chosen were symbols of freedom or democracy—not the Statue of Liberty, not the Liberty Bell, not Independence Hall, nor the home of Congress, nor the house of our elected president. I found myself thinking, "They have got us wrong." Well, if the meaning of America is not simply wealth and power, what is it? Who are we as a people, and how can we defend that core identity against terrorists and our more insidious enemies: sloth, greed, and arrogance?

Conjure in your own mind an apparition of America and you will soon be surrounded by a host of spectral forms,[1] no single one of which is adequate to represent something as complex as our nation. On the other hand, however various those representations may be, they are likely to feature images of motion, talismans of travel—sailing ships

---

1. See *Talk to Me*, a documentary film by Andrea Simon, Arcadia Pictures, New York, NY.

that brought the first Europeans to these shores, covered wagons that took others across the continent, railroads spanning the land between the great oceans, automobiles on the open road, airplanes in "the wild blue yonder," spaceships carrying astronauts to explore the last frontier—suggesting not only the mobility of Americans geographically and socially, but also the idea that America is more about departures than arrivals, more about destinations than the here and now, more about going there than being there, more about hopes than memories. Whatever the goal is, we agree that we are not yet there. We are still becoming.

Not only are we moving, but we are going in various directions at the same time. Hints about the Idea of America are to be found in the paradoxes that mark the frontlines of cultural conflict like the muzzle flashes of opposing armies. We are materialistic, yet we are the most religious people in the developed world. Our economic system is proudly based upon selfishness, yet large-scale philanthropy was invented in America. We believe in the common man and disdain people who put on airs of superiority, yet we are fascinated by celebrities. Hard work is a cultural commandment, yet we are always looking for get-rich-quick schemes. Our middle-class virtues stress delayed gratification, but we avail ourselves of instant coffee, fast foods, and quick marriages. We are optimistic to a fault, but the jeremiad is a major motif of our intellectual life. We admire the heroic perseverance of championship athletes because they represent the triumph of individuals over great obstacles, so we set up a system to mass-produce those exceptional individuals for Olympic competition. We are famously pragmatic yet we are also the land of utopian experiments—the largest of those experiments being the nation itself.

I am amused that the motif of the lonely hero, the unconstrained individual, looms so large in the American imagination, from James Fenimore Cooper's Natty Bumppo to the Hollywood heroes played by John Wayne or Clint Eastwood. As powerful as that virile image of splendid isolation is, the real genius of America is to be found in large-scale organization: the transcontinental railroads, the great business corporations, mammoth philanthropies, the effort to send men to the moon and robots to Mars, not to mention the logistical efforts of World War I, World War II, and, currently, Operation Iraqi Freedom.

Something important about America is to be found in the conversations between opposing terms of a few binary opposites that lie at the center of our being: liberalism and republicanism, individualism and community, the One and the Many, in the sense of our being one nation and many cultures, and, especially, liberty and equality. That we used "freedom" as the name of our current effort in Iraq is a clue to the way we understand ourselves.

Freedom as National Purpose

Freedom is the most powerful word in the American vocabulary, centrally implicated in the meaning of America (Foner 1998; Kammen 1986; Potter 1976; Wiebe 1995). Freedom's alter ego, liberty, is prominently present in the Declaration of Independence. The Preamble to the Constitution asserts that securing its blessings for ourselves and our posterity is a major purpose of government. When President Thomas Jefferson two hundred years ago sent Meriwether Lewis and William Clark to explore the Louisiana Purchase, he called the vast acquisition an "Empire for Liberty." Our patriotic songs invoke the nation as "sweet land of liberty." We pledge allegiance to the flag as the symbol of a republic devoted to "liberty and justice for all." When our leaders want to summon up "the better angels of our nature," freedom is usually there. President Abraham Lincoln, when dedicating the military cemetery at Gettysburg in 1863, hoped that the Civil War would lead to a "new birth of freedom." Woodrow Wilson called his program of reform the "New Freedom." Franklin Delano Roosevelt invested World War II with transcendent significance by enunciating four freedoms as global goals: freedom of speech, freedom of religion, freedom from fear, and freedom from want. Martin Luther King Jr. in 1963, at the March on Washington, had a dream of an America that would truly "let freedom ring" because in that America all God's children would be reconciled and therefore would be able to proclaim, "Free at last! Free at last! Thank God almighty, we are free at last!"

Problems begin to arise only when we pause to wonder what "freedom" means and who is included in its embrace? As Isaiah Berlin noted, "Almost every moralist in human history has praised freedom. Like happiness and goodness, like nature and reality, it is a term whose meaning is so porous that there is little interpretation that it seems able to resist" (Berlin 2002). Freedom has meant different things at different times and places, and it has meant different things to different people at the same time and place (Hirschmann, chap. 9 in this book). Scholars have identified more than two hundred different meanings of freedom (Berlin 2002, 168). That does not include Janet Joplin's definition: "Freedom's just another word for nothing left to lose."

Freedom for the Group

For the Puritans in seventeenth-century New England, freedom in the first instance was the ability of their communities to establish a society that was in accord with their understanding of the Bible, the kind of biblical commonwealth they were not permitted to create in Great Britain, where the king was the Defender of the Faith and the Church of England was the established church. The first kind of freedom for them belonged to the group. As they proved over and over, it certainly did not imply religious toleration for other groups within the Massachusetts Bay Colony. Nor did it imply the absence of communal supervision of individual behavior and belief.

For individuals, what was offered was freedom from enslavement to sin, which freedom was to be achieved by strict conformity to the will of church and community. As the long-time leader of Massachusetts Bay, John Winthrop, put it in his speech to the General Court in 1645, "On Liberty," moral liberty is to be understood in terms of the covenant between God and man, and it is the "liberty to that only which is good, just, and honest. . . . This liberty is maintained and exercised in a way of subjection to authority; it is the same kind of liberty wherewith Christ hath made us free" (Kammen 2001, 20).

Colonial America, in general, was not devoted to religious toleration. Anglicans in Virginia had very different religious ideas from the Puritans in New England, but they agreed completely about the need of the society for uniformity of worship. Yet, by the time of the making of the Constitution in 1787, religious toleration was no longer a controversial subject. Freedom of religion is announced in two critical clauses of the First Amendment, adopted in 1789, though part of the motivation was to reassure the states which still relied on established churches that the federal government would not intervene. In the realm of ideas and values, few things are simple or simply straightforward.

Freedom from Bondage

Something of the explanation for the historic progression from uniformity to toleration is suggested by the experience of the state of Pennsylvania. In 1689, after the Glorious Revolution of 1688 that brought

Mary, the Protestant daughter of James II, and her husband, William of Orange, to the throne, Parliament passed the Act of Toleration, which allowed nonconformists to worship without breaking the law, though atheists, Jews, and Catholics could not vote or hold public office. The English had grown weary of killing and persecuting each other, to determine who could prescribe the mode of worship, and to exercise other aspects of sovereignty.

During the Commonwealth period (1649–1660), Independents and orthodox Anglicans had made common cause to demand toleration from Oliver Cromwell's Puritan government. William Penn and the Quakers were shaped in their thinking about church–state relations by their experience during the Commonwealth period. The Quakers aligned themselves with the Independents, and in favor of religious toleration.

William Penn originally had been confirmed in the Anglican Church, but he became a Quaker in 1667 at the age of twenty-three. He was a zealous convert and was repeatedly arrested for preaching in public, which was considered to be incitement to riot. On one such occasion, in 1670, the jury found him not guilty, an early case of what we might now call "jury nullification." The judge sent him to jail anyway. In fact, the judge sent the jury to jail as well. However, a higher court reversed these rulings and set William Penn free.

While in jail on this occasion, Penn wrote a tract, "The Great Cause of Liberty of Conscience," in which he argued in favor of freedom of worship. Consequently, Penn founded his colony in 1682 explicitly on the theory of religious liberty for all who professed a belief in a supreme being, though Jews could not vote or hold office, nor could Africans or Indians, and atheists were not knowingly allowed residence.

Despite the toleration, even William Penn thought that government was a religious undertaking. Pennsylvania was thus a "Holy Experiment," and the sorts of personal behavior that would draw God's wrath (swearing, cursing, lying, profane talking, drunkenness, whoredom, etc.) were against the law. On the other hand, Penn also believed that, "Force can make a hypocrite, but only faith can make a Christian." Consequently, his proprietary colony was to be a refuge for Quakers and other victims of religious persecution—though there were limits on who was included in the freedom of self-governance.

A representative Assembly, required by Penn's charter from Charles II, existed from the start, as well as a Council whose members were appointed by the Proprietor. In the Preface to the Frame of Government of 1682, Penn wrote that there is a truth that is shared by Monarchy, Oligarchy, and Democracy: "Any Government is Free to the People under it (what-ever be the Frame) where the Laws Rule, and the People are a Party to those Laws, and more than this is Tyranny, Oligarchy or Confusion. . . . For Liberty without Obedience is Confusion, and Obedience without Liberty is Slavery" (Dunn and Dunn 1982, 213–214).

In 1701, after years of bickering about the powers of the Assembly, Penn yielded, abolished the appointive Council, and issued a "Charter of Liberties." It was interchangeably called the "Charter of Privileges," revealing the unspoken assumption of the time that rights were privileges that were granted by one's superiors in the great hierarchy descending from the sovereign monarch. The Charter of 1701 established a unicameral legislature with substantially enhanced powers of local self-government. Henceforth, an elected unicameral legislature and a Governor appointed by the Proprietor ruled over the colony. In 1705, with Queen Anne on the throne, Parliament forced the colony to apply the Test Oath to office holders, thus prohibiting Catholics as well as Jews and nonbelievers from holding office.

In 1751, the first Jubilee of the Charter of Liberties of 1701, the Assembly commissioned a bell to be struck. It was to hang in the statehouse in Philadelphia, and to be rung on important ceremonial occasions. The Speaker of the Assembly ordered an inscription to be engraved on the bell. It was from Leviticus 25:10: "Proclaim LIBERTY throughout all the land unto all the inhabitants thereof." The liberty that the Speaker and the Assembly had in mind was the liberty of "freemen" to participate in the making of the laws under which they were to live (cf. McInerney, chap. 2 in this book). It was the "home rule" nature of the Charter of Privileges that was being celebrated.

The inscription from Leviticus is a commandment through Moses from God to honor Jubilee, which was to be celebrated after a week of Sabbath years, or every fiftieth year. In the year of Jubilee, believers are to free their slaves and to forgive their debts. Jubilee thus was about freedom, but not about freedom from the tyranny of government. It was about freedom from men oppressing each other. It was also about duty. This takes us back to the most prevalent notion of liberty in the colonial period: freedom from sin, which is obtained by perfect obedience to the Word of God.

Nevertheless, the protean word "Freedom" was inscribed on the Bell. It was rung in Philadelphia in 1776, to announce the Declaration of Independence—a document that commenced the struggle of the colonists for freedom in the sense of "home rule" but that also initiated a quest that has continually discovered new meanings of liberty. Most important, the Declaration and the Constitution located sovereignty in the people; no longer would rights and liberties be viewed as privileges that flowed down from above, granted by kings or lords. The Declaration also proclaimed the radical notion that "all men are born equal, that they are endowed by their Creator with certain unalienable Rights, that among these are Life, Liberty, and the pursuit of Happiness."

It was this universal but unrealized promise of freedom that abolitionists picked up in the 1830s. They began using the Bell as the symbol of their effort to abolish human slavery and began referring to it as the Liberty Bell.

Freedom as Self-Reliance

In the course of the eighteenth century several varieties of freedom were at play in Colonial America. Republican theory, deployed by British dissenters, emphasized that the source of authority was to be found in the citizens. Everyone was subject to the law, but subjects were to participate in the making of the laws. Since one did not want laws that served the interests of a particular person or faction, it was important that the representatives of the people be citizens of great virtue, and virtue was to be found among those who were independent enough to discern the common interest and to resist the pressures of self-interested individuals and factions. In short, virtue was to be found among gentlemen of property and standing. Without property, a man was dependent on others, and thus not fully free.[2] At the time of the Revolution, most colonists were un-free in the sense that they were dependent upon someone, usually the patriarchal head of a household: women, children, apprentices, indentured servants, and slaves. Property, argued John Locke in "The Second Treatise of Government," was the guarantor of freedom. "Man being born, as has been proved, with a Title to perfect Freedom, and an uncontrolled enjoyment of all the Rights and Privileges of the Law of Nature, equally with any other Man, or number of men in the world, hath by Nature a Power, not only to preserve his Property, that is, his Life, Liberty and

---

2. See J. J. Mulhern (2008) "The Political Economy of Citizenship: A Classical Perspective," in Jose V. Ciprut, Editor, *The Future of Citizenship*, Cambridge, MA: The MIT Press.

Estate, against the Inquiries and Attempts of other Men; but to judge of, and punish the breaches of that Law in others" (quoted in Gerber 2002, 229).

The First Great Awakening, exciting the colonies in the mid-years of the eighteenth century, emphasized the direct and personal relationship between the individual and God, which one might see as the beginnings of theological individualism. At the same time, the great free market revolution was also causing people to begin to conceive of freedom in individualistic, as opposed to communal, terms. With the free market as the model, the new vision was that a just society should not depend on the republican ideal of leaders with sufficient virtue, authorized to choose policies that would serve the general interest of society as a whole. A just society more reliably was the product of the automatic balancing that would occur if every individual pursued his own self-interest. Indeed, in liberal theory, there is no such thing as the "general interest." After the Revolution, and then rapidly in the nineteenth century, as immigration, industrialization, and urbanization continued to transform America, individualism, understood as self-reliance, became the dominant mind-set of America (Appleby 1992a; Sandel 1998; Shain 1994).

Not surprisingly, the tycoons of the Gilded Age who built the modern industrial and financial corporations, and amassed the great American fortunes, found this notion of self-reliance very attractive, even flattering, especially when combined with the then-fashionable Darwinian idea of the survival of the fittest. When confronting labor unions, conservatives used the liberal argument that each worker had "freedom of contract," which is to say that the union ought not to interfere with the worker's right to sell his labor to the employer. Progressives responded with a new view of freedom that recognized that individuals could be as oppressed by other human beings as they could be by government—and especially so by these new aggregations of economic power. The progressive notion was that the government should be used as the democratic balance wheel of justice, regulating the free market and providing those things, such as education, that would allow the individual to have a chance to realize his full potential. From the late nineteenth century to this day, the role of government has been at the center of political conflict in the United States.

Meanwhile, back in the eighteenth century, our Revolution was fought to protect the old British notion of freedom as being the right of "freemen" to participate in making the laws under which everyone would live. If the king and Parliament insisted on taxation without representation, then perhaps liberty could only be found when the colonies were free from the control of the empire. In the process of explaining themselves to the world, and of rallying support among the American colonial population, the Founding Fathers chose to resort to "natural rights" philosophy, and to use the concepts of "liberty" and "equality," which contained a powerful capacity to grow, to include more and more people in their protective embrace, and slowly to reduce the conflicts between the theory and practice of freedom.

From Subjects to Citizens

With "liberty" and "equality" joined together by the founding documents,[3] it was natural that Americans during the Revolution would shift from referring to themselves as "subjects" of the crown to seeing themselves as "citizens" of the United States of America. Citizenship has an equalizing aspect to it. The rights and privileges of citizenship are enjoyed equally by all, are they not? Actually, the Constitution was originally silent on the question of what the precise "privileges and immunities" of citizenship were, and on the matter of who is a citizen and who is not. The assumption of the government was that every free person who did not flee the country during the Revolution was a citizen (Smith 1997).

Women occupied a particularly anomalous place inasmuch as their status generally followed that of their father or husband, the male head-of-household on whom they were dependent. Widows and spinsters with property were in most matters exceptions because they were independent. They could not vote, however, until the Nineteenth Amendment was ratified in 1920. Indians also occupied an ambiguous position until they were specifically declared to be citizens by act of Congress in 1934 (Kerber 1997).

A further hint that Americans had a racialized notion of national identity came in the Naturalization Act of 1790, which restricted eligibility for naturalization to "free white persons." This restriction was not changed until the McCarren-Walter Act of 1952, though that act left in place the "national origins quota" system that was itself the

---

3. For a discussion of the democratic dilemma created by these two terms see Mark P. Gaige (2008) "Citizen: Past Practices, Prospective Patterns," in Jose V. Ciprut, Editor, *The Future of Citizenship*, Cambridge, MA: The MIT Press.

public policy embodiment of a racialized notion of the American identity.[4]

Free blacks were not as free as free whites, a fact confirmed by countless discriminations suffered by people of color in nonslave states in the antebellum period. Then, in the infamous Dred Scott decision in 1857, Chief Judge Roger B. Taney wrote for the majority of the Supreme Court that people of African descent were not citizens of the United States and did not enjoy the "rights of privileges of citizenship."

The Fourteenth Amendment, ratified in 1868, was the second of the three great Civil War amendments. It voided Dred Scott and created a national citizenship, along with state citizenship, and declared that all "persons" had a right to the "equal protection of the law." Though violated in letter and spirit, this provision, over time, has been a powerful tool in the development of a more inclusive and tolerant society. In that atmosphere, in 1870, the Naturalization Act of 1790 was amended to allow the naturalization of African immigrants.

Thousands of Chinese came to the United States in the 1840s and 1850s, mostly to the West Coast and to work on the transcontinental railroads. They were not eligible for naturalization, though their children born in the United States were automatically citizens. The Chinese Exclusion Act in 1882 wrote into immigration law the prejudices of European Americans: it barred Chinese laborers. During World War II, the Chinese were allies. Congress repealed this insulting restriction, leaving Chinese immigration to be governed by the national origins system, under which China's quota for 1943 was 105 people.

Japanese started coming to the United States in significant numbers in the 1890s and in the first decade of the twentieth century, stirring up the same sort of anti-Asian sentiment. The result was the Gentlemen's Agreement of 1900, in which the United States promised not to exclude Japanese by statute if Japan drastically limited the emigration of laborers. This arrangement was made stronger and more explicit through a series of diplomatic notes in 1907 and in 1908. The racial assumptions of this policy became apparent in particularly ugly form during World War II when the U.S. government interned thousands of Japanese-American citizens, as well as Japanese aliens, while placing German aliens under a very loose monitoring system.

---

4. There were, and are, three ways to obtain American citizenship: being born in the United States (*jus soli*); being born of American parents (*jus sanguine*); and being naturalized.

Meanwhile, after the Civil War, during the 1880s and after, the magnitude and character of European immigration changed, increasing dramatically and shifting from northern and western Europe to eastern and southern Europe. The "New Immigration" stimulated a vigorous immigration restriction movement, as well as aggressive cultural assimilation efforts. While, in principle and in effect, immigration policy remained open to all Europeans, in practice the more one could look like and act like an Anglo-American, the more welcome one was.

World War I interrupted the flow of these "huddled masses yearning to breathe free," as they were described in the idealistic lines of the poem by Emma Lazarus (1849–1887) and inscribed on the base of the Statue of Liberty in 1903. Following the Great War, in step with the growing isolationism of the time, the immigration restriction movement was successful in getting the Congress to pass the National Origins Quota Act of 1921, amended in 1924. The new policy set a low limit on overall annual immigration (350,000 per year at the beginning, as compared with almost one million per year in the first decade of the century) and provided that the quota be allocated to countries based on their proportion of the U.S. population in 1890. This was intended to freeze the ethnic character of the American population at its 1890 composition.

First the Great Depression and then World War II limited the flow of immigrants to a trickle, even fewer than the official quota, but the National Origins Quota system remained in effect until it was replaced in 1965 by a new immigration law that was in tune with the newly ascendant racial egalitarianism. Since that revolutionary act, increasing numbers of Hispanic and Asian immigrants have found their way into the United States, giving rise to struggles over the meanings of the multiculturalism that increasingly is the reality of American life. Racial nationalism, dominant from the Revolution to the 1960s, had been replaced by civic nationalism, under whose dispensation we currently live.

Individualism and Community

When the French aristocrat Alexis de Tocqueville visited the United States during Andrew Jackson's presidency, he entitled his brilliant analysis of the society he found there *Democracy in America*. First published in 1835, it is so full of deep insights that the America it describes is still recognizable almost two centuries later. Tocqueville was not always right, of course. For instance, he thought the passion of Americans for equality would always win out in the competition with liberty, yet the United States today has the greatest internal disparity of wealth and income among the industrialized nations.

On the other hand, de Tocqueville did see many things clearly. In particular, he saw the reciprocal relationship between individualism and community. He coined the term "individualism" to describe the self-reliance and self-rule that he found in America, and he worried about it, as you might expect a European aristocrat to do: "Thus not only does democracy make each man forget his ancestors, but it hides his descendants from him and separates him from his contemporaries; it constantly leads him back toward himself alone and threatens finally to confine him wholly in the solitude of his own heart" (Tocqueville 2000, 2:484).

Yet, de Tocqueville also noticed that Americans are a "nation of joiners," as Arthur Schlesinger Sr. has termed it—a society in which voluntary associations are a way of life:

Americans of all ages, all conditions, all minds constantly unite. Not only do they also have commercial and industrial associations, in which all take part, but they also have associations of a thousand other kinds: religious, moral, grave, futile, very general and very particular, immense and very small; Americans use associations to give fetes, to found seminaries, to build inns, to raise churches, to distribute books, to send missionaries to the antipodes; in this manner they create hospitals, prisons, schools. Finally, if it is a question of bringing to light a truth or developing a sentiment with the support of a great example, they associate. Everywhere that, at the head of a new undertaking, you see the government in France and a great lord in England, count on it that you will perceive an association in the United States. (Tocqueville 2000, 2:489)

This dialogic relationship between individualism and community is one of the main themes of American history. It is not really a tension because Americans in public opinion polls express the same level of enthusiasm for the notion of individualism as for community. Yet it seems paradoxical that we live utterly alone, but have no meaning, no identity, apart from the social context in which we are embedded. It is this two-ness in our natures that makes us long for "community" (see Arcenas, chap. 3 in this book). The connection, as Gordon Wood has argued (1993, 220), is that "social love" derives from "self-love." And as Robert Wiebe suggests (1995, 40), "Free individuals formed democratic communities [and] democratic communities sustained free individuals." Americans continue to live their lives in this conversation between individualism and community.

Creating a National Sentiment

Meanwhile, the young United States had to create a sense of nationhood that other nations inherited. Living as they did in local communities and separate colonies, without any collective memory other than the heroic struggle for independence, ordinary citizens had little idea of what it meant to be an American. George Washington, speaking the words written by Alexander Hamilton, noted in his Farewell Address that Americans needed to develop a "national sentiment" if they were to survive as a nation in the family of nations. What was that sentiment to be? He did not say.

European intellectuals had always seen the New World as a place, where one or one's group could escape the corruptions and restrictions of European society and build a society that would avoid or correct all of the perceived problems of Europe. Alternatively, the colonies were seen simply as the land of opportunity, of second chances, or of first chances for second sons—a place open to talent and industry. America served as a projection of European dreams and nightmares.

It is not surprising, therefore, that the "national sentiment" in the late eighteenth century came from the "party of hope" in Europe. Joyce Appleby finds the seeds of American "exceptionalism" in the way European intellectuals viewed the newly founded United States. She quotes a French progressive as saying of the United States, "They are the hope of the human race; they may well become its model." Denis Diderot called the new republic an asylum from fanaticism and tyranny "for all the peoples of Europe," and Thomas Jefferson's secretary, still in France after Jefferson's return home, compared Americans to a group of prisoners who have broken out of a "common gaol" (i.e., Europe) and are being watched by their fellow inmates with "an anxious eye" to see if they make good their escape. Bernard Fay, the French historian, wrote later that "not a book on America was printed between 1775 and 1790 but ended with a sort of homily on America as the future of mankind" (Appleby 1992b, 419). To European dissidents of all kinds, the United States represented the possibility of social reform. In a sense, Americans learned who they were from these Europeans, who were using America to their own rhetorical ends (Appleby 2000; Greene 1993; Woodward 1991).

These reveries of Europeans were popular in the United States because they offered eighteenth-century Americans a collective identity before they had any other basis for spiritual unity. As the politics of the 1790s grew more heated, the "exceptionalism" that was latent in colonial experience was reformulated into a specific destiny for the nation, a destiny that was tied to European dreams as well as to the political principles enunciated in the Declaration and the Constitution, as ambiguous as those were. This was the beginning of the conscious conception of American "exceptionalism"—the making of a new "imagined community" that forms the nation. The United States was in reality an insignificant country. In the American imagination, however, the nation became the vanguard of human progress, the very exemplar of liberty—"the last best hope on earth," as Lincoln said.

This Grand Narrative of American history has been under attack for the past two generations as being triumphalist, and Eurocentric, which is to say, oblivious to the gaps between creed and reality, forgetful of the bitter conflicts among Americans, which have offered alternative outcomes for America at every step along the way. One can think of realities that are at odds with the innocence of our myth: slavery, the genocide of Native Americans, anti-Catholicism, nativism, anti-Semitism, xenophobia, anti-Asian feelings, the exploitation of "wage slaves," adventures in imperialism, and the repression of dissidents during the Red Scare in 1919–1920 at the time of the Russian Revolution, or during the McCarthyism of the 1950s. Nevertheless, we are still inspired by our commitment to the Revolutionary ideals of liberty and equality, even as we continue to try to understand their meaning.

The most obvious example of a disjunction between theory and practice, of course, was human slavery. A number of the signers of the Declaration and drafters of the Constitution were slave owners. Even though an abolitionist movement already existed, the Constitution tacitly recognized slavery in order to bind the slave states to the Union. Besides, at the time of the making of the Constitution, many expected slavery to die of its own inefficiency. The invention of the cotton gin and the steamboat, however, breathed new life (profits) into the corpse.

The argument over human slavery, in a country devoted to human freedom, intensified during the debates that led to the Missouri Compromise in 1820. It posed a moral question that was increasingly difficult to avoid. Finally, the election of Abraham Lincoln in 1860 was taken by white southerners to convey a signal that the national government was in the hands of forces hostile to their "peculiar institution," the popular euphemism for slavery. Eleven of the fifteen slave states decided to leave the Union.

And the war came. Though initially the North fought simply "to preserve the Union," it is clear that the reason for war having been slavery, freedom from human bondage became the meaning of the war. Concluding that the federal government in the hands of Republicans threatened the institution of slavery, the South seceded to protect the freedom of states and local communities to determine their own social arrangements. The Civil War in this sense was a contest between two opposing ideas of freedom (Foner 1998, 95; McPherson 1988, vii).

The Civil War settled the question of chattel slavery, but Reconstruction did not settle the question of what "freedom" would mean for the former slaves. By 1877, the white South and the white North were reconciled at the expense of African-Americans, who were abandoned; their second-class citizenship was to be defined by white southerners in legally prescribed segregation and through political disfranchisement, a system of racial subordination put into place in the twenty years that would follow 1890—the year of the Mississippi Constitutional Convention, held to curb black voter participation by seemingly legitimate means, such as the imposition of a literacy test.

The long struggle by African-Americans and their allies toward achieving equal citizenship produced notable victories in the first half of the twentieth century, albeit no dramatic change in racial discrimination. Then, under the slogan of "Freedom Now," the Civil Rights movement of the 1950s and 1960s, together with the other social justice movements that it inspired, led to the erasure of legally prescribed discrimination from the statute books, fostering a shift toward cultural diversity and social inclusiveness, with equal rights and opportunities for all.

Parallel to the efforts in the 1960s of previously marginalized groups (blacks, American Indians, women, Hispanics, gays, lesbians, and people with disabilities) to overcome the hitherto oppressive external roadblocks to individual achievement was the effort of the counterculture to free individuals from equally oppressive internal roadblocks posed by cultural constraints. "If it feels good, do it," was the mantra. The counterculture ridiculed every middle-class tenet: hard work as its own reward, postponement of gratification, self-control, responsibility for family and community, and so forth. What the counterculture was asserting was that it was not enough to strive for a society in which everyone could become whatever they wanted to become. We should create a society in which people were free to want to be whatever kind of person they could imagine being. This raises an interesting question about the "freely choosing autonomous self" of liberal theory: who is the "real" self that is doing the "wanting," the "imagining," and the "choosing"? And is that real "self" free of oppressive cultural commandments?[5]

Freedom as Self-Invention

This invocation of the liberty of self-invention did not begin with the counterculture, and surely not with singer-actress Madonna's multiple personalities. As an early self-fabricator, Benjamin Franklin comes to mind. Perhaps the story of Frederick Douglass can illustrate this dimension of the malleability of freedom.

Douglass was born a slave on a Maryland plantation. At the age of about eight, sent to Baltimore to live with a family there, he had a transforming experience, which he described in the first of his three autobiographies, written at different points in his long life:

Very soon after I went to live with Mr. and Mrs. Auld, she very kindly commenced to teach me the abc. After I had learned this she assisted me in learning to spell words of three or four letters. Just at this point of my progress, Mr. Auld found out what was going on, and at once forbade Mrs. Auld to instruct me further, telling her, among other things, that it was unlawful, as well as unsafe, to teach a slave to read. To use his own words further, he said, if you give a nigger an inch he will take a mile. A nigger should know nothing but to obey his master; to do as he is told to do. Learning would spoil the best nigger in the world. Now, said he, if they teach that nigger (speaking of myself) how to read, there would be no keeping him. It would forever unfit him to be a slave. He would at once become unmanageable and of no value to his master. As to himself it could do him no good but a great deal of harm. It would make him discontented and unhappy. . . . These words sank deep into my heart, stirred up sentiments within that lay slumbering and called into existence an entirely new train of thought. It was a new, a special revelation explaining dark and mysterious things with which my youthful understanding had struggled in vain. I now understood what had been, to me, a most perplexing difficulty; to wit, the white man's power to enslave the black man. It was a grand achievement, and I prized it highly. From that moment I understood the pathway from slavery to freedom. (Douglass 1993, 57–58)

---

5. For a detailed account see David R. Williams (2008) "Ego and Ethics," in Jose V. Ciprut, Editor, *Ethics, Politics, and Democracy: From Primordial Principles to Prospective Practices*, Cambridge, MA: The MIT Press.

Mr. Auld was right. Though Mrs. Auld ceased to teach her young slave, Douglass continued to learn on his own. Soon, he escaped to New York. From that point of physical emancipation, he started the process of becoming the Frederick Douglass that we know. This story of self-liberation through learning has two meanings: he left physically and escaped chattel slavery. Then he exercised his liberty (see Williams and Barber, chap. 4 in this book) to make himself into the kind of free man that he wanted to be.

I believe that when Frederick Douglass composed this first self-presentation in 1845 at the age of twenty-seven, he knew exactly what he was doing. He knew that he was creating a persona. He was not only creating himself, but he was portraying someone in print. I infer that from the way the *Narrative* is written, but also because Douglass was writing fairly soon after William Ellery Channing published a widely read book, in 1837, entitled *Self-Culture*—a set of lectures that he had been giving to working-class audiences. Channing was preaching not the virtue of rags-to-riches (that would come later, in the 103 novels and books for juveniles to be written by Horatio Alger in the last third of the nineteenth century); he was preaching the virtue of the self-made man in its original sense: how to master oneself, and build character, and lead a moral life.

The liberty of self-invention is a characteristically American phenomenon, reflected in the power of the myth of the frontier; recognizable in our therapeutic culture; in television programs such as *Extreme Makeover* that, however superficially, trade upon our desire to start anew; in the consumer culture that invites us to buy at the store the identity that we want; in our commitment to second chances; and even in our religious desire to be "born again."

Liberty Ordered and Balanced

All of this is to say that, historically, we have argued over what liberty means and who should enjoy its blessings. Those struggles were made inevitable by the very fact that liberty has been at the core of our self-image from the birth of the nation to the present. A prize so precious is bound to attract suitors and protectors, both noble and profane.

We have therefore thought of liberty as freedom from sin, the kind of freedom that is to be achieved through perfect obedience to some authority's interpretation of God's word; personal independence, which can be secured by owning property; freedom from chattel slavery; the absence of wage slavery; the ability to reinvent oneself; freedom from discrimination because of one's group identity; participation in self-governance; religious toleration; local self-government; and countless other definitions.

As a society, we have learned how to hold in dynamic tension the notion that liberty has to do with the absence of governmental constraints and the Progressive Era idea that, in a complex and interconnected economy, with vast powers over the individual wielded by invisible forces and distant people, the government must act in positive ways that should help the individual to free himself and to achieve self-realization.

A constant theme throughout has been the need for "ordered liberty":[6]

America the beautiful
God shed his grace on thee.
Confirm thy soul in self control,
Thy liberty in law.[7]

Or, as the eminent jurist Learned Hand put it in 1944 in his address, "The Spirit of Liberty," when addressing the question, "What is liberty?": "It is not the ruthless, the unbridled will; it is not freedom to do as one likes. That is the denial of liberty, and leads straight to its overthrow. A society in which men recognize no check upon their freedom soon becomes a society where freedom is the possession of only a savage few" (Kammen 2001, 171).

Several years ago the billionaire financier George Soros, who is active in encouraging the growth of capitalism and democracy in the countries of the former Soviet Union, wrote that unregulated free markets do not breed democracy; they breed thugs (Soros 1997). In a similar vein, though somewhat more elegantly, the historian of ideas Isaiah Berlin wrote: "Both liberty and equality are among the primary goals pursued by human beings through many centuries; but total liberty for wolves is death to the lambs, total liberty of the powerful, the gifted, is not compatible with the rights to a decent existence of the weak and the less gifted" (Berlin 1990, 12).

A constant worry through these centuries of freedom is that it would degrade into some form of uncivilized society. Thus, eighteenth-century

---

6. See Viet D. Dinh, chap. 12 in this book, for the connection between the internal and external contexts, in globalizing settings.
7. Words by Katherine Lee Bates, a professor at Wellesley College, written during a trip to Colorado, 1893.

commentators worried that liberty would undermine the authority that they assumed was necessary to keep order. Theodore Adorno and other social scientists of the twentieth century, who were trying to explain totalitarianism, theorized that freedom breeds such feelings of insecurity and anxiety that many ("authoritarian personalities") will seek security in submission to some strong authority. In two hundred years, the American people progressed from worrying that too much freedom would lead to anarchic disorder to fearing that too much freedom would lead to regimentation.

It is both wonderful and worrisome that freedom is so variegated in its meanings and so powerful in its appeal. It tells us who we are and reminds us of whom we must not become. It gives Americans a standard by which we can measure the worth of proposed policies, and it allows our leaders to mobilize support for actions that require sacrifice but that will be beneficial in the long run. At the same time, it also allows our leaders to mask less altruistic motives, to lead us in directions in which we should not be going. The task of the citizen is to discern the difference between those two rhetorical uses of the idea of freedom. It depends on an alert and healthy democracy. If citizens fail in that task, freedom will fail.

Liberty, in short, is a communal enterprise. Whatever it means, whether it is the absence of governmental or social intrusion into the space in which the individual is autonomous (freedom from . . .) or the availability of governmental and social support to overcome barriers like poverty or ignorance (freedom to . . .), it depends on the active commitment of the members of the society. If liberty is not cherished and nurtured by the community to which we belong, so that it is expressed in the laws that apply to everyone equally, and if it does not include all citizens alike, it will soon not exist for any but the fiercest animals in the urbanized jungle. Furthermore, since liberty changes its meaning from time to time, and place to place, it will always be unfinished and contingent—forever in need of being remolded by our very selves, to defend against new threats, but also to take advantage of new opportunities for each civic participant.

References

Appleby, Joyce (1992a) *Liberalism and Republicanism in the Historical Imagination*, Cambridge, MA: Harvard University Press.

———— (1992b) "Recovering America's Historic Diversity: Beyond Exceptionalism," *Journal of American History*, 79(2) (September):419–431.

——— (2000) *Inheriting the Revolution: The First Generation of Americans*, Cambridge, MA: Harvard University Press.

Berlin, Isaiah (1990) "The Pursuit of the Ideal," in Henry Hardy, Editor, *The Crooked Timber of Humanity*, London: John Murray.

——— (2002) "Two Concepts of Liberty," in Henry Hardy, Editor, *Liberty*, New York and Oxford: Oxford University Press.

Douglass, Frederick (1993) *Narrative of the Life of Frederick Douglass, An American Slave, Written by Himself*, edited with an introduction by David Blight, Boston: Bedford Books of St. Martin's Press.

Dunn, Richard, and Mary Maples Dunn, Editors (1982) *The Papers of William Penn*, vol. 2: *1680–1684*, Philadelphia: University of Pennsylvania Press.

Foner, Eric (1998) *The Story of American Freedom*, New York: Norton.

Gerber, Scott Douglas, Editor (2002) *The Declaration of Independence: Origins and Impact*, Washington, DC: CQ Press.

Greene, Jack P. (1993) *The Intellectual Construction of America: Exceptionalism and Identity from 1492 to 1800*, Chapel Hill: University of North Carolina Press.

Kammen, Michael (1986, 2001) *Spheres of Liberty: Changing Perceptions of Liberty in American Culture*, Jackson: University Press of Mississippi. [First published in 1986 by the University of Wisconsin Press.]

Kerber, Linda (1997) "The Meanings of Citizenship," *Journal of American History*, 84(3) (December):833–854.

McPherson, James M. (1988) *Battle Cry of Freedom*, New York: Ballantine Books.

Potter, David (1976) *Freedom and Its Limitations in American Life*, Stanford, CA: Stanford University Press.

Sandel, Michael (1998) *Liberalism and the Limits of Justice*, 2nd ed., Cambridge: Cambridge University Press.

Shain, Barry Alan (1994) *The Myth of American Individualism: The Protestant Origins of American Political Thought*, Princeton, NJ: Princeton University Press.

Smith, Rogers (1997) *Civic Ideals: Conflicting Visions of Citizenship in U.S. History*, New Haven, CT: Yale University Press.

Soros, George (1997) "The Capitalist Threat," *The Atlantic Monthly* 279(2):45–58. Available at: http://www.theatlantic.com/issues/97feb/capital/capital.htm.

Tocqueville, Alexis de (2000) *Democracy in America*, Harvey Mansfield and Delba Winthrop, Editors, Chicago: University of Chicago Press.

Wiebe, Robert (1995) *Self-Rule: A Cultural History of American Democracy*, Chicago: University of Chicago Press.

Wood, Gordon (1993) *The Radicalness of the American Revolution*, New York: Vintage Books of Random House. [Originally published by Knopf, 1993.]

Woodward, C. Vann (1991) *The Old World's New World*, New York: Oxford University Press.

12

Outside In/Inside Out: The Ordering of Liberty in a Globalizing International Political Economy

Viet D. Dinh

In the search for the elusive balance between liberty and security, and short of platitudes, commentators often resort to the stand-by dictum from Benjamin Franklin that "they that can give up essential liberty to obtain a little temporary safety deserve neither liberty nor safety." With this thought, there can be no disagreement. One should not trade liberty (let alone "essential liberty") for safety (let alone "a little temporary safety"). That is so, because security should not be—and in U.S. constitutional democracy is not—an end in itself, but rather merely a means to the greater end of liberty.

Oft-quoted and incontrovertible, Franklin's truism is not very illuminating. For the essential question is what does one mean by liberty. Here, I think Edmund Burke puts it best: "The only liberty I mean is a liberty connected with order; that not only exists along with order and virtue, but which cannot exist at all without them" (1996, 64). Order and liberty, under this conception, are symbiotic; each is necessary to the stability and legitimacy that is essential for a government under law.

To illustrate this symbiotic relationship, consider liberty without order. Absent order, liberty is simply unbridled license: men can do whatever they choose. It is easy enough to recognize that such a world of liberty without order is unstable, but I would argue that it is also illegitimate. The essence of liberty is the freedom from subjugation to the will of another. In a world of unbridled license, the strong do what they will, and the weak suffer what they must. One man's expression of his desires will deprive another of his freedom. Liberty without order is illegitimate because one man may infringe, by force as necessary, another's freedom. True liberty only exists in an ordered society with rules and laws that govern and limit the behavior of men.

Just as liberty cannot exist without order, order without liberty is not only illegitimate but also unstable. The first of these propositions is widely accepted, so I will not dwell on it here. But it is important to recognize that where there is only order but not liberty, force must be exerted by men over men in an attempt to compel obedience and to create a mirage of stability. Most people are familiar with Rousseau's dictum: "Man is born free, and everywhere he is in chains." But often neglected is the sentence that immediately follows in his *On Social Contract:* "Anyone who believes himself the master of others is no less a slave than they. . . . [F]or, either this people, in recovering its liberty by means of the same right as the one by which it was stolen, is entitled to regain it, or no one was entitled to take it away" (1988, 85).

Order without liberty is unstable precisely because it is illegitimate. In an apparent order maintained by brute strength, the ruler has no greater claim to the use of force than his subject, and the master and slave are in a constant state of war—one trying to maintain the mirage of stability created by his use of force, the other seeking to use force to recover his lost freedom. Order and liberty therefore are not competing concepts that must be balanced against each other to maintain some sort of democratic equilibrium. Rather, they are complementary values symbiotically contributing to the stability and legitimacy of a constitutional democracy. Order and liberty go together like love and marriage and horse and carriage—and, as the song says, "you can't have one without the other."

In his 1998 book, *The Structure of Liberty*, Randy Barnett distinguishes liberty structured by order from unbridled license by comparing it to a tall building, the Sears Tower. License permits thousands of people to congregate in the same space, but only with the order imposed by the structure of the building—its hallways and partitions, stairwells and elevators, signs and lights—would those thousands be endowed with liberty, each to pursue his own end without trampling on others or being trampled on. Like a building, every society has a structure that, by constraining the actions of its members, permits them at the same time to act toward accomplishing their ends. To illustrate the essential necessity of that structure, Barnett posits this hypothetical: "Imagine being able to push a button and make the structure of the building instantly vanish. Thousands of persons would plunge to their deaths" (1998, 2).

Osama bin Laden pushed that button on September 11, 2001, and thousands of persons plunged to their deaths. Just as Randy Barnett's building was only a metaphor for the structure of ordered liberty, al

Qaeda's aim was not simply to destroy the World Trade Center; its target was the very foundation of ordered liberty.

Appreciating the exceptional nature of the threat, government in the United States has embarked on a thorough campaign to contain and to defeat the international terrorist conspiracy. At home, that strategy is one based on the paradigm of prevention. Abroad, the strategy manifests itself as the doctrine of preemption.

The twin manifestations in domestic and foreign policy of the preventive strategy have attracted much comment—some nuanced; most, rather critical; and a few even apocalyptic. Despite their variety and predominantly critical approach, these commentaries generally adopt the administration's premise that what happened on the day of September 11, 2001, was so unprecedented and unimaginable that it rocked our world—and that world would change forever.

In some ways this premise is correct. We were awakened from our democratic innocence, from what a law professor, from a perspective much different from mine, called our "puerile arrogance" (Young 2003, 28). We realized that there are people out there who would not only reject our institutions, ideals, and values, but also find them so offensive that they would give up their lives to take the lives of innocents and to upend all that we hold dear.

Others reject the notion that 9/11 was special; they perceive political conspiracy lurking in the shadow of 9/11 exceptionalism. Accusing the Bush administration of engaging in a "plot against history," historian Marilyn Young concludes that "its ruthless cunning is demonstrated everywhere" (2003, 28). Hyperventilating rhetoric aside—and it is rhetoric, because I do not think that a respected scholar could actually *believe* this ludicrous charge—I do think that 9/11 exceptionalism can be taken too far: "9/11" was an event, not a justification in and of itself. It is, more precisely, a challenge for scholars and policy makers to discover its meaning, and to draw from it some lessons for the twenty-first century.

As Marilyn Young poses that intellectual project, "This use of the idea of change to justify new policies requires that we examine critically whether this justification rests on a firm foundation, whether the idea of transformation holds up under closer scrutiny, and whether any changes are of the sort that would justify these new government policies" (2003, 8). It is to this task that I now turn.

The attacks of September 11, 2001, and the composition of its perpetrators, should make one lesson crystal-clear: Nation-states no longer possess a monopoly on warfare or warlike violence (Ciprut, 2000). Nineteen individuals, with several hundred thousand dollars, inflicted more damage, took more lives in one day, than even the most mighty of armies would—and, I should add, against the most powerful nation on earth. That there are people who would wish such damage on the United States and on its people is neither new nor surprising. What is surprising, however, is that they have both the will and the means to do so—that they were able to do that which no enemy nation has ever been willing or able to do in the history of the United States.

There were signposts leading to the lesson of 9/11. For many years, individual terrorists and terrorist organizations have sought, and have even articulated their desire, to obtain statelike force. Did not Timothy McVeigh illustrate the ease of mass violence even in his very own country? In that sense, the breach on September 11 of the monopoly on force of nation-states is not a watershed. Rather, it merely marked a turn, even if in a most dramatic and catastrophic manner. Just as— dominated by wars among nation-states—the twentieth century gave way to the twenty-first, so did the day of September 11 threaten the replacement of the world order with a long period of disorder.

In this new era, the Age of Terror, the threat to national and global security comes not only *from* nation-states individually. In a far more striking way, the threat is now posed *to* nation-states collectively, by terrorists who believe fervently in their cause, owe no allegiance to any particular place, social space, or polity, and place no value on civilized human life, including their wretched own.

This phenomenon of ideology unmoored from geography, coupled with the means to inflict mass destruction, poses a pervasive and asymmetric threat to the international order. It is pervasive because the international terrorist movement is not really a movement at all, only a loose network of complicitous objectives and ideals. The threat from the shade is asymmetric because the new warriors would exploit the vulnerabilities of liberal democracies, all the more hatefully to inflict terror on their easily accessible masses.

They have engendered fear by undermining the stability of consequence. Acting without the tethers of a geographic base or the restraint of a national polity, the enemy is faceless and, in this way, impregnable.

This central lesson of 9/11, that nation-states no longer have a monopoly on the motives and means of war, has ominous implications in a whole host of areas of law, policy, and international relations.

My comments here focus on the fundamentals, examining how terrorism threatens not only American freedom or Western democracies but also the entire world order. That order is predicated on the nation-state as the organizing unit of sovereignty—a predication that is being challenged by organizations and individuals who operate statelessly, employing terrorism as a means to advance their personal designs and preferences or their ramified, complicit ideological ends.

I first examine the development of the sovereign nation-state as the basic unit of political organization and scrutinize how transnational terrorism threatens the international order predicated on such sovereignty. I follow this outside-in analysis with an inside-out look at how patriotism—or, put more bluntly, nationalism—contributes to the maintenance of sovereignty and international order. I will conclude with some thoughts on where all of this may lead us and, perhaps more important, where a recommitment to national sovereignty and dedication to national ideals should not lead us.

The Nation-State and the Westphalian Order

We start at the beginning, or to be precise, before the beginning of the political system as we know it. The year is 1612. Rudolf II, Emperor of the Holy Roman Empire, dies. Five contentious and tumultuous months later, on June 13, his brother Matthias is elected to the imperial throne.

But what the new Emperor Matthias inherits is hardly an empire as we would imagine it. In this presovereignty age, political power was split among cities, duchies, kingdoms, leagues, unions, and . . . empires. That power was further split between religious and secular authorities, with no clear lines demarcating where God leaves off and Caesar takes over. Warfare was a way of life, as rulers competed for territory, vied for power, and sought revenge for personal insults. Amidst this hodgepodge of overlapping allegiances, vague boundaries, and parchment compromises, the Protestant Reformation swept through Europe, challenging the religious authority of the Catholic Church and dislodging its political authority over temporal matters. These were the times that inspired Hobbes to posit the state of nature, in which he aptly described life as "solitary, poor, nasty, brutish, and short" (1994, 76).

So it was that six years later, in 1618, "a war of succession for a duchy near Schleswig-Holstein" (Ward et al. 1907, v) grew like a brush fire on a hot summer day, spreading everywhere and consuming all. As *The Cambridge Modern History* puts it:

The quarrels of the Alpine leagues and those about the Mantuan succession, the rivalries of the Scandanavian north and of the Polish north-east, the struggle, only temporarily suspended, of the United Provinces against Spain, the perennial strife between Spain and France for predominance in Italy and elsewhere—all contributed to the sweep of the current. Even the Ottoman Empire was concerned in its progress; for the 'Turco-Calvinistic' combination announced by the pamphleteers was by no means a mere hallucination. "All the wars that are on foot in Europe," wrote Gustavus Adolphus to Axel Oxenstierna in 1628, "have been fused together, and have become a single war" (1907, v).

This *single* war, the Thirty Years' War, wiped out the old Europe and ushered in a new one. On June 1, 1645, delegates convened in Munster for a peace conference with France and in Osnabrük for a peace conference with Sweden. The two towns, thirty miles apart, in Westphalia, were chosen to permit communications between the two Congresses, thus perchance to facilitate a global peace. On October 24, 1648, signatures were apposed on The Treaty of Peace between the Holy Roman Emperor, the king of France, and their respective allies, and also on The Treaty of Peace between the Holy Roman Emperor, the king of Sweden, and their respective allies.

One would wade through the pages of these treaties and search in vain for any mention of "sovereignty." Like most peace treaties, this one, too, was concerned with the terms of cessation of hostilities and the redivision of territories among the various warring parties. Unlike the ambiguous and often meaningless treaties that preceded it, however, the Peace of Westphalia delineated the limits of authority and the bounds of territory between the emperor and the kings and among the kings and lords. As John Jackson puts it, "the compact represented the passing of some power from the emperor with his claim of holy predominance, to many kings and lords who then treasured their own local predominance. As time passed, this developed into notions of the absolute right of the sovereign, and what we call 'Westphalian sovereignty'" (Jackson 2003, 786).

From these beginnings one can trace an unbroken intellectual and diplomatic lineage to our current system of international law and relations—from the Vienna peace treaty settling the Napoleonic Wars to the Paris Peace Accords of 1919, through the League of Nations, on to the Charter of the United Nations (Gross 1948, 21–24). In the words of a commentator in 1948, about the time when the United Nations was born, the Peace of Westphalia was the first to establish "something resembling world unity on the basis of states exercising untrammeled sovereignty over certain territories and subordinated to no earthly authority" (Gross 1948, 20).

This system of unity grounded in sovereignty seeks not to impose global authority from one central ruler directly upon his subjects, as the Holy Roman Emperor sought haplessly to do in the face of competing claims to authority. Rather, it disaggregates political authority into discrete units—each one a hypothetical and juridical person with the autonomy to determine its own actions and to check the actions of its others. Through bilateral agreements and multilateral organizations, and by force as necessary, these discrete units interact with each other to sustain the uneasy if comparatively stable social compact that we have come to call 'world order'.

To qualify for international personhood, would-be nation-states must prove their autonomy. In the precise language of the Montevideo Convention on Rights and Duties of States (1933): "The state as a person of international law should possess the following qualifications: (a) a permanent population; (b) a defined territory; (c) government; and (d) capacity to enter into relations with other states." Evidently, each of these requirements serves to ensure proper disaggregation, and to support the critical assumptions of autonomous personhood—that each unit internally can govern its territory and subjects, and externally can interact with fellow units.

By so transforming the universe of billions of actual persons into a club of far fewer juridical persons—191 states, or 193 if one counts the Holy See and Taiwan—the international community can seek to bring order to the chaotic task of governance. Citizens are answerable to nations, and nations in turn are answerable to each other. The value of the nation-state as the basic unit of political organization is perhaps best, and most relevantly, illustrated by the use of force. Each sovereign has an *internal* monopoly on the use of force within its jurisdiction. Each nation can project suasive force externally in order to wage war. Because preventing and limiting war is the whole point of the exercise, what the law of nations—as it has traditionally developed—governs is, first and principally, use of force.

Richard Haas (2003) summarizes well the concept of order grounded in sovereignty, highlighting also well the many challenges to that vision:

Historically, sovereignty has been associated with four main characteristics: First, a sovereign state is one that enjoys supreme political authority and monopoly over the legitimate use of force within its territory. Second, it is capable of regulating movements across its borders. Third, it can make its foreign policy choices freely. Finally, it is recognized by other governments as an independent entity entitled to freedom from external intervention. These components of sovereignty were never absolute, but together they offered a predictable foundation for world order. What is significant today is that each of these components—internal authority, border control, policy autonomy, and nonintervention—is being challenged in unprecedented ways. (Haas 2003, 2)

The modern challenge to sovereignty comes from many sources: the ascendancy of international institutions, the development of regional unions, the delegation of governmental authority to non-state actors, the impotence of weak or failing states, and other factors auguring the increasing irrelevance of the sovereign nation-state. Some scholars saw national sovereignty as an obstacle to regional and global governance, or at least as unnecessary, in light of such governance structures (Chayes and Chayes 1995; Friedman 1999; Liftin 1998; among others). Some even have identified in the increasingly interdependent world the seeds of cosmopolitan citizenship superior to claims of national allegiance (Nussbaum 2002, 3–17). And for some others, sovereignty is an empty vessel, "of more value for purposes of oratory and persuasion than of science and law" (Wright 1968, 278). The title of one book seems to summarize the prevailing assault: *Sovereignty: Organized Hypocrisy* (Krasner 1999).

These criticisms share the common trait of posing the challenge to sovereignty-based order, from within—by arguing, as they do, that nation-states by their actions or inaction have so manipulated or abused the concept of sovereignty that it has very little if any enduring analytical value. One strand of criticism even explores sovereignty as a social construct, arguing that "[n]umerous practices participate in the social construction of a territorial state as sovereign" (Biersteker and Weber 1996). Once it is freed from its inherent characteristics and requirements, sovereignty can be next reconstructed to fit the policy or political needs of the day.

The Terrorist Challenge

Whatever the validity of these criticisms, they fundamentally differ from the *external* assault on sovereignty-based order—mounted by stateless terrorism. Armed with the means and motives of war, and yet operating outside the community of nations, the terrorist poses an external threat to the ordering structure of that community. His access to means of mass violence breaks the monopoly on force held by sovereign nation-states. His illicit use of those means elides the nation-states' internal exercise of that monopoly of power, eludes criminal law, and escapes their external projections—the legality of war. This modern terrorist threat goes beyond ideology unmoored from geography. Even more accurately, it is in fact: force unchecked by sovereignty.

The use of nonstate force, however, is not a new phenomenon. This aberration of the world ordered by nation-states draws from the advent of piracy, mercenary forces, and, more recently, transnational criminal organizations, each of which—like the terrorist and his act—is an affront to principles of sovereignty, thus to legal recourse by a state to its legitimate monopoly on the use of force.

Today, terrorism, piracy, and transnational organized crime are all considered contrary to a world order grounded in sovereignty. Specifically, terrorism has been called "an attack on legitimate transnational order" (Perdue 1989, 8). In *Terrorism and the Liberal State*, Paul Wilkinson (1977, 80) concludes that "terrorism constitutes a direct repudiation of liberal and humane values and principles" and that "terrorist ideology is inevitably and constantly deployed in a struggle to defame and discredit liberal democracy." As important is what Martin Van Creveld (1991, 294) sees to be part of the danger that terrorism and other affronts to sovereignty comprise: "Once the legal monopoly of armed force, long claimed by the state, is wrested out of its hands, existing distinctions between war and crime will break down." In this way, stateless force leads to worldwide anarchy.

Little wonder, then, that the *Training Manual* of the most reviled enemy today in the War on Terror, al Qaeda, states its primary goal to be: "The overthrow of the godless regimes and their replacement with an Islamic regime" (p. 12). This chilling decree was translated from a manual uncovered in an al Qaeda operative's home. In this manual, al Qaeda most explicitly rejects diplomacy, discourse, or debate as means of effectuating change: "The confrontation that we are calling for with the apostate regimes does not know Socratic debates . . . , Platonic ideals . . . , or Aristotelian diplomacy. . . . But it knows the dialogue of bullets, the ideals of assassination, bombing, and destruction, and the diplomacy of the cannon and machine-gun" (p. 12).

Loosely translated, al Qaeda means "base" or "foundation," but "[i]t can also mean a precept, rule, principle, maxim, formula, method, model or pattern" (Burke 2003, 7). As an organization, al Qaeda began to take form during the Soviet invasion of Afghanistan and in the subsequent resistance movement by local Afghans and Muslims throughout the Islamic world. Jason Burke notes that "al Qaeda" is a common Arabic word and was probably employed to describe *the base* from which Muslim fighters and local Afghani militia operated (2003, 7–8). After the withdrawal of the Soviets in 1989, however, al Qaeda would emerge as a radical Islamic terrorist organization. The rebirth was devised in an effort to unify the geographically and ethnically disparate groups (Burke 2003, 8; see also Gunaratna 2002, 87) that had taken part in the Afghan war, with the specific purpose of forming "an 'international army' which would defend Muslims from oppression" (Burke 2003, 8).

While terrorists have long directed their actions outside the known borders of the nations or states sheltering them, al Qaeda has distinguished itself by its effort to "globalize" terror operations. According to Yoram Schweitzer and Shaul Shay (2003, 49), al Qaeda "disputes Western cultural concepts on every level." And as Vincent Cannistraro, former Chief of Counterterrorism Operations, U.S. Central Intelligence Agency, put it in his statement at a Hearing before the House Committee on International Relations of the 107th U.S. Congress in 2001, regarding al Qaeda and the Global Reach of Terrorism: "This terrorist organization is not merely bent on achieving geographically limited political success; it seeks to isolate the Islamic world from global society and to reorder it under the beliefs of radical Islam as well."[1] In this way, al Qaeda is not only a vital threat to Western nations, which are seen as obstacles to unifying the Islamic world, it is also an existential threat to all Islamic nations deemed impure and corrupted by Western ideals and precepts.

In his testimony before the Senate Subcommittee on International Operations and Terrorism, the U.S. Federal Bureau of Investigation's Acting Assistant Director of Counterterrorism, J. T. Caruso (2001), listed four reasons why al Qaeda is opposed to the United States:

First, the United States was regarded as an "infidel" because it was not governed in a manner consistent with the group's extremist interpretation of Islam. Second, the United States was viewed as providing essential support for other "infidel" governments and institutions, particularly the governments of Saudi Arabia and Egypt, the nation of Israel and the United Nations organization,

---

1. Cannistraro 2001, 19. See also *Al Qaeda Training Manual.*

which were regarded as enemies of the group. Third, Al Qaeda opposed the involvement of the United States armed forces in the Gulf War in 1991 and in Operation Restore Hope in Somalia in 1992 and 1993, which were viewed by Al Qaeda as pretextual preparations for an American occupation of Islamic countries. In particular, Al Qaeda opposed the continued presence of American military forces in Saudi Arabia (and elsewhere on the Saudi Arabian peninsula) following the Gulf War. Fourth, Al Qaeda opposed the United States Government because of the arrest, conviction and imprisonment of persons belonging to Al Qaeda or its affiliated terrorist groups or with whom it worked, including Sheik Omar Abdel Rahman, who was convicted in the first World Trade Center bombing. (Caruso 2001, 4–5)

Besides its leadership, al Qaeda's unifying rule appears to be its members' unwavering adherence to a form of radical Islam. The *Al Qaeda Training Manual* states that all members must be Muslim. But this characterization-qua-requirement must be qualified by the other requisites for membership: A member must be committed to the organization's ideology—the "overthrow of the godless regimes," including the overthrow of most Arab nations, "and their replacement with [a single, utopian] Islamic regime." Not least, members also must "be willing to . . . undergo martyrdom for the purpose of achieving" al Qaeda's goals.

As a religion-centered ideology would limit its violent tactics, al Qaeda sheds the morality of religion: individuals and nations that stand in its way are dehumanized, subordinated—the cause is promoted above all else. In this way, no tactic falls outside of the realm of the acceptable. As explains the *Training Manual*: "Islam is superior to all human conditions and earthly religions, it permits [means and ways] for itself [that are not available] for others" (p. 77).

In no uncertain terms, al Qaeda's extremist and fundamentalist ideology is a direct affront to liberal-democratic ideals. Al Qaeda seeks to subjugate women; democracy works for their liberation. Al Qaeda seeks to deny choice; democracy celebrates the marketplace of ideas. Al Qaeda seeks to suppress speech; liberal democracy welcomes open discussion.

Were al Qaeda a nation, a government would deal with these differences in the same way that it does vis-à-vis nations with which it may have fundamental disagreements. Subject to certain limits, it would respect their sovereignty—even though it would use its own sovereignty to bring upon them every political, diplomatic, and economic pressure legitimately practicable, the more effectively to cajole and/or to coerce them into adopting a more humane and civilized exercise of their sovereign power. But even if al Qaeda were a "nation," many of its actions would fall outside the limits of sovereignty. Václav Havel (2002) reminds us that "human rights, human freedom and human dignity represent higher values than State sovereignty." As Kofi Annan (1999) has said, "If states bent on criminal behaviour know that frontiers are not an absolute defence—that the [United Nations Security C]ouncil will take action to halt the gravest crimes against humanity—then they will not embark on such a course assuming they can get away with it."

Of course, al Qaeda is not a nation, and its offence to the United States and to other nations is not limited to its extremist ideology. By adopting the way of terror, it has attacked not only U.S. citizens on U.S. territory but also and especially the very foundation of world order grounded on state sovereignty.

The terrorist does not seek to destroy a social construct—the *idea* of a world ordered by sovereign states. The terrorist seeks to destroy that *reality*. In this sense, the terrorist is fundamentally different from the criminal offender normally encountered in the criminal justice system. By attacking the foundation of order in civilized society, the terrorist seeks to demolish the institutional structures on which the lives and well-being of citizens depend. By fomenting terror among the masses, the terrorist seeks to incapacitate them from exercising the liberty to pursue their individual ends. This is not mere criminality. It is an outright warlike attack on the polity.

In waging this war, the terrorist employs strategies that diverge fundamentally from those used by nations. The terrorist does not abide by recognized rules of war; those rules were established among nations. Rather, the terrorist exploits those rules to his advantage. Civilian life is no longer sacred; military installations are not necessarily the primary targets. By way of comparison, an enemy nation targets its foe's instruments of defense; rather, the terrorist targets the core of society. And unlike a nation, exposed to the vulnerabilities of its geographic territory and of its population, and therefore appreciative of the costs of war, the terrorist appreciates only the moral hazard he inflicts—his undertakings do not absorb the *costs* and therefore cannot internalize the *risks* (see Kleindorfer, chap 6 in this book) of his bellicose actions. The world becomes his battleground—no country is immune from his attacks—and all innocent civilians are henceforth exposed to the threat of wanton violence and of incapacitation by the fear of terror.

This, then, is the enemy in the Age of Terror: a criminal whose objective is not crime but fear; a mass murderer who kills only as a means to a larger end; a warrior who abuses the rules of war; a war criminal who recognizes no limits or boundaries, and who aspires to reach all parts of the globe. Neither endowed with the rights nor in the least encumbered by the responsibilities of being a legal *person* in the international community, terrorism attacks that community as a virus does—moving from one person to the next, infecting each and every one on its path indiscriminately, with poisonous lethality.

National Pride, World Order

Faced with such an external threat, naturally a nation turns inward to uphold its spirit of national unity and resolve. Thomas Paine (1925, 263) captured well that spirit when he wrote, on a drumhead, words that were read to every soldier in the Continental Army: "These are times that try men's souls. The summer soldier and the sunshine patriot will, in this crisis, shrink from the service of their country; but he that stands it now, deserves the love and thanks of man and woman. Tyranny, like hell, is not easily conquered, yet we have this consolation with us, that the harder the sacrifice, the more glorious the triumph."

These are, indeed, times that try men's souls—and their hearts, and their minds, too. For under attack are not only yesterday's targets—the World Trade Tower, the Pentagon, the White House, or the Capitol—but also the institutions and ideals that they represent (cf. Hackney, chap. 11 in this book) still now, and for the future. The public expressions of resolve that have followed those lowly attacks evoke the assent of U.S. citizens, precisely because Americans share a commitment to those institutions and ideals—and to the land of their birth that continues to nurture them.

The same spirit of pride fortifies each metaphorical-citizen, member in the international community, through strengthening the body politic of nations and through the building of the civilized world's defenses against harmful illegal infections. Nations are not built overnight. The very history, institutions, and memories of peoples help to cultivate and reinforce their commitment to each other. As Michael Walzer (1992, 54) describes the process in his classic *Just and Unjust Wars*, "Over a long period of time, shared experiences and cooperative activity of many different kinds shape a common life. 'Contract' is a metaphor for a process of association and mutuality, the ongoing character of which the state claims to protect against external encroachment."

In his celebrated essay *Qu'est-ce qu'une Nation?* Ernest Renan (1994, 17) answers the question posed in his title as follows: "To have common glories in the past and to have a common will in the present; to have accomplished great things together, to wish to do so again—is the essential condition for being a nation. . . . A nation is [therefore] a grand solidarity, constituted by the sentiment of sacrifices which one has made and those that one is disposed to make again."

A national identity can be born from a shared commitment to its core principles as the American example amply demonstrates. George W. Bush, as incoming U.S. president, put it best in his Inaugural Address (2001): "America has never been united by blood or birth or soil. We are bound by ideals that move us beyond our backgrounds, lift us above our interests and teach us what it means to be citizens."

But patriotism means more than just intellectual and emotional attachment to a set of principles. It is a rational commitment to the polity and to a shared sense of belonging. It is the very spirit that Stephen Decatur voiced in 1816 in his famous toast: "Our country! In her intercourse with foreign nations may she always be in the right; but our country, right or wrong" (Decatur 1816, 295). The reflexive and unyielding patriotism that this toast manifests has been criticized and even (maybe justly) scorned for the unconditional pledge of allegiance that it embodies—one that leaves practically no room for exit or voice and demands absolute loyalty. But then loyalty there must be, and even in dissent. "For patriotism," in Professor Wilfred McClay's own eloquent words (2001), "like any love, withers and dies if it is not accorded some degree of instinctive assent."

If patriotism is a kind of love, then it is unfortunately a love that often dares not speak its name—assuredly not in cosmopolitan academic circles.[2] In a highly influential essay, written in 1994, Martha Nussbaum (2002) argued that "this emphasis on patriotic pride is both morally dangerous and, ultimately, subversive of some of the worthy goals patriotism sets out to serve—for example the goal of national unity in devotion to worthy moral ideals of justice and equality." Labeling

---

2. George Orwell (1968, 56, 75) wrote that "almost any English intellectual would feel more ashamed of standing to attention during 'God Save the King' than of stealing from a poor box." Wilfred McClay (2003) makes the same observation in reference to contemporary American academia, where patriotism "must face a disdain even more deeply rooted than the incest taboo."

nationality as "morally irrelevant," she advocates an identity of "citizen of the world"—"the person whose allegiance is to the worldwide community of human beings" (Nussbaum 2002, 4, 5).

These are by no means trivial objections, for we know all too well the atrocities committed in the name of nationalism. But they underestimate the value of the nation-state as the basic political unit of international order. International presupposes national. As Michael Walzer (2002, 125) answers: "I am not even aware that there is a world such that one could be a citizen of it. No one has ever offered me citizenship, or described the naturalization process, or enlisted me in the world's institutional structures, or given me an account of its decision procedures (I hope they are democratic), or provided me with a list of the benefits and obligations of citizenship, or shown me the world's calendar and the common celebrations and commemorations of its citizens."

Nussbaum acknowledges, of course, that there is no world state; she does not necessarily advocate for one. Instead, she argues that nationality does not stand in the way of cosmopolitanism—nationalism does. But much as we like to *think* globally, we can only *love* locally—as in Burke's little platoons (McConnell 2002, 82): "To be attached to the subdivision, to love the little platoon we belong to in society, is the first principle (the germ as it were) of public affections. It is the first link in the series by which we proceed toward a love to our country and to mankind." Or, as Michael McConnell puts it: "We do not love those distant from us more by loving those close to us less" (2002).

That we love those close to us does not necessarily mean that we cannot love those distant from us. And it certainly does not suggest that we may disrespect them. Indeed, loving one's country allows one to love others even more. Liberal democracy requires a healthy dose of mutual commitment. Do not countermajoritarian norms, protection of minority rights, and redistributive justice go against parochial self-interest and demand much enlightenment—the immense *empathy* (see Williams and Barber, chap. 4 in this book), and commitment, that national identity and unity do, indeed, facilitate?

Loving "our" country—for us Americans, loving the United States—allows and, indeed, requires of each of us, as citizens, to show love for others, who are not. As U.S. President George W. Bush (2002) has expounded: "Unlike any other country, America came into the world with a message for mankind—that all are created equal and all are meant to be free. There is no American race; there's only an American creed: We believe in the dignity and rights of every person." And Walter Berns (2001) sounds the same theme in his book, *Making Patriots:* "What makes us 'one people' is not where we were born but, rather, our attachments to those principles of government, namely, that all men are created equal insofar as they are equally endowed by nature's God with unalienable rights to life, liberty, and the pursuit of happiness, and that the purpose of government is 'to secure these rights'" (cf. Cameron, chap. 13 in this book).

Loyalty to nation thus fosters commitment to universal precepts. It is not at all evident that rejection of national identity would foster global brotherhood—indeed, quite the opposite is plausible. Nussbaum (2002, 15) acknowledges that "being a citizen of the world is a lonely business. It is . . . a kind of exile—from the comfort of local truths, from the warm, nestling feeling of patriotism, from the absorbing drama of pride in oneself and one's own." Frankly, I am not sure that the destination justifies the journey. I would submit that, rather than aspiring to universal cosmopolitanisms, statelessness may well foster mere reversion to selfish individualism. Worse still, and highly relevant to our discussion here, a rudderless person in search of a universally grounded fundamental identity may—these days, even more quickly—find oneself in the dubious comforts of zealotry in a community of terror.

In Closing

In many ways today, the global community is navigating uncharted territory—we are at war with nihilistic terrorists instead of rogue nation-states. During these times, when the very foundation of liberty is under attack, it is critical that each nation-state celebrate the stability of order grounded in sovereignty. Stability is fostered by the nation-state as the basic building block of world order. Each of these blocks forms an element of a communal wall against terrorism: a wall fortified from within by each state's desire to purge internal challenges to sovereignty; a wall fortified from without, the better to stand up to the terrorist challenge to global order. As any structure with a function, a wall is dependent on the strength of its component blocks from which it derives its strength and stability. Weak blocks make weak walls. Likewise, weak states leave us all more susceptible, surely more vulnerable to terrorist attacks. Strong states serve not only to protect us from the terrorist threat, but also to preserve that order essential to the continued stability of liberty.

References

Al Qaeda Training Manual, available at: http://www.usdoj.gov/ag/manualpart1_1.pdf.

Annan, Kofi (1999) "Two Concepts of Sovereignty," *Economist* (September 18), available at: http://www.un.org/News/ossg/sg/kaecon.html.

Barnett, Randy (1998) *The Structure of Liberty: Justice and the Rule of Law*, Oxford: Clarendon Press.

Berns, Walter (2001) *Making Patriots*, Chicago: University of Chicago Press.

Biersteker, Thomas, and Cynthia Weber, Editors (1996) *State Sovereignty as a Social Construct*, Cambridge: Cambridge University Press.

Burke, Edmund (1996) Speech at his arrival at Bristol in 1774 before the election in that city, quoted in Robert H. Bork, *Slouching Towards Gomorrah: Modern Liberalism and American Decline*, New York: ReganBooks/HarperCollins.

Burke, Jason (2003) *Al Qaeda: Casting a Shadow of Terror*, London: I. B. Tauris.

Bush, George W., U.S. President (2001) Inaugural Address, January 20, 2001, available at: http://www.whitehouse.gov/news/inaugural address.html.

——— (2002) Remarks at Ripley, West Virginia, July 4, 2002, available at: http://www.whitehouse.gov/news/releases/2002/07/20020704-3.html.

Cannistraro, Vincent (2001) Statement in his capacity as former Chief of Counterterrorism Operations, U.S. Central Intelligence Agency, on the matter of *Al Qaeda and the Global Reach of Terrorism: Hearing Before the House Committee on International Relations*, 107th U.S. Congress, 19.

Caruso, James T. (2001) Statement in his capacity as Acting Assistant Director, Counterterrorism Division, U.S. Federal Bureau of Investigation, on the matter of *The Global Reach of Al Qaeda: Hearing Before the Senate Subcommittee on International Operations and Terrorism*, 107th U.S. Congress, 4–5.

Chayes, Abram, and Antonia Handler Chayes (1995) *The New Sovereignty*, Cambridge, MA: Harvard University Press.

Ciprut, Jose V. (2000) "The Quest for Certainty and the Newer Equations of Security," in Jose V. Ciprut, Editor, *Of Fears and Foes: Security and Insecurity in an Evolving Global Political Economy*, Westport, CT: Praeger.

Convention on Rights and Duties of States (1933) Article 1. Seventh International Conference of American States, December 26, 1933, Montevideo, Uruguay.

Decatur, Stephen (April 1816) Toast at a dinner in Norfolk, Virginia, in Alexander Slidell Mackenzie, *Life of Stephen Decatur* (1848), Boston: Little, Brown.

Friedman, Thomas (1999) *The Lexus and the Olive Tree: Understanding Globalization*, New York: Farrar, Straus and Giroux.

Gross, Leo (1948) "The Peace of Westphalia, 1648–1948," *American Journal of International Law* 42:20–41.

Gunaratna, Rohan (2002) *Inside Al Qaeda: Global Network of Terror*, New York: Columbia University Press.

Haas, Richard (2003) "Sovereignty: Existing Rights, Evolving Responsibilities," Remarks at the School of Foreign Service and the Mortara Center for International Studies, January 14, 2003, Georgetown University, available at: http://www.georgetown.edu/ sfs/documents/haas_sovereignty_20030114.pdf.

Havel, Václav, President of the Czech Republic (2002) Opening Speech, NATO Prague Summit, November 20, 2002, available at: http://www.nato.int/docu/speech/2002/ s021120c.htm.

Hobbes, Thomas (1994) *Leviathan*, Edwin Curley, Editor, Indianapolis: Hackett.

Jackson, John (2003) "Sovereignty–Modern: A New Approach to an Outdated Concept," *American Journal of International Law* 97:782–802.

Krasner, Stephen (1999) *Sovereignty: Organized Hypocrisy*, Princeton, NJ: Princeton University Press.

Liftin, Karen T., Editor (1998) *The Greening of Sovereignty in World Politics*, Cambridge, MA: The MIT Press.

McClay, Wilfred (2001) "America—Idea or Nation?" *Public Interest* (Fall):44–58.

——— (2003) "The Mixed Nature of American Patriotism," *Society* 41(1):37–45.

McConnell, Michael (2002) "Don't Neglect the Little Platoons," in Martha C. Nussbaum and Joshua Cohen, Editors, *For Love of Country?* Boston: Beacon Press.

Nussbaum, Martha C. (2002) "Patriotism and Cosmopolitanism," in Martha C. Nussbaum and Joshua Cohen, Editors, *For Love of Country?* Boston: Beacon Press.

Nussbaum, Martha C., and Joshua Cohen, Editors (2002) *For Love of Country?* Boston: Beacon Press.

Orwell, George (1968) "The Lion and the Unicorn: Socialism and the English Genius," in Sonia Orwell and Ian Angus, Editors, *The Collected Essays, Journalism, and Letters of George Orwell*, vol. 2, London: Secker and Warburg.

Paine, Thomas (1925) "The American Crisis," in *The Life and Works of Thomas Paine*, vol. 2, New Rochelle, NY: Thomas Paine Historical Association.

Perdue, William (1989) *Terrorism and the State: A Critique of Domination Through Fear*, New York: Praeger.

Renan, Ernest (1994) "Qu'est-ce qu'une Nation?" (Ida Mae Snyder, Translator), in John Hutchinson and Anthony D. Smith, Editors, *Nationalism*, Oxford: Oxford University Press.

Rousseau, Jean Jacques (1988) *On Social Contract or Principles of Political Right*, in Alan Ritter and Julia Conway Bondanella, Editors, *Rousseau's Political Writings*, New York: Norton.

Schweitzer, Yoram, and Shaul Shay (2003) *The Globalization of Terror: The Challenge of Al-Qaida and the Response of the International Community*, New Brunswick, NJ: Transaction.

Van Creveld, Martin (1991) *The Transformation of War*, New York: The Free Press.

Walzer, Michael (1992) *Just and Unjust Wars*, New York: Basic Books.

——— (2002) "Spheres of Affection," in Martha C. Nussbaum and Joshua Cohen, Editors, *For Love of Country?* Boston: Beacon Press.

Ward, A. W., et al. (1907) "The Thirty Years' War," in A. W. Ward et al., Editors, *The Cambridge Modern History*, vol. 4, Cambridge: Cambridge University Press.

Wilkinson, Paul (1977) *Terrorism and the Liberal State*, New York: Halsted Press.

Wright, Quincy (1968) *Mandates under the League of Nations*, New York: Greenwood Press.

Young, Marilyn (2003) "Ground Zero: Enduring War," in Mary L. Dudziak, Editor, *September 11 in History: A Watershed Moment?* Durham, NC: Duke University Press.

13   Beyond Ideology, Toward a New Ethic of Freedom?

Kevin Cameron

In this chapter I search for a new ethic of freedom—one beyond the limits imposed by ideological definitions of freedom. After examining the relation between freedom and ideology within the contested framework of an emerging global economy, I look for the possibilities of freedom against the terms laid out by the dominant ideology accompanying the contemporary political-economic processes broadly known as globalization. This ideology is what Manfred Steger refers to as "globalism" (Steger 2002). Globalism is a rehashing of the nineteenth-century liberal free market ideology, except that—unlike its ancestor, revolving mainly around the emerging industrial societies at the time—globalism has reached the status of a truly universal hegemony, mainly because it accompanies the ongoing breakdown of particular inter-societal economic barriers that marked the preglobalizing world. Globalism purports to promote universal freedom, for all societies to share—a concept of freedom that promises to put an end to another, always already engaged, struggle for freedom.

In the face of this ideological hegemony, I argue that ideological definitions of freedom tend to cloud the relationship between reason and freedom, so central to more rigorous definitions of freedom such as that offered in Kant's critical philosophy: I submit that ideology functions to impart to deterministic or heteronomous acts (non-free acts in the Kantian sense) only the appearance of being transcendentally free acts. In this sense, the goal of ideology, I think, is to prevent the subject from recognizing itself as free in any way other than that prescribed by ideology. If freedom is defined through constraints (be it human nature, the rational ego, or the "good"), such definitions can be utilized by ideological means to make the subject's non-free acts seem authentically willed by the subject. Utilizing Kant's theory of freedom, this chapter seeks to demonstrate how ideology causes subjects to

presume they are free when in fact they are not; and how employing
Kantian ethics could allow the subject to reach a *transcendental* stance
of freedom—beyond impassive compliance with imposed ideological
constraints. In closing, a glance at the future scans the prospects for a
novel ethic of freedom from inside a globalizing political economy and
against the backdrop of the terms laid out by the dominant ideology
driving the realities of economic globalism.

Transcendental Freedom

The tenets of globalism espouse "the primacy of economic growth; the
importance of free trade to stimulate growth; the unrestricted free
market; individual choice; the reduction of government regulation; and
the advocacy of an evolutionary model of social development anchored
in the Western experience and applicable to the entire world" (Steger
2002, 9). Globalism is, thus, neoliberalism on a global scale. Neoliberal
globalists aim to cultivate in the popular mind the connection between
free markets, rising global living standards, and the enhancement of
individual freedom. As ideology, globalism seeks to generate an imaginary relation to real political-economic forces; thus, to shape a particular social understanding of authority.

   As with any ideology that seeks to fuse a relation between the individual and the dominant social forces, globalism cultivates a particular
view of the subject: in this case, one modeled on the nineteenth-century
homo economicus (Steger 2002, 9). Economic (wo)man is an isolated
being whose actions reflect his/her economic self-interest. Thus,
freedom is found in the unbounded exercise of rational egoism. If
unencumbered by extraneous political forces only the free market can
offer the space to maximize our freedom. I shall return to globalism
later; for the moment, I will say that globalism offers a theory of freedom
where freedom can be exercised in a nonmechanical but nevertheless
deterministic universe. In this manner, *homo economicus* can be said to
be 'determined' by its own nature—in the form of desires and inclinations special to one's self, or to a particular concept of human nature
that all people share—otherwise by nothing external to one's nature.
In contrast to this view of freedom, one may explore the objections
raised to such a formulation by Kant's theory of transcendental freedom.
Kant argues that freedom can only be exercised by a self that is not
determined by anything outside of reason including causal antecedents, be they individual desires, personal inclinations, social constraints,

moral codes, or even human nature. For Kant, "transcendental freedom" is freedom without qualification.

Kant's theory of transcendental freedom arguably remains the most philosophically rigorous definition of freedom available to date. This is due to the endeavor central to his critical philosophy to understand both freedom and morality on nondogmatic grounds. Kant contributes two major adjustments to traditional moral philosophy: he rejects the traditional impulse that understood moral obligations in terms of what is possible for an agent to fulfill. Moral obligations are not derived from what is possible, but from a point beyond our understanding of cause and effect. This is not to say that duty is based on the impossible, but merely that the criterion of possibility plays no role in the formation of our duty. He also rejects the view that ethics is concerned with the good (Kant 1996, 82), for to be morally free means to be completely disconnected from any presupposed conception of the good, including all those offered by traditional or even nontraditional moral codes—if 'good'ness justifies the act, or is imposed on the agent, then the agent cannot be said to act freely.

Confronted by Hume's skeptical empiricism, Kant argues that we have access to patterned cause and effect relations because of our cognitive ability to project the dimensions of time and space onto the world of phenomena (Kant 1996, 71–72). However, because we impose time and space upon phenomenon through our own experience, we do not have access to any transcendental relation between things, we do not have access to what Kant calls the noumenal world—we are forever cut off from cognating the true nature and relations of things. Thus, what is 'possible' for us in terms of ethics, say, a notion of the "good," in no way partakes of the ultimate order of things: traditional ethics is limited by our cognitive capacities. Any possible good that we can construct as a basis for duty will always reflect dogma. Kant, on the other hand, seeks a definition of freedom that is not reduced to the limited scope of the human mind and thereby limited by human custom and/or dogma. To be free in the transcendental sense means to be free of our very relation to the phenomenal world.

Kant notes that freedom exists in a reciprocal relation with what he calls the moral law or the categorical imperative. As opposed to speculative reason, practical reason is concerned with the grounds of determining one's will in relation to objects. Practical principles are propositions or rules containing the general determination of one's will. The rule I set up to guide my will, to cause it to move in a certain direction, is a principle of practical reason. Such principles can take one of two forms: maxims, which are guided by subjective principles, and laws, which are guided by objective principles. Maxims as rules are determined by inclinations particular to oneself—say, choosing the course of action necessary to optimize one's happiness, riches, or recognition. Laws, on the other hand, are rules of the will that hold universally for all wills and thus are not particular to one's own inclinations. While maxims can vary because of the variety of particular inclinations representative of all our different wills, there is only one law. That is the categorical imperative: "act so that the maxim of thy will can always at the same time hold good as a principle of universal legislation" (Kant 1996, 46).

To be free, my will must be determined by *the* moral law, not by my subjective inclinations. To act on a subjective maxim is to make myself a product of the phenomenal world—the sensible world in which I understand the laws at work because of my cognitive capacity to impute dimensions of space and time onto that world. Thus, when my will is determined by these laws, I become a passive agent of "them"— of my own nature. Autonomy, in contrast, comes when my will is determined by a principle universal for all rational agents. This entails that an agent determine oneself beyond the confines of phenomenal causation. We know we have subjected ourselves to the laws of nature when we can *experience* the achievement of our own maxim. If it is my maxim to enrich myself, I can test whether the actions I chose under this maxim in fact have been successful. Such phenomenal causes of the will are what Kant referred to as pathological causes. Pathological causes include our desires, social goods, moral codes, and even human nature. All these determinations for moral action can be tested by our experience. As they are all registered in the phenomenal world, they cannot be the basis for autonomy—a state in which one is not subject to the laws of nature, say, as an animal is. Phenomenal causes determine the will heteronomously; they determine the will from something outside the will, not by the will itself. So as determinants, they cannot hold universally for all agents at all times; they are particular to my position in space and time.

A free will is a will that is entirely self-determining. It is not determined by any external causes, but only by reason. Thus, the free will is reciprocal to the law that one must act as if the maxim of one's will were tantamount to a principle of universal legislation. The free will wills itself not in terms of a particular desire, but in terms of its capacity to be universal. It is important to note that the moral law exists only as formal edict (Kant 1996, 41). Were it to possess or offer any content or object, it necessarily would partake of the phenomenal world. Any content to the law would mean also that the law is merely an instrument that guides the will toward something beyond the law and away from the autonomous use of reason. Traditional moral systems act in precisely this way: they presuppose a good, and offer maxims that direct the will toward that good. Likewise, the rational ego of globalism merely employs reason for some other end. Such systems do not allow for freedom. Freedom entails that the will determine the law for the agent without any external causes or antecedents. The only form this law can take is that of the categorical imperative— because only it offers the free will rather than something phenomenal as its object. The object of one's will is freedom itself. This further entails that to be free means to do one's duty (obey the moral law) not for any reason other than out of respect for one's duty. It is not enough to conform to one's duty, for this does not necessarily close the door to antecedent determinants; one must do one's duty solely for the sake of duty. This respect for duty is the only content or motive associated with the moral law. Only such a disposition can make one aware of oneself as a free agent distinct from an instrument of the laws of causation as they function in the phenomenal world (Kant 1996, 92).

Here another distinction between autonomous and heteronomous wills needs elucidation. A will can be said to be free of all subjective desires yet still be subject to some fundamental drive or natural impulse such as self-preservation, or maximization of pleasure, that functions to limit the agent's actions without thereby necessitating a given choice (Allison 1998, 287). Such a drive is often what is referred to as human nature, an impulse common to all humans and which limits the choices we make. This situation might produce what Kant calls the *possibility* for practical freedom, but would be incompatible with transcendental freedom since it outlines the contours of a heteronomous will by remaining determined by nature and, therefore, not free. Transcendental freedom demands that I transcend my natural limits no matter how much of a hold those limits have on me as a member of my species. Freedom entails that I be capable of acting upon a law that is imposed by my will alone, even if that law runs counter to the natural limits to what humans are capable of. This does not mean that one is free to choose any law, since the choice of any law cannot preclude pathological motives. Only the categorical imperative can serve as the basis of freedom because only it can be discovered by reason alone.

These requirements of transcendental freedom raise a peculiar problem for Kant's theory. Can an agent who chooses not to obey the moral law still be considered a free agent? The rejection of freedom can be a free act in the practical sense, but not in the transcendental sense. One freely can choose to disregard the moral law, but only if one is aware of the moral law: being aware of what transcendental freedom entails is not incompatible with the failure to actualize it. Yet, this failure should not be construed as a definition of freedom. I am not necessarily free by dint of having disregarded my freedom: after all, to be pathologically motivated, I do not have to be aware of my capacity to be free. Thus, practical freedom can be viewed as an expression of freedom; not as the definition of freedom. Let us look at Kant's famous example of freedom from the *Critique of Practical Reason*: "if his sovereign ordered him, on pain of the same immediate execution, to bear false witness against an honorable man, whom the prince might wish to destroy under a plausible pretext, would he consider it possible in that case to overcome his love of life, however great it may be. He would perhaps not venture to affirm whether he would do so or not, but he must unhesitatingly admit that it is possible to do so. He judges, therefore, that he ought to do certain things because he is conscious that he ought, and he recognizes that he is free—a fact which but for that moral law he would never have known" (Kant 1996, 45–46). As one can see from this example, Kant's definition of freedom does not concern the agent's choice. It is merely concerned with the agent's awareness of the possibility of his choice. If the agent in this case were to choose to bear false witness, this would *only* be a free choice if the agent were also aware of the fact that he could have chosen his duty not to bear false witness, that is, chosen to sacrifice his pathological desires. Thus, it is not the choice that makes one free, but the awareness that one is doing one's duty to the moral law that sets one free. The *freedom* to disregard the moral law is conditioned by the moral law. Once one is aware of one's duty, one realizes that in choosing to disregard that duty, one has chosen to place a constraint upon oneself. Only in one's awareness that one has failed to do one's duty, that one has failed to be free, can the disregard for duty be conceived as a free (deliberate) choice.

This is without question a very rigorous definition of freedom. It demands that one disregard one's self-interest, as well as one's ties to nature. It is seemingly incompatible with rational egoism—the idea that free choices are determined by rationally calculating the means necessary to further one's self-serving ends—since it reveals that such egoism is something other than rational. Relegating the agent to the phenomenal world, rational egoism makes the will a mere conduit of natural forces (Korsgaard 1996, 168). As noted above, transcendental freedom is one that is not concerned with what is possible for the agent. So, what possible bearing or value can transcendental freedom have for us who are relegated to the phenomenal world? It is a definition of freedom that opens the door for the agent to transcend the cognitive and sensible limits of the phenomenal world. In placing oneself—by means of an act of will—beyond the phenomenal world, one can find oneself in a position actually to effect rational change in that world rather than just make oneself a mere subject of it. When one puts oneself in this position, one effects a change in the world through a change in the self. Transcendental freedom is essentially subversive toward the phenomenal world because it transforms "rational" from something external to the agent into something internal. In contrast to globalism, the agent is rational in terms of its own will and not in terms of the economic forces that determine the rationality of its will in advance. Such action does change the phenomenal world—if by transforming the subject's practical orientation toward that world. Eventually, any ends adopted under the influence of pathological inclination no longer appear to be one's own (Korsgaard 1996, 168); the loss of the pathological ceases to feel like a sacrifice at all. The value of Kant's rigorous definition of freedom is that it demonstrates how all definitions of freedom that relegate the agent to phenomenal motives, such as those subject to the rational ego or some moral good, necessarily impose upon that subject desires that are foreign to its true self-determination as a rational being. When compared with transcendental freedom, all other constructs of freedom merely serve a world that seeks to constrain the agent. Kant's definition of freedom, on the other hand, seeks to free the agent from such worlds.

Ideological Freedom

Although transcendental freedom may reveal the limits to freedom entailed in the heteronomous freedom associated with the rational ego, we should not therefore underestimate the ability of ideologies such as globalism to make heteronomous freedom feel transcendental to the subject. Ideology is commonly thought of as a system of ideas about the world (Love 1998, 4). It is a mechanism by which we integrate our view of the world into a belief system. Although ideology contains ideas that refer to the world, it is usually viewed as lacking scientific viability. This lack grants ideology a political dimension in that it aims at not merely understanding the world, but at affecting it no less. Many nineteenth-century theorists, Karl Marx the most pronounced, became increasingly critical of this political dimension of ideology (Love 1998, 5–6). These critiques of ideology sought to expose the manner in which ideology was used by political-economic regimes toward manu-facturing the consent of political subjects. From the general critique there emerged two different positions as to just how the power dynamic of ideology works. The first position espoused the view that ideology constituted an illusory image of the real conditions of social existence. Although ideology refers to reality, it represents it in an imaginary form. The purpose of this illusion is to veil the real power structure underlying political relations. For example, ideology allows the people to serve the power of kings and priests under the illusion of thereby serving God (Althusser 1971, 163). The second position represents Marx's more sophisticated understanding of ideology. For Marx, ideol-ogy represents an illusory representation of reality because the real conditions under which people live are themselves alienating (Marx 1978, 148–150). Ideology as a fabrication is the natural product of a social system that estranges people from their true nature. Ideology follows from a division of labor that alienates people from the product of their labor. Men generate ideology not so much for the purposes of gaining power, but because the power relations in which they find themselves estrange them already from the world. The point here is not, as the first position would have it, to challenge the truth claims of ideology, but rather to transform the real relations of production—the very transformation that would make ideology superfluous.

Louis Althusser seeks to go beyond these two positions, both of which hold out the possibility for a humanist insurgency against the hold of ideology. In the end, he rejects humanist criticisms of ideology as in themselves ideological. For Althusser, it is not their real conditions that people represent to themselves in ideology, but their *relation* to those conditions (Althusser 1971, 164). It is our relations and not our conditions that are imaginary (165). Here, ideology does not start from a view of the world, but from the constitution of the individuals who populate that world.

Although ideology promotes imaginary relations, still it possesses a very real material existence. Ideologies always exist as part of ISAs—ideological state apparatuses. ISAs are practical extensions of the dominant ideology of any regime. They are both governmental and nongovernmental institutions that promote the legitimacy of a given regime, not through force, but through ideologized practice. In modern capitalist societies, the dominant ISAs are the schools and the family, but they can also be found in such spheres as the law [courts], politics [parties, elections], religion, media, and, yes, culture [literature, arts, sports] (Althusser 1971, 143). Instead of being repressive mechanisms of state power, such as the police and the army, ISAs offer us the opportunity to participate actively in rituals and practices such as school attendance, jury service, dieting, family planning, voting, and so forth, in the service of ideological homogeneity. By participation in ISAs, we adopt a practical attitude in favor of the dominant ideology. Ideas are transmitted through these material practices, thus granting ideology a palpable hegemonic existence. We develop ideas of the world even as we are inserted into material practices that impart form to those ideas. The ideas have no independence from the corresponding material practices. In this manner, we participate in the material world by constituting our imaginary relation to that world actively.

Central to this theory of ideology is the concept "interpellation"—the means by which ideology transforms individuals into subjects. In this concept, there is no ideology except for subjects. The "subject" is the material extension of ideology into the world. Ideology transforms the pre-ideological individual into a subject by creating a space through material practices by which the individual can recognize oneself as a willing subject. For example, serving on a jury transforms one into a subject of justice. Such self-transformation takes place when ideology recruits individuals as subjects through "hailing" (Althusser 1971, 174). Hailing begets the common everyday occasion of recognizing oneself in a call. No sooner does one recognize oneself in a gesture, than one has turned oneself into a subject. One murmurs, in effect, "mmm . . . that's me." It is in the act of recognizing oneself from a perspective outside oneself, from the position of that which hails, that one becomes a subject. Hailing-and-recognition as process is entirely constituted ideologically. It is through ideological practices that we recognize ourselves in an external gesture. Ideology thus functions to constitute subject positions for individuals. This is why those in ideology cannot recognize themselves as subjects. Ideology bases itself on a necessary illusion that one has been always already a subject. In this illusion, the individual never realizes that s/he has just become a subject, for ideology hushes the birth of its newborn.

The external place from which the ideological subject recognizes oneself functions as if a higher Subject of sorts. Its interpellation of numerous subjects portrays that Subject as a different, unique, entity in whose name the individual was transformed into a subject from the outset. Depending on ideological practice and purpose, the higher Subject can be Anything: God, Nation, Democracy, and, oh yes, Freedom. One's subjectivity becomes mirrored in, has a home in, that Subject. And the mirror relation guarantees four features of ideology simultaneously: (1) The interpellation of individuals into subjects; (2) their subjection to the Subject; (3) the mutual recognition between subject and Subject, the subjects' recognition of themselves as one entity, yet each subject's recognition of oneself; and (4) the absolute guarantee that reality is really what it looks to be. This last feature is the true key to ideology's success: it attests to ideology's ability to create a world that seems "obvious" to the subject. When everything—from the world, to the meaning of a political event, to one's own subjectivity—seems obvious, that is when surely ideology is at work. The function of ideology is to create the illusion one is at home in one's subjectivity. By focusing on constituting a subject, ideology works on creating an illusory relation to the world, not on generating an illusory world. Interpellation reveals the near-seamless nature of ideology; it does not merely foist a world onto the subject, it allows the subject to come into being. Ideology does not seek to monopolize reality, only to monopolize the soul.

Through its relationship to freedom, ideology offers its subjects the illusion of choosing one's own subjectivity whereby the choice feels natural—the more natural it feels, the more ideological it is. A free subject in the ideological sense is one who functions as the "center of initiatives, author of and responsible for its actions"—in appearance only (Althusser 1971, 182). Since a subject only comes into being by way of a mirror relation to a Subject, the "free" subject can only come into being by way of Freedom. Think of a good-natured customer who—upon the nod solicited from a waiter eager to sell his boss's overstock of fish—finds himself eating the fish he believes to have freely ordered because it is Friday and, yes, because the fish served everyone else smells good.

In regard to interpellation, globalism makes five central claims (Steger 2002). Concern here is not with how accurately they represent the true nature of globalization, but with how they articulate an illusory relation to globalization from which the subject can be interpellated:

1. *The spread of markets enhances human freedom because markets rely on a set of rules that apply equally to all people.* Yet rules do not emerge from markets, they result from individuals acting on markets. Echoing classical liberal ideology, globalists argue that the market is an "institutional framework for the fulfillment of voluntary agreements" (Steger 2002, 48). Since markets are voluntary and not coercive, the spread of markets can minimize and even counteract coercion throughout society. A spread of markets through globalization hence can assure the spread of human freedom in general; thus the opening of economies is advocated as a project of universal applicability since it reflects the dictates of human nature in general (Steger 2002, 52). The notion of universal applicability is grounded on subjects' participating in their own freedom by means of material rituals and market practices known as voluntary exchanges. These exchanges serve as ideological reinforcements in which subjects come into being as voluntary and, therefore, free beings. With the spread of global markets these exchanges become dominant ideological practices. They end up constituting the rational subject.

2. *Globalization is inevitable and irreversible. These qualities owe themselves to the development of new technologies which in themselves force the spread of global markets.* The claim to inevitable/irreversible nature ideologically functions to heighten the "apolitical" character of globalization. Not being the product of overt human design, then, in terms of freedom, globalization becomes a kind of forced choice: since it is so inevitable, one might just as well participate in it. Here the market encapsulates a human inclination toward the technological that parades as the natural propensity of humans. Since we find our nature in the market, the choices offered in the market are heteronomous. The subject can exercise its will freely, but only under the laws of the market. Here the subject becomes the conduit for phenomenal market forces.

3. *Neither does globalization reflect the arbitrary agenda of a particular group or groups: nobody is in charge of globalization—surely people are not, only markets and technology are.* Globalization in this claim comes very close to positioning the market under the parameters of what Kant called the laws of nature. Although this may appear to relegate the global market

to the phenomenal realm, globalists endow this process with a transcendental element. Since globalization spreads human freedom throughout the world, would acting on impulses in the global market not be one's way of conforming to a transcendental force that one might even call the "invisible hand"? What this ideologically would signal is that in following my heteronomous maxims as a duty, I am actually spreading freedom throughout the world. There is an element of interpellation here, wherein one has a moral obligation to conform to one's pathological imperatives. Of course, in this interpellation one relinquishes one's will in the transcendental to the mechanisms of the market. Not only do we become free under the rules of the market, we become also subject to a moral duty to our heteronomous freedom. When I consume, I have furthered the freedom of countless unseen people throughout the world. This transcendental mechanism may not be visible in my everyday exchanges; but these exchanges, so the logic says, partake of a noumenal realm that affects the phenomenal existence of countless others. In this manner, both I and my others serve as the means rather than the end of freedom. We are the conduits through which the market is free. Is that not more efficient than torturing oneself over duty?

4. Moral duty to the pathological parlays into the fourth claim of globalists: that *globalization benefits everyone—not merely by spreading economic benefits but in so doing also easing individual self-realization on an exponential scale*. Globalists tout the emergence of a global village, and with it, of the universal subject. Even if this might amount to nothing more than a subject who lives a fulfilling life of mindless consumption, it nevertheless is a universal entity embodied in the very real material practices of the global market. Is it not by partaking in the material practices of the market that we recognize each other in our common humanity—also known as the interpellated Subject of Humanity? The sacrifice we are required to make in order to enter this universal is not a sacrifice of the particular—of our individuality—but the sacrifice of our particular local political-economic connections. It is under this ideological guise that concrete human community becomes a sacrificial token of entry in modern society.

5. The final globalist claim is that *globalization spreads democracy around the world*. This claim is anchored in the premise linking free markets with democracy. However, this connection hinges on a limited definition of democracy, one in which democracy is embodied by a set of

formal procedures (voting, etc.) which serve to trigger direct and broad participation by the majority of the citizenry, hence one limiting it to what Max Weber calls "democratization," a process by which citizen participation is reduced by bureaucratic injunctions necessary for the concentration of the means of administration and the smooth functioning of the capitalist economy (Weber 1946, 224–226) but insufficient for democratic freedoms fully to blossom. Full democratic decision making is surrendered to political and economic elites in the name of safeguarding freedom, in the latest version of an older tale that the people cannot be trusted with the power democracy would grant them. Procedural democracy serves as safeguard for rational ego's moral duty, in the best of cases.

Such ideological practice of globalism mimics the Kantian notion of transcendental freedom. Freedom, the Subject for the free subject, takes on the aegis of the moral law, except for being ideological fabrication—a determinant that propels the subject, not something discovered by the subject's autonomous use of reason. What fools the "free" subject into thinking it is free is its coming into being only by means of the Subject of Freedom (the global Market), just as for Kant the autonomous agent can come into being only by means of the moral law. Because the subject owes its recognition of itself to the Market—to the ways in which the Market hails one—one fails to recognize one's choice as a heteronomous choice: a forced choice, since as subject, I have no choice but to elect the ideological course of my rational ego if I am to recognize myself as a subject. Being a forced choice, the actual constitution of the subject works by the means of phenomenal laws. By the same token, the fabrication of the subject in Freedom allows the subject to see this choice as the obvious choice for a free subject. Here, ideology manufactures the illusion of transcendental freedom. The transcendental illusion lies in the very recognition that the subject is awarded for subjecting oneself to Freedom. I, as subject, am granted the appearance of becoming "other" by my own choice. It appears to me to have entered the noumenal world. Whereas mere heteronomous choices reveal that I, as subject, am limited by the laws of nature, ideology covers up this feature of its functioning by offering me, the subject, the illusion of freely choosing my place in the world, of choosing my practical orientation to the world, in this case, through voluntary exchanges. It may be the case that the formal character of the Kantian law makes it susceptible to the phenomenal content offered by ideology and, thus,

Kant was unaware of the manner in which ideology could undermine the possibility of transcendental freedom by making heteronomous choices feel as if they were transcendental choices. Yet, as we will see, ideology fails to undercut completely the possibility of transcendental freedom: unlike ideology, transcendental freedom does not function by means of the subject's recognition of itself, but by means of the very limits of this recognition.

Freedom and the Absurd

The common criticism of the theory of interpellation is that it denies any space for free agency. Freedom becomes nothing more than a necessary illusion in the constitution of the subject. But for me, it is precisely this uncomfortable and disagreeable element of the theory that gives it its value. After interpellation, any talk of "free agency" must always carry the taint of this illusion. Thus, it is a theory of ideology that represents a brilliant stumbling block to any theory of freedom. In this section, I want to argue that there is a space for human freedom beyond interpellation, beyond the "universal" space delimited by globalism. Yet, this is not a space from which one can easily recognize oneself.

Ideology undermines the possibility of rational self-determination by usurping the transcendental position, while still allowing the subject the illusion of self-transparency. Althusser's criticism of Kant would be that the rational agent of transcendental freedom is always already an ideological construction. Ideology prefigures the ethical space in which the "free" subject is to find itself. Thus, to get beyond interpellation and to salvage transcendental freedom, one must search for freedom not in the ethical act, as Kant would have it, but in what Kierkegaard calls the "teleological suspension of the ethical" (Kierkegaard 1985).

In his study of Abraham, in *Fear and Trembling*, Kierkegaard argues that human existence occupies three possible realms: the particular, the universal, and the absolute. The particular is the realm of desire in which the individual acts on the force of one's particular interest. This is synonymous with Kant's understanding of pathological motivation. It would include any individual who seeks to promote one's own pleasure, riches, or even one's self-preservation. The particular includes the rational egoist who employs self-interest as a maxim of the will. The particular denotes a realm of heteronomy. Freedom then cannot be realized in the particular.

The universal represents the realm of the ethical. It entails renouncing one's desires in order to accomplish one's duty. The universal allows the subject the opportunity to transcend the particular. It opens the space for the individual to become part of humanity rather than just to serve its own animal inclinations. The individual has its telos in the universal and the "individual's ethical task is always to express himself in this" (Kierkegaard 1985, 83). As soon as the individual resorts to the particular, s/he has sinned. Only in recognizing this can the individual understand her/his duty to the universal. The archetypical agent in this realm is the tragic hero. The tragic hero demonstrates his/her duty to the universal by making a sacrifice for some greater good, most commonly the greater good of the community. Ethics entails that the individual sacrifice what is dear to one in one's universal duty, say, Agamemnon's sacrifice of Iphigenia for the greater good of the Greeks or a soldier's sacrifice for his/her country. The universal, then, has its expression in what Kierkegaard calls the ethic of resignation. The ethical hero gives up what is dearest to one in order to find one's telos in the universal, to become an expression of the universal. Humanity itself is expressed in the individual's duty to the universal and the resignation that comes in renouncing the particular. As we saw above, with globalism, it is the market that allows the particular individual to partake of a universal humanity.

At first glance, this understanding of the universal has certain affinities with Kant's understanding of the universal and transcendental freedom thereof. Both entail a sacrifice of all pathological motivation, including one's relation to those one holds dearest. In both cases, the universal allows one to transcend the phenomenal determinants of the will in favor of something greater that holds for all wills. This affinity ends, however, when one views the universal from the point of view of what Kierkegaard calls the absolute.

The absolute is the realm of faith, encapsulated most perfectly in the example of Abraham. When God commands Abraham to sacrifice Isaac, God not only commands him to sacrifice the particular, his love for Isaac, but to sacrifice his duty to the universal as well. His duty to the universal is found in God's covenant with Abraham that he is to become the founder of a nation among nations. Isaac is the embodiment of the future of this nation so that in sacrificing Isaac, Abraham is renouncing his duty to the greater good. God's command, when viewed from the point of view of the universal, is absurd. Nothing in the universal possibly can benefit from Abraham's taking on the task that God has placed before him. What Kierkegaard finds so astonishing about this episode is not so much God's command as the manner in which Abraham carries it out. Abraham does not obey God in order to demonstrate to God that he is willing to sacrifice everything for Him, much as the tragic hero might; rather, he obeys God under the faith that he will get Isaac back. If Abraham had acted under the assumption that he would have to sacrifice Isaac in this life—that God was demanding resignation from him—then Abraham would be merely partaking of the universal. By acting in terms of the faith that he will get Isaac back, however, Abraham is not sacrificing for the universal, but is sacrificing his place in the universal. He is willing to carry out a deed that can only be deemed to be murder from the perspective of the universal. Thus, there is something beyond resignation in Abraham's action.

The act of faith suspends this ethical teleology in its rejection of the individual's duty to the universal. It does this by transcending the act of resignation. Even though Abraham is willing to kill Isaac, he never becomes resigned to losing him because he knows he will get Isaac back on the strength of the absurd. In suspending the ethical, Abraham demonstrates the ideological pathology that supports the universal. He rejects the "peace and repose and consolation in the pain" that comes through resignation (Kierkegaard 1985, 74). In differentiating faith from ethics, Kierkegaard says: "The knight of faith knows it gives inspiration to surrender oneself to the universal, that it takes courage to do so, but also that there is a certain security in it, just because it is for the universal" (1985, 103–104). From the angle of the absolute, the universal takes on the dimensions of a forced choice of interpellation. The act of resignation belies a certain pathological desire to partake of humanity. Resignation provides rationalization. In doing so, it offers the individual a position in the phenomenal world, thereby subjecting it to all the laws thereof. Yet, by offering such a position in the name of sacrifice, it makes the act of resignation appear transcendental. Unlike the act of faith, the act of resignation makes sense. As Kierkegaard notes, the realm of the absolute transforms ethics from duty to temptation (1985, 88). Abraham must have been tempted to kill Isaac for a reason that could be understood by others, but this is precisely what he does not do.

The act of faith demonstrates that there is something higher than the universal. That *something* is the single individual who transcends the pathological motives opened up by the universal. The universal allows the individual to get beyond its particular desires in the name of humanity, but the absolute allows the individual to get beyond the heteronomy that continues to structure "humanity." It is his faith in the absurd that allows Abraham to stand alone beyond any justification. Had he relied on a justification for his act, he would not be free, but merely tempted by the meaning offered by ideology. Kierkegaard has argued that all moral philosophies balk at the act of faith precisely because they can find no justification in it (Kierkegaard 1985, 84). But quite unlike the act of resignation, the act of faith does not offer a forced choice. There is no greater good at stake. It rejects any pathological surrender to the Subject of humanity. It is the absurd, impossible act—an act completely disconnected from any good—that makes the act of faith consonant with the autonomous will in Kant. From the universal, one cannot recognize an act of faith as a duty, just as a will that partakes of the noumenal cannot be fathomed from the phenomenal world. The "absolute duty can then lead to what ethics would forbid" (Kierkegaard 1985, 101). Abraham's faith is an affront to humanity. And as with transcendental freedom, the act of faith is potentially subversive to the phenomenal world.

This raises a question concerning the parallel between God's command to Abraham and the moral law in Kant: How can something as absurd and personal as God's command to Abraham share the same structure as that which is universal for all rational and autonomous beings? However, the nature of God's command seems absurd only when seen from the perspective of the universal. From the perspective of the phenomenal world—that is, from inside ideology—the moral law appears every bit as absurd as God's command. Likewise, those who determine themselves by means of the moral law look every bit as inexplicable and monstrous as Abraham. An act of faith requires a renunciation of subjectivity. What Abraham does with his faith is not to destroy his place in the phenomenal world, but to restore it on new grounds: he does not simply reject the things of this world (including his phenomenal nature); rather, he reconstitutes their value as springing from the very *source* of existence itself. Does this not parallel directly Kant's understanding of the free subject who refashions the phenomenal order of things practically, along rational lines, by partaking of the noumenal? With both Kant and Kierkegaard, one transforms the nature of the phenomenal realm by making oneself to be determined by something beyond that realm.

In terms of the relation between freedom and interpellation, what Kantian autonomy and Kierkegaardian faith demonstrate is that one can be free only prior to uttering one's "freedom" in the phenomenal/ideological realm. Kierkegaard, I think, echoes the problem at the heart of Kant's critical moral philosophy: How is the good that is to serve as the basis for moral action ever established? How can moral action or freedom ground themselves as thus? As we have seen, ideology appropriates this grounding gesture for us by offering a space in which we can readily recognize ourselves as free. Through hailing, it frees us from this seemingly impossible task. Transcendental freedom, on the other hand, reminds us that our ideological choices are in fact not free. It is we—as free beings—who precede the establishment of freedom, in any sense of the term. Heteronomy and ideology offer only a forced choice masked as freedom. They transform us into instruments of ideological power. Transcendental freedom demands that only we, as individuals, can establish the very grounds for freedom. Nothing phenomenal can make this decision for us. Thus, only in this transcendental gesture can freedom be expressed on non-dogmatic grounds. Freedom *is* this founding gesture. The teleological suspension of the ethical demonstrates that there is an element to us that cannot be completely subjected—that, therefore, there is something beyond our subjectivity that eludes the hold of ideology. It is this element and not some recognizable core of our self that is the basis for freedom.

Against the ideologically interpellated rational ego and the "good" that it serves, one should make the radical Kierkegaardian gesture. In the face of globalism, freedom requires nothing less than the suspension of the ethical. This suspension entails not just sacrificing one's pathological interests in the name of the greater good (since, as we have seen, globalism very cleverly and conveniently links these two), but sacrificing one's place in the universal as well. This means nothing short of sacrificing one's freedom in the global market, but not out of duty—rather, out of the absurd faith that in sacrificing your freedom, you will get it back. When faced with the forced choice offered by globalism—*choose the freedom of the global market or suffer the certain slavery of a world without free markets*—we should choose to strike out at the rational ego, that very thing that supports our interpellation. As Abraham did, we must be willing to sacrifice that which in our present political-economic condition is dearest to us. Only by shedding the skin of the rational ego can we be capable of an authentically free act. To found freedom on our own terms as humans, we must sacrifice the subject of "freedom."

This gesture may carry with it a spirit of the impractical or even the impossible. In a sense, where does the subject stand once it destroys itself? However, one must remember that the rational ego is nothing more than the symptom of our imaginary *relation* to globalization. It is the conduit through which the free market passes. Furthermore, transcendental freedom is not concerned with what is possible, since the "possible" is always delimited ideologically. To be free, then, we must renege on our obligation both to our pathological interests and to our duty to the good. Yet, we must do this, not in terms of a resignation to the loss of our freedom, but under the faith that only in this gesture will we found freedom on our own terms. Transcendental freedom precisely is this very Kierkegaardian step into the abyss—the freedom to determine freedom. Politically, this act changes the very coordinates of freedom. If you no longer recognize yourself as a rationally calculating ego, then you will not locate your freedom in voluntary exchanges or be guaranteed freedom in the global market. Rather, you will be handed an economic straitjacket and the good you once served will now be pathological and alien. The rational ego is that part of us that makes life in the global market bearable. When we sacrifice this crutch, we open the space for something different—albeit a space that can appear as fantasy from the perspective of globalism and its rational ego. This gesture would entail embracing the symptoms of our alienation from the global market, embracing the "this is not me" embedded in the radical dislocation of globalization. For it is through this alienation that the true route to our freedom lies. It would require a politics not only without the rational ego, but one against it, since we would seek to transform our practical orientation toward the phenomenal world. In terms of transcendental freedom, what could be more practical than this?

The example of Abraham demonstrates the absurdity of this gesture. Nevertheless this is what Kant's moral law invokes—that we treat others as ends, and not as means. As Kant's moral theory connotes, this is a change that cannot be brought about by elites, but only by individuals themselves. The Kierkegaardian gesture can perhaps inaugurate what Kant would call the "kingdom of ends," a kingdom beyond ideology. Of course, there is no guarantee that such a kingdom will appear in the phenomenal world. All we know is that globalism only offers us a world where we are the means and not the ends of freedom. To become free, one must undertake the revolutionary gesture of which Kant speaks—toward a future utopian Otherness. Freedom is not found in deferring this utopian gesture to some unseen external forces, but by enacting it in the present. For only in this gesture can freedom begin to transcend the forced choice of ideology.

References

Allison, Henry E. (1998) "Morality and Freedom: Kant's ReciprocityThesis," in Paul Guyer, Editor, *Kant's Groundwork of the Metaphysics of Morals*, pp. 273–302, New York: Rowan and Littlefield.

Althusser, Louis (1971) "Ideology and Ideological State Apparatuses," *Lenin and Philosophy and Other Essays*, New York: Monthly Review Press.

Kant, Immanuel (1960) *Religion Within the Limits of Reason Alone*, New York: Harper and Row.

———— (1996) *Critique of Practical Reason*, Amherst, NY: Prometheus Books.

Kierkegaard, Sören (1985) *Fear and Trembling*, New York: Penguin.

Korsgaard, Christine M. (1996) *Creating the Kingdom of Ends*, Cambridge: Cambridge University Press.

Love, Nancy (1998) *Dogmas and Dreams*, Chatham, NJ: Chatham House.

Marx, Karl, and Friedrich Engels (1978) *The Marx-Engels Reader*, Robert C. Tucker, Editor, New York: Norton.

Steger, Manfred (2002) *Globalism: The New Market Ideology*, New York: Rowan and Littlefield.

Weber, Max (1946) *From Max Weber: Essays in Sociology*, H. H. Gerth and C. Wright Mills, Editors, New York: Oxford University Press.

Zupancic, Alenka (2000) *Ethics of the Real: Kant, Lacan*, London: Verso.

14

Freedom? Beware What You Wish For(!)

Jose V. Ciprut

here in this carload
i am eve
with abel my son
if you see my other son
cain son of man
tell him that i[1]

When political-economic settings do not allow vibrant public space for it and even social-cultural interstices cannot somehow accommodate it, "freedom" lives on: albeit in the residual hopes and suppressed yearnings of human imagination. Were freedom a conferrable private privilege or an acquirable public right, "being free" would mean never sensing a need to write home about it. And we may forget sometimes that freedom is not always liberating. Whenever the basic personal freedoms of the many intersect or collide, a select few may end up becoming far freer than others. Where only a few winners take all and "l'économie du bonheur" demands that they act parsimoniously because there is so very little of it to pass around, freedom finds ways of hiding itself in the wishful longings and the numbed utopian rationalizations of the many for which it has become but a nominal password to nowhere.

When the self-serving passions of rulers reject or retard the aspirations to liberty of those ruled, a search for solace in mass revolution, wherever reforms are dismal, dormant, or dead, usually augurs little more than the crudest of reversals in fortunes, often resulting in others now doing to selves what selves a while ago did to others, in turn

---

1. Dan Pagis, "Written in Pencil in the Sealed Railway-Car," *The Selected Poetry of Dan Pagis*, trans. Stephen Mitchell and with an introduction by Robert Alter, Berkeley: University of California Press, 1996.

necessitating what next must pass for a counterrevolution. Endless spirals in the not so distant lands of successive military coups; monotonic change in the oppressive jurisdiction of now dynastic now contra-dynastic regimes; cyclical continuities in quasi-sultanic top-down democracies or in born-again paternalistic tyrannies legated from nine-teenth-century world politics to the twentieth, and in parts of the world somehow still afoot in the twenty-first century, continue today to justify their anachronisms by portraying their politics of continuity to insiders and outsiders alike as "steadily moving" if "understandably" (necessarily?) all too slowly progressing "pursuits" of freedom. As if freedom ever assumes a linear trajectory, let alone a monotonic unidirectional line of progression, in any socioeconomic or cultural-political context, under any attenuating circumstances.

Responding to a childhood classmate of mine, become author of fiction turned radical ideologue of the Left, and a vociferous critic of the "U.S. invasion of sovereign Iraq," I surprised myself by my spontaneous reaction in my e-mail to him, when military action was about to begin: "Tough and uncomfortable as it may seem to be in the eyes and minds of those who pride themselves for smoking unfiltered Gauloises to their bitter butt while feverishly discussing the human condition and the world's fate in the low-lit caberdouches of the Left Bank, only defeat—decisively quick, final, publicly irrefutable defeat—can teach those in perpetual denial, once and for all, that there is room for democracy (voice, unimposed loyalty, active and responsible civic participation); for humane acknowledgment of those not born to one's own faith; for respect toward those who do not share one's obtuse if grandiose worldviews, farfetched ambitions, or deadly prejudices; for human freedoms of the first, second, third, and n-th kind as well . . . be it for women, Sunnis, Shiites, non-Arabs, and yes Jews, too. A born-again Baghdad (caesarean birthmark to boot) will serve as a model for a once self-deluded and now self-defeating Tehran; as example to the tyrannically cocky neighborhood; as new beginning indeed—for those sagacious enough to recognize a new 'tide in the affairs of (wo)men,' and to seize that unique opportunity to their greatest advantage. Left to themselves, they could not do it: Iraq is not alone. See Venezuela, Zimbabwe, Myanmar, or North Korea. Tough luck for Left Bankers! This too shall come to pass. Mind you, I do not reside on the Right Bank either. Rather, I prefer to breathe 'ailleurs—avec mon Prochain, qui n'est ni nécessairement ni toujours mon Autre' (elsewhere—with my Next, who is neither necessarily nor always my Other)."

At the time of this cry from the heart in the guise of a sincere, spontaneous exclamation expressed before-the-(f)act, who would have known, or—coming from the world's mightiest military, and the oldest young democracy—who even remotely could have imagined that routinely avoidable errors, wholly unnecessary shortcomings, circumventable consequences, eminently eschewable gaffes, and surprisingly innocent oversights should come to complicate and retard what both in theory and practice would have been a decisive, willed, welcome, and surely long-overdue self-transformation on the part of those long resigned to their fate, and too reticent to risk change, lest they lose atavistic controls over their women and their own children's future and as a consequence come to face themselves. The queues formed by the death-defiant electors in Iraq on "election day," on one of the last days of January, 2005, may augur well for the future of freedom, in the area, across the region, and worldwide, too: even if surely more so in the longer run, as Keynes might have retorted. But then, who said that freedom could be had for free.

The greatest personal satisfaction that one truly derives from conceptualizing, conducting, and bringing to fruition such a timely cross-disciplinary seminar, and from putting together the ensuing comprehensive volume, comes from the human learning experience that has benefited us all. First, the obvious: "conquering any difficulty always gives one a secret joy, for it means pushing back a boundary-line and adding to one's liberty."[2]

Second, as Foucault once remarked,[3] "for a long time, I have been trying to see if it would be possible to describe the history of thought as distinct both from the history of ideas (by which I mean the analysis of systems of representation) and from the history of mentalities (by which I mean the analysis of attitudes and types of action [schémas de comportement]). It seemed to me there was one element that was capable of describing the history of thought—this was what one could call the problems or . . . problematizations. What distinguishes thought is that it is something quite different from the set of representations that underlies a certain behavior; it is also quite different from the

---

2. Henri Frédéric Amiel [1821–1881] (1922) "Préface," in *Fragments d'un Journal Intime*, Geneva: Georg & Cie; Paris: G. Crès & Cie. [See Amiel's Journal (1889) translated, with an Introduction and notes, by Mrs. Humphry Ward, London and New York: Macmillan.]
3. Copyright Paul Rabinow, *Michel Foucault*/Interview, May 1984, to the question "What is a history of problematics?" Translated by Lydia Davis and published in *Ethics*, vol. 1 of *Essential Works of Foucault*, New York: The New Press, 1997.

domain of attitudes that can determine this behavior. Thought is not what inhabits a certain conduct and gives it its meaning; rather, it is what allows one to step back from this way of acting or reacting, to present it to oneself as an object of thought and to question it as to its meaning, its conditions, and its goals. Thought is freedom in relation to what one does, the motion by which one detaches from it, establishes it as an object, and reflects on it as a problem."

We saw in our initiative a potentiality—a unique opportunity to tackle the thought of freedom in the very way that we here did—truly an extraordinary possibility, enabling to address not only a complex systemic problématique by way of a multilateral problematization, but perchance also permitting to hold a conversation among (very) unlike minds, stands, and visions, in turn allowing to articulate the more edifying of its attending schémas de comportement: polyphonically, unabashedly, and head-on.

Last, yet perhaps foremost—and not simply because we all at one time or another might have heard and taken the words of U.S. Supreme Court Justice Louis D. Brandeis to heart—I think to speak for all of us when I confess that only the very sincerest of concerns for the future of freedom made us do it: in his great sagacity, Brandeis had cautioned that "[e]xperience should teach us to be most on our guard to protect liberty when the government's purposes are beneficent. Men born to freedom are naturally alert to repel invasion of their liberty by evil-minded rulers. The greatest dangers to liberty lurk in insidious encroachment by men of zeal, well meaning but without understanding."[4] It should serve the world well to heed his words; and whenever and wherever possible, to help those not born to freedom to wish to acquire a taste for liberty, to want to spread the felicitous thought, share the sentiment of mature responsibility, and taste the sense of being born again that comes with it. The future of freedom will depend not so much on the present promise of liberty for the so many already liberated from the tyranny of others as on the palpable prospects of liberation for the few who, for their own reasons, often out of fear of fear itself, insist on remaining enslaved to themselves.

---

4. Justice Louis D. Brandeis, dissenting, *Olmstead v. United States* 277US479 (1926).

About the Authors

Elvira Arcenas (PhD Penn) is currently CEO of ThinkActPeace (TAP) Foundation, the Phillipines. She was Assistant Professor/Coordinator of the Master's Program in Communication Education at the Pontificia Facolta di Scienze dell'Educazione "AUXILIUM" in Rome. She worked as an educator for several years in Hong Kong and in Italy and traveled widely in Asia and Africa on educational projects. Her *Curriculum Design of Media Education* (1979) is in the third reprint; her *Study of Communication* is forthcoming; and her *Media Studies* (with G. Gerbner) was in the making when her co-author died.

Jacques P. Barber (PhD Penn), Professor of Psychology in Psychiatry at the University of Pennsylvania School of Medicine and Associate Director of the Center for Psychotherapy Research in the Department of Psychiatry, has published over seventy scientific papers, thirty chapters, and co-edited three books. Dr. Barber serves on the boards of *The Journal of Clinical Psychology, Psychotherapy Research*, and the *Journal of Psychotherapy: Practice and Research*. He has a private practice integral to the Department of Psychiatry at Penn.

Kevin Cameron (PhD SUNY) became Instructor of Political Science at Chaffey College, in California, after teaching political theory in the Department of Government and Law at Lafayette College, in Pennsylvania. He studies the interrelation between political theory and psychoanalysis, the psychoanalytic underpinnings of the development of the early modern democratic subject in the writings of Thomas Hobbes, and the affinity between perversion and democracy in the works of John Calvin and Alexis de Tocqueville.

Jose V. Ciprut (PhD Penn) is Founding Director and Convening Editor of *Cross-Campus Conversations at Penn,* a series of transdisciplinary inter-faculty seminars. Educated in the humanities and trained in industrial

technology, he pursued a full career in international industrial market-
ing development before returning to academe. He specializes in comparative international political economy, international relations, and
global security. Dr. Ciprut has authored journal articles and book chapters and has edited several cross-disciplinary books.

Viet D. Dinh   (JD Harvard) is Professor of Law at the Law Center;
Founding Director, Center for Security and Technology; and Deputy
Director, Asian Law and Policy Studies, Georgetown University. A former
U.S. Assistant Attorney General, he has led a comprehensive review of
U.S. Department of Justice policies, priorities, and practices to protect
the United States from terrorist acts; has assumed a key role in develop-
ing the USA Patriot Act; and is revising the U.S. Attorney General's
Guidelines on law enforcement and national security investigations.

Sheldon Hackney   (PhD Yale), Professor and Chair of History at the
University of Pennsylvania, is a former provost of Princeton University
and a former president of Tulane and of Penn. He served as Chair of
the National Endowment for the Humanities in Washington, D.C.; is
focused on the history of the U.S. South since the Civil War; and has
researched U.S. utopian and social movements, the American Civil
Rights movement, and the 1960s. A prolific author, his next book will
be about U.S. identity, from precolonial days to the present.

Roger Haight   (PhD Chicago), Professor of Systematic and Historical
Theology, and Jesuit Fr., has taught in graduate schools for training
for ministry in the church, in Manila, Toronto, Chicago, Cambridge,
Massachusetts, and New York. In the 1970s and '80s, he was attentive
to Latin American liberation theology. Since then his books and articles
have focused instead on basic Christian doctrines and on the nature of
theology, on the understanding of Jesus Christ, and on a doctrine of
the Christian Church as a pluralistic community in history.

Levi Y. Haskelevich, a scholar of the Talmud, the Bible, Jewish law,
and Jewish theology, has taught and conducted workshops on Judaism
in public schools and Jewish community retreats. He is the campus
rabbi-cum-spiritual leader and Associate Director of the Chabad-
Lubavitch House in West Philadelphia, Pennsylvania. He studies the
esoteric teachings of Judaism, in Chabad Chassidic texts on mystical
reasoning, and, as an ordained rabbi, seeks to heighten a sense of
Jewish awareness and identity in students of Jewish lineage and faith
living on the Penn campus.

Nancy J. Hirschmann (PhD Johns Hopkins), Associate Professor and past Vice-Chair of Political Science at the University of Pennsylvania, teaches modern political theory and feminist theory. Her essays, in the contexts of political theories of freedom (i.e., on political obligation, welfare, domestic violence, and Islamic veiling), have been published in books and professional journals. She has authored and co-edited several books and her latest book, *Gender, Class, and Freedom in Modern Political Theory*, was published in 2007.

Paul R. Kleindorfer (PhD Carnegie-Mellon) currently serves as Distinguished Research Professor at INSEAD. He was the Anheuser Busch Professor of Management Science at the Wharton School, Professor of Business and Public Policy, Member of the Graduate Group in Economics, and the Co-Director of the Risk Management Center at the University of Pennsylvania. He specializes in regulation, managerial economics, restructuring initiatives in network industries (energy, postal delivery services), industrial risk management strategies, and catastrophe coverage for the P&C insurance industry. Newly retired, he now works out of Europe.

Jeremy McInerney (PhD Berkeley) is Associate Professor of Classical Studies and Greek History and Chair of the Graduate Group/Ancient History, Art and Archaeology of the Mediterranean World at the University of Pennsylvania. He is the author of *The Folds of Parnassos: Land and Ethnicity in Ancient Polis,* and has written for *Greek, Roman and Byzantine Studies*, *American Journal of Archaeology, Hesperia*, and *California Studies in Classical Antiquity*. He serves on the Managing Committee of the American School of Classical Studies in Athens.

William Parberry is Director of the University of Pennsylvania Choral Society and Choir and Co-director of Early Music at Penn. As conductor of the Penn Madrigal Singers and of Ancient Voices, he has conducted nearly every major work in the choral repertoire and has also taught courses in music theory and history, including one of the most popular courses at Penn: "Jazz—Style and History." He has been a guest lecturer on jazz at many universities and in other departments at Penn, relating jazz to several managerial and scientific disciplines.

Greg Urban (PhD University of Chicago) is Arthur Hobson Quinn Professor of Anthropology, was Chair of the Anthropology Department at the University of Pennsylvania, serving as head of the Folklore and Folklife Graduate Group as well as resource faculty for the Latin American Cultures Program. He is consulting curator of the American

Section, University Museum. He has written or edited seven books and published essays or chapters in the *International Journal of American Linguistics*, *Semiotica*, the *Latin American Research Review*, and *American Anthropologist*.

David R. Williams   (PhD Yale) is Emeritus Professor of Psychology, former Director of Clinical Training at the University of Pennsylvania, and a licensed psychotherapist. He is interested in combining the psychology of brain and behavior with personality theory and clinical psychotherapy, toward constructing an experimental psychology that reaches to the innermost layers of a person's private experience and hidden capacity for voluntary action. After working in B. F. Skinner's laboratory, Dr. Williams joined Miller and Sheffield's to pursue learning theory and human behavior.

Name Index

Subject Index